lure

A BIOGRAPHY BY Munroe Scott

Canec Publishing and Supply House, Toronto

Canadian Cataloguing in Publication Data

Scott, Munroe, 1977—
McCLURE: The China Years

ISBN 0-919000-12-6

Printed in Canada for
CANEC Publishing and Supply House,
47 Coldwater Road, Don Mills, Ont. M3B 1Y9

Book Design by Bryan Mills & Associates

Printed and Bound in Canada by the John Deyell Co.

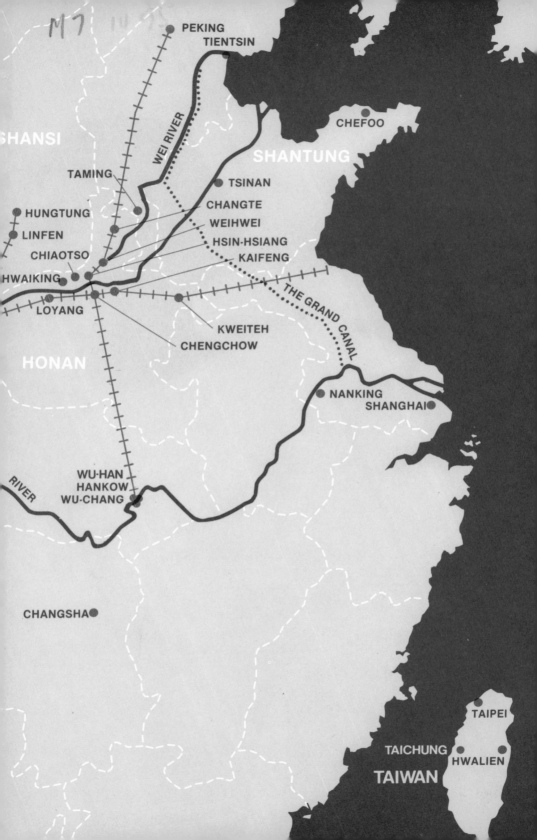

McCLURE

McC

THE CHINA YEARS OF DR. BOB McCLURE

To Amy and Hilda

CONTENTS

Foreword

This book started out to be a full biography of Dr. Bob McClure from his birth in 1900 up to the present time. It gradually transformed itself into something that may seem to fall halfway between an adventure story and a history of China through the first half of the twentieth century.

I make no excuse for this transformation because the first forty-eight years of Bob McClure's life were very tightly woven into the fabric of events in China. His Chinese career was too varied, his adventures too many, and the scene against which it was all carried out far too vast to allow compression into a book that would *then* follow him into the second half of the twentieth century and on to the Gaza Strip, India, Sarawak, Peru, St. Vincent, Africa, *and* a term as Moderator of The United Church of Canada.

I have been fortunate in that many people who participated with Bob McClure in the "China years" are still very much alive, including Bob himself and his wife, Amy. I am indebted to all those who have assisted me so generously with their time, reminiscences, suggestions, and advice. Dr. and Mrs. McClure have been unstinting with their co-operation and they gave me full and unconditional access to personal correspondence from the period. Their daughter, Norah (Mrs. David Busby), generously turned over material that she herself had been gathering throughout the years. Mr. A. E. 'Sandy' Nicholson gave me full access to interview material he, too, had been laboriously gathering. I have received correspondence and tapes from as far away as England and Switzerland.

I have been particularly fortunate to have as two special "China advisors" a couple who have been close friends of the McClures for years and who worked and lived in China, one from childhood and one from 1923. They are the Rev. and Mrs. Bruce Copland, and their assistance has been invaluable. They have been embarrassed to find themselves wandering through the pages of my manuscript.

In spite of the help from my advisors and correspondents there may be some errors of fact and interpretation. For those I apologize and hasten to add that all such errors are undoubtedly mine.

An author reads many books in preparing for a project such as this, but I am particularly indebted to C. P. Fitzgerald for his *Birth of Communist China*; to Immanuel C. Y. Hsu for *The Rise of Modern China*; to A. Tegla Davies for *The Friends Ambulance Unit* "The Story of the F.A.U. in the Second World War"; to Margaret Brown for *A History of the Honan Mission 1882-1951* (United Church Archives, unpublished), and to Marnie Copland for her memoirs *Moon Cakes and Maple Sugar* (unpublished).

A final and very important acknowledgement is due to Norman Vale, whose idea it was that this book should be written and that I should write it, and to The United Church of Canada that has made it possible for me to write it. The United Church has approached this project the same way it has always approached Bob McClure himself—by providing support without attempting to exercise any control.

An acknowledgement that is never final, but that is on-going, continuous, never-ending is to my wife who works at my side, types my scribbles, and keeps me organized, filed, sane, and happy.

M.S.

Lindsay,
Ontario.
August 1977

McCLURE

Prologue

In the year 1900, news of events elsewhere in China travelled into the little Presbyterian mission station at Chu Wang in fits and starts. The local peasants who came to the Canadian doctor's bottle-lined dispensary seldom had any definite news at all. There was rumour in plenty, some of which a callous patient would pass on to the "Big Nose" foreigner or to his Chinese assistants in order to watch their discomfort. Some patients were more sensitive. A few appreciated the alacrity with which the Doctor had learned to speak their Mandarin language and were loath to torment such a scholar with rumour. Besides, fact was hard come by and most of it was of an unpleasant nature that was difficult to relay to a foreigner who had just alleviated one's physical suffering.

Occasionally newspapers came through from the "Forbidden City" Peking or from its seaport neighbour, Tientsin. In the best of times it took mail two weeks from Tientsin to the mission. The Doctor refused to be alarmed by out-of-date articles written by Western journalists. They wrote from the foreign "Concession" territories of the major cities and probably knew little of the mind of China. He was much more interested in letters from other missionaries and he listened intently to any information he could glean from the boatmen who travelled the six hundred winding river miles inland from Tientsin, following the ancient Grand Canal and the Wei River.

Early in the year the information the Doctor pieced together, much of it already alarmingly out of date, indicated that a general uprising was gaining momentum. It seemed to be aimed against foreigners. To the immediate north, in the Province of Shansi and on up into Manchuria, some mission stations had already been burned. Missionaries and their converts had been attacked. Around Christmas time an English missionary had been murdered.

The Doctor had a wife and two small daughters. As a family man he had to give full consideration to the implications of both news and rumour. He also had to put the present into perspective with the past. He knew that in 1870 there had been a massacre of foreigners in Tientsin. The majority of those killed were French and Catholic, but the Doctor, having been raised on a farm near Lachute, Quebec, could easily identify with the victims. Was 1900 bringing a more widespread version of the 1870 massacre?

He himself had come 'out' in 1888, one of a sturdy handful of men and women answering the first call of The Presbyterian Church in Canada for workers to go to China. He remembered the crushing of their initial naive optimism. They had met with opposition ranging all the way from the threat of mob violence to outright robbery and organized vandalism. Two years later there had been anti-Christian riots in the Yangtze Valley, only a few hundred miles to the south. Those riots had continued into a second year.

The year 1894 had been thoroughly etched into his memory. That year there had been smallpox, typhus, floods and war. All but the war took place right at Chu Wang and even the war made its impression. The Japanese had attacked key points in Manchuria and during the wettest summer in years Chinese troops had flowed back and forth on their way to and from the northern war zones. China had lost her key Manchurian cities and all of Taiwan to the Japanese and after that foreigners had become even less popular.

Now, in 1900, the Doctor could easily believe that the new uprising was indeed nationalistic in character. After all, the foreign Powers, backing their commercial interests with military might, had been carving up China's major cities like some communal pie. They treated her with less respect than their own colonies and Britain in particular had never been forgiven for forcing the opium trade, at gunpoint, upon the Chinese. He also knew that the uprising was anti-Christian. Although regrettable, it was not surprising. Missions always ran the risk of being too closely identified with their Western governments. Any moderately intelligent Chinese could hear the Western missionaries preaching one thing and see the Western Powers doing the contrary, to the great discredit of both. And already the variety of missions was proliferating, with an equal variety in approach and doctrine. The religion they were preaching was a religion that, if followed, demanded change throughout the whole structure of society and the more fundamentalist among the missionaries were not particularly tolerant in the presentation of their views. Being a tolerant man himself, and also a colonial, the Doctor had an inherent respect for the rising wave of Chinese nationalism.

The uprising took its momentum from units of the Chinese village militia. The rebellious units called themselves the "Righteous Harmonious Fists". The fists were portrayed so graphically on posters that the foreign press shortened the name to "Boxers".

It seemed that the Boxer Rebellion was in support of the Manchu Dynasty and specifically of the old Empress Dowager who had just had a reforming Emperor put away. It was also, by all accounts, widespread and popular. Moreover, there was a mystical hysteria to the movement and its more ardent supporters were convinced they were immune to knives and bullets. The Boxer slogan made their objectives quite clear. It was brief and explicit—"Protect the Country, Destroy the Foreigners". The Boxers identified missionaries as being "Primary Foreign Devils".

The Doctor's wife was about three months pregnant. Pregnancy was not a condition that adjusted itself to the requirements of other phenomena, either natural or political. The Doctor and his family headed downriver toward Tientsin taking the risk of a river dash through the heart of Boxer territory rather than accept either of the alternatives—to ride out the storm in Chu Wang or to head south on a ten day cart journey followed by a long river trip. Those who remained to temporize at Chu Wang wished they had not. The mission homes were attacked and destroyed. The occupants escaped and joined their associates from the other centres. Two dozen men, women, and children from the little Canadian missions of North Honan began the long overland journey south, travelling by ox cart. Ahead lay angry mobs, bandits, and hostile cavalry.

The Doctor's group on the river trip were alerted to the fact that the foreign controlled seaport of Tientsin, for which they were headed, was now under siege. The Boxer lines lay between them and their haven. The Doctor's party, too, struck south on an overland journey complete with its own special nightmares.

Before long most of the earlier rumours were only too well confirmed. Boxers were laying siege to the Roman Catholic Cathedral in Peking. The German Ambassador had been murdered. Other foreign diplomats and missionaries, along with hundreds of Chinese Christians, were blockaded in the embassy quarter of Peking. Over in Shansi Province and up in Manchuria thousands of Chinese Christians, the unpopular "Secondary Foreign Devils", were being slaughtered. The Foreign Powers had attempted to send additional troops into Peking and had been thrown back. And then, to top it off, the Empress Dowager issued an Imperial Edict calling for the death of *all* foreigners.

The city of Shanghai was to be the Canadians' rendezvous, but it seemed impossible that many would make it. Members of the multi-national China Inland Mission (C.I.M.) had also been escaping from North Honan and they were already counting their dead. Eventually the C.I.M. survivors would raise a bronze plaque carrying the names of 56 men and women and 19 children, all murdered in the exodus.

The Canadians began to arrive at Shanghai. Some came singly. Some came in small groups. Others arrived in parties. Families had been broken up. The father of one family and the son of another had been lost. One of the doctors had been terribly mutilated in a bandit attack. But the lost turned up and the wounded survived. The entire personnel of the Canadian Presbyterian Mission of North Honan came out of the heart of the Boxer Rebellion without a single loss. During the process they developed a highly intimate awareness of what is referred to as Divine Providence.

The Canadian missionaries had survived but a pessimist might have been pardoned for assuming the work of a decade had been totally wiped out. In the meantime their lives had been changed and their careers disrupted. As berths on ships became available many of the missionaries sailed for home. The Doctor's wife, now well on in her pregnancy, was given passage with her two daughters on a Japanese ship, the S.S. *Shinano Maru*, bound for the United States. Before members of the mission dispersed from Shanghai a council meeting was held and it was decided that the Doctor should remain to look after whatever was left of mission interests.

It was not long after his little family had sailed that the Doctor decided the best interests of the mission coincided with the interests of the Chinese Christians and foreigners who were in immediate need of his medical and surgical skills. He joined the medical section of a British naval unit headed for Peking.

And so it was that Doctor William McClure of Lachute, Quebec, graduate of McGill University, ex-superintendent of Montreal General Hospital, recently mission doctor in Chu Wang, finished the year 1900 as a naval surgeon in a British unit commanded by a young officer with the unusual name of Jellicoe.

And so it was in the latter part of the same year that the S.S. *Shinano Maru* touched at Portland, Oregon, and landed Dr. McClure's wife, Margaret, and her two daughters. There at Portland on November 23rd, 1900, on her own native soil but still three thousand miles from her home in Pennsylvania, Margaret McClure gave birth to her first and only son, Robert Baird McClure.

And so it was that Robert McClure was born a refugee.

The Allied Powers managed to suppress the Boxer Rebellion without declaring war on China. The result was a further subjugation of China, more concessions, further encroachment upon her sovereignty. Once again, faced by foreign force and internal corruption, the Chinese had to swallow their pride and suppress their nationalism. Up in Manchuria Japan's hold had been shaken loose but Russia seized the opportunity for a military occupation of much of that northern area. Japan would be back into Manchuria almost immediately. All of this, although violent, was politics, and of no immediate concern to Dr. William McClure. By mid-summer of 1901 his wife had rejoined him, bringing with her the two girls, Janet and Margaret, ages 3 and 6, and the baby.

Many of the former missionaries returned. New ones came out. Even before the rebellion, land had been purchased in North Honan near the cities of Changte, Weihwei, and Hwaiking.* Here the Canadian Presbyterians were determined to establish larger, more permanent missions. The McClures were among the handful of families who were sent to Weihwei.

*See map on front end paper.

At Chu Wang the missionaries had attempted to live in Chinese houses on a Chinese street. There Dr. McClure and his wife had lost two infant daughters to epidemic diseases. During the rebellion the houses had been destroyed by mobs. Now, the Weihwei mission station was retreating behind the brick walls of a compound. Here the missionaries would build their own sanitation systems, something Chinese municipalities were not doing, and they would have at least the psychological protection of walls. Other missions all over China were taking the same precautions. Later generations would criticize the 'compound' mentality without pausing to marvel at the fact that these people had returned at all. But here they were.

Dr. William McClure and his wife Margaret had returned to China in spite of its chaotic past, dangerous present, and unpromising future. They had no idea that their son would cling to China for the next forty-seven years—in spite of years of anarchy, a ten year civil war, three revolutions, the Sino-Japanese War, the Second World War, and a final revolution.

1

First Decade

In the beginning Robert McClure's world was contained in the Weihwei compound and the world was surrounded on all sides by a brick wall broken only by the 'bell tower gate' on the east and by the 'water gate' on the west. Within the walls were the plain, square homes of the married missionaries, the house for the single lady missionaries, store-house, stables, the goat yard and gardens. This world was peopled by many shadowy figures as well as by Robert's mother, father, and sisters Janet and Margaret; but mostly there was Maria Sloan.

Miss Maria Sloan was from Ontario. She had been raised in the pretty Great Lakes port of Owen Sound, on Georgian Bay. Maria had trained as a school teacher. She came to China as a combination nanny and governess, not just to teach the McClure family but to teach the children of the other Canadian families living in the Weihwei compound. Maria's presence released several women for evangelical work in the community. Her knowledge, gentleness, affection, skill and devoutness were to be major influences on the early life of young Robert. She changed him as a baby, fed him as an infant and taught him his prayers as a child. Maria read him to sleep at night and taught him his three r's in the daytime.

Robert's mother was an important presence, and he would remember her in later years, affectionately, as a very "motherly" woman; but she kept disappearing. She would leave the compound riding under a canvas shade in a two-wheeled cart drawn by a mule and a bony horse. There would be a Chinese woman with her and a couple of Chinese men following carrying her baggage suspended from long poles over their shoulders. Robert would not see her again for days. One of the men might turn up in a week or so and Robert would hear him reporting that Mrs. McClure was at such and such a village thirty miles away and had run out of coffee. If they wanted the Work of the Lord to continue would they please send out more coffee right away!

It was only as his own world expanded that Robert realized his mother was teaching in those remote villages. Her disappearances were most frequent in the winter time when work in the fields was at a minimum and the Chinese peasant women had the time to learn to read and to talk about health and other home matters and to listen to stories about a carpenter boy from a place called Nazareth. Except for her beloved coffee his mother took few western supplies with her. She would eat the same porridge or steamed bread that the peasants ate and sleep as the peasants slept. It was only years later, as a man, moving furtively through a war-ravaged country and himself living off the land that her son would come to appreciate his mother's dedication and fortitude. In these early years his mother was an important, powerful, but somewhat enigmatic background figure. It was Maria who occupied the foreground.

Robert's father would sometimes leave for several days, too, saying he was going to Presbytery at another mission station called Changte or Hwaiking, or that he was going to a village to hold a clinic. But no matter where he was going the doctor would don his felt hat with the side brim turned up and would disappear through the bell tower gate. As Robert grew he discovered that a long lane led from that bell tower gate to the great wooden doors of a main gate covered by a roof with curving eaves. The walls which bordered the lane enclosed another world where the Chinese nannies, the "amahs", lived and where the men servants had their quarters and where a primary school was being built for Chinese boys and another for Chinese girls. Here, too, was the mysterious place called a "hospital" with an equally mysterious "chapel" attached to it.

Even to a toddler the hospital was a most marvellous place. The local people came and went all the time. Outside the hospital there were open areas where cooking fires were tended by relatives of patients who were being cared for inside the building. The relatives cooked the meals and carried them in to the patients. It was the customary system.

There were always children in the compound. There were

Robert's two sisters, plus the children of the other missionaries, the Grants and the Mitchells, plus the ever changing flow of children in the hospital yard. There were also the children of the Chinese staff and the boys and girls of the two schools in the outer compound. No child could have had a more ready made supply of playmates than had young Robert.

In the home Robert learned, formally and informally, from his parents and from Maria. Out in the yard he learned from the Chinese children. Out there he was not Robert McClure. He was "Pao-pei" (pronounced "Bough-bay"). It was what the Chinese referred to as a "milk-name" and was an approximation, in sounds, of "Bobby". When he grew older a teacher or special friend would re-name him.

In the house and with Maria, Robert spoke English. Outside in the yard Pao-pei spoke Chinese. It was a very practical Chinese and it became even more practical as he grew old enough to explore beyond the compound. He learned that there were certain words that seemed to be able to penetrate the skull of a Mongolian pony. There were certain words that, when used with the proper emphasis, would stampede a herd of goats. Pao-pei's informal language studies continued at such a pace that his father took him aside one day and, trying to keep from actually mouthing the forbidden words himself, explained that there were certain Chinese expressions that must never be heard inside the walls of the compound.

Dr. McClure also objected to his children speaking any Chinese inside the house. To Pao-pei this seemed a little strange. After all, every day began with household worship. His mother, if she was home, his father, Maria, Janet, Margaret and he himself would all gather in the dining room before breakfast where they would be joined by the cook, the houseboy and the gardener. The doctor would then read from the Bible and lead in a short prayer. The reading and the prayer were always in Chinese. And yet his father began an outright campaign to cure his own children of speaking Chinese in the house! To Pao-pei it was a puzzler.

The trouble was that for Robert Chinese was a first language and as such was easy. And there were Chinese words for which there were no English equivalents. Chinese was expressive, adaptable and always right there on the tip of the tongue. Finally, his father, frustrated, declared open warfare on bilingualism in the home. Muttering strange expressions about "pidgin" and "banana ridge English" he marched Robert to the main doorway of the house. With a large piece of chalk he drew a firm white line across the threshold.

"There will not," said the doctor, "be any Chinese spoken by you on this side of that line. Or else!"

Although the doctor's moustache always made him look fierce, his eyes suggested bottomless compassion. Even as a child Robert had an instinct for reading eyes. The first time the chalkline rule was broken he received a caning he remembered for the rest of his life. After that he paid more attention to moustaches. It was several years before he came to understand that his English had to be protected so he could use it effectively when the time came for him to visit his mother's people in Pennsylvania or to go to Canada. That there could be a culture where people spoke only English was something Robert would not fully appreciate until he was ten years old.

In the meantime the mission 'family' of the compound was expanding. Rev. and Mrs. Lochead arrived with their three year old daughter, Marnie, who had been born at the Changte mission. A new 'sister' came to live with the McClure family. Her name was Jean Menzies. Jean's father was the doctor at the Hwaiking station, a hundred miles farther inland. Jean's parents felt that rather than teach an only child themselves she would receive a better education as a member of the little group that was growing around Maria Sloan. Jean came knowing of a world that was far bigger than Robert had imagined, although his mother had a habit of coming home bringing part of that larger world with her.

Mrs. McClure's homecomings were sometimes more of an avalanche than a homecoming. She would arrive from a distant village, accompanied by a dozen or so women, each woman bringing quilts and children. Some would come hoping to gain the courage to take an ailment to the Big Nose doctor at the hospital. Others would come out of curiosity to see the inside of the mission station. Still others followed out of a growing affection for the bustling white woman with her strange supply of useful knowledge and her fund of stories.

At such times the living room would be full of women from morning until night and the kitchen would give off the smell of Chinese cooking and there would be children absolutely everywhere. It was great fun for Pao-pei and all rules having to do with chalklines were suspended. There were hazards to these invasions that would not have been acceptable to many Western housewives. Most of the women had never seen such luxury as a rug on a floor. Even the gardener coming in for instructions would carefully walk around the edge of it. Visiting peasant women, duly impressed, would see to it that their children did not pee on the rug. They would whisk them away to a corner where the floor was bare. When that happened, the doctor's wife could demonstrate a volatile temper and a seething tongue.

Mrs. McClure had a vocabulary almost as broad as her son's and a fine disregard for logic. She maintained that good Christians made poor cooks and when faced as an employer with a choice between a 'good Christian' and a backsliding scallywag, she would inevitably choose the latter. She chased beggars out of the compound and scolded patients for touching the children but it was all froth on the surface. The gardener, the cook, the water-carrier, the patients and the peasant women all had the truth of her. They called her "Bitter-lips, Sweetheart".

It was on one of the occasions when Mrs. McClure and her Chinese cohorts returned from the countryside that she brought home the Wolfboy. She had been up into the hills that led into mountain country. In that area, so she told her son, many people lived in caves. A cave was not necessarily an uncomfortable place to live. They were well insulated, dry, and not much darker than the average peasant house. But where wolves would not enter a house they would enter a cave. They would slink in at night and carry off the youngest child. It was instinct. It was also instinct for a wolf to attack a child by seizing it by the upper lip and the nose. Even if the child was rescued, the resulting wound was horrible, the upper lip being sliced upward and much of the nose being torn away. A survivor lived his life with a disfiguring hole in the centre of his face.

The victim Robert's mother brought in had not only survived but was now already in his teens, about eight years older than Robert. He was a sturdy, intelligent youth but marked for life. Mrs. McClure hoped her husband might be able to help him. If he could, there were many other similar victims who would stand to benefit. It was a time when surgeons like Dr. McClure were already doing good work with harelips and cleft palates. The McClures kept the boy with them and the doctor operated several times, but the injury defied his best efforts. He was able to make a partial improvement but not a complete repair. There was still no nose tip to shelter the nostrils. It was said by the Chinese that a wolf victim could drown in a heavy rain.

Robert was fascinated by the youth from the hill country and called him "Wolfboy". The tendency to name people by their afflictions rather than their names was to remain with him throughout the years. By the time surgery had gone as far as was advisable, Wolfboy liked the mission and the McClures liked Wolfboy. He stayed on to assist the gardener, and Pao-pei became his shadow. To Pao-pei, Wolfboy was a hero of no ordinary dimensions.

When Robert was not in class with Maria, or doing home-work, or attending to household chores, he was allowed as much freedom as his Chinese playmates but unlike them he did not have to work in the fields or carry grain to the threshing floor or help man the pole that turned the upper stone of the grinding mill. But even for the Chinese boys all was not work. In the summer one would see a raggle taggle bunch of Cana-dian and Chinese boys swimming in the Wei River. Before the summer rains, the Wei wound its way rather amiably between low bare banks relieved by occasional higher ground and rows of tall willow trees. The banks were hard slippery mud and dif-ficult to negotiate but just upstream from the compound there was a bend in the river where access was easier. The swimmers would plunge in there, come down with the current, and climb ashore at the water gate steps. Dr. McClure laid down strict rules about swimming. Not only was one never to swim alone but there must always be an adult supervisor. It was a rule that was difficult to remember particularly on very hot days when Pao-pei and the gang had wandered completely out of sight of the mission.

Even in the winter the Wei was a playground. Snowfall was seldom heavy but the temperature dropped well below freezing for days on end. At such times the river froze and there were memorable days of skating on the Wei River.

Saturday was freedom day and in that one respect Robert's lifestyle coincided with that of children in the Canadian homeland he had never seen. And, once every month, Saturday was "Allowance Day"; at least for the white children. They each got one Chinese silver dollar (about 50c. Canadian). Their Chinese playmates had no allowance but often managed to earn a little spending money by collecting peanut and bean straw for the mission goats and horses. Allowance Day had an aura of adventure. Robert and one of the other mission boys, Bill Mitchell, would head for the Christian village that had grown up just beyond the compound and would round up Wolfboy and other playmates. They would then head for the city of Weihwei, half a mile away.

There was always a sense of impending magic as one passed through the gate in the city wall. The gate with its curving sweep of tiled roof and huge iron studded doors that were closed at nightfall always seemed to suggest mysteries beyond imagination. Even in the daytime one passed through the open gates only to be confronted by a solid wall forcing an abrupt turn to the right where another equally formidable gateway loomed over the cobbled street. The abrupt turn, it was said, was built to confound demons. And inside the walls, the city always seemed so busy, so full of people, so loud with the noise of human voices that it was like another world. Clutching their silver dollars the boys would head for the street of the money changers and here the real sport would begin. A naive foreigner would assume that there would be one hundred cents to a dollar but, under tutelage from their friends, Robert and Bill learned the monetary facts of Chinese life. Sometimes they could haggle their way as high as 134 copper cents in exchange for one silver dollar. That left them with 34 coppers in pure profit.

It was always understood that all profits would immediately be shared with their Chinese friends. The favourite treat was a kind of deep fried soya bean 'meat ball' served in a violently hot red pepper soup and sold by street vendors. After consuming the profits they would usually go on to squander some of the capital and once again the same bargaining principles were used. It was a system that gave everyone full value for money. A Chinese merchant would consider it a dull day indeed if he had not had a few good bargaining sessions. The boredom of fixed prices and fixed exchange rates was not for them.

On the way home from the city the boys would pass along Horse Market Street which took them outside the city gate. Here was a full-fledged Asian market full of noise, colour and activity. Here merchants sold fruit, pottery, cloth, birds, goats, in fact everything except horses. One could watch jugglers, snake charmers, or magicians and one could buy more little gastronomical delicacies, particularly if one chose to ignore warnings from one's father, the doctor, concerning parasites, bacteria and other contamination. It was here in Horse Market Street towards the end of a happy Allowance Day that the boys first realized the full power of the Law.

They heard the Law coming even before it arrived. It was heralded by loud shouts of "Make way! Make way!". There was also the sharp crack of a whip, repeated and approaching. Then over the heads of the scattering crowd they saw an officer in full uniform, mounted on a spirited horse, emerging through the city gate. It was he who wielded the whip, flailing out on either side of him as he spurred his mount through the crowd toward an open area just beyond the city gate. The boys, frightened at first, were suddenly intrigued. They noticed that the whip seldom made contact. People ran but only a few steps. There was an artificial ferocity to the officer as though he, like the merchants with whom they had just been haggling, was playing a role on the marvellous stage of this Chinese street. Instead of running the boys pushed forward to find out what was happening.

Behind the officer came a squad of men moving at a fast jog. Each man wore a wide belt with ammunition clips. Stuck in each belt, ready for instant use, if need be, was a long Mauser pistol. Wooden pistol holders slapped empty by their sides. Each man carried a large broadsword. The afternoon sun gleamed from the blades and highlighted colourful strips of red bunting streaming from each hilt. In the midst of this squad creaked an open two-wheeled farm cart with five male prisoners squatting within. Each prisoner had his hands tied behind his back. Large Chinese characters painted on a placard announced to the world that the prisoners were convicted bandits. The bandits were shouting loudly but whether in desperation, defiance, or fear the boys could not quite tell, there was so much noise and confusion and excitement.

As the parade stopped in the open square the crowd, having parted like the Red Sea, now surged in again and the boys were momentarily separated from the action. They knew the parade had stopped but could not see what was happening. They struggled forward through a crowd that seemed momentarily to be frozen.

Suddenly there was a hush of expectation and then, almost in unison, an explosion of breath, a great "Ai yah!" from hundreds of human throats.

The boys struggled and wormed their way forward and in a moment their progress was no longer impeded. It was as though the forward edges of the crowd were retreating like the Wei River after the spring floods. And then the boys were almost alone, looking at the scene that marked the end of the pageant. On the ground lay the bodies of the five bandits. Each had had his head severed by the blade of a broadsword. Each body and each head lay where it had fallen, grotesque, bloody and ghastly. Robert Pao-pei McClure was eight years old and childhood had come to an end.

For many days afterwards the boys talked among themselves about the execution they had witnessed. Thereafter and for many months whenever they would pass along Horse Market Street they would point out the execution site, each pointing it to the other as though he alone had been a witness. Bob himself was to be present at many more public executions, legal murders and mass slayings but the emotion of that first occasion was unique, as though every single individual who made up that crowd had been violated by the grossness of the performance. That first execution was to be a lasting memory, searing its way through all other childhood experiences, obliterating many of them. There was to be only one other incident to equal it and, like the executions, it was an incident that happened at the height of a happy occasion and came suddenly, ruthlessly, bringing death.

It, too, happened on a Saturday afternoon. It was a warm spring day and Pao-pei, Bill Mitchell, Wolfboy, and several of their friends had wandered along the Wei River well beyond contact with the compound. They had been watching the river traffic, the houseboats, barges, and great long bamboo rafts.

They had watched crews of boatmen toiling upstream along the towpaths as many as twelve men to a crew, each man wearing a harness attached to a long rope leading to the mast of the boat. They had listened to the song of boatmen poling lighter craft against the same currents and they had stomped their feet along the mud paths in rhythm with the bare feet stamping along the wooden decks. They had lain on their bellies in the long grass, quietly, to watch the fishermen launching cormorants into the water from the gunwales of twin-hulled boats. They had run footraces along the footpath trying to keep abreast of flat scows bubbling along with a favourable breeze filling patchwork sails. Finally, tired, hot and happy they had all gone swimming. Strict injunctions against unsupervised swimming could easily be overlooked with the mission station well out of sight and even further out of mind.

How it happened they never knew. Whether he was struck by the end of a passing barge pole or caught unawares by a sudden wave no one saw, but Wolfboy, victim of his upturned open nose cavity, drowned. One minute he was there, happy with the rest of them, and the next minute he was gone. The river, silt laden from the vast expanse of flatlands through which it wandered, was the colour of mud and just as opaque. By the time the boys found their companion he was dead. The mission boys were soundly caned and had their privileges withdrawn for weeks but no arbitrary punishment could equal the affliction of suddenly losing a friend nor could one escape the punishment meted out by one's own conscience. Sunday words and catch phrases, that had been so familiar as to be meaningless, gained a new importance. Words like "obedience" and "responsibility" required some thought. Rhetorical questions like "Am I my brother's keeper?" now demanded an answer.

It was early summer of 1910 when Dr. and Mrs. McClure took their first furlough since returning to China after the Boxer Rebellion. Bob was nine years old going on ten and ready for the first great journey of his life.

They travelled by train, Doctor and Mrs. McClure, Janet, Margaret, Bob and Maria Sloan. The first part of the journey was north up the new Peking-Hankow railway that had been completed a mere six years ago and was still a novelty. Gone were the days when it required ten days to three weeks on a houseboat to get out to Tientsin or Peking. Weihwei to Peking was now a matter of a day. The second day took them to Harbin in northern Manchuria. Here in the strange semi-Russian city of Harbin they caught the weekly train that was to carry them via the newly-opened Trans-Siberian railway to Moscow from where they would journey across Europe to England and by boat across the Atlantic to America.

It was a trip that left strange fleeting memories isolated in the boy's mind. There was something exotic about ice on the shores of Lake Baikal. Trips to churches and art galleries in Moscow were so boring as to be memorable. The dead treasures of the Hermitage could not equal the Warsaw station platform where there were live pickpockets. The English summer was incredibly warm and the whole country somehow comfortable. But all these experiences were to remain as isolated pearls of memory, not really strung together on the continuous thread of one journey. It was as though all lesser memories were once again forced into limbo by the trauma of a larger experience.

It happened when they were on the Trans-Siberian railway. Their train pulled into a small station out on the vast Russian steppes. Another train was already there, waiting on a siding. The passengers from the other train had disembarked and had scattered over the nearby fields. There seemed to be literally hundreds of people. Some were clustered in family groups around small fires while others were lying down, resting. Yet others were walking restlessly to and fro and some children, more energetic than the adults, were playing in the distance. At first the McClure children did not even notice the presence of armed guards, but their father noticed and quietly left the compartment. He returned after a few moments, having asked a few discreet questions. His report made the whole scene look even more exotic.

The train beside them was carrying exiles to Siberia. It had been waiting here almost two days for clearance to proceed. It was grossly overcrowded and the guards had permitted the passengers to take advantage of the fresh air and open spaces.

As Bob and his sisters watched, thinking that the exiles did not look so very much like prisoners because no one was being shot, or clubbed, or was in chains, the exile train whistled for departure. Guards shouted urgent orders. Men, women, children, and guards hurried from the fields, some even dropping their belongings in their haste to clamber aboard. This sudden, incredible haste seemed very strange.

The adults were on board, as were the guards, but children were still running in from the farther fields when the train whistled once more and began to move away.

The McClure children watched in uncomprehending disbelief as those other children ran screaming after that accelerating train. They watched as parents struggled to leap from the train and were held back by the guards. They watched as the train vanished and only the children were left running into the vast prairie perspective. They watched, through glass, looking out from within an upholstered compartment but those screams, faces, running feet and reaching hands would be part of Bob's memories for the rest of his days.

For many miles the three McClure children sat subdued, brooding dark thoughts. When they finally started to discuss what they had witnessed, talking quietly between themselves, they used juvenile words but their thoughts had to do with the idea that Oppression must eventually breed Revolution.

Bob had no idea that they had left China just in time to miss a real Revolution and that it would be two years before he would be back 'home' again in Honan. Nor did it mean anything to him then that five years earlier Japan had trounced Russia, driving her out of southern Manchuria and confirming Japan's claim to Korea and the southern half of the Manchurian railway. As usual others had been warring over China's territory; but something had changed. Japan, an Oriental nation, had thoroughly defeated a 'Western' one. The secret obviously lay in the acquisition of Western techniques. Chinese students had started to flow abroad in search of those techniques. Thousands went to Japan and many went to Europe. By now, 1910, those students were returning, and Chinese nationalists were again taking heart.

2

American Interlude

Bob's mother had been born and raised in Pennsylvania. The Bairds had been a farm family with a modest holding near Uniontown about fifty miles south of Pittsburgh. Grandmother Baird had proved to be more fertile than the soil and consequently Bob's mother, Margaret, was one of a family of twelve children. The farm, however, had not been without its resources. The low productivity of the topsoil was more than compensated for by the contents of the lower strata, for the farm was in Pennsylvania coal country.

Long before 1910 the farm had been completely taken over by coal interests and eventually the railroad had struck across it. There had been no big cash financial settlement but the Bairds had been given stock in the Pennsylvania Railroad. There was certainly no fortune involved but in the early years there was a rather solid growth to that railroad that made it's stocks comfortable to own.

Now, however, it was not to Uniontown that Margaret McClure and her husband headed with their children, but a little farther west to Wooster, Ohio. This was within the orbit of the Baird family and was one of those mid-West towns that seemed to have accumulated more than its fair share of missionary families. Here, in Wooster, the McClures bought a small frame house at 666 Beaver Street and Mrs. McClure, Janet, Margaret and Bob settled in to ride out the lean period of furlough while Dr. McClure went off in pursuit of his studies.

During the next two years the doctor's studies in tropical diseases and, particularly, in encephalitis would take him to London and to Africa. They were demanding studies for a man in his mid-fifties. The doctor, however, had come to his career at a more mature age than most. Before studying medicine under William Osler at McGill he had already acquired an M.A. in mathematics and a teaching certificate. In his maturity he had shown great ability in learning the Chinese language. Now, as he went off to further his medical studies, he was merely continuing a lifelong habit of self-improvement.

His little family set in to adapt to life in mid-West America. Janet and Margaret were both in high school. Bob was inserted into the midst of the Ohio primary school system and life in Wooster proceeded at a leisurely pace.

In later years Bob would remember all the Bairds as kindly, tolerant folk, some quite poor and others almost wealthy, with no barriers between them of either money or station. But the two who made a lasting impression upon him and who were to remain vivid in his memory were Uncle Will and Uncle Jim, the two black sheep of the family. It was a source of tribulation to Bob's missionary minded, evangelistic mother to know that of all her many brothers and sisters the two her son idolized were the two who had strayed the farthest from the narrow path to salvation. She admitted that a third brother had strayed, too. He had been bitten with the gold fever and had participated in the Klondike Goldrush. He, however, had come to his senses and had settled down on a farm in Kansas. It never occurred to her that she herself, a lady who was known on the other side of the world as "Bitter-lips, Sweet-heart", was not exactly orthodox.

Will Baird had been married but was now divorced. Those were the days when to be divorced was legal but not respectable. Will had had two children and they were raised by his brothers and sisters leaving him free to roam the country. Uncle Will would turn up every now and then enjoying sudden affluence. Bob and his sisters had the impression the affluence came from successful real estate deals. The source of it was quite unimportant compared with the fact that Uncle Will usually came bearing small treasures such as turtles, chipmunks, and rabbits. This was enough to establish any uncle's niche in memory, but Bob's mother clinched it one day in a sudden burst of honesty. She confided sadly to her son that Uncle Will "gambled". There was a tone in her voice that imbued the word with decadence and depravity. Uncle Will was instantly enshrined in his nephew's heart.

Mother permitted herself few really scathing descriptions of fallen people but her judgement could be read from her tone. If she said of a man, "He drinks," her tone suggested a whole world of unspeakable horrors.

Uncle Jim drank; quite liberally. He was also a bachelor, a state for a grown man that carried its own air of indecency. He had been a marine in the Spanish-American War in the Philippines. He now drove a freight locomotive on the Pennsylvania Railway. In short, to a ten year old boy going on eleven, Uncle Jim was about as exotic as an uncle could be. To a missionary sister, he was about as exasperating as any brother could be. Not only would he drop in for a visit with booze on his breath but he actually taught her boy to play poker. She also had trouble with her brother's language. Uncle Jim had trouble with it, too, and had to watch it carefully when he was visiting "Maggie" and her brood. He lapsed frequently enough for his nephew to learn the English equivalents for the words that were already part of his unofficial Chinese repertoire. Bob found it an intriguing game to ask his mother for definitions of the new words that would be left as a kind of murky residue after one of Uncle Jim's visits.

It speaks well for Maggie McClure's basic tolerance that these two brothers who must have tried her sorely were always welcome and were permitted to contribute to her son's informal and liberal education. Given the times, her vocation and that of her husband, a lesser woman might have refused to tolerate Jim and Will. As for Bob, if contacts with adults during his impressionable years had been solely confined to the missionaries of North Honan (few of whom listed drinking, gambling or profanity among their vices) he would not have grown up with the same ability to overlook such peccadilloes.

While Dr. William McClure's family were living in the provincial peace of Wooster, Ohio, back 'home' in China the Manchu Dynasty was coming to an end. The old Empress Dowager had died in 1908. The new Emperor was but a child and the country was now ruled by a Regent. In October, 1911, the accidental explosion of a bomb revealed a republican conspiracy among officers of the Wu-chang garrison. Instead of the plot being foiled it was accelerated. The Wu-chang garrison revolted, capturing the local mint and arsenal. Wu-chang, one of a great complex* of cities, was strategically located on the Yangtze River at the very heart of China. From Wu-chang the revolution spread southward. City after city declared against the Manchus. A popular republican revolutionary leader returned from abroad. His name was Sun Yat-sen. He became provisional President of the new Republic with the provisional capital being Nanking, near the delta lands of the Yangtze. The southern half of China had gone republican. The Western Powers were delighted. The Republicans represented a new wave of Chinese, interested in change and in Western ways and therefore more open to trade, commerce and exploitation. In addition, Sun Yat-sen was a Christian.

In the north the Manchu Dynasty hung on. The Regent called an old general, Yuan Shih-k'ai, out of retirement and placed him at the head of the army. It was an army that the general himself had created in the aftermath of the old Taiping Rebellion of the 1850s and his presence alone was sufficient to keep the northern army loyal. Militarily Yuan Shih-k'ai and his army were superior to Sun Yat-sen and his rebels in every way except one. Yuan Shih-k'ai did not have the support of the Western Powers. Being a man unwilling to let personal loyalties frustrate sudden opportunity the old warrior made full use of his bargaining position. He ignored the Regent and came to terms with the rebels. The principal terms were that he himself would be the first President of the New Republic. Secondary terms were that the Emperor could retain his title, the Summer Palace, and some revenue. This was not to Sun Yat-sen's liking but Yuan Shih-k'ai, being farsighted, wished to preserve the throne so that he himself could one day occupy it. The Republicans, in a generous burst of trustfulness and apparently hoping to ease China along the road to democracy without unnecessary bloodshed, agreed to Yuan's terms on February 12, 1912.

Word of all this had swept the Western world and even penetrated to Wooster. The McClure adults no doubt heard it with relief and approval; relief that a major rebellion had occurred without their beloved China being plunged into endless months of devastating civil war; approval of the new regime because of the moderating influence of Sun Yat-sen, a Chris-

*Including Hankow

tian. True, several Manchu garrisons had been massacred and the new regime, particularly with General Yuan Shih-k'ai as President, was not dedicated to non-violence, but Dr. and Mrs. McClure had learned to keep China in perspective. Even violence was a relative thing.

By the spring of 1912, the McClures were facing a major decision. Furlough was over. It was time to return to China. The complicating factor now was that their daughters were growing up. Janet, seventeen, was already taking Arts in Wooster Academy. Margaret, fifteen, was well on in high school. The McClures knew that during their absence a school for missionaries' children had been built in the compound at Weihwei but it was designed to take its students only to the end of first year high school.

Bob was quite aware of his parents' dilemma, but he was not aware of any great family trauma in deciding it. There was never any suggestion that his father was being 'called by God' but it was accepted without question that the doctor had work to do in Honan. The only question was how to organize the family in the best interest of all its members.

It was decided the family would split up. The girls would remain with their mother. They would stay in Wooster until Janet had completed her studies at the Academy and then they would go to Toronto where Margaret would finish high school and Janet could enter university. Bob, now eleven years old, would accompany his father back to China. Dr. McClure did not want his son to be separated too long during these formative years from his natural environment. It is highly significant that in the minds of both Dr. William McClure and his son, Bob's 'natural environment' was unquestioningly accepted as being North Honan, China.

3

Return to China

In the fall of 1912 a CPR Empress liner nudged her way into Shanghai harbour. Among the passengers lining the rails to view the never ending spectacle of this great Asiatic port were Dr. William McClure and his eleven year old son.

Bob could barely contain himself with the sheer excitement of it all. Within the last two years he had seen several European and American seaports but none could compare with Shanghai for sheer spectacle. He watched in wonder as the Empress slid past warships flying the flags of Britain, France, and Japan. They looked sombre, solid and threatening, which was their intent. He watched as tiny sampans scuttled out of their way and he peered down onto their flat decks where cooking fires burned just astern of the sleeping shelters. Old rusting hulks of coasters, grimy with the coal trade, smoked their laborious way out of harbour. Deep sea freighters off-loaded into lighters, their sides swarming with coolies. A gleaming liner aflutter with pennants, rails lined with waving passengers, a band playing on the hurricane deck, was moving out even as the Empress was moving in. Past liners, battleships, freighters, cutters, longboats, and sampans sailed stately Chinese junks, each rear deck towering high like the after-deck of an ancient galleon, each ribbed sail looking like a great single wing of a prehistoric insect. Bob had seen junks before around Tientsin but still marvelled at them. They were a floating paradox. They appeared to be clumsy while being amazingly elegant. They were cumbersome but functional. They were dwarfed by the ships around them but moved with inherent dignity. Off in the distance the slanting rays of the sun backlit an entire fleet whose fan-shaped sails seemed to stretch to the horizon. They were incredibly incongruous and achingly beautiful. They were China.

Dr. McClure had seen variations of the whole scene many times before. He always enjoyed it, always felt a surge of excitement. This time, however, he detected a difference. On shore there were signs of new constructions. New piers were being built, new loading facilities, new godowns.* Dredges were deepening the entrance to the Whangpoo River. The republican revolution was only a few months old but apparently already China was moving, building, looking outward to the West. As the thought crossed his mind he could not restrain an inner smile. Being linguistically oriented it always amused him not only the way "West" was used to mean both North America and Europe, but that "to look to the West" from, say, Shanghai meant to look east. English was indeed a strange almost mystical language. It would be pleasant to get ashore and be able to converse again in the cultured flowing Chinese tongue.

Dr. McClure was in for a rude awakening. He knew that many of the officials in the customs sheds could talk English but out of courtesy he always spoke Chinese. He did so now only to have his overtures proudly ignored. He had the distinct feeling he was insulting them by implying they might not be comfortable speaking English. They even brushed aside the usual formal courtesies and went straight to the business at hand. This was unnerving enough but there was another change that was so unbelievable the doctor thought at first he was over-tired after the voyage. In the great long customs godown not one single Chinese official was wearing the traditionally indispensable pigtail!

These two changes, in manner and in tradition, were incredible and yet inevitable. By now many Chinese had received Western educations, either abroad or in mission schools. They had been radicalized by the very civilization that had been exploiting them and were determined to demonstrate that China was no longer quaint, old-fashioned, and incompetent. The republican radicals had now formed a new political party under Sun Yat-sen. Its aim was to achieve nationalist ends by using

*Warehouses

Western technology to create a New China. The new party was called the "People's National Party", the *Kuomintang*.

China's politics were of no interest to young Bob when faced with the physical presence of Shanghai.

Even two short years in small town Ohio had deculturized Bob to the point where it came as almost a physical shock to move once again into the midst of so many people. The harbour had had its own sounds of whistles, horns, thudding engines, rattling chains, shouted commands, even brass bands, but the city had a sound he had almost forgotten. It was the sound of Shanghai and of Peking and Tientsin and Weihwei and even of the little village outside the Weihwei compound. It was the sound of human voices, not the cry of a multitude nor the roar of a crowd but the sound of individual human voices blending into an all pervasive seething chatter that was both background and foundation to everything else. It could frighten a Westerner when he first realized what he was hearing but it came over young Bob more like a warm wave. The sound, too, was China, and Pao-pei had come home.

The pigtail phenomenon haunted them even on the train trip north through Honan to Weihwei. Deep in the interior it was not unusual to see gangs of men waiting at the stations to ambush unwary countrymen who had not yet fully embraced the new republican freedoms. There was usually more merriment than roughness but the result was invariably the same. The pigtail would be removed with an enthusiastic snip of the sheers and the offending object would then be handed back to its owner with suitable mocking ceremony. As the train pulled into each station, Bob scanned the platforms with increasing interest, watching for waiting radicals.

There was a larger group than usual at one station but as the train slowed to a crawl, the youngster soon realized that most of this gathering were onlookers. Then, as the train stopped, he saw the focus of their attention. A handful of men were standing in isolation, their hands tied behind their backs. Facing them was a squad of soldiers, each man standing smartly to attention. There was a bugler with them and an officer. Looking out from inside the train Bob could not hear the officer but he could hear the bugle. Its off-key, strident call cut through the autumn air and the soot-smeared glass. The soldiers, mechanical toys responding to a mechanical officer, snapped through silent movements that took rifles to the horizontal. Bob heard the volley and saw the silent crumple of victims. A new China indeed. The rifle had replaced the broadsword for public executions.

Bob was only eleven, going on twelve, but thanks to a two year absence in America he was able to see China with new eyes. The country the child had taken for granted was suddenly now, to the boy, unique, primeval, and wildly fascinating. The pageant that unfolded beyond the train windows was like the beginnings of a great Oriental tapestry that was being woven especially for him. Eventually that tapestry would include republicans, monarchists, anarchists, communists, bandits, warlords, merchants, peasants and scholars, and would be coloured with the strange hues of both paradox and compassion.

The train trip home to Weihwei was merely the first passage of the shuttle across the loom.

4

Life with Father

Weihwei had changed. There was no mother, no sisters, and no Maria. Cook was still there, waiting for them, and coming home to Cook was like coming home to family. The gardener was there, too, but it made Bob sad to see him because the gardener reminded him of Wolfboy and it was all wrong not to see the strong youth with the hideous face. It was good to see Bill Mitchell again and surprising to see how some of the little kids, like Marnie Lochead, had suddenly become bigger.

It was not only the children that had grown. The compound had been enlarged and now included a house for the Locheads and a big two storey boarding school for the children of missionaries. It was typical of Mr. Lochead that he had refused to have his new house quite as big as the others and had had the standard design reduced to a mere three bedrooms. Across the road from the main gate and just a few hundred yards closer to the city gate was the beginning of another compound. There was only a wire fence around it but there was a bridge leading to it across the road and already there was a large residential school there, almost completed. It was a Secondary School for Chinese boys and Bill Mitchell's father was the principal. Next to the school, construction was underway on a large Chinese church that was already being referred to as "Rosedale Church" because the money for it was being provided by the folk of Rosedale Church in Toronto.

For Bob the presence of a residential school for missionaries' children took some getting used to. It seemed somehow strange to think that this massive two storey building with a double verandah running the entire length of two sides had been built to replace Maria Sloan. There was a matron to look after the boys and girls who were in residence. There was also a full time teacher who was assisted part time by several of the evangelical missionaries. In this new school Bob resumed his public school studies following the curriculum of the Province of Ontario. He also took violin lessons from the Rev. Harvey Grant.

The school had been set up to serve the mission families of the North Honan field and there were children there from the sister stations of Hwaiking and Changte and the smaller satellite stations of Tao-k'ou, Hsiu Wu and Wu An. But Bob McCann came all the way from Tientsin where his father, treasurer of the American Congregational Mission, had acted for several years as customs broker and general expediter for the Canadian Presbyterians.

Bob McClure, Bob McCann, Bill Mitchell and the other boys became firm friends. At first, Bob regretted that he could not join the gang and move into residence at the school but as it turned out life with his father was to have its own diversions.

The big, square, spartan mission house reserved for the Hospital Administrator would have been a dismal barn of a place for a father and one boy if Dr. McClure had not turned it into the Mission Language School. Now when new missionaries for North Honan arrived from Canada they were sent to the McClure house at Weihwei for several months of language study and acclimatization. The principal was Dr. McClure himself. It meant that the house was never empty and Bob began to experience at first hand the variety of personalities that went to make up the staff of a mission field. There were the "evangelicals" and the "medicals"; among the former were the clergymen and their wives and some of the single lady missionaries while the latter included the doctors, and those single lady missionaries who were nurses rather than educators.

Bob soon learned that some medical people could be more pious than some evangelicals and some evangelicals more skeptical than some medicals. It gradually dawned on him that the entire field was staffed not just by individuals but by individualists and that one should never generalize about missionaries. Even the fact that they were all Presbyterians was no guarantee they would conform to any pattern. There were the ones like the Rev. and Mrs. Harvey Grant who would expect to see the very gates of hell yawn open if anyone so much as mentioned the use of alcohol as a drink and there were those who would shun Roman Catholics like they would shun the Devil himself, while there were others like the Rev. Arthur Lochead who would cheerfully face both evils simultaneously by sharing a bottle of wine with the Roman Catholic Italian priests. Some missionaries could get themselves quite used to servants, comfort and good food, while others would eat porridge and drink hot water for dinner. Some delighted in holding earnest prayer sessions while others, finding their knees getting stiff, would suddenly get up and go home.

Bob gained his impressions by hearsay, by participation and by osmosis. He came to realize that his own father, while being a regular and faithful participant in Sunday worship, had his own views as to what was good theology. Bob himself rather liked hearing sermons from someone with a lot of pulpit fervor who could thunder on exhorting the faithful to move mountains by means of prayer and who would describe the most awesome of miracles in minute detail. As Bob and his father would stroll across the compound, however, the doctor would gently administer the antidote.

"Enthusiasm is a great thing," he would say. "Mind you, for myself, I'd rather not put too much reliance on miracles. To my mind the real miracles are not what the Lord can do when man prays for it but what a man can do when he lets the Lord push him to it."

The doctor was a devout man but had his own thoughts about presbytery meetings that resolved into long theological debates.

"I don't really care whether the whale swallowed Jonah. What I want to know is whether Jonah carried out any gastrointestinal investigations while he was down there."

He knew that his observations could lower the tone of theological deliberations and felt that it was not his role to do that to the evangelical missionaries any more than it was their role to intrude into his operating room. He would attend presbytery meetings, submit his reports, and then vanish at the first opportunity.

Bob never knew what his father would talk about at the dinner table. The doctor could appal guests one minute by displaying a trophy fresh from the operating room, or delight them with some anecdote. Newcomers would be shocked to hear the doctor describe how a rich merchant might disguise himself as a beggar to con the hospital into giving free medical care. Then they would find the doctor considered it as much of a game as did the Chinese themselves.

Bob and his father had never been 'chums'. Bob could not remember his father ever having read him to sleep back in childhood years. His father had not been the centre of games of family tag. But what his father did do was to treat him like an adult. Whether telling stories or answering questions the doctor was always forthright. He never tried to smudge the facts of life. He carried truth the same way he carried a big Marlin rifle, in the open. That rifle was just as unpopular as the truth. There were many who felt a missionary had no right going around armed. The doctor had reasons that were good enough for him. The villages were always full of dogs. The dogs, beaten and ill-cared for, ran in packs. They had a selective sense of smell that differentiated between Chinese, whom they feared, and white men, whom they terrorized. The doctor wore leather boots and had found that a few well directed kicks usually curbed any canine belligerency but there would be the occasional beast that he would observe weaving strangely, or drinking compulsively, or attacking in a direct line. Up would come the big Marlin 30-30 rifle and over would go the dog.

"That poor beast has rabies," he would tell his son. "If you're in doubt never give the dog the benefit of the doubt. Hydrophobia is a terrible way to die."

Bob noticed that even the most ardent arms prohibitionist would be quick enough to call the doctor if he knew of a rabid dog. Apparently there was a dividing line between good and evil that was somehow adjustable. Bob understood there was a certain practicality in having a sliding scale of values when faced with a mad dog. It was a lesson which, once thoroughly understood, made it difficult for him to accept philosophical absolutes.

During these years Dr. McClure was Weihwei's only qualified physician and surgeon. He would occasionally be relieved or assisted by Western doctors in for language study or seconded temporarily from one of the other stations. There was a Chinese medical staff but at this stage the Chinese 'doctors' were still unqualified in that they had taken no formal training. Some of these medical assistants had apprenticed with practitioners who themselves were products of the apprentice or 'preceptor' system. It was a system that had only recently passed out of use in Canada and both there and in China had produced practitioners of great practical knowledge and skill. It was not a system, however, that could fill the demands of modern medicine as hospitals began to be equipped with X-rays, aseptic operating rooms and better laboratory facilities. This was all beginning to happen at Weihwei and everything from the introduction of new nursing techniques to the use of modern anaesthesia put more and more of a strain on the hospital's medical chief, Dr. McClure. In addition to administration, surgery, teaching and routine medical work, the doctor was putting his recent post-graduate studies into practice and was beginning to build a reputation as one of China's leading diagnosticians of early encephalitis and of Parkinson's disease.

Dr. McClure was also the Mission Treasurer for Weihwei and as such was responsible for all mission expenditures including the thirty or so salaries that supported seventy to eighty people. This task was made interesting but time consuming by the transformations Canadian currency had to undergo in transit from Toronto to the pockets of Weihwei. It was a transformation that went from dollars to English pounds to Chinese *taels* to Chinese silver dollars, with the *tael* (a weight measurement, not a currency) being the only constant in the whole process. Dr. McClure put his M.A. in mathematics to good use.

It was the doctor's duties as treasurer that brought him and Bob into contact with Building Contractor Wang and his family. Mr. Wang was an entrepreneur of sorts who had a temporary home in the Christian village and a permanent one on a farm some miles away. In the past he had contracted with the mission to provide various construction services and at the moment was involved in what was by far the biggest job of his career. Contractor Wang was building "Rosedale" Church. This was to be a big church with a soaring vaulted roof supported by great Douglas Fir timbers from Canada's own forests. There had already been a gala day when those same timbers had arrived at the mission, a great raft of them having been poled the 600 miles up the Wei River. There had been a terrible day, too, when one of the stone masons had fallen from a dizzy height and been killed. But the work had continued to progress.

It was only during the stages when the roof itself was going on that Dr. McClure, as treasurer, discovered that Mr. Wang was going bankrupt. He had miscalculated in his estimates. He was, however, not complaining. He had already mortgaged some property and was continuing to build the church, paying for it from his own pocket. Dr. McClure was both impressed and appalled. This was not the way a church should be built. After assuring himself that Mr. Wang's losses were very real he saw to it that the mission absorbed the loss. General Contractor Wang was also impressed.

It so happened that Mr. Wang had a son the same age as Bob. A missionary in a fit of enthusiasm had named him George Washington. George was enrolled in the Weihwei Chinese Primary School. George Washington Wang and Bob Pao-pei McClure became good friends and visits to the Wang home enlarged Bob's domestic horizons.

The summer of 1913 was to be marked by two mileposts, one for China and one for Bob. That summer the doctor decided Bob was old enough to learn to handle a firearm. They found an isolated spot and Bob was initiated into the mysteries of the big lever action Marlin. That same summer the republicans of the Kuomintang decided they had outgrown subservience to President Yuan Shih-k'ai who was acting more and more as though he was intending to found a new dynasty rather than a new democracy. The Kuomintang, under Sun Yat-sen, rebelled and launched an expedition to chastise the President. The expedition seized Nanking but the rebellion was soon put down. Yuan Shih-k'ai was astute enough to notice that the Western Powers had not rushed to the aid of the Kuomintang simply because it advocated democratic republicanism. He deduced, quite accurately, that they were much more interested in a strong man at the helm of China and he set his face resolutely toward becoming, if not the next emperor of China at least the first of the modern warlords. It was quite possible that the gentle, farsighted doctor was not thinking entirely of canine mad dogs when he chose that same summer to teach his son the maintenance and use of the Marlin.

In November, 1913, after little more than a year of existence, the Kuomintang was outlawed, but whether the revolution was dying or still suffering birth pangs only time would tell. In that same month, November 1913, Bob celebrated his thirteenth birthday and his life took on new dimensions as his father began to let him see more and more of the work at the hospital. Bob became an interested observer and soon a participant.

It was about this time that a young Canadian doctor arrived on the China field. He was a junior of the juniors but he was brilliant. He was highly eccentric but highly capable. His mind seemed unable to understand the Chinese language but quite able to understand the Chinese ailments. He had worked at other mission hospitals but at each one his eccentricities were such that his medical chiefs, each in turn, saw fit to recommend him in the highest terms and pass him on to the next unsuspecting station. In this fashion Dr. F. F. Carr-Harris came to Weihwei. He took up residence in the McClure house and Bob gradually became his unofficial interpreter thus permitting the education of both to continue apace.

Dr. Carr-Harris was to become something of a mission field legend. People could dine out on stories of Carr-Harris and the true stories were usually more bizarre than the apocryphal so it became difficult to separate one from the other. A tall, gaunt, homely young man he had a winning warmth about him that attracted the patient's trust. Missionary wives who were fortunate enough to have Carr-Harris supervise their confinements described his bedside manner as "loving". The fact that he might well abandon a hospital full of patients to give loving care to one confinement was merely one of his little eccentricities. When he gave his mind to anything he gave it totally, without reservations. They said he could become so engrossed in a medical textbook that he would not notice the lamp burning incorrectly and would read on while the flame vanished behind a wall of carbon and the house rolled with smoke. They said he would turn up at the hospital in the middle of the night wanting to do an operation and not be able to comprehend why the medical assistants were not on hand.

Bob always took pleasure in the fact that he had met Carr-Harris in the latter's formative years. They even worked together as colleagues during the course of one long heroic night when Bob, as interpreter, was the middle man in a night long argument between Dr. Carr-Harris and the senior medical assistant as to the lengths to which a doctor should go to save an old man's life. Dr. McClure was away and the old man under discussion was an opium addict who had taken a large overdose by mouth. For some strange reason the medical assistant seemed to think they were interfering and the old man should be permitted to die. Bob, as interpreter, admired the firmness with which Carr-Harris over-ruled all opposition while prescribing a shot of atropine, the use of a stomach pump, and large doses of expensive and very rare coffee. That the patient lived was entirely due to Dr. Carr-Harris and it was an object lesson for Bob. Obviously an eccentric could still be a good doctor.

A few days later the ex-patient was beheaded for dealing in opium and that, too, was an object lesson for Bob. He realized that to interpret a case one needed to understand more than the words. The Chinese part of his mind wondered if perhaps the assistant had been right and they had been interfering. The activist, Western part of him decided there was something equally interfering in the use of a broadsword, and that one could still make a case for Fate being man-made.

Dr. Carr-Harris moved on to other parts carrying another sterling recommendation to add to his portfolio. (He eventually went away to World War I and absent-mindedly won almost every medal except the Victoria Cross. He finally left the mission field in order to bestow his amazing gifts upon the people of Kingston, Ontario.) Before long two more Canadian doctors joined the Weihwei team. They were Dr. Fred Auld, a surgeon from Montreal, and Dr. Gordon Struthers.

The demands on the Weihwei hospital were increasing with every year and for some time Dr. McClure had been thinking about the need for re-building and re-organizing. Dr. Auld had the vision of a thoroughly 'modern' hospital using up-to-date nursing and teaching techniques. Dr. McClure was enthusiastic and felt that Fred Auld and Gordon Struthers were just the men to carry out the vision. As for himself, he was no longer a young man but he knew there was a mountain of work to be done in translating English language medical texts into Chinese, and that there was a tremendous need for professors of medicine who could teach in Chinese. While Dr. McClure encouraged Auld and Struthers to draw plans for a new hospital he himself was drawing plans for a new career.

It was just about this time, as his father was beginning to make decisions about the next stage of his medical career, that Bob made the first decision about his own.

It was a Sunday morning and Bob and his father were coming out of chapel after having attended the Chinese church service. A panic stricken father was hurrying across the compound toward the hospital carrying his little eight year old daughter in his arms. Dr. McClure and Bob joined him and learned that the child had been bitten by a rabid dog. She was already in an advanced stage of hydrophobia, convulsing horribly and in much pain. The doctor took the child in his arms, ordered Bob not to follow, and vanished into the hospital.

The little scene took place so quickly that it was virtually impossible in later years for Bob to recall the specific points that made such an overall impact upon him. Was it the child herself, eyes wide with fear and clouded with pain, her mouth opening and closing with jawbreaking spasms? Was it the father, looking slight and helpless in his worn baggy trousers and threadbare quilted jacket, holding his child to him and running, too late, to the foreign hospital? Dr. McClure had taken the child and carried her inside but what was he going to do? And why had the doctor ordered Bob, almost brusquely, not to follow? Bob went home, his imagination haunting the interior of the hospital. He had heard of hydrophobia victims having to be lashed to their beds, literally, during the final stages. Surely with morphine and other drugs his father would at least be able to rescue the pathetic little victim from that fate!

When his father finally came home Bob was stunned. His father was moving slowly and suddenly looked so old. He merely reported that the child had died and said no more. What he had no need to report in words, for it was written on his face and in every weary movement, was that her dying had drained him. For the first time Bob began to understand that compassion was something active, that one human being gave to another, that it was a life force that sprang from one's very vitals and in the extreme moments of its passing over could leave the donor physically exhausted. He also understood that in the face of one of the monstrous afflictions of this world compassion alone had not been enough. It was at that rather strange moment when his father, having lost a patient, was in the depths of depression that Bob McClure decided he, too, would be a doctor.

As public school drew to a close Bob and his pals tried the Ontario Departmental examinations to qualify for high school 'entrance'. The Rev. Harvey Grant was their examiner and he eyed the McClure results with sorrow. The Missionary Childrens' School could take pride in the academic accomplishments of young William Mitchell but it was sadly apparent that Bob McClure had been spending more time haring around the countryside than studying. He would have to pull himself together if he was serious about medicine.

During 1914 President Yuan Shih-k'ai had himself proposed as emperor. He ploughed at the Temple of Agriculture and sacrificed at the Altar of Heaven. He humbly kept refusing the crown with the artfulness of Shakespeare's Caesar and in compliance with Chinese tradition, while at the time moving closer and closer to the throne. There was still enough respect for the stylized rituals of Confucian society that the wily general did not move with undue haste. Unfortunately for Yuan Shih-k'ai, World War I intruded itself into his schemes.

While Western Powers were concentrating upon self-annihilation in Europe, Japan used her alliance with Britain as justification to occupy the German concessions in Shantung, a province bordering on Honan. She was given the moral support of a small British force. Japan then went beyond anything that had been granted the Germans and claimed a railway zone along which she set up a Japanese civil administration. By January of 1915, Japan was quietly presenting the Emperor-elect of China with a list of "Twenty-One Demands". If accepted these demands would have had the effect of eliminating China's independence and of making her a Japanese protectorate. Yuan Shih-k'ai temporized and stalled, hoping for Western support, but the Western Allies at the moment wanted Japan's help more badly than they wanted China's survival. Yuan showed signs of yielding.

Before the Boxer Rebellion, Yuan Shih-k'ai had betrayed

the reforming Emperor Kuang Hsü to the reactionary Empress Dowager. Later on he had betrayed the Regent to the Republic. Next he had betrayed the Republic to himself and it now looked as though he was about to betray China to the Japanese.

It was not the republicans who rose first in protest but the generals. There was a massive military revolt and by early 1916 generals were jockeying for power, the Kuomintang had declared a provisional republican government at Canton and Yuan Shih-k'ai had died, according to a usually reliable source*, of "chagrin and rage". China had well and truly passed from Confucious into confusion and the Age of the Warlords had begun. The McClures, however, were not present for this final stage of transition. In the summer of 1915 the doctor and his son had returned to Toronto, Canada. Not long after that most of the male medical staff of the Honan mission and many of the evangelical missionaries were on the slaughter fields of France and Bob himself was entering the academic years that would be the final step in preparing him to serve in the chaos that was China.

*Encyclopedia Brittanica.

5

The Higher Education of Bob McClure

It was the summer of 1915 by the time Bob and his father rejoined Mrs. McClure, Janet, and Margaret. The McClure womenfolk were in Toronto where they had migrated two years before in order to enroll Janet in Arts in the University of Toronto. Margaret was attending Harbord Collegiate. As for Bob, he was finally, at the age of fourteen, taking up residence in Canada, his official homeland. The family rented a house at 83 Kendall Avenue, Toronto, and Bob, too, attended Harbord Collegiate.

In the school in the Weihwei compound Bob had completed first year of high school, known as First Form. Now, in wartime, everything was accelerated and *haste* was the by-word. Bob found himself projected forward into Third Form. At one step he missed the Second Form grounding in French, Latin, Algebra and Ancient History. There was, unfortunately, no scope for his Chinese language.

To a boy who had just come from the intimate atmosphere of the school in the Weihwei compound, where students and teachers were all part of an extended family, the aloofness of the staff in the big city collegiate was chilling. Any teacher-student relationship was strictly within the classroom. Bob knew nothing about his teachers as individuals except their names and their most obvious personality traits. He did not know where they lived, what they did in their spare time, whether or not they had families, or how they felt about social issues. Even his fellow students vanished at four o'clock. It was only the ones who resurfaced again at the Bloor Street Presbyterian Church Sunday school that he really got to know. It was the Sunday school teachers who opened themselves to questions and who would talk about the peculiar ways of the world that had nothing to do with Latin or Algebra. They were the teachers who were destined to remain in his memory throughout the years.

In the summer of 1916, Bob was introduced to the working class, a group that was missing from the middle class pews of Bloor Street Church. In the spring of that year, with the June exams on the horizon, Dr. McClure asked his son what he intended to do with himself during the summer holidays.

"Work in a war plant," said Bob, promptly.

"Well then, son, hadn't we better decide what plant you'd like and who's in charge and make an appointment to do some negotiating?"

Bob knew only too well what his father meant. Any respectable Chinese father of means would make a proper contact for his son and would negotiate the terms and conditions of employment.

Bob tried to explain the Canadian way. "When exams are over you just go someplace where there's a sign on the fence saying they need workers. That's all."

He protested in vain. The doctor went down to the Russell Motor Car Company factory on King Street and stood unhappily eyeing the premises. Like all industrial plants in the country it was in the midst of a wartime boom, expanding its facilities and working three shifts a day. It was large, busy and impersonal. The doctor never penetrated beyond the main gate. He talked to the security man there and explained that he had an intelligent son whose services were about to become available to the war industry.

"Little bugger wants a job does he? Send the little sod down. We'll fix'm up."

Doctor McClure came home in a rather thoughtful mood. He apologized for not having been able to see the Manager and warned Robert that the employees of the Russell Motor Car Company were a rather rough lot. It was effective advertising and Bob chose to honour the Russell Motor Car Company with his fifteen year old enthusiasm for the summer of 1916.

In comparison with the missionaries of Weihwei compound the employees in the factory down on King Street were indeed a "rough" but cheerful crowd. The doctor, still worried that his son might not be working with 'nice' people, quizzed him carefully concerning his fellow workers' language and morals, both of which Bob found to be fascinatingly loose. Bob answered all such questions but developed skill in the use of euphemisms.

The Russell Motor Car Company proved to be a happy choice. Bob worked ten to twelve hours a day six full days a week and sometimes on Sunday. He was making brass fuses for artillery shells and while doing so he received an apprenticeship in the use of machine tools. The result was the development of a skill in metal work that was to be a major asset in the years ahead.

Fourth Form high school made little more intellectual impression upon young McClure than had Third Form. Margaret had now finished high school and was training as a nurse. Janet was still at Varsity but had transferred to medical college. Bob ploughed ahead trying to keep some balance between sports, Sunday school, studies and the Cadet Corps. He made several attempts to enlist in the army but ran into two obstacles which, when combined, proved insurmountable. He was under age and his parents wielded an iron veto.

During this fourth year of high school the family moved again. It was the shortest move of their career being two blocks along Kendall Ave., to number 32.

Bob knew before he completed Fourth Form that if he were to continue on to university he would have to pay much of his own way. The combined efforts of his family and of the Foreign Mission Board of the Church could only provide him with about $350.00 a year. The secret of survival was obviously going to lie in part time jobs and summer employment.

The wartime system permitted students with good academic standing to leave school in the spring before the final examinations, provided they were employed in what was exuberantly known as the "Soldiers of the Soil" programme. Dr. McClure felt that farmwork was definitely character building and Bob felt that even character building was better than writing exams. His term achievement in Fourth Form, however, was such that he could only be relieved from the spring exams if he would undertake to write four supplementals in September. It was an ingenious device that enabled the nation to get labour onto the land when it was needed and permitted the same labour to postpone the inevitable moment of academic truth. There was a distinct impression among the students that the supplementals would be marked more leniently than would the spring exams.

Bob shovelled manure all summer for eight dollars a week, survived the four supplementals, and was granted his Junior Matriculation. There was something paradoxical about qualifying for Junior Matric on the end of a manure fork but paradox was part of life to anyone with a good Chinese background.

In the autumn of 1917, Bob enrolled in first year medicine at the University of Toronto. That same autumn Dr. McClure returned to China to teach medicine at Cheloo University in Tsinan and Mrs. McClure and Margaret went to Oberlin, Ohio, where Margaret could study kindergarten-teaching. Soon, they would rejoin Dr. McClure in China. Janet was still in Toronto, in third year medicine.

Young Bob McClure was among the last group of students to be permitted to enroll in medicine in Ontario with only four years of high school as a pre-requisite. Soon one would require five years of high school in order to enter university, and honour standing in order to study medicine. Since Bob had skipped Second Form, he actually had had only three years of Ontario's much vaunted secondary education, and that, with final marks so low they had had to be elevated on the tines of a pitchfork. But, with an entire generation being slaughtered on the battle fields of France, doctors were in short supply. Bob McClure, not yet turned seventeen, was considered to be ready for 'higher education'.

During the next five years Bob managed to improve his academic standings, although he was never destined to achieve the heady triumph of being 'top of the class'. As usual, his education continued to be based on experiences broader than the curriculum.

As the son of a Presbyterian missionary, Bob was given a free room in the men's residence of Knox Theological College, but the financing of food, books, tuition and incidentals was his responsibility. Family resources were limited and Bob estimated that he would have to earn about $1000.00 a year from part time employment. As it turned out, part time employment added valuable depth to his education. The most useful experience was that of a dockyard stevedore.

Toronto harbour, even in those pre-Seaway days, was a busy port. The city had had an early career as the capital of Upper Canada partly because of its excellent natural harbour. Since 1914 the facilities had been expanding and improving with new warehouses, wharves and piers being constructed to accommodate the increasingly large Great Lakes vessels. In those pre-forklift, pre-containerized days the principal qualification for a stevedore was that he have good muscles, a strong back, and no fear of hard work. The Chinese summed it all up in one word, "coolie" meaning "bitter-strength". The real coolies of North Honan would have been amazed to see Pao-pei of Weihwei working as a coolie on the Toronto harbourfront, but it was a weekend occupation that helped put the same Pao-pei through college.

The docks at the bottom of York Street were singularly free of red tape. Bob would head down after his last lecture on a Friday afternoon. There were no forms to fill out and no applications to be made. He would be given a brass identification token with a number on it and could start right in on the six o'clock shift. From there on for the rest of the weekend it was up to him. The stevedores worked five hours on and one hour off. They could put their shifts end to end for as long as they were able to keep their eyes open, stand up, and work. At the end of the first shift the sixth hour was usually spent eating sandwiches and chatting. At the end of the second shift one ate a sandwich and looked for the nearest bale to sleep on. By the end of subsequent shifts even a sack of potatoes made a most comfortable bed indeed. When the stevedore had had all he could take he simply handed in his brass token and was paid off in hard cash. It was 50¢ an hour in the daytime, 55¢ at night, and 60¢ an hour Saturday afternoon and evening with no deductions and no questions asked.

It was with considerable surprise that Bob learned that most of his fellow coolies were ex-convicts who were not using their correct names. It was with fascination that he listened to casual conversations concerning the life inside such venerable institutions as Kingston Penitentiary and Toronto's Don Jail. Bob was impressed by the genuine humanity of this group of men. Most were knowledgeable and some had wide interests. Occasionally, after an all night shift, one of the married men would invite him to share breakfast in a dingy one room flat on Sherbourne Street. While Bob ate his fried egg and toast the man's chatty wife filled in the domestic details of an ex-convict's life.

That wife, her husband, and the other stevedores of the Toronto harbourfront had a more profound effect on the young medical student than they ever knew. They reinforced in him a tendency, already planted in China, not to assess people by the sometimes arbitrary judgements of society.

During the Christmas and New Year period, with the harbour frozen over, Bob shifted his part time earning endeavours to the Union Station and put his stevedore muscles to work as a baggage handler. The job was known affectionately as "baggage smashing". That was the era when the railroads held a monopoly in that gentle art.

He spent another summer working on a farm. He spent two summers in the office of the Lake Simcoe Ice Company and one summer as chauffeur and mechanic for Sir William Gage's* motor launch on the Muskoka Lakes. He also took up barbering and did a stint as a hod carrier for bricklayers. Hod carrying was a union job and so McClure became a card carrying, dues paying member of The Construction Workers' Union of Toronto. There was something reassuringly proletarian about his union card and it remained in his wallet for many years.

During the academic year, lectures, labs, studying, and part time employment filled most of McClure's waking hours but he did manage to play some basketball. He also found time to play second violin in the Meds orchestra. He joined the Student Volunteer Movement which had a most optimistic motto: "Evangelization of the World in This Generation". Summers were more relaxing and he acquired a second hand canoe along with a fairly strong biological urge. He and his friends used the canoe to prowl the recreational waterfront area at Sunnyside beach. After one depressing occasion led young McClure panting to a girl's home just in time to help put her drunken father to bed in most miserable surroundings, Bob decided that per-

*Publisher, philanthropist, and founder of several TB sanitoria.

haps the choosing of the correct person and place for the biological rituals deserved more thought than he had given it.

Bob also acquired wheeled transportation. It was a powered vehicle of the most elemental sort consisting of a small buckboard body mounted on four bicycle wheels and propelled by a fifth wheel driven by a tiny gasoline engine. It was one of a number of such vehicles that had been supplied at war's end by a philanthropist who hoped they might be of use to double amputees. As it turned out an operator needed to be blessed not only with both legs but with mechanical ability as well. Bob found the machine derelict, bought it cheaply and rebuilt it himself. It carried him from Knox College to clinics at Toronto General Hospital at a maximum speed of twenty-five miles per hour and became a familiar sight on campus. *Varsity* magazine, delighted by the oddity of a machine with a fifth wheel, dubbed it the "pentacycle" and poked fun at it for several years. The story went around that a dear old lady standing on a street corner as the McClure pentacycle trundled by was heard to exclaim, "That poor boy, is he crippled?" A laconic reply came from a passing medical student. "Not physically."

The jokesters were no doubt envious. The pentacycle had a certain quaint charm in a high wheeled way and just a touch of dash. It was, romantically speaking, a landgoing canoe with the added advantage of being able to travel more genteel areas. A young man and a lady friend could cut quite a swath on a Sunday afternoon on the pentacycle just so long as they kept away from the hills on Avenue Road and Yonge Street south of St. Clair.

There was still a problem, however, for an impecunious young Lothario even with five wheels. Although the pentacycle cruised a better area of town than did the canoe the unfortunate fact remained that girls of the 'nice' type were inclined to have expensive tastes. They liked to attend the cinema and go to concerts at Massey Hall. A fellow could very easily slide into a whole social life geared to high living and high expense. Bob had not developed any particular antipathy toward high living but the Scottish Presbyterian ancestors lurking in his genes drew the line at high expense. The primary target was "education" and he knew it instinctively in every ancestral drop of blood.

In spite of the physical demands made upon him by the pressures of studies and part time employment, Sunday mornings usually found Bob McClure occupying a pew at Bloor Street Presbyterian Church. There he came under the influence of that institution's patriarchal pastor, Dr. George C. Pidgeon.

Dr. Pidgeon was one of those big, quietly virile clergymen who gave the lie to every cliche ever devised about men of the cloth. He exuded authority without domination, confidence without assertiveness, devoutness without piousness, and was able to demonstrate that holiness could be compatible with efficiency. To begin with, however, his main contribution to Bob was that of a reassuring sounding board for the latter's gradually broadening theological concepts.

Although Dr. William McClure had always been somewhat impatient with ecclesiastical pedants, and was certainly not inclined to take the whole Bible quite literally, he had never suggested any personal hesitation in the complete acceptance of Jesus as the Messiah foretold in the Old Testament and as the Only Son of God as proclaimed in the New. Nor had any others of the Weihwei family shown any waffling on this point. But at university Bob met, for the first time, the Humanist idea of Christ as a man. What upset him was the realization that it seemed to make such good sense! For a while he went around feeling vaguely guilty as one does who thinks he is turning his back on the faith of his fathers. Then he had the good sense to talk to Dr. Pidgeon.

Dr. Pidgeon reassured him, told him not to be afraid of the Humanists and not to be intimidated by the Conservatives, but to search for his own Truth and, if he found it, to follow it. It was counsel that was followed to the letter; had it not been, the unique career of Bob McClure would not have been possible.

It was at Bloor Street Church in the early spring of 1920 that Bob and the rest of the congregation received sad news, the import of which would eventually affect Bob's career. The news was that Dr. James Menzies, the father of Jean Menzies, Bob's 'sister' of Weihwei days, had been murdered in the North Honan mission station of Hwaiking.

There were two sections to the old Hwaiking compound in those days, the area where the single lady missionaries lived being separated by a double wall from the main area. Between the double wall ran a cart track. Over the track, spanning the gap, ran a footbridge joining the compounds together. One night bandits invaded the ladies' quarters causing loud cries of both indignation and fear. It was probably money they were after, although rape was frequently on the agenda for such nocturnal raids. Dr. Menzies rose from his bed and ran to the rescue. He had a revolver in his study but whether he forgot to take it or refused to take it no one would ever know. He was totally unarmed when he found his path across the footbridge blocked by a bandit. A hand to hand struggle began up on the footbridge and Dr. Menzies, a robust, versatile man of wide experience, might well have triumphed had a second bandit not fired upon them. It was typical of the impartiality of Chinese bandits that the gunman fired on both men, killing his own man and wounding Dr. Menzies in the leg. The gunman fled, but James Menzies lay haemorrhaging from a severed femoral artery. By the time his associate and former apprentice, Dr. Chang Hui-ting, could get him down from the bridge and into surgery Dr. Menzies was dead. It was perhaps unfortunate that the hospital facilities were so tantalizingly close. First aid up on the bridge might have saved Menzies' life. On the other hand, minutes wasted groping in the darkness to discover the nature of the wound could have been just as fatal. It had not been an easy choice for Dr. Chang.

The congregation of Bloor Street Church held a memorial service for Dr. James Menzies on March 28th, 1920. As reported by one participant it was "a sad, yet triumphant" occasion.

It was that same year, 1920, that Bob met Amy Hislop. That event, too, would affect the remainder of his life. Amy's older sister, also a Janet, was teaching school in Toronto and going out with a medical student, Stan Montgomery, who was a close friend of Bob's. Janet and Stan brought Bob and Amy together at a corn roast on a Toronto beach.

The Hislop girls were from Whitby, a small town not far from Toronto. Their father was a retired farmer who was now working as grounds keeper at the Ontario Ladies' College in Whitby. Their mother had been a school teacher. Both parents were devout Presbyterians and Amy and Janet had been brought up in an atmosphere as religiously oriented as had Bob. Bob wanted to be a doctor, Amy wanted to be a nurse, and both were thinking of serving on the foreign mission field. At the moment Amy was working as a secretary at the

Goodyear Tire and Rubber Company where she was becoming proficient in the new secretarial speciality of transcribing dictation from the wax cylinders of Mr. Edison's Dictaphone. Her hope was to enroll in nursing as soon as she could save enough money to finance the three year course.

It was not unnatural that Amy Hislop should be quite impressed by her first encounter with the sandy-haired extrovert with the Scottish name who had been born when his mother was fleeing the Boxer Rebellion and who spoke Chinese, played a mandolin and sang pleasantly sacriligious songs.

It was only natural that Bob McClure should be attracted to the good looking, dark-haired girl with the pensive eyes whom he found liked a good time just as much as he did and was just as unable to squander ready cash to achieve it. Here was a girl with whom one could relax. They started going out together, not frequently but whenever it was practical. They went to free university concerts and to meetings of the newly formed Student Christian Movement. They would attend the evening service at Bloor Street Church and then enjoy the long walk back to Amy's lodging without either one feeling pressured. Amy got the distinct feeling that Bob was just a little *too* casual.

The courtship continued at an amiable pace during Fifth Year Medicine but Amy was never under any illusions concerning young McClure's intentions. Medical training took top priority and everything else was of secondary consideration. So far sentimentality had not been a prime mover in the lives of William McClure and his progeny. Singleness of purpose and tenacity was much more in the McClure line.

It was during this Fifth Year that the scope of Bob's medical training was suddenly broadened, quietly but significantly. Dr. Parsons, a faculty member, was a practising doctor who would often enter the lecture hall having just come from the bedside of patients in the final stages of TB. He confided to his class that the patients who upset him the most were half a dozen young people who were at home dying of TB. The problem, as Dr. Parsons saw it, was simple but very real.

"They're too weak to come to the hospital for check-ups. They can't afford to have a doctor call on them regularly and the fact is that medically there is nothing more one can do for them. But what a help it would be if a final year medical student were to drop in on them, regularly!"

Bob was puzzled.

"Sir, if a patient's past your help—well, I don't see how a student can do any good?"

"McClure, they need to know that *somebody* cares!"

It was with considerable misgivings that Bob set out to make housecalls where he knew he could contribute literally nothing but himself. He had a stethoscope sticking out of his jacket pocket and he carried a little black bag that had nothing in it. The young patients and their grieving parents called him "Doctor" although they knew he was not, and they associated him, through Dr. Parsons, with the hospital. There was a Catholic family out east of the Don River in the Beaches area whose fourteen year old daughter, Mercy, was a victim of advanced bilateral tuberculosis of the lung. Mercy, a tiny little thing already down to skin and bones, was also plagued with asthmatic attacks which would strike in the night. The family had Bob's phone number at Knox and he had his pentacycle. Whenever they called him, he went. It was a subtle experience for the young medical student and difficult to analyse. There was no doubt it was a venture that gratified his ego. After four and a half years of being a nonentity, there being nothing in the medical profession lower than a mere student, here he was suddenly being called "Doctor" and being treated with deference. On the other hand here he was, far from hospital or clinic, entering poor private homes where small families were waging the age old and unequal struggle against indiscriminate and undignified death. Here the "doctor" had a role to fulfill that had very little to do with the official parchment of graduation and had a great deal to do with those strange inner vibrations known as compassion.

Mercy died, as Dr. Parsons had said she would, but her passing etched a message deep into young McClure's being. Even though in the final stages medical science had been powerless to help Mercy, there had still been a real need for a representative of that science to be there with the patient, far from the institutional base. As the ridiculous pentacycle burbled its way homeward through the dingy industrial area near the mouth of the Don River, the young man at the helm was beginning to formulate a concept of medical work that would go far beyond hospitals and even beyond the nebulous area known as "Public Health". It was a concept that would eventually lead him and his associates to medical pioneering that would have unsung ramifications in the history of Chairman Mao's China. Never would Bob McClure view with equanimity any hospital that had no outreach.

Before the end of Fifth Year he made a decision concerning his future. He was still going to be a missionary but he would go about it in a way that would build some financial independence. Young McClure had never pretended to *enjoy* a low standard of living and some financial independence would permit him to concentrate on the areas of service where, in his opinion, he had the most to contribute. The short term route to reach the long term goal appeared to lead through the British Colonial Service. The Service offered a good salary, security, and a great deal of experience in tropical medicine. Bob applied and was accepted on condition he was willing to do some post-graduate work in Public Health at Harvard after graduation. He was more than willing and for a brief period it looked as though he was controlling his own destiny.

"Graduation Day" for Bob was on a May morning in the year 1922. This was not the graduation day of processionals and distinguished guest speakers and the ritual of cap, gown and hood with the University Chancellor droning, "Rise, Doctor of Medicine". That was an official ritual in which Bob and many of his friends never participated. Real graduation was the morning the entire class of '22 gathered, perspiring with nervousness in the main hallway of the Old Medical Building. They clustered at the foot of the big staircase and tried to appear nonchalant and unconcerned while the Dean's secretary, Miss Russell, came down the steps. She paused while still at a nicely elevated vantage point and gazed upon them like some aging Establishment Vestal Virgin about to bestow largesse upon the peasant masses. She had in her hands a list of names of those who had passed and this list she opened and read, not too slowly, lest it be thought that she herself approved of the fact that any member of such an obviously unworthy group should be given the accolade of M.D. The name "McClure, Robert Baird" was on Miss Russell's list.

Bob headed off for the Y.M.C.A. summer camp at Geneva Park on Lake Couchiching. The Y.M.C.A., optimistically assuming that he would graduate, had hired him for the summer as camp Medical Officer. After his arrival at camp he had sev-

eral hours before attending to his first patient. He confessed
many years later that those few hours were the only time in his
long career when he knew all there was to know about medicine. He was twenty-one and knew it all.

He returned to Toronto the first week of September and
began to pack his bags for Harvard. The next Sunday morning
found him attending Bloor Street Church for what might well
be the last time in many years. After the service Dr. Pidgeon
asked Bob to step into the vestry. It was nice of him, thought
Bob, to want to say good-bye.

"Bob," said Dr. Pidgeon, "it's two years since Dr. Menzies
was killed. How would you like to go out to China and take his
place?"

The hospital at Hwaiking had been built by Bloor Street
donations added to an original seeding of $25.00 donated by a
lady dying of cancer. Dr. Menzies himself had been designated
by the Presbyterian Church as "the special missionary of Bloor
Street Church". Now, if Bloor Street Church was asking young
McClure to replace Dr. Menzies it was no idle request. Bob felt
a tremendous surge of excitement. For him North Honan was
certainly not an unknown country. He knew from first hand
that there the disease was real, the bandits were real, and the
adventure was real. The thought of possible adventure was
powerfully attractive but prudence took hold and he back-
pedalled. After all, there was Harvard and the British Colonial
Service, and the idea of making himself financially independent.

"There's a problem, sir," said Bob. "I can't go to China
without post-graduate work. From what I know of Honan I
shouldn't go to Hwaiking without a year of surgery."

This was a real problem. Internships were hard come by
and all the openings would have been snapped up in July.
These things followed an established pattern that was as un-
changing as the Laws of the Medes and the Persians. It would
be virtually impossible for Bob to be accommodated now.

Dr. Pidgeon ignored the problem. He named four of the
leading surgeons in the city and asked young McClure which
one of these mighties he would like to work under.

"Sir," said Bob, "this is ridiculous. I'd be honoured to
work with any of them. But it's too late, I don't think it can be
arranged."

"Well, how about Dr. Perfect at Western Hospital?"

"Of course," said Bob, knowing it was quite impossible, "that would be lovely."

Dr. Pidgeon picked up the telephone, got the operator, and in a few moments was interrupting Dr. Perfect's Sunday dinner.

The two men chatted about how nice it was to have a volunteer willing to replace a murdered missionary and agreed that it would be unkind to release him upon the unsuspecting Chinese without first giving him more surgical training. After a few moments Dr. Pidgeon turned to Bob.

"Dr. Perfect says you're his man. You begin tomorrow morning at Western Hospital. Eight o'clock."

6

The Intern

Dr. Kenneth Perfect, Chief of Surgery at Toronto Western Hospital, was a quiet, almost bland man, not given to imbibing strong drink, to giving pyrotechnical displays of temperament, to the telling of off-colour jokes, or to any other memorable eccentricities. In the rather free-wheeling medical circles of the '20s his very blandness was enough to mark him as a singular man. In his early days he had lost his right index finger from an infection but now he simply wore a special surgical glove that had the short finger moulded into it and he could tie delicate surgical knots with a skill that was the envy of other men. He had not followed the academic post-graduate route to success and was not a "Fellow" of anybody's college, Royal or otherwise. He had come up through the ranks as a general practitioner who gradually did more and more surgery and conscientiously took refresher courses in the States until now, in 1922, he was quite simply one of the best surgeons in Toronto. Dr. Perfect had earned an enviable reputation for his thyroid and goiter operations but he was not a 'specialist'. Very few surgeons were.

The idea of specialization was just beginning to gain ground. There was an Eye, Ear, Nose and Throat man associated with Toronto Western, but that did not mean other doctors would not remove tonsils. They would and they did, in the hospital, at their offices, or on farmhouse kitchen tables. Bob McClure was one of the last disciples of this old informal order.

Dr. Perfect was, in every sense of the word, young Dr. McClure's mentor. For the next year, Bob assisted at ninety-nine percent of Dr. Perfect's operations. While they were scrubbing up they would talk about the pending operation and then Dr. Perfect would discuss it in detail while he was doing it. If he had opened an abdomen for a ruptured appendix and found it to be a gynaecological condition he would carry right on and attend to that without anyone thinking it necessary to call for the Head of the Gynaecological Department. He recommended technical reading, loaned Bob textbooks, and then grilled him about their content. When McClure chafed at the fact Perfect was no longer doing genitourinary work, because it was one of the areas that had become specialized, Perfect told him to "go see Abe".

Dr. Abraham Isaac Willinsky was head of Urology at Toronto Western and had a large practice in genitourinary work that came to a focus in a clinic at the corner of Bloor and Spadina. He knew Bob McClure was headed for the mission fields of China and McClure's Presbyterianism did not bother him, which was more than could be said for Toronto medical circles concerning Willinsky's Jewishness.

"What you're going to need out there is cystoscopic work," said Dr. Abe. "Come up and help me at the clinic Friday evenings."

Cystoscopes, those delicate little instruments that made it possible to view the urinary tract and explore the inside of the bladder, were a recent development. By faithful and diligent work every Friday night alongside Dr. Willinsky, Bob received cystoscopic training that in later years would only be available to an intern specializing in genitourinary work. Dr. Willinsky gave young Dr. McClure a complete set of cystoscopes to take with him to China.

There were eight interns in Toronto Western. Two others, like Bob, were very young to be graduate doctors. The others were all World War I army and navy men who had finished their medical studies after being overseas. Returning from the naval sick bays and the army field hospitals they had brought with them a broad experience and an unquenchable thirst. They were in the correct profession to make full use of both.

Prohibition, like income tax, had been introduced as an emergency measure during the war and was proving just as difficult to eliminate. Ontario was destined to remain superficially 'dry' until 1927 but in the meantime there were some chinks in the prohibition armour or, depending upon one's point of view and taste in metaphors, there were some oases in the desert. One of these oases was the interns' quarters of Toronto Western Hospital.

A licensed doctor with a medical practice was permitted to buy several gallons of alcohol every month for office use. Some of it could be in the form of whisky and the rest straight ethyl alcohol. He could also write fifty prescriptions a month with no questions asked, each one good for a bottle of liquor for 'medicinal use only'. The interns, being intelligent men trained to use their minds in an analytical way, soon saw to the heart of the matter. The secret lay in having a 'medical practice' and a practice consisted of having an office address and a shingle outside with one's name on it. There was a boarding house just across Bathurst Street and for a modest fee it became their mailing address. They festooned a verandah pillar with almost illegible 'shingles' and they were in business. It was a multi-faceted business involving bootlegging, parties and hangovers.

"Bootlegging" was a nasty word that had just been coined, conjuring up pictures of illicit stills, dark alleyways and furtive men. Some of the gallon stuff, the straight ethyl alcohol, the interns retailed as bathtub gin more or less out the back door in a manner not incompatible with the meaning of the word. The more sophisticated part of the business was not a traffic in alcohol at all but simply a traffic in prescriptions *for* alcohol, a delicate distinction. A prescription, signed by the doctor but with the name of the patient conveniently left blank, was almost as good as cash. An intern wanting to attend a dance and feeling the need of a new pair of shoes could go to the store of his choice, price the pair of shoes he wanted, then go to a nearby hotel, sign enough prescriptions to cover the purchase, sell them to a bellhop at two dollars apiece, and then pop back to the store to complete the original transaction. The system was kept within bounds by the arbitrary limit of fifty prescriptions per month and by the interns' own thirst and scruples. The scruples belonged almost exclusively to Bob and the other two youngsters.

It was not unusual for an older doctor to seek post-operative refuge in the interns' private territory bringing a bottle as a kind of visa. This could either be the beginning of an amiable period of conversation between colleagues or it could escalate into a cheerful soiree, an all night poker game, or an out and out drunk. There was an interesting unpredictability to it all that called for a rather flexible outlook on day to day living. Bob learned to enjoy a party while still shunning alcohol. He also became proficient in studying and sleeping in the midst of noise and chaos, a part of his post-graduate training that was going to be almost as useful in China as surgery.

It was not surprising that one frequently found one or two or most of the interns suffering from large hangovers. At such times the custodians of the throbbing brains, queasy stomachs and trembling hands, if faced with duty in the wards or operating rooms, would turn hopefully to the abstemious youngsters. Bob looked upon his colleagues' self-inflicted incapacitation as a heaven sent opportunity for him to broaden his base. By being amiably available, he was able to get twice the experience he normally would have encountered, not only in the Emergency Department but in Obstetrics and Gynaecology. Without the presence of booze the internship of Bob McClure would have been far less comprehensive.

There was no Internship as yet in Eye, Ear, Nose and Throat but there was a "Nose and Throat" specialist affiliated with the hospital, Dr. N.K. Wilson. Mastoid operations were something that the general surgeons, like Dr. Perfect, had already abdicated to the specialist. Bob knew that in China he would have need of mastoid experience. He also knew that Dr. Wilson was being called upon to go as far afield as Orangeville, Pickering and Oshawa to perform radical mastoids, a most refined operation. Bob suggested to Dr. Wilson that he go along on the out-of-town work. The idea of having his own intern out in the boondocks was most appealing to Dr. Wilson. "One condition," added Bob. "Every mastoid you do in Western Hospital you let me work with you and nobody else. In time, when you think I'm ready, you let me do some and you assist."

Not only did Bob get his mastoid training in the operating room but after a while he discovered that his mastoid mentor liked to take the occasional week off and on such occasions was pleased to leave Dr. McClure in charge of all the post operative cases.

In those days there was no X-ray Department in Toronto Western. There was an X-ray machine and an X-ray technician but no department with its own diagnosticians. Bob was fascinated by X-ray. He wanted to learn how the machine worked and he wanted to learn the technique of using it. Again the obvious answer was to make a deal. The technician lived up near St. Clair Avenue and was not fond of coming down during the night to do routine emergency work. He agreed to teach Dr. McClure provided Dr. McClure took the emergency work at night. Dr. McClure had already come to the conclusion that night was a very educational part of the day and was swift to agree. It was the first time at Western that an intern had been given the keys to the X-ray room.

Whether or not the X-ray technician talked to the pharmacist, Bob was never sure, but the pharmacist came along one day with a suggestion of his own. "I sometimes have to come down here in the middle of the night to make up something that's very simple. Nobody is supposed to have the keys to the pharmacy but if I leave the keys with the head nurse how'd you like to make up these prescriptions? If you're not absolutely sure what you're doing telephone me but if you are sure— well—you can save me a trip down at night." If the head nurse had no objection Bob knew he had no objection.

Already a very clear pattern was emerging. In spite of institutional rules and in complete disregard of his own comfort and convenience, McClure was relentlessly going after whatever training and experience he could find that would be of use in Honan.

It was not unnatural that in the course of such an intense year Bob's extra-mural social life suffered. Bob and Amy went out together as often as he could afford the time and money and before the end of the year Bob even yielded to temptation and 'cashed' a few prescriptions. But a 'night out' never took priority over 'the work'. There were also built-in distractions in the hospital in the guise of young nurses.

There was something almost mystical about the bond that could form between a young intern and a young nurse trying to shepherd a patient through one more night, or quietly helping each other lay out the body of a patient who had not made it. There was the creation of a mutual reliance that could lead to a lessening of ties with the outside world and to a certain amount of socializing in the darkrooms. The year at Toronto Western was the one time in Bob's career when he came perilously close to becoming trapped in the insular isolation of an institution. Subconsciously he shied away from making any firm personal commitment to Amy. As for Miss Hislop, she was not sitting around on the doorstep waiting for Dr. McClure to come off shift.

Amy still had her heart determinedly set upon nursing and early in the New Year of 1923 she felt the time had come. She applied to Toronto General Hospital. In those days, one made a personal application and she found herself in front of the Superintendent of Nursing, Miss Jean Gunn. Miss Gunn was a person of great depth, with an austere outer shell, who was already becoming a legend in nursing circles. She did not approve of young women who simply wanted to wear an attractive nurse's uniform in order to capture a husband. Amy had always been enthralled by the femininity of a nurse's uniform and she even had a husband in view but fortunately she had more cogent reasons to give Miss Gunn when the latter fixed her with an even stare, suspicious no doubt of the applicant's good looks, and said, "And why, Miss Hislop, do you want to be a nurse?"

"Because," said Amy, "I want to go overseas and work in a mission hospital."

Miss Gunn approved. In March, 1923, Amy began her training at Toronto General Hospital as a member of the Class of '26. Amy, too, was now immersed in the institutional life of a city hospital. The next year and a half was to be for her, in her own words, "a thrilling experience".

By the time Amy was meeting Miss Gunn it had already been impressed upon Bob McClure that the members of the nursing hierarchy were indeed powers to be reckoned with. There was a great aura of authority surrounding a man like Dr. Perfect but it was an aura that inspired awe in the heart of an intern. There was equally no doubt what was inspired by the aura surrounding a head nurse. It was absolute fear. There was good reason for this craven feeling because a head nurse had the authority to decide when a case had gone beyond the competence of the intern. Even in Emergency O.R., Bob only had to glance over his shoulder to see a head nurse balefully watching his every move. He was always braced for an interruption from a cool female voice.

"Just a minute, Doctor McClure. We'll just call the Chief if you don't mind. The intestine may be ripped. I'm sure the Chief would like to have a look."

Even the Chief knew that when a head nurse summoned there was only one acceptable reaction. He would soon appear by the intern's side.

"What have you got there, Robert, what have you got there? Ah, I see—yes, yes. Tell you what, you just take it easy. I'll scrub up and join you."

If the situation were messy and urgent even the Chief might attempt to hurry his preparations. It was not lost upon Bob that the head nurse ruled the Chief, too, and was as capable of enforcing O.R. regulations upon him as upon anyone else. Young Dr. McClure was astute enough to realize that not only could a head nurse make or break an intern but that she was, in a very real life and death sense, defending the patient. The concept of the head nurse as defender of the patient was not a concept that appealed to the ego of many doctors. Some of his fellow interns were never at ease with the idea. McClure was pragmatic enough to come to the conclusion early in his internship that perhaps for once the Establishment had devised a correct system. He worked in undisguised awe of head nurses who obviously knew so much more than he did. More than fifty years later he was asked if he remembered any of their names from those days in Western.

"Yes. Oh yes! There was Mary Thomas in the Operating Room. There was Betty Duff in Emergency, and there was Marjorie Agnew in the Obstetrical Department." There was still awe in his voice, tinged with reverence. "Oh, I'll never forget those names to my dying day!"

On June 17th, 1923, there was a special service in Bloor Street Church. At this Sunday morning service Bob McClure publicly committed himself to serve on the foreign mission field in North Honan. He was "designated" by the congregation for such service which meant it was a two way street and that the congregation was committing itself to him. It was to be a long association, all the more remarkable because it was not unique. Not only did other congregations designate other missionaries but at this June service the Bloor Street Church also designated Miss Jean Menzies, Miss Coral Brodie, Mrs. Harold D. Brown, Miss Marjorie Webster and Dr. Victoria Chung. All were destined for China. In ecclesiastical jargon such people were now "set apart" for service. It was an old tradition. Even the Romans had set Christians apart in the Coliseum.

Bob's internship came to an end in August, but there was still a gap in his formal education that bothered him. From what he already knew of the work awaiting him in North Honan he was certain there would be a great deal of eye work to be done, particularly the surgical removal of cataracts. Cataracts had been a major affliction when his father first went to China. Indeed, Bob had been brought up on the story of Chou Lao Chung, the first convert made by the Canadian Presbyterians. Mr. Chou, a one time strong arm constable, drinker, gambler and general bully-boy was blind at the age of fifty-five and on the discard heap. Bob's father had diagnosed the problem at a travelling clinic but Mr. Chou was not about to let anyone cut into his eyes with a knife. Upon reflection, however, and much against the advice of family, he finally allowed a Dr. Smith to perform the miracle. The mission doctor "made the blind to see" in the best New Testament tradition and Chou Lao Chung became an ardent booster of the Christian faith. The evangelical missionaries liked to point out that "Old Joe" (a term of respect not patronage) was so keen on Christianity that he had memorized many verses of the Bible while waiting for the bandages to be removed. It had been suggested to Bob, however, that one should consider the possibility that Old Joe might well have thought the Bible verses were part of the cure. Whatever the truth of the matter, it in no way lessened the importance of the operation. Bob scraped all his savings together and took off for Chicago to attend a three month crash course on the Eye.

It was a good course run by a private practitioner who, being highly motivated by greed, liked to process a great many patients in order to get enough wealthy ones to more than compensate for free work done on the poor ones. The students were allowed to work on the free patients with the master supervising. (The advent in later years of pre-paid medical plans must have greatly complicated the process of choosing human guinea pigs.)

Chicago was an interesting place in those prohibition days when everything was wide open except the bars. A cross-section of Chicago came through the eye clinic. A frequent cause of blindness was the drinking of wood alcohol. Although there was no remedy, Bob could never quite get used to the senior doctor's laconic advice to the victims. "Buy your pencils and shoelaces and try to find an unoccupied street corner. There are not many left."

While Bob was in Chicago a huge labour union rally was held at the "Cow Palace". Having already begun to develop some socialist thoughts of his own Bob thought it would be interesting to attend. He lacked identification and was being turned back at the gate when he remembered the Construction Workers' Union of Toronto card that had been in his wallet since the summer of 1918. It not only got him past the guard but suddenly he found himself being passed on to a committee member as a delegate from Canadian Labour. It was too late to turn back. The great labour assembly continued that evening in the Fall of 1923 with Dr. Robert Baird McClure on the platform as a fraternal delegate from Toronto, Canada. He had the good grace to be embarrassed and that, too, was a novel experience.

The Chicago studies ended in November and Bob took a fast trip to Oberlin, Ohio. His mother and his sister Margaret had returned from China and were staying with his mother's sister. It was a brief visit and a difficult one. Although his sixty-nine year old mother was as buoyant as usual she was far from well. She knew, and her husband knew, that she had a mitral-valve lesion of the heart, a condition that in those days was fatal. Like other crises in the lives of Margaret and William McClure it had been the occasion for both introspection and prayer before she and her husband had come to the conclusion that she should return to the comfort of her sister's home and that William should continue with 'the work' in China. And now both China and 'the work' were calling her son, too. Mother and son embraced for the last time on a bright November day in Ohio in 1923.

Bob returned to Toronto to make his final preparations. He had numerous things to attend to, not the least of which was the result of a casual request from his father to take with him to China "a few pathology specimens". Bob had agreed without investigating the implications of the request. He investigated now.

Dr. William McClure, thoroughly entrenched in the medical faculty of Cheloo University in Tsinan, Shantung Province, was teaching in the best tradition of his own mentor, Sir William Osler, who had founded all his teaching upon a sure knowledge of pathology. In China, specimens for the teaching of pathology were very difficult to come by because the Chinese were not in favour of post mortems and were inclined to take offence at the idea of mutilating or dissecting the bodies of ex-patients even in the interests of science. Bob's father had discovered that the Pathological Museum of the University of Toronto was being re-organized and that it had a great many duplicate specimens which were cluttering up the shelves. These had been generously donated to Dr. William McClure who cheerfully consigned them to the temporary care of Dr. Robert McClure. There were hundreds of specimens, each sealed in a glass bottle of formalin solution. Glass bottles were not the ideal shipping containers in which such precious cargo should make a winter crossing of the Pacific. It was up to Bob and to a Medical College handyman, George, to solve the problem.

They made a waterproof, zinc-lined packing case which they filled with sawdust soaked in formalin solution. Into the sawdust went the precious specimens. When the case was packed full the top sheet of zinc was soldered carefully in place. The whole was then put into a pine packing case and carefully re-inforced. This box of human remains measured three feet by three feet by six feet long and was very heavy. It seemed best not to put any label on it that would advertise the contents.

Bob's time in Toronto was moving toward its final few days as Amy gained the courage to approach Miss Gunn with a request for a few extra late leaves. In those days such a request was viewed with disapproval if not outright hostility, but once again Miss Gunn thawed at the mention of missionary work. There was little doubt but that the austere Miss Gunn wished Miss Hislop well in the staking out of McClure territory.

By the time Dr. McClure had left for China there was still no formal engagement, no exchange of ring or pledges, but Amy had no personal doubts. "We had an understanding. I was not wearing an engagement ring but certainly as far as I was concerned Bob was the only person that meant anything to me." Amy knew where she stood, but much was to happen to both of them before she would find out where *he* stood.

Bob's first reaction to Dr. Pidgeon's challenge had been that it would be a great adventure. His ship had hardly left Vancouver in mid-December before he felt adventure snapping at his heels. The ship was only a few hours out before events occurred that made him think he ran a fair chance of being apprehended as a trunk murderer.

7

Loa Ming-yuan

Radio in those days was still in its pioneer stage. Only about half the licensed stations broadcast on more than an intermittent basis but radio was becoming an exciting novelty for the owners of crystal sets, more and more of whom could be found encased in their headphones listening to music and news bulletins. As the CPR Empress ship left Vancouver in December of 1923 she offered her passengers the luxury of listening to broadcast music, weather reports, and news bulletins. They were within range of the signals for two or three days.

The music was enjoyable and the weather was self-evident. It was the news bulletins that gave young Dr. McClure pause for reflection. Back on the mainland there had been a series of grisly murders. The victims had all disappeared without a trace as had the murderer but the police had been given a lead that indicated the bodies had been dismembered and stowed in a trunk or trunks. Speculation was that the murderer had left the country. Police of the world's ports had been alerted and there was confidence the murderer would be apprehended at his destination. Bob thought of that large unlabelled pine box with the soldered zinc liner in the baggage hold. He alone on that entire ship knew the contents of that box. His imagination raced ahead to the Port of Shanghai where the police had a reputation for somewhat ruthless efficiency. The best that could happen would be that he would be hauled before a magistrate in the British "Concession" and at least be given a chance to explain how he came by all those spare parts. On the other hand, if there had been another one of China's overnight shifts in political jurisdictions he might find himself in Chinese hands. Young McClure had not-too-distant childhood memories of summary Chinese Justice. An over-active imagination was not conducive to sound sleep for the remainder of the voyage and it got no less active as the ship entered the Yellow Sea.

One day out from Shanghai the Purser issued Customs Declaration Forms to each of the passengers. They were told to fill them in with attention to detail. One must list not only one's pieces of baggage but the contents of each piece. There were severe penalties for making false declarations. This seemed to be an unnecessary admonition to a young doctor whose passport clearly indicated his occupation as "Missionary" but the same missionary went to bed that night feeling his career was about to get off to a very muddy start.

As so often happens, inspiration came cradled in the arms of sleep. Bob arose next morning and filled in the declaration form and indicated both his occupation and the contents of the box with a boldness that would have led a knowing observer to assume he was attacking the problem via a McClure frontal assault.

The ship moved into the river off Shanghai and dropped anchor. The ship's launch shuttled back and forth with passengers and baggage and soon Bob found himself in the musty humidity of a Shanghai customs shed. An efficient Chinese officer in an immaculate white uniform went through the hand baggage with meticulous care and finally came to the large pine box. He glanced at the declaration made out by missionary McClure and listened politely as McClure apologized for the fact that the zinc lining was soldered tight against humidity. The officer smiled understandingly. He knew all about the Jesus people. He ran his fingers over an imaginary key-board and put his clearance stamp upon the box. The declaration form had quite honestly stated "ORGANs". The "s" was large enough to be seen in a court of law and small enough to be missed in a customs shed.

Bob's first destination inside China was neither the old stamping ground of Weihwei nor his new headquarters of Hwaiking. Like all new missionaries he was headed first of all to Peking and to Language School. Just about everything had changed since the days his father had conducted the Canadian Mission Language School in the McClure residence at Weihwei. Now the Language School was in Peking and was a co-operative institution run on an inter-mission basis.

It was obvious that someone who had been raised in China would not be inserted at the bottom of the language system. As soon as he arrived Bob was given an oral test to determine his level of efficiency. He was puzzled to see his Chinese teacher blushing.

"What is the matter, honourable teacher? Do you not understand what I am saying?"

"I understand some words only too well, young sir."

"To which words does my honoured teacher refer?"

"They are words which I would rather not mention."

The days of Pao-pei's childhood spent in the goatyard at Weihwei had caught up with Dr. Bob. It was not only that his fluent Chinese was what the Chinese themselves called "dirt talk" or, as the poet would say, "of the earth, earthy", nor was it just because it was apparently enough to make a mandarin blush, but he was, unfortunately, neither able to read nor to write in Chinese. It was a modest oversight in his early education that applied to most of the missionary children of his generation. It would apply to Bill Mitchell. It applied a few months earlier to Jean Menzies and would apply before long to Marnie Lochead. They were what the more envious students cheerfully referred to as "the illiterates".

Bob settled in to learn the rudiments of reading and writing the beautiful Chinese characters and to make his spoken language more suitable for the wards of a mission hospital. He made little effort to overcome his Honan accent because it was an accent that spoke of the sandy soil, the sorghum fields, and the great plains of the Yellow River, and he was proud to be a son of Honan and very soon was to return home. In the meantime Peking was a wonderful city in which to live and study. There were the beautiful western hills, and the lakes, and the Summer Palace with incredible sights like the 'floating' marble boat inlaid with precious stones. The palace had been built with money diverted from the Chinese navy and was a lasting reminder of the whims of the old Empress Dowager who had once ordered the death of all foreigners including, in her sweeping enthusiasm, Bob's parents and sisters.

Now, in the opening months of 1924, it seemed to be such a very civilized city full of gracious, civilized people. The shopkeepers and their assistants spread an air of quiet friendliness as they showed customers precious gems or fine silks and they were just as polite to the appreciative customer who bought nothing as they were to the one who spent a thousand dollars. One day in a fit of friendly co-operation Bob guided some blatantly rich tourists to a gem merchant with whom he had become friendly. The merchant spread out a few of his less precious gems. Bob's 'friends' were insulted by the low prices and loudly demanded to be shown, not "more beautiful" but "more expensive" stones. When they had gone, the merchant scolded Bob for bringing such barbarians to his premises, and then invited him to the courtyard to repair their friendship over fragile cups of fragrant tea. In this manner did the people, scenery, sounds, and architecture of Peking contribute, each in its own fashion, to the civilizing of the 'barbarians' who attended Language School. These barbarians were not only young missionaries, but older missionaries back for refresher courses, members of the various diplomatic corps, army men, businessmen from Western establishments, and wives who were learning the language and the customs alongside their husbands. There were, in all, some hundred students.

In a few short months the rougher, more uncouth edges that were to be expected on a young man brought up in both Ontario and Honan were more or less polished smooth. Even the Language School could not make any impression upon the McClure brashness and unbounded energy but that was not the object of the exercise. The Language School did, however, begin to change his name. "Pao-pei" had been Bob's milk name. No one would dream of using that name for a twenty-three year old graduate doctor. The term for "doctor" was "Tai-fu". Among the millions of Chinese people there were only about one hundred surnames. There was one that sounded a little like McClure, particularly if one dropped the "mc" and slid over the "r". The name was "Loa". To the Chinese teachers Bob very quickly became "Loa Tai-fu"*—"Dr. Loa". His first name posed a more delicate problem. The Chinese were not in the habit of taking liberties with one's personal name. The giving of it and the using of it were very private matters. As it turned out the solution was in the hands of an-

*Pronounced: "Low-ah die-foo"

other young doctor who knew all about first names having a melodious supply of his own. He was none other than Dr. George Washington Wang.

Bob and George Wang found each other in Peking soon after Bob arrived at Language School. It was not an accidental meeting. Each knew of the other's studies and in a very real sense both had been part of the same family even though separated by one ocean and a continent. Not long after Bob and his father had gone to Canada back in 1915, George had gone to Peking where he had taken his undergraduate degree in Arts. After the War, when Dr. William McClure had returned to teach medicine at Cheloo University in Tsinan, George Wang turned up on the roster of medical students. When Bob's mother arrived she took George into the McClure home as a surrogate son. George had graduated from Cheloo and was now in Peking serving his internship at Rockefeller Hospital.*

Bob soon discovered that George and his fellow interns were having difficulties. The Rockefeller Hospital functioned entirely in English. It was superbly equipped and was staffed with fine American personnel, but even in class situations the Americans talked so fast the Chinese interns had difficulty following. Even George, who had been exposed to English most of his life, was having difficulty because his medical training at Cheloo had all been in Chinese and the medical terminology was difficult. Before long Bob was having a weekly bull session with George and the other interns to translate into Chinese what they had heard, or thought they had heard, in English. Anyone eavesdropping on these sessions would have been impressed by the understanding rapport between Drs. Wang and Loa. Only a sudden ribald translation would have betrayed the fact that under the sophisticated medical veneer there might still lurk two rascals from Honan.

Bob completed the one year Language School course in five months. He was not as "illiterate" as the immigrant missionaries would have liked to pretend and by now it was becoming quite apparent that he had not only inherited his mother's "bitter-lips and sweet-heart" but his father's brain. Bob always felt that George Wang was much brighter than he was. If so, it was a formidable progeny that had emerged from

*The Peking Union Medical College

the McClure nest and it was not surprising that George Wang one day came up with a suggestion.

"Bob, we should become brothers, you and I."

The Chinese were a very pragmatic people. They would joke and say that one could not expect to be responsible for all the offspring one's mother might choose to produce but that in a country of four hundred million people if you actually chose a brother you should be able to choose a good one. One could discount the joking because family ties were very close but one could not discount the fact that a chosen brother was considered a closer relationship than that of natural brother.

There was a ritual involved in becoming brothers. George and Bob gave a 'feast' and announced that from now on they were "exchange-of-treaty" brothers. The important part of the ritual was an exchange of first names. These were new first names that from then on would be their official ones.

Bob renamed George as Kuo-pao, "Treasure of the Nation". George renamed Bob as Ming-yuan, "Far Shining Brilliance". Wang Kuo-pao and Loa Ming-yuan then went their separate ways, each to serve his Chinese people in his own fashion. Wang Kuo-pao finished his internship and headed off to pioneer in Manchuria. Within a very few years reports would filter back that he was the leading doctor in the city of Chang-chuin and the owner of a flourishing private hospital.

Loa Ming-yuan set off by train for Hwaiking. He had, as travelling companion, one goat that had been ordered by Dr. Reeds, the Administrator of the Hwaiking hospital.

More than a decade ago the young Bob McClure had felt excitement upon his first return to China, but it was nothing to equal the excitement now felt by Loa Ming-yuan upon this second return to North Honan.

From Peking south-west through Hopeh Province the foothills and the mountains of the Tai-hang range were never far to the west of the railway line. As the train reached North Honan, however, it was difficult to tell whether the hills veered farther west or the train veered more directly south. Here there was mile after mile of fertile plain composed of stone-free loess soil, that fine yellowish-gray loam that could drift and blow and ride on the wind like sand and yet, when properly irrigated, could be amazingly fertile. Through here it was partly irrigated and had been for several thousand years. Now, in June,

North Honan had the appearance of one vast wheat field, flecked as far as the eye could see with the figures of hundreds, thousands, of peasants toiling at the harvest. There were donkeys and mules plodding toward the threshing floors carrying bundles of wheat sheaves tied to their backs. There were Peking carts with their squealing axles and five-foot high wheels so over-loaded they were cutting grooves in roadways already worn many feet lower than the surrounding countryside. The passing eye caught rhythms of constant motion from the village threshing floors. There was the slow rhythm of the great stone rollers pulled by donkeys, mules, oxen, even people. There were the faster, sharper rhythms of the threshers swinging sheaves up and down, beating the full heads against the hard packed ground to finally loosen the grain. There were sweeping rhythms from the muscled arms of the winnowers throwing the same loosened grain high into the air so the wind could blow away the light chaff and husks and let the grain itself fall back to the ground. In some areas the wind was aided by great fan-like mats being swung slowly backward and forward. The whole great plain beat with the pulse of harvest as far as the eye could see.

As the train rolled farther south it entered areas where the wheat harvest had already been completed but now other thousands of figures were reworking the soil and planting new crops. The crops were as varied as the needs of the peasants or the demands of the landlords dictated. Peas, beans, corn, millet, rice, sesame, melons, squash, egg-plant, cabbage, peanuts, yams, carrots, turnips, all would grow in fertile North Honan, but all had to be planted quickly now because the rains would come in July and it would be difficult even to walk to the fields let alone work in them. Rivers would swell into torrents, fields become lakes and some houses would literally dissolve between now and September. After the inundation those same patient myriads would be out harvesting the new crop.

To the eyes of Bob McClure, recently arrived from Southern Ontario, it seemed strange to see no farmhouses, but simply village after scattered village and town after town, many of them walled. These communities had long since spilled outside their walls, not that the need for protection was no longer felt but because walls were not the same protection against warlord artillery as they had been against arrows and spears. It was not long, however, before even the great chimneys of the brick kilns looked familiar again and Ming-yuan was soon trying to recall from memory how to identify travellers journeying on the roads. They travelled by foot, mule, Peking cart, sedan chair, or rickshaw. He could spot the prosperous merchants and gentry. There was little difficulty identifying a company of soldiers but no way to tell whom they represented. He spotted a country mandarin being sped along in a sedan chair and speculated as to the nature of a case that could cause such apparent haste on the part of an official. As the train clattered across a shallow tree-lined ravine he caught a glimpse of several poorly dressed fellows confronting a merchant and his coolies. There was a glint of sunlight on a rifle barrel and Ming-yuan decided it was quite possible, even probable, that there was a robbery being conducted in broad daylight with several hundred studiously uninterested field workers within earshot. The pastoral scene of this North Honan tapestry was not as placid as the first superficial glance might imply.

China was, in fact, deep in the midst of the Age of Confusion and was even now moving with increasing momentum toward the Second Revolution. It was already eight years since Yuan Shih-k'ai had died of rage when the generals prevented him from establishing his own Imperial Dynasty. The infant Republic had been struggling on but it was a political Siamese twin. One head was at Peking, which was under warlord rule. The other head was down south in Canton where Sun Yat-sen and the Kuomintang were still trying to establish a democracy based upon Greek and Roman ideals most of which were foreign to the cultural traditions of China and, as had become more and more apparent, equally foreign to the Western Powers.

The Peking Government had been more or less bullied into declaring war upon Germany during World War I. China had had no more quarrel with Germany than she had with any of the other predators, but with China in the war the Allies had been able to confiscate all German shipping in Chinese ports and to take over all German business interests within the country. Japan, one of the Allies, had taken over all German interests in Shantung Province. After the war she never bothered returning them thus demonstrating that there had been no change in the hundred year old game of robbing China.

After World War I the only generous act on the part of any of the Allies that made any impact upon the Chinese was carried out by an Ally that had dropped out of the war because of its own revolution. It was Russia. Imperial Russia had been one of the wolves at the door but things had changed. When Bob was at Language School, the Chinese were still talking about the envoy the new Soviet government in Moscow had sent down to Peking in 1920. He had come with an offer from Russia renouncing her Concessions, her extra-territorial rights, and her privileges in Manchuria. Members of the Western diplomatic corps boycotted the Russian envoy and failed to participate in the many banquets that were given by Chinese officials and intellectuals in his honour and in celebration of the Soviet proposal. Being absent they could not read the handwriting that was beginning to appear upon the walls.

Much of this background Bob had picked up from George Wang and the other Chinese interns in Peking. Some of it, on a less impassioned level, had permeated through from Chinese lecturers. There was anger and frustration. Much of the frustration had to do with the sheer chaos of government-by-warlord. Bob had been told that the interior was completely controlled by generals with private armies and in the next few years he would come to understand the system in some detail. The essential fact he had already grasped—the predators were not all outside China looking in. This fact had been impressed upon Ming-yuan by his treaty brother in Peking and it had been no accident that the same brother was intending to head for Manchuria. It was also no accident that young Dr. Loa, embarking upon a missionary career dedicated to relieve physical suffering, carried in his personal baggage a Webley automatic pistol.

8

Weihwei

The main line of the Peking-Hankow railway went through Weihwei. To get to Hwaiking one had to detrain at Weihwei, wait overnight, and catch a train on a branch line. Weihwei to Hwaiking was some 100 miles. Young Dr. McClure was quite pleased at the thought of a stopover at Weihwei. It would give him a chance to see the old homestead, to renew acquaintances and of course to make his first contacts out on 'the field' in his professional capacity. Even though he was not stationed at Weihwei, it was quite possible that he would have some occasion to work in its new hospital with Dr. Struthers and Dr. Auld. Now would be a good time to let them know he was available if they had any difficult problems in the genito-urinary, mastoid, or cataract line. He knew that he was some-what unique in that he was already destined for Hwaiking be-fore he even left Canada. The usual system was for a new missionary to complete language study and to apprentice at one of the stations. Then the Mission Council, that gathering of wise heads from the various stations, would deliberate over his abilities and designate the station where he should serve. This was not for Bob McClure. *He* had been singled out to replace Dr. Menzies, one of the most irreplaceable men on the Cana-dian field. For just a few moments, as the train pulled into Weihwei, young Dr. McClure felt a sense of well being that was vaguely reminiscent of that feeling he had had upon arrival at the YMCA camp immediately after graduation from medical school. It was a feeling of being God's Gift to the Ailing and the feeling remained with him all the way down the platform to the baggage car where he collected Dr. Reeds' goat.

The Weihwei mission station had delegated one of their members to meet the newcomer's train. It was a customary courtesy. The emissary this time was Bruce Copland, a Canadian from Montreal one year younger than the man he was meeting. Copland knew that his translation services would not be required and that the newcomer probably remembered more about Weihwei than he would ever learn but he was curious to meet Bob McClure and anxious to extend the hand of friendship. He had very little difficulty identifying him.

Dr. Robert Baird McClure, Loa Tai-fu, Ming-yuan, he of "the Far Shining Brilliance", was engaged in a debate with a goat who did not want to disembark at Weihwei and who thought the baggage car a most comfortable abode. As Copland came up, the amazingly muscular, red-haired, bullet-headed young doctor was in the process of removing said goat by force and wrestling it to its knees on the station platform to the accompaniment of verbal endearments imported from the dockyards of Toronto and adorned with Honanese goatyard sayings that brought smiles of appreciation to the faces of the Weihwei railway coolies. The goat-wrestler, having just won the main round of his first professional assignment in China, looked up and beamed a friendly smile.

"Hello, you must be Bruce. They said you'd probably be here to meet me. I'm Bob." He had a handshake that could crack bones.

On the way to the Weihwei compound Bob had a chance to assess the new man from Montreal. Bruce was not a Varsity graduate but a graduate of McGill. He could be forgiven that. He was not, however, either a doctor or an evangelist. He had been sent to the mission field as a hospital business administrator. Bob felt slightly offended that a mere business administrator could be a medical missionary although he had to admit to himself that a professional administrator could have saved his own father from hours of administrative work. He discovered that Bruce had been sent out specifically to work at the new Weihwei hospital. So there was another one who had bypassed the Mission Council! The McClure ego was having to make some swift re-adjustments in perspective. Bob assumed that Bruce did not have any missionary connections, or at least not in China, since the name Copland was not familiar to him. Bruce admitted that he came from a fairly well-established Montreal business family. He had been impressed, however, by his mother's brother, a Dr. Percy Leslie. Dr. Leslie had come to Honan in the 1890s. Dr. Leslie was the Canadian who had been so savagely carved up by bandits on the historic flight during the Boxer Rebellion that it had been a miracle he had lived. He had not only lived, he had returned to Honan. Bob decided, grudgingly, that Copland's credentials were not bad, "not bad" being as close as any Canadian of Scottish ancestry could ever bring himself to saying "good".

"Met a friend of yours, Bob. Last summer before leaving home."

Bob could not imagine who it would be.

"A girl from Weihwei. Folks were home on furlough and spent some time in the Laurentians at Lac Marois where my folks have a cottage. She was going to start university that fall."

Bob could not remember any Weihwei girl from Montreal.

"The Lochead's daughter."

"Marnie!"

"Yes, that was her name. Mother insisted I be friendly. 'Be nice to the missionary's daughter!' You know the routine."

"How was Marnie?"

"Well, you know, seventeen, long hair all down her back. A pain, naturally."

Bob could remember, years ago, trying to lasso little Marnie from a tree. She had thought *he* was a pain. He wondered idly what she had thought of this tall, good looking, rather slightly built young man with the finely structured cheek bones and the high forehead that the Chinese would interpret as a sign of the intellectual.

By the time the stopover visit in Weihwei was completed McClure and Copland had become good friends. They were already planning a hinterland tour for the holiday at the end of the summer. Bob was full of the idea he would like to make his way far up the old Yellow River to its headwaters in the mountains and come back down by raft or sampan or even canoe if one could be found. Even Bruce knew that just after the rainy season that would be a suicidal trip. He liked the idea but was already trying to divert the McClure enthusiasm toward a less self-destructive hiking tour and, as it turned out, that was what they eventually took. Bruce was not an administrator for nothing. This friendship, begun at Weihwei, would continue for many years.

It was not long after Bob had re-embarked aboard the train for Hwaiking that Weihwei mission station welcomed another 'old' arrival from Canada. Summer was just nicely underway when Marnie Lochead returned to her childhood home. Marnie, she of the "long hair all down her back", had decided, almost two generations ahead of the times, that after one year of university she was not sure she wanted another. She would stay a year in Weihwei and study music and Chinese.

Bruce Copland decided that if his mother's instructions to be nice to Marnie Lochead were valid at Lac Marois they should be equally valid at Weihwei. There was, after all, such a thing as filial obedience.

9

Hwaiking and the Path to Chinghua

The Province of Honan lies mainly south of the Hwang Ho, the "Yellow River". It comprises about 81,000 square miles and in 1924 contained a population of roughly 32,000,000 people. The name Honan means "South of the River" although a portion of the province lies north of the river. It is this northern area, a triangular region thrusting up from the Yellow River valley more or less following the edge of the Tai-hang mountain range, that is referred to as North Honan. It was in this triangle that the Canadian Presbyterians had put down their roots at the most northerly station of Changte, the mid one of Weihwei and, off to the south-west, at Hwaiking.*

As the train approached Hwaiking, Bob became more and more aware of the hill country pressing in from the north. If he could have taken a high level, bird's eye view he would have verified that it was pressing in from the south as well, but this was not as self-evident from ground level. The Yellow River valley was in fact being pinched in here by the Tai-hang mountains to the north and the Tsin-ling mountains to the south. To the casual observer the river was still wide and placid and the valley still wide and fertile but it was in effect a narrow corridor leading outward from the vast interior plateaus of Shansi and Shensi Provinces. The city of Hwaiking was tucked away almost at the western end of the triangle that was North Honan. The northern mountains, the provincial border and the Yellow River all intersected very close to Hwaiking. This seemingly irrelevant geo-political fact was going to have a considerable

*See map on front end paper

short term impact on the type of surgery carried on by Dr. Loa and his associates in the Hwaiking mission hospital. The long term impact would come from the fact that the Yellow River corridor route across China and into the interior was one of the most strategic military routes in all China. The Yellow River, longer than Canada's longest river, almost completely bisected China's ancient heartland, an open invitation to military travel from either direction. Moreover, not only were the marshy plains fertile but this was coal country! There was also some tin, iron, and lead with a silver content. The combination of water for transport, food for sustenance, coal for energy, and metal for cannon would be an irresistible attraction to an invading army. At the time of Bob McClure's arrival it was already an irresistible attraction to warlords.

It was nice to 'own' a city like Hwaiking, not as yet heavily industrialized but one that had possibilities and was certainly strategically situated. It and the surrounding countryside were just prosperous enough to be a good source of tax money. A general with a modestly small army could take Hwaiking, and one usually did, in the summer after the first harvest and before the rains. The really big generals were still more interested in places like Chengchow where the north-south Peking-Hankow railway intersected with an east-west main line, and where there was heavy industry. Or better still a place like Hankow that had its own arsenal and supportive industry. The warlord who owned an arsenal was really into the big time. Hwaiking was fortunate not to have an arsenal. Hwaiking was also fortunate to be a quite formidable distance from coastal cities like Shanghai where the Western Powers had their Concessions and still exerted their extra-territorial rights. The big warlords rather liked the Concessions. If one had a turn of bad luck one could always retreat to a foreign Concession, send one's money to a foreign bank, and await a more opportune time to sally forth. Hwaiking's local warlords tended to work the area over in a modest fashion while praying to their ancestors to keep the big boys busily occupied farther east.

The tendency of local warlords to take over after harvest when it was taxation time, and then to abdicate during the rougher seasons, made for a certain amount of political instability. Indiscriminate and ruthless taxation also made for a population more impoverished than nature had intended. This in turn led by a quite logical process to the creation of a large population devoted to banditry. Just as there were communities where the craftsmen tended to follow village specialties such as carpentry, pottery, and leatherwork, there were communities that specialized in robbery. Whatever their trade the Chinese were noted for being industrious and the people of North Honan were said to be particularly so.

The Hwaiking area was of even more interest to bandits than it was to warlords and the reason lay in that happy confluence of river, plains, mountains and provincial border. The only lasting, year-round authority rested in the hands of the local magistrates and police. Their jurisdiction did not cross provincial boundaries. At Hwaiking the good pickings were one side of the boundary and the haven of the mountains was the other side. Compared to the constant to and fro of police and bandits the seasonal sweep of the warlords was stately indeed.

It was to Hwaiking, then, that the Canadian Presbyterian Church in its wisdom and the congregation of Bloor Street Church in its generosity sent young Bob McClure, a doctor of untried ability and undeniable potential, with a forthright manner and an irascible temper. Those who knew him were already surmising that the only thing he had sense enough to fear was a head nurse, but time, and Hwaiking, would tell.

The mission station at Hwaiking was not unlike the other Canadian stations. It was architecturally and aesthetically uninspired. It was not as big as Weihwei, not having the same central boarding school facilities and other amenities. It was one compound now since the wall that had divided it at the time of Dr. Menzies' murder had been removed. It did not have the attraction of a river flowing in front of the rear gate as had Weihwei. The Hwaiking mission station was what its Presbyterian lineage dictated it should be—solid, functional and drab. Fortunately, however, the real character of the mission station was not made by the family homes standing two-storey, square, immovable, identical, but rather by the families that inhabited those homes and who comprised the larger Hwaiking mission family. This larger family was composed of a number of married couples, one widow, several single ladies and bachelor Bob.

Bob already knew some of them. Two of the single women

were nurses who had been 'set apart' at the very same Bloor Street Church service that had done the same for him. One was Miss Coral Brodie. The other was none other than his 'sister' from childhood days, Jean Menzies. Jean Menzies, who had lived with the McClures while attending the boarding school at Weihwei; Jean, whose own father had been murdered in this very mission station, the man whose shoes Bob was eventually supposed to fill; Jean, whose mother, the widow of the martyred doctor, was still here, refusing to leave either the 'field' or 'the work'.

Some observers were quite sure that Mrs. Menzies saw in McClure's presence a happy evidence of predestination. She took the young bachelor under her wing and into her home where he would be in close proximity to her daughter. The presence of bachelors on the mission field was not common and this arrangement would bridge the time until more suitable quarters could be arranged for Dr. McClure. The fact that the Menzies were living in the single ladies' quarters made it a somewhat unorthodox situation. The good lady could not have pondered all the odds because there were some factors of which she was ignorant. One, a dangerous one, was that young Dr. McClure had for quite some time been of the opinion that the creation of an opposite sex was one of the Lord's happier inspirations. The other, a frustrating one, was that Bob could never view any of the girls from Weihwei, and there were some charmers, as anything more than sisters because of the very nature of that close mission 'family' of his childhood. In addition to all this, Jean's and Bob's time in Language School had over-lapped and Bob knew Jean had been more than casually interested in a certain young Englishman. As events would prove, Mrs. Menzies may have been correct about predestination but had been wrong about time, place, and participants. Jean was destined to marry Dr. Handley Stockley, not only an Englishman but, shudder, a Baptist. Before long Dr. McClure escaped, unscathed, to a mission house of his own.

Dr. McClure had been sent out to 'replace' Dr. Menzies. The appointment had had a certain drama to it when announced in the Toronto newspapers. It had also been flattering to a young doctor's ego. Dr. Menzies had been the top man of the Hwaiking medical hierarchy. Dr. McClure was intended for the top but he would have to get there through a process of either osmosis or attrition because there were two doctors senior to him and already entrenched. The most senior man was Dr. Robert Reeds, a fellow Canadian. The other was Dr. Chang Hui-ting, a fellow Chinese.

Dr. Reeds was a married man with children. He had graduated from the University of Toronto about 1912 and had volunteered for the China work. World War I had soon deflected him to the battlefields of France. His main achievement as a medical student had been to win the inter-varsity wrestling championship. His main achievement as a surgeon had been to survive his 'internship' in France as surgeon with a Chinese labour battalion. Neither of these achievements was conducive to developing a surgeon with a delicate touch or an eye for the niceties.

Dr. Chang Hui-ting was a man in his mid-thirties. He was a widower with a family of small children. Dr. Chang had not graduated from an institution of higher learning but had learned his medicine through the apprenticeship or 'preceptor' system. He had learned it well and was constantly augmenting his knowledge through a personally imposed reading programme.

The doctors were backed up, not only by the Canadian nurses, Coral Brodie, Jean Menzies, and head nurse Janet Brydon, but also by a formidable team of highly experienced Chinese male medical assistants who, like Dr. Reeds, their Chief, had 'interned' in France. Several of these men had journeyed to France via North America, crossing Canada by train. Because they had been locked in a box car from coast to coast, they had not been favourably impressed by Canada. After the war the medical dressers, the dispenser, even the hospital accountant had all come back home again with Dr. Reeds.

All together the male medical staff of the Menzies Memorial Hospital at Hwaiking formed quite a crew. A superficial observer might have thought they were the ideal team to be functioning at that unstable corner of society at that particular time. The observer would have been wrong. Dr. Chang was handicapped by the very fact that he was Chinese. Here he was at a time of rapidly escalating nationalism working in an institution that was patently Western. He did not have a university degree which would have given him status in the eyes of the Chinese official and intellectual community nor did he enjoy the British 'extra-territorial' immunity which gave the Canadians some protection. Dr. Chang found it wise to keep a low profile and to bend himself assiduously to his work. As for Dr. Reeds, he was a living paradox. In the operating room he was fearlessly willing to confront anything. He and his lads were a blood and guts team who would prepare for a mastectomy or an amputation by spreading sawdust on the operating room floor to absorb the gore. But outside the surgery Dr. Reeds was one of the kindest and gentlest of souls. In spite of World War experience, he still thought the best of all of his fellow men and would accept any hard luck story at face value. He was the proverbial 'soft touch'. To top it all off this was a time when it was not unusual to have wounded police and wounded bandits sharing the same ward and extreme diplomatic complications would arise during visiting hours. There was a solution for this problem but Dr. Reeds was not devious enough to spot it. It was a problem to which Ming-yuan would eventually have to bend his mind.

This, then, was the medical team into which Dr. Bob McClure had to insert himself in the summer of 1924. The insertion proved to be painless. In many ways the three doctors all complemented each other. Dr. Chang did not have high academic qualifications but was extremely able. Dr. Reeds had had the broadest experience. Dr. McClure, thanks largely to Drs. Perfect, Willinsky, and Wilson, had had the best training. Being three mature and well motivated adults they soon worked out a division of labour that made the best use of their respective talents and that downgraded no one. It so happened that Dr. Reeds and Dr. McClure had both taken the identical high pressure eye course in Chicago but at different times. Dr. Chang tossed a coin for them and Dr. Reeds won the eye cases. Almost immediately, however, Dr. Reeds began to hand over much of the abdominal surgery and genitourinary work to Dr. McClure. It was an amicable arrangement.

Establishing a working arrangement with the living doctors was far easier than coming to terms with the ghost of the dead one.

The presence of Dr. James R. Menzies permeated the compound, subtly impinging upon the consciousness of the young doctor who was being groomed as his successor. It would have taken an enormous ego indeed on the part of that same young doctor not to have been impressed by his predecessor almost to the point of inhibition. There was no escaping Menzies. Everybody around still remembered him as clearly as though he had just left the room. The man's widow had practically appointed herself Bob's foster mother and she was kindness personified, but Bob could not escape the feeling she was watching him to see that he was worthy of the mantle he had inherited. He could imagine everyone else feeling the same way. The nurse at his side making ward rounds was the late doctor's daughter. The head nurse, Janet Brydon, watching him with an efficient practiced eye during operations, was one of the women Dr. Menzies had rushed to aid the night he was murdered. The Chinese medical assistant so expertly administering open-ether anaesthesia in the operating room had learned the fine points of his art from Dr. Menzies. Nor was there any escape from the results of Dr. Menzies' handiwork. Chances were that when Bob peered into a patient's mouth to examine an inflamed throat his tongue depressor was resting on teeth that had had their cavities filled by Dr. Menzies. Many of the missionaries had had to do dental work, nor had they always been members of the medical fraternity, but Dr. Menzies was a double doctor: Doctor of Medicine and Doctor of Dentistry. When Bob went to the villages to participate in evangelical tent meetings he knew the chances were very high that even the local Chinese evangelist was a Menzies man, because James Menzies had also been an ordained minister. He even had a Doctor of Divinity degree. Menzies was a 'doctor' three times over!

The Rev. James Menzies, M.D., D.D.S., D.D., had not been content to confine his missionary efforts to the healing and preaching ministries. Dr. Menzies had designed and engineered most of the buildings within the Hwaiking compound. What those buildings may have lacked in aesthetics they possessed in durability. It was not easy to construct foundations for large buildings in that area. The mission was about a quarter of a mile away from the Chin River* but it was on land that was fifteen feet lower than the bed of that same river. There was nothing unusual about this because much of the area was below river level and the river itself had been lined with dikes since time immemorial. The water table, however,

*A tributary of the Yellow River.

was only about three feet below ground level. Dr. Menzies had taught the local builders how to overcome these problems so that they could build foundations capable of supporting the large, two-storey, eight-room, brick mission homes. He it was who had first installed running water in the mission compound not so much for convenience as for fire protection. He it was who cast his eye around the countryside and realized that even the very good homes were using inefficient heating, relying as they did on open fires, fireplaces or, at the best, upon very crude furnaces. Menzies imported a McClary furnace, took it apart, made wooden patterns from it and taught the local workers of cast iron how to make their own McClary furnace. That action raised the eyebrows of those tuned to the idea of copyrights and patents, but it was an action that for once permitted the Chinese to exploit the West.

Bob McClure could not escape James Menzies. The doctor's name was over the hospital doorway in English and on the tip of the patients' tongues in Chinese. Even his Chinese surname was in itself enough to inhibit a successor. It was Meng, a name that was also that of the ancient Chinese sage Mencius.

McClure was sensitive enough to realize that by sending him as Menzies' successor the Church had unwittingly set him an almost impossible task.

Bob McClure had not been at Hwaiking very long before he began to eye the little Delco plant that had been another one of Dr. Menzies' inspirations. There was no municipal power plant at Hwaiking and Dr. Menzies had quite correctly come to the conclusion one could not run a modern hospital without some electricity. Rural electrification was making tentative beginnings back home in Canada and there many farmers and some cottagers were using private Delco generating systems composed of a small gasoline motor, a generator, and storage batteries. The missions always worked on a shoestring budget but Dr. Menzies had managed to import a tiny Delco system that ran on kerosene. It's electrical output was somewhat minimal but if there was an emergency operation at night the Delco could run the operating room fan and the light. It had been a godsend to the hospital and had been quite literally a lifesaver for many patients. But the Delco was wearing out and becoming unreliable and the cost of kerosene was escalating. What the station really needed was a Diesel generator, but the cost was so prohibitive there was no use wasting time contemplating such glories.

There was a coal mine twenty-two miles away from the compound. Ever since Dr. Menzies' death the hospital had been relying on the coal mine workshop for assistance in repairing the Delco. Bob McClure saw more potential in a coal mine than mere access to a repair shop. He saw coal. The inquisitive mind that surveyed the resources at hand and then adapted them to fill an urgent need was to be one of his outstanding attributes. Before many years had passed it would have him playing strange roles in outlandish locations but to begin with it took him post haste to the local coal mine. Unconsciously Bob McClure was setting out firmly in the footsteps of James Menzies.

The easiest and fastest way to get to the coal mine was to take a fifteen mile bicycle ride to the town of Chinghua and there catch a ride on the railway spurline to the Chiaotso mine itself. Dr. McClure did so and soon established friendly and professional contact with the mine doctor. That contact proved to be a bonanza.

Being a doctor on the staff of a coal mine in North Honan in the mid-twenties was not one of the world's great jobs. Being a Chinese miner in a coal mine lacking even the most primitive safety devices was an even less enviable job. Hard hats and safety boots were unheard of. The result was twofold. The miners had a high incidence of injuries, particularly head wounds, fractures, and brain injuries, and the mine doctor, not being a surgeon, had acquired an alcohol problem through sheer frustration. It was not long before he was inviting Dr. McClure up to the mine to attend to the more difficult cases. It was not long before Dr. McClure was trying to talk the mine management into helping finance some electrical development work he had in mind. He never managed to get the financing but he did manage to obtain a greatly reduced price for coal for the mission and full co-operation from the mine machine shop. It was enough to launch Bob into Project Producer Gas.

Bob wanted to use the energy from coal to create electricity. This was not too big a problem if one had unlimited money. It took on large dimensions in the face of a non-existent budget. Ignoring money, one solution would be to build a steam generator. The water in the area, however, was very hard. A steam system would require the services of a full-time expert just to scale boilers. The 'producer gas' system appeared to make more sense. In this system one passed steam through a bed of live coals. The resulting product was hydrogen and methane gas. The methane gas could be led to an internal combustion engine and that in turn would drive the generator and light the hospital and the compound. If there was a surplus they would encourage local people to use electricity and perhaps even run lines out to surrounding villages. Bob was dreaming of great projects, all of which required vast sources of money, before he discovered the mine management did not have the same broad vision as himself. However, by dipping into his own savings and by adding money sent to him from well wishers in Toronto, he managed to import a small engine from England. Then he began devoting his spare time to the challenge of economically producing a small amount of producer gas. As far as he knew the only big gas plant in China at that time was in the municipal electrical plant at Peking. It ran a huge engine developing hundreds of horsepower. Out in the south-western tip of North Honan Bob McClure knew he would be lucky to achieve five or ten horsepower.

The project escalated. Gradually he improved the mission station workshop, cannibalizing cast-off equipment from the mine and anything else that came to hand. He needed an assistant mechanic but as soon as he taught one the merest rudiments the local bus company would lure him away as an expert. Then Chou Teh-kwei joined him and stayed. Chou had been in France with a coolie labour battalion and had served as batman to the Rev. Herbert Boyd, now of Hwaiking. Soon Dr. Loa was passing on to Chou the machine-tool skills that young Bob McClure had picked up at the Russell Motor Car Factory. As the two of them struggled together with the little English engine McClure was reaching back to his pentacycle days at Varsity and to the summer as motor mechanic for Sir William Gage's powerboat.

There were problems associated with the project that were not in the least bit mechanical. They were human and dangerous and had to do with the bamboo groves that bordered the fifteen mile bicycle route to Chinghua. Those bamboo groves were inhabited by bandits who had already killed the occasional wayfarer and had even attacked the postmen. An attack on a postman was an attack on the official Establishment and would result in punitive police action, but no one really expected the police to take much interest in the sudden demise of the odd private traveller.

The train to the Chiaotso mine left Chinghua every morning at 8 o'clock which meant that if McClure was to catch it his bicycle journey had to be accomplished mostly in the dark and empty hours. When he realized he was in a fair way of becoming the mine's regular surgeon, and that the trips would be frequent, he decided he could do without the suspense of wondering whether or not there was an ambush waiting for him in the heart of the next grove. It seemed to be a good idea to try a frontal assault.

It was easy enough to learn who the bandits were. For one thing they were Moslems. The entire bamboo area was inhabited mainly by Moslems, a remnant from an early migration within the Mongol Empire. There was nothing unusual about this, there being a sizeable Moslem population in China, its members being quite easily identifiable by the turban headgear topping otherwise ordinary Chinese garb. So distinct and separate had they kept themselves that even facial characteristics helped identify a Moslem, particularly the high bridge nose which was not typically Chinese.

Bob had not been working in the Hwaiking hospital very long before it was drawn to his attention that a tropical disease, kala-azar, was prevalent in the area. It was a disease that struck particularly hard at children. There was nothing unique about it being in the Hwaiking area. What was interesting, however, was that here it seemed to be most prevalent among Moslem children.

Kala-azar was certainly easy enough to detect. The victim would become weak and anaemic, with an enlarged spleen. One could feel the spleen, hard and swollen, coming right across the abdomen, resting in the abdominal fossa. If not treated the victim would die. The condition was caused by a parasite and could be cured medically with an arsenical compound. It occurred to Bob that he had a unique opportunity to solve two problems at once.

By discreet questions in the hospital wards it was not very difficult for Dr. Loa to find out where the Moslem villages were and then to find out which ones were the bandit villages. The inhabitants were all in the bamboo industry, making baskets, weaving scoops, cutting poles for scaffolding, fashioning dippers, spoons, fans and water buckets. Being a region with a good product it was also carrying a large tax load. Where a warlord's taxmen trod most heavily there grew the bandits.

Dr. Loa mounted his bicycle and, with his heart just slightly in his mouth, went bandit hunting along the road to Chinghua.

In daylight this was good bicycle country, being almost as flat as the Dutch polders. There were the main roads, often deeply rutted, a quagmire in wet weather. There were footpaths, worn smooth by centuries of barefoot travel, that followed the irrigation ditches. There were other footpaths running straight as arrows along the tops of earthen dikes. On the footpaths a cyclist had to keep his eyes open for sudden interruptions in the pathway caused by intersecting drainage ditches and the like. If he strayed off the paths in dry weather the fine loess soil could drag at him like the sands of the Sahara. If he had a headwind the force of it coming across those plains could make him work mightily on the pedals, but taken all in all it was good cycling terrain. One thing about the bamboo groves, they certainly broke the wind. Bamboo grew so thick as to be almost impenetrable. That was one reason bamboo country was so beloved by bandits. Bamboo grew high, some of it soaring almost a hundred feet in the air. It grew fast, sixteen inches a day being not at all unusual. You could build an entire house with it, beams, planks, walls, roofing, right down to the kitchen utensils, and you could eat it. The outer cuticle was hard enough to be turned into a cutting tool and, like sandstone, bamboo contained enough silica to be used as a whetstone. You could bore out the diaphragms and use long running lengths of it to pipe water or cut it in cross sections to make buckets. If lead and gunpowder were hard come by you could make spears out of it, and bows, and arrows. Bamboo groves also contained splendidly isolated nooks along lonely pathways in which robbers could hide and there were private pathways carved through the depths along which they could disappear.

Dr. Loa paused on his bicycle only long enough to ask occasional discreet questions of bamboo cutters. With his directions verified he sped on again, praying that he would not be ambushed before he had a chance to make verbal contact. Finally, deep in the heart of bamboo territory, he came to a village whose inhabitants he had good reason to believe specialized in highway robbery as their principal trade.

The arrival of the young Canadian on his bicycle actually looking for Ali Baba was somewhat disconcerting. There was no doubt he was a Westerner. McClure never tried to disguise that fact. He never adopted Oriental garb, nor had his father before him. He was already in the 'uniform' that would be his customary China garb—a khaki shirt, brown shorts (breeks in winter) and on his feet the knee-high leather high cuts so familiar to Canadian lumberjacks. It was functional gear that provided complete freedom of movement on foot, horseback, or bicycle. The high leather boots gave protection against both fleas and dogs. The uniform, the red hair, the blue eyes, the 'big nose', everything shrieked foreign 'barbarian'. Then he introduced himself as "Loa Tai-fu" and the language and the voice and the tone, even the pitch of it, was Chinese. The words were colloquial and the accent was from North Honan. While the Elders were still pondering the meaning of this apparition, Loa Tai-fu spotted an ex-patient and made immediate inquiries concerning the child's health. Before long he was by a village hearthside, no longer a potential victim, but a guest.

The Chinese of North Honan are a very logical people who are quick to appreciate the merits of a good argument and Moslems are a very tough direct people who are quick to appreciate similar qualities in others. In that village Loa Tai-fu found himself among kindred spirits. He pointed out that, as some of them had already discovered, the hospital of the Jesus people could cure their children of kala-azar. He also pointed out that since bamboo cutters often injured themselves and since bandits sometimes got shot it seemed only logical to assume that they might have need of his surgical skills. Whatever the ailment or injury they should feel free to call upon him at the hospital. They should not hold back thinking they were not welcome because the hospital was Christian and they were Moslem. The hospital was there for all. The villagers seemed to feel that this was not a bad offer. It required very little dialogue to point out the obvious corollary, that Loa Tai-fu would be permitted to travel bamboo territory with impunity. By the time Loa Tai-fu mounted his bicycle to head back to Hwaiking he had paved the way for hundreds of children to come to the Hwaiking hospital and he was already planning a counter attack against kala-azar in that difficult area. He had also secured his own route to Chinghua and to the ill and injured at the Chiaotso coal mines.

Ming-yuan knew by instinct and by upbringing that if the Tai-fu part of him was to function fully in China he would have to tread some very narrow paths indeed. The road to Chinghua was merely the first of many lonely paths McClure would travel in order to deal with Violent Ones on behalf of Ailing Ones. His willingness to negotiate for the good of his patients would at various times alienate everyone from evangelicals and fellow doctors to officials and generals. But after every such 'journey to Chingua' there would always be one group who would not be alienated—the sick and the suffering.

10

News From Home

There was one habit that had been thoroughly implanted in all members of the McClure family. It was that of writing letters. No matter what was happening, an hour or so every week was always set aside for letter writing. Bob found it difficult because he was always asking questions without receiving up-to-date replies. By the time return letters crossed Canada by train and the Pacific by ship and then took the train trip to the interior of China weeks could go by. If he received bad news in a letter the suspense of waiting for the follow-up was rather unpleasant. Of course the telegraph had come to China along with the railroads and really bad news travelled as fast there as anywhere else. It was not long before Bob received the sad but expected telegram telling of his mother's death. A following letter said that his sister Margaret was joining their father. Soon the McClure family was once again all in China, Dr. William and Margaret at Tsinan, Dr. Janet at Chengtu, West China, and Dr. Bob in Hwaiking.

Bob wrote regularly to all of them and, less frequently but consistently, to Dr. Pidgeon and others at Bloor Street Church. He discovered, as had so many before him, that the best thing about writing letters was receiving them. And somehow or other the letters most anticipated of all originated from the nurses' residence of Toronto General Hospital.

Amy had started into training at a high pitch of anticipation. She was not disappointed. The experience was thoroughly enjoyable and socially, too, her life was far from drab. By reading between the lines Bob got the distinct impression she was not sitting around pining for him. Eventually, however, her letters began to indicate that all was not well with the Hislop family.

Amy's father, now retired, had been plagued for some time with pain in his right wrist. It was thought at first to have originated with a slight infection in a finger and then the diagnosis suggested arthritis or a touch of rheumatism. After a while the diagnosis was changed to tuberculosis of the bone. He had to have his right hand amputated above the wrist. To a man who had spent his entire life working with his hands it was a hard blow.

Amy, too, fell ill. In the autumn of 1924, after completing a year and a half of her training, she developed pleurisy. There were no miracle drugs. Pleurisy was a lung condition that often signalled tuberculosis. There was already tuberculosis in the Hislop family and her physician, Dr. George Young, took no chances. Amy became a patient in the very hospital in which she had been training. She was in bed for many weeks. When she was finally released it was to go home to Whitby for six months of rest and very light exercise.

Eventually the news in Amy's letters improved and she announced she had recovered from her pleurisy to the point of being judged fit to return to training. Then on the heels of this good news came more bad news. Her mother had taken ill and the diagnosis was cancer of the stomach.

Almost the very next letter from Amy reported her mother's death. From diagnosis to death had taken only three weeks. Her mother was sixty-three.

Mrs. Hislop had made a dying request of her daughter. "Amy, you will look after father, won't you?"

Amy had said, "Yes."

Originally Amy and her older sister had had an understanding that if Amy went to the Foreign Mission Field Janet would take responsibility for the parents in their old age. Janet was at that time already married to Dr. Stan Montgomery and comfortably settled in Canada, but things had changed dramatically. Stan had received the missionary call himself and he and Janet were now off in Africa, in Rhodesia.

Amy gave up any hope of returning to training and settled in to look after her father. It was a decision which at that time and in that society seemed only right and proper and dark-haired Amy was of a nature that could make such sacrificial decisions with grace. In later years she would question the validity of such a total surrender to 'duty' and wonder whether it might not have been possible to find a compromise that would have permitted her to complete training without necessarily deserting her father.

One thing appeared certain. Any initiative that Amy might have had for the continuation and culmination of romance with Bob McClure was now totally out of her hands. As for Bob McClure, he was a mere junior officer in the army of Christ, stationed at a far off frontier outpost, and he was only beginning to participate in a final epic struggle between the world's great religions, both the old and the new. The prize was the mind and the heart of China.

11

Religious Background

Five hundred and eighteen years before the birth of Christ a thirty-four year old Chinese scholar borrowed a carriage and horses from the Duke of Lu in Shantung Province and drove up the broad valley of the Yellow River to the city of Loyang. He was a philosopher-teacher sprung from a poor but noble family called Kung. He would become famous as Grand Master Kung, "Kung 'fu' tzu"—Confucius. He journeyed to meet with an elderly sage called Lao Tzu who was keeper of the royal archives in that capital city of Loyang. Since one was to enter history as the founder of Confucianism and the other as the founder of Taoism, the meeting is cited by scholars as an interesting moment of convergence between two great personalities. It is cited here by way of emphasizing that North Honan was not so much in the hinterland as in the heartland of China. Hwaiking was only fifty miles by crowflight from Loyang where the two sages met to discuss and study the ancient rites of their own already ancient civilization. When Bob McClure began his missionary career in Hwaiking as a representative of Christianity he was working in an area that had cradled Taoism and helped nurture Confucianism.

Confucius was a humanist. He taught that it was up to man to understand nature and that man had a duty to his family and to society. He put great store in education, stating as an almost sacred precept that any man who had the ability had a right to be educated. The ultimate aim of education was the achievement of personal moral perfection. Confucius saw an orderly universe involving man and nature. He taught that from individual moral perfection all good would follow, moving outward from the individual through the family to the state. "When the personal life is cultivated, the family will be regulated; when the family is regulated, the state will be in order; and when the state is in order, there will be peace throughout the world," said Confucius. He taught rules of behaviour designed to achieve this personal morality. The emphasis on education eventually resulted in the creation of an immensely important social class in Chinese society, that of the scholar-official. It became what we would call the civil service and, as such, indispensable to the rulers. Since Confucianism depended heavily upon a codified system of rules of conduct the scholars became the custodians of Confucianism. There was no priestly hierarchy. There were also no gods and no heaven. Confucius refused to be drawn into mystical speculation. This is evident in the "Analects", a collection of his sayings compiled by his followers. There one reads that when asked about the worship of ghosts and spirits Confucius said: "We don't know yet how to serve men, how can we know about serving spirits?"

"What about death?" came the next question, and Confucius said: "We don't know yet about life, how can we know about death?"

A significant statement was made in answer to a suggestion that one should not kill a sacrificial lamb at the beginning of each new moon. "You love the lamb", Confucius is reported to have said, "but I love the rite."

So strong was the Confucian love of ritual that his code of behaviour gave China a formalized pattern of governmental and social behaviour that lasted until after 1900. The emphasis on education and the creation of a scholarly class of civil servant resulted in the creation of a bureaucratic feudalism.

The religion of Taoism, founded by the contemporary of Confucius, Lao Tzu, complemented Confucian ethics with Taoist mysticism. Lao Tzu taught that by observing nature one could understand man. In this he was exactly opposite to Confucius. He saw an orderly universe. In this he and Confucius were in agreement. Lao Tzu propounded the theory of the mystical Tao, "the Way", as the fount of all being. He called not for action but for reaction on the part of man. Man should let things happen to him as nature wills and then respond selflessly.

The philosophies of Confucius and Lao Tzu were in sharp contrast to the beliefs that had held firm sway in China throughout the preceding millenium. Those beliefs were centred on an elaborate concept of heaven in which Shang Ti, a god in human form, supervised the doings of mankind and administered rewards and punishments. Around Shang Ti swarmed myriads of mystical creatures and lesser gods. Men's lives were thought to be controlled rigorously by spirits but priests could intervene and, if not change the spirit's will, could at least divine the course of future events. The gods and spirits refused to be suppressed by Taoism and Confucianism.

When Buddhism reached China from India in the first century A.D. via the silk routes it met with great favour. Gautama Buddha himself, when teaching around 500 B.C., had made no claim to divinity nor had he suggested any particular reliance on gods. He taught that by accepting certain "Noble Truths", and by seeking insight through meditation, one could eventually not only achieve enlightenment but a state of infinite bliss resulting in the total extinction of self. As preached by Gautama, Buddhism could be said to be atheistic. It was also said to be a religion for monks. The version, however, that came over the trade routes into China was Mahayana Buddhism which stressed that the doctrine of personal salvation was open to all, not just to the priest and scholars. It had also acquired a pantheon of saints. A Buddhist could pray to the gods for a good harvest, or protection, or rain, but the path to personal salvation lay through meditation.

From dynasty to dynasty, Confucianism had been the official 'religion' of China. It was the religion of scholarly officialdom and of the heads of state. It was the religion through which the power structure of the orderly society was maintained, but it could easily tolerate Taoism and Buddhism which were both mystical, meditative, and non-activist. Indeed, scholars and rulers alike felt that Taoism and Buddhism were good for the masses. It was not difficult for the pious to find a temple dedicated to all three sages within which one could approach the local gods for assistance, appeal to one's ancestors for protection, and cast divination sticks to pierce the veil of the future. Long before the Christians arrived on the scene China had already absorbed three of the world's great religions. The universe was orderly and was unfolding as it should.

About the year 570 A.D. the prophet Mohammed had been born in the Arabian city of Mecca. The religion of Islam that sprang from his visions and teachings was rigidly monotheistic. The holy book, the Koran, prescribed practices aimed principally at the glorification of the One God, Allah. A doctrine known as "Jihad" encouraged conversion by the sword.

The faithful could reach a delectable Heaven if killed in battle. Even during the prophet's lifetime Islam spread like a prairie fire. Within a hundred years of Mohammed's death Islam was entrenched on three continents, having swept across Africa to the borders of Spain and from Syria across to the borders of China.

Islam arrived inside China, however, not by the fervid thrust of Jihad but, like Buddhism, as baggage. Foreign mercenary troops were occasionally brought into China and enrolled in the service of the Emperor. Some of these troops were Mohammedan and many settled, marrying local women. They clung to their religion and converted their wives but being tiny minorities among millions they were in no position to proselytize by the sword. The rigid monotheism of Islam with its daily periods of worship of a supreme being, and firm intolerance of idolatry in any form, was of little interest to the Chinese. The Chinese did not absorb Islam and did not reject it. They tolerated it.

The first Christian missions were established in China about the year 636 by followers of Nestorius, a fifth century patriarch of Constantinople who had preached heresy. "Let no one call Mary the mother of God, for Mary was a human being," proclaimed Nestorius in an oration prepared by himself but thoughtfully delivered by another. "That God should be born of a human being is impossible." Nestorius was expelled from the priesthood. His followers were expelled from the Roman Empire but they preached zealously in the Orient. Nestorian missions stretched along the trade routes from Baghdad to Peking in what is said to have been one of the greatest Christian mission campaigns ever launched. Princes and powerful ministers of the T'ang Dynasty patronized the new faith and eventually so did their emperors.

A thousand years after Nestorius, Roman Catholic missionaries studied a stone tablet found in North China. On it was inscribed in both Chinese and Syriac an account of the

Nestorian missions in China. They studied that tablet with disbelief, and well they might. There were no other indications of Nestorian Christianity still to be found in China. There were no traces of it in literature or in traditions. There was only the silent stone. Reluctantly the scholars had to accept the stone's authenticity. Christianity had once flourished in China and had then vanished.

That lonely stone monument to total failure stood at the city of Sian, 230 miles west of Hwaiking. Centuries before McClure's time the area had already spawned Taoism, endorsed Confucianism, accepted Buddhism, tolerated Islam, and had obliterated Christianity.

Those 17th century missionaries decided that because the Nestorians had been heretics, it was just as well they had failed. China was still open to conversion. It appeared that the ruling class were pagans, interested in ethics not in religion, and that the masses believed in a whole pantheon of gods and ancestral spirits whom they placated with ritual. The missionaries convinced themselves that the prospects for Christianity, the stone to the contrary, were very good.

The Roman Catholics understood China's ruling mechanism very well, and understood how Confucianism interlocked the scholar-officials with the ruling class. As a result, in the 18th century, the Catholics concentrated on the court itself, assuming that to convert the Emperor would be to convert the nation. The French and Italians in particular had great success. By using their scientific skills they gained acceptance at court. They passed on their knowledge of astronomy, engineering, even warfare, and in turn they themselves became Chinese scholars. They began to adopt Chinese customs, to conform to Confucian practices, to tolerate the observance of religious rituals before ancestral tablets, and to set off fire-crackers while celebrating mass. China was converting the missionaries. The Vatican, alarmed, condemned such easy tolerance, lost Imperial favour, and the church found itself in a period of persecution. Another Christian wave had been broken on the beaches.

The next wave of missionaries, in the early 1800s, was primarily Protestant. They entered China with permission. It had been wrung from the Manchus by the military might of the Western Powers. In the Protestant democratic tradition these missionaries ignored the Manchu court and virtually ignored officialdom. They went after the peasant masses. They translated the scriptures into Chinese and held literacy classes to teach the unlettered farmers and lowly merchants so that they might read those scriptures. The Protestants taught on street corners and ventured off on evangelistic tours from village to village. Suddenly in their midst there appeared a Chinese Christian prophet, Hung Hsiu-chuan. Unlettered, and inspired by visions, he rose like a meteor from the labouring Hakka people of Canton. He was soon at the head of a religious sect and leading the Tai-ping Rebellion of 1853. China ran with blood as the rebels entrenched themselves in most of southern China, turned Nanking into their capital and almost captured Peking. This 'Christian' wave was on the verge of crashing over the dikes and inundating China at last. All it required was help from the Western Powers. The missionaries, however, and through them the Western Powers, viewed this uprising with alarm. To the Roman Catholics, Hung was a heretic spawned by Protestant teachings. To the Protestants he was unbaptized and doctrinally dangerous. His inspirations and interpretations rose from his readings and illnesses rather than from their direct teachings. Some of his beliefs they knew would be rejected vehemently by the churches back home. Everyone hesitated and demurred until too late. The Great Peaceful Heavenly Kingdom Movement launched by Hung was overcome by the Manchus, with an assist from Britain's General Gordon. The third Christian wave had broken on the rocks of its own orthodoxy.

Bob McClure's own parents had been part of the fourth assault which was both Catholic and Protestant. This was the first time the Canadians had been involved. This time the force was broken on the nationalistic shoals of the Boxer Rebellion. But now there was a difference. Each Christian wave was following closer and closer on the heels of the preceding one and each time more and more of a residue was being left in the form of hospitals, schools, churches and universities. That more and more inroads were being made was evidenced by the increasing numbers of Chinese who called themselves Christian.

The fifth wave, which had borne the McClure family back to China, appeared to be given tidal dimensions by the formation of the Republic in 1911. Sun Yat-sen, the founder of the

Republic, was himself a Christian. The universities that had been founded by missions were much admired. Their graduates and young converts returning from abroad were gaining influential positions. To the educated youth Buddhism was exhausted, Taoism was mumbo-jumbo, and Confucius was being dethroned as quickly as possible.

But by the time Bob McClure was established in the Hwaiking mission station this fifth wave had already crested and was coiling inward and disintegrating upon the rocks of nationalism, greed, corruption, and political anarchy. (It was said that parliamentary votes were being bought and sold on the open market with opening and closing quotes like any other stock.) But all was far from lost. If the Christians could press forward, consolidate positions, make more gains, the next wave would be along at any moment and at last China would be 'won for Christ'.

The whole map of China was dotted with mission stations. They were Roman Catholic and they were Protestant. They were supported by Jesuits, Fransciscans, Oblates, Presbyterians, Baptists, Lutherans, Anglicans, Methodists, small sects and large sects. They were manned by Scandinavians, French, Italians, Germans, Canadians, Americans, British, Australians—a list that read like the roll call of squadrons in some twentieth century crusade. But when one disposed of the rhetoric and looked at the charging edge of those squadrons, the cohorts of Christ were thinly spread and lamentably lacking in over all co-ordination or grand strategy. Their strength really lay in quiet personal endeavour.

In its own way the McClure family was a little microcosm of the hundreds that were working quietly away within the borders of China. Each member was simply doing the work that came to hand without looking for spectacular results or questioning the enormity of the larger task.

To Bob and the other Hwaiking doctors the specific work at hand was clear enough. There was surgery to perform and there were diseases to treat. There was suffering to alleviate and, hopefully, to prevent. For the evangelistic missionaries the work had changed little through the decades. They had literacy classes to conduct, followed by teaching, preaching and, hopefully, the winning of converts.

They were all trying to demonstrate that, through the love

of God and the power of faith, the nature of man and the quality of life could be changed. They were powerfully motivated by their concept of the divine origin of the universe and of man, and they were driven by an activist compulsion to meddle with details in that universe which were patently not functioning in an orderly and loving way. Some of these Christians would attack anything from a rampaging cell to an oppressive social system. The younger men, like McClure, were restless, aggressive, intolerant of the status quo and eager for change. They were alien.

Or were they?

Off in Peking there was a library assistant in the Peking National University by the name of Mao Tse-tung. Among Chinese students in Paris there was a man called Chou En-lai. He had gone to France in 1916 as a literacy teacher in the Chinese labour battalions. Chou, Mao, and others had founded the Chinese Communist Party in 1921. Their religion was Marxism which, in keeping with Chinese tradition, did not recognize a powerful divine imperative. They were, however, every bit as aggressive, restless, and eager for change as were the Christians. As a result of Communist Russia's magnanimous gesture of relinquishing its Chinese claims the Chinese Communists were now being permitted to enter the nationalist party, the Kuomintang, as individual members. Many of the leaders of this new 'religion' came from the mountainous north-west hinterland, just beyond Hwaiking, where the ancient system had deteriorated most rapidly and where Western ideas had penetrated least deeply.

Christianity had been coming in waves. Communism was growing up out of the ground.

Communist tools were mass organization, propaganda, and infiltration.

The Christian doctors had their hospital as their principal tool. The Christian evangelists had literacy classes, the chapel and the school. They also had a very large tent.

The tent was, in a way, a kind of mousetrap.

12

The Tent

It was autumn of 1924. In the Hwaiking area the farmers had reaped the year's second harvest. The cold winds were starting to sweep down from the Mongolian desert, across the province of Shansi, skirting the western end of the Tai-hang mountains, funnelling down the Valley of the Yellow River, passing over Hwaiking, and blowing on into North Honan. Children were out collecting sorghum stubble for the cooking fires of winter. Peasant, merchant and mandarin were all now wearing heavily padded clothing, the labourers with long pants bound tightly at the ankles, and snug fitting jackets, the scholarly officials with long skirted robes over their pants, all quilted against the common foe—the cold.

In the compound the evangelistic members of the Hwaiking mission station, assisted by their gardeners and house-boys, hauled the tent out of storage and inspected it carefully in preparation for the weeks ahead. It was a large tent made of strong cotton canvas. The roof was in a single piece, forty feet long by twenty feet wide, rising to two peaks with a twenty foot ridge between them. The peaks were supported by poles sixteen feet long and the outer edges by six-foot poles. A six-inch scalloped border hung down from the roof edge and behind it, sewn firmly into the joining seam, were the hooks from which the sidewalls were suspended. The sidewalls, six feet high, came in two great lengths of continuous fabric that could be hung to totally enclose the roofed area or to leave much of it wide open depending on the dictates of weather. It was a small circus tent. Its direct descendants can still be seen next to the midway at any Fall Fair in rural Canada giving shelter to the food enterprises of the local churches.

The connotations of 'midway' and 'circus' were quite apt.

The reverend gentlemen of the Hwaiking mission, Herbert Boyd, Stuart Forbes and Jack Mathieson were preparing for a kind of Christian circus. They would be assisted by the evangelistic single women and had already told young Doctor McClure how he could get into the act. They were very pleased that their new colleague had appeared so amenable to their suggestions. They assumed that, since this was a slow period in the hospital, he would be itching like themselves to get out and preach the gospel. What he really itched for was adventure.

The purpose of this foray with the tent was to recruit potential converts for the church. It was also an admirable way to extend the reach of the hospital. Bob packed his diagnostic kit for eye, ear, nose and throat and other useful paraphernalia of the medico's trade and added the warmth of a leather jacket to his personal uniform.

It was quite a cavalcade that departed from the compound via the bell tower gate. There were three high-wheeled Peking carts, two pulled by oxen, one by a mule. There were two mules and two donkeys following as pack animals. There were Chinese evangelists, cart drivers, cooks, and baggage coolies. There were Chinese preachers and Canadian evangelists; and there was McClure Tai-fu. Bob had debated with himself whether to ride in a Peking cart, ride a pony, take his bicycle, or walk. At the speed this procession would travel there was nothing to be gained in speed one way or the other. He had settled for his bicycle as the transportation that gave him the most freedom of movement. They made such a fine show as they went creaking and clanking out through the main gate that he almost regretted he had not ridden the pony. There would have been a more splendid Kiplingesque feeling of outpost-of-empire to the whole show to be leaving sitting tall in the saddle instead of cranking away on a bicycle. And there were no cheering crowds bidding the troops adieu. There were, alas, no fifes, pipes, drums, or trumpets, all of which was too bad because trumpets at least were not unknown at the tent meetings of North Honan.

Over in Weihwei the Rev. Jack Bompas had been known to round up an instant audience by an enthusiastic trumpet rendition of "Bringing in the Sheaves". With the harvest completed and everyone going into the semi-hibernation of winter the prospi ~t of entertainment as announced by the trumpet was highly enticing. The Rev. Harvey Grant of Weihwei was not only skilled on the trumpet but performed quite passably on the violin. He could not bring himself to perform outside like some kind of a musical barker but he played either instrument with considerable enthusiasm inside the tent once the seekers had been lured within. Honanese ears were not well tuned even to Oriental music let alone to the jubilant rhythms of "Jacob's Ladder" or the stately tones of "Old Hundredth" and it said much for the power of their curiosity that they would stay and submit. The Hwaiking team did not go in for trumpets and violins but they did have the usual portable pedal organ. It was an instrument that most missionaries could play with some degree of skill. Many considered it to be an absolutely essential part of the evangelists' equipment and the Chinese identified the little organ with the Jesus people the way others identify bagpipes with the Scots. Unfortunately the organ did not lend itself to the pomp and splendour of departing legions.

On a winter foray, like this one from Hwaiking, it was not the evangelists' intention to hold a tent meeting in every village, but to set the tent up in strategic areas, accessible from many villages, so as the news of their presence spread people could be drawn in from various communities. Arrangements had been made ahead of time for the team to be invited to set up tent. The extending of an invitation fulfilled the requirements of Confucian courtesy and propriety. This was important. The first fine flush of pro-Western sentiment after the Revolution of 1911 and the establishment of the Republic had by now, 1924, worn very thin. In these chaotic times nationalism was again gaining strength and all Westerners were again being eyed with suspicion and even hostility. It was wise to work very carefully within the framework of such a society.

Now, even though they were armed with an invitation, there was a certain amount of suspense. Would curious villagers come to watch, and stay to listen, or would students come and level the tent to the ground? Fortunately student harassment tended to be seasonal and much more likely to occur after the spring exams. Winter was not a favourite time for marches, demonstrations, and riots.

The tent was put up without incident. The poles were guyed and the walls pegged. It was with a sense of elation that Bob saw the tent gradually fill with the idle, the curious, and the proverbial seekers after truth.

The tent meeting lasted for several days and gradually structured itself into small gatherings. Those who heard part of the Christian story for the first time one day could come back the next day to join a smaller group to hear more details and to ask questions. Those who might be on the point of becoming converts could have in-depth classes organized for them. Those who had a desire to read their own language would find literacy classes beginning within the big tent. Such classes, begun now, would continue on a regular basis long after the tent had been moved to another area.

The big tent, during a portion of each day, became a medical clinic. Bob soon found that the clinic could go almost nonstop. During the evenings while the tent was bursting to overflow with whole families, grandfathers, parents and children, all come to see the show, the doctor could continue on outside by the light of a Coleman lantern. It was a circus atmosphere anyway, with children underfoot everywhere who, the more they saw their friends being inspected by the foreign doctor, the more willing they were to submit themselves.

McClure and his medical associates carried out more inspection than treatment. Certain ailments could be helped on the spot—eyes cleansed, a boil lanced—but for others it was a matter of trying to convince the sufferer to visit the hospital for proper treatment. There was a parade of infections, ringworm, boils, benign cysts and lumps, and always abdomens painfully distended with kala-azar. There were old fractures that had been improperly set resulting in twisted limbs that could benefit from the surgeon's skill, *if* the person could be induced to spend a few of the barren weeks of winter in the mission hospital. There were the ravages of poliomyelitis. There were running ears and enlarged, inflamed tonsils. And always there were diseases of the eye.

Bob had thought he had reacted to Dr. Pidgeon's challenge out of a sense of adventure. Now, by the light of a Coleman lantern in front of that tent, with the organ blowing away inside and Chinese voices cheerfully murdering the Welsh tune

"Cwm Rhonddha", it began to occur to him that there was a tremendous sense of personal fulfilment in having gone forth 'to heal the sick'.

Bob could not follow the tent on its entire itinerary but when the hospital workload permitted, and if the tent was functioning, he would peddle off to join in. The opportunity to hold a country clinic was too good to be missed. Ever since Dr. Parsons had sent him out as a medical student, on his pentacycle, with a stethoscope and an empty bag to visit the child Mercy in Toronto's east end, he had known that no hospital could ever hold him.

Bob realized that as a medical missionary he was fortunate. He could assess the tent meetings by a simple yardstick. If, after the meetings, more patients came to the hospital for treatment then obviously the meetings had been a success. The fact that the mission chapel and the hospital waiting room were one and the same room, and that the evangelistic missionaries would make every effort to make some kind of spiritual contact with patients while they were in hospital, was an acceptable part of the technique; but medical success was not measured by the evangelical success. If the lame could walk and the blind could see that was a fact that could be entered on the triumph side of the ledger. The medical people knew when they were functioning well. The evangelists merely hoped.

Another problem for the evangelists in preaching Christ's message of brotherly love was that Christians had had a very strange way of demonstrating it amongst themselves. The same myriad denominations, branches and sects that had proliferated in the Western world had migrated to China with much of the same confusing doctrines, schisms and intolerances. The Chinese tended to group the Westerners into two basic groups, English and French. They further simplified it by thinking all Protestants were English and all Catholics were French. It was not too great a leap of the imagination to assume that Protestantism and Catholicism were two different religions. Most Canadians thought the same.

In China the various Protestant denominations tended to stake out areas where they would work and often were not at all happy when another denomination encroached on 'their territory'. Gradually, over the years, there had been some pooling of resources. The new Language School in Peking was the result of co-operative effort as was Cheloo University where Dr. William McClure was teaching. And as early as 1910 Canadian Methodists had participated in the founding of West China Union University at Chengtu. To the young liberals like Bob anything that would lessen inter-denominational conflict was all to the good. It was a problem, however, that had its roots not here in China but in the Western countries.

Back home in Canada some of the Protestant churches had been eyeing the basic absurdities of denominationalism and had decided to do something about it. The Methodists, Presbyterians, and Congregationalists had been talking about forming a united church and finally, on June 10th, 1925, the inaugural service was held for the new United Church of Canada.

It had been an emotional time in the Canadian churches leading up to 1925, particularly among the aggressively democratic Presbyterians. Congregations split down the middle. Ministers split with congregations. Speeches were made on both sides of the question that were undiplomatic and divisive and sermons were preached that were un-Christian and intolerant. It often appeared that Unionists and anti-Unionists could both quote scripture to support the unsupportable. The end result of the turmoil was that all the Methodist congregations, most of the Congregational, and two thirds of the Presbyterians joined together to form The United Church of Canada.

The United Church of Canada inherited the Canadian Presbyterian mission field of North Honan and the Canadian Methodist mission field of West China.

The United Church of Canada also inherited Bob McClure.

There had been little 'Union' trauma in the North Honan field and almost none at Hwaiking. Most of the missionaries, like Bob, were unionists by instinct. Bob was a protege of Dr. Pidgeon. Dr. Pidgeon and Bloor Street congregation both joined the new church and Dr. Pidgeon became its first Moderator.

Regardless of what decision their supporting congregations might take, to join or not to join was a personal choice for each missionary. Jonathon Goforth, the founder of the North Honan Mission and still a member of it, was now active up in Manchuria. He remained Presbyterian and, diplomatically, the

Manchurian field was allotted to the continuing Presbyterian Church in Canada. With one other exception, everyone else on the North Honan field joined The United Church of Canada. Thus the personnel of the North Honan Mission had experienced two miracles of survival in the first quarter of the century, the Boxer Rebellion and "Church Union". Only those who knew the early 20s in Canada could appreciate the comparison.

The Chinese in the North Honan Mission were almost unaware of the great organizational change. Those involved in the work of the mission recognized an increased impetus and even optimism. The aim of the Presbyterians had always been to create an indigenous church. They had played down the "Presbyterian" label. It was certainly now not the intention of anyone to create a United Church of Canada in China. The name itself conveyed the absurdities of such an idea. The same applied equally to the former Methodist Mission of West China. The new name and the new structure, The United Church of Canada, was important to the missionaries, but only indirectly to the Chinese.

Bob and his associates at Hwaiking were now part of a Canadian family that was working not only on the stations of the North Honan triangle but a thousand miles to the south-west at Chengtu.

It was an interesting field the new Canadian church had inherited. It was a field staffed by interesting people. They formed a microcosm of Protestant Canada and in some ways were quite unlike any other group of missionaries in China. Although sheltered by British power they were critical of exploitive colonialism and were sympathetic to Chinese nationalism; they tended to be theologically liberal and tolerant; they tended to be puritans who regarded drinking, smoking and womanizing as outright works of the devil; they were radicals who could bring themselves to believe that schools and hospitals were as important as churches.

These missionaries now represented the outreach of the largest Protestant Church in Canada and Canada was a rising young nation in the Western World. With their new found enthusiasm and drive it was just possible it might be their destiny to help give the fifth wave of Christian endeavour in China the final impetus to hurl it over the dikes of Chinese indifference and tolerance. Much would depend upon the outcome of the mounting political chaos around them.

During the same month that The United Church of Canada held its inaugural service in Toronto, Chinese students were firing old cannon at foreign shipping on the Yangtze River.

Time was running out.

13

Loa Ming-yuan and the Warload of Hwaiking

Early in 1925 the prospect for some semblance of peace and order in China had looked slightly promising. The Kuomintang's republican government was still holding its firm base in Canton and a somewhat progressive warlord had taken over in Peking. His name was Feng Yu-hsiang. Feng was a Christian, a Protestant, and a nationalist with strong inclinations to the Left. Both he and his 40,000 man army were highly disciplined. General Feng frowned upon tobacco, alcohol, loose women, rape, and plunder and, remarkably, had created an army of like mind. Feng, in uneasy alliance with two other warlords, announced a new provisional government in Peking and called for a re-organizational conference. Far off to the south in Canton, Sun Yat-sen, the founder of the Republic, rapidly ageing and ill, but still a visionary and still dreaming of a peaceful, united, democratic China, followed his personal grail to the Peking Conference.

The Conference accomplished nothing except the final depletion of Sun's physical resources. On March 12, 1925, Sun Yat-sen died in Peking. In addition to founding the Republic he left a legacy in the form of a last will and testament in which he set forth a three fold doctrine. It called for democratic government, a higher standard of living for the masses, and the recovery of rights granted to foreigners. There was another legacy. He had sent a young general to Moscow for advanced military training and upon the general's return had allowed him to set up a military college, which had rapidly become the best in the country. The general's name was Chiang Kai-shek. The Dean of the College had also returned from Europe. He was Chou En-lai.

Immediately upon their leader's death the Kuomintang proclaimed Sun to be a national hero and enthusiastically ex- pounded his final doctrine. Sun Yat-sen had also suggested that the realization of unification and democratization should be preceded by temporary dictatorship by a single party—the Kuomintang. The Kuomintang, restlessly shifting and chang- ing in search of a new leader but already possessing a disci- plined well trained army, was filled with renewed revolution- ary fervour. Then, in Shanghai, just a little more than two months after Sun Yat-sen's death, one of the minor agitations organized by the Kuomintang's communist partners had a vio- lent and unexpected result.

Shanghai, the largest, wealthiest, most dynamic of all China's great cities was also the one most under the control of foreign powers. Here were the largest of the "Concessions" of Britain, France, Belgium, and Japan. And here, in May, there was a strike in a Japanese owned cotton mill. Strikers were ar- rested. Students gathered in front of a police station in the In- ternational Settlement to protest the arrests. Although the mill was Japanese controlled, the police of the International Settle- ment were British controlled. As the demonstration escalated the police read the statutory warning. After first firing into the air they then fired into the crowd of students, killing several of them.

China went into convulsion.

There was no telephone service in the interior and only rudimentary telegraph but the news of the Shanghai shootings of May 30th, 1925, spread like a prairie fire down to Canton, up to Peking and into the far interior. There were riots, demon- strations, strikes, and boycotts aimed against all foreigners, but principally against the British and Japanese. Even warlords came under attack, particularly the incumbent master of Shanghai, for not having the courage to attack the foreign con- cessions and obliterate them. Many warlords were designated as "running dogs of imperialism", a label that was not without justification. During June, students marshalled some old can- non and began firing upon foreign ships on the Yangtze. Residents of the foreign settlements in the coastal cities petitioned home governments for troops and more gunboats. Foreign business men withdrew temporarily from the interior. Married missionaries and single lady missionaries went on early summer leave to Tientsin or the coast. Even in far off Hwaiking students from the government secondary school surged out to the mission compound to wave placards, to shout anti-foreign slogans, to throw stones, and to urge the Chinese employees to boycott the mission. There was a brief, partial evacuation of the married folk and the single ladies. It would become an almost annual event.

This roar of rage, this cry of pain from the lungs of China was nationalistic and anti-foreign. The Kuomintang's 'doctrine' was nationalistic and anti-foreign. Economics and standard of living or even basic freedoms had little to do with anything now. This was a gut issue of 'China for the Chinese' and the Kuomintang saw itself as the instrument of deliverance. The Party began to organize itself for a military sweep north out of Canton. General Chiang Kai-shek rose to the leadership. Up in Peking the 'Christian General', Feng, ousted by intriguing warlords, was being harried into Mongolia. The time was rapidly becoming ripe for the Second Revolution.

As the initial flurry of demonstrations, violence, and outrage died down the business men and missionaries returned to their posts. Off in the Canadian mission station at Hwaiking things returned more or less to normal.

"Normal" was a word that had to be interpreted in context.

The to and fro of police and bandit activity in the Hwaiking area was tied to economics and had little to do with nationalism or any other sentiment. There was a constancy to it that created a certain norm of violence, action, and bloodshed as a base, the way a crackling fire or a loud fan created a foundation of sound in a room. The arrival of a warlord's army or a mob of students was simply a peak rising out of this already violent base. Consequently, although common sense dictated the occasional tactical withdrawal, there was no thought in anybody's mind of complete and permanent evacuation. It was a matter of trying to accommodate to each problem as it arose.

The initial accommodation had begun to take place not long after Bob McClure's arrival. It had to do with the obvious fact that the spectacle of police chasing bandits might be funny in a Mack Sennett movie but lost some of its charm when transferred into a hospital ward. The police had, on occasion, raided the hospital, rousted post-operative bandits out of their beds, and taken them outside for summary execution. Nor was it unusual for wounded police and wounded bandits to be in the hospital together. This was awkward enough in itself but when their respective relatives arrived at the same time it made for violent scenes during visiting hours.

There was obviously nothing the missionaries could do about the basic problem, which was banditry. The police from south of the river would drive the bandits north across the river. The Hwaiking police would drive them into the hills or across the borders into Shansi province. Later the Shansi police would drive them back again. The bandits, not being hampered by political jurisdictions, could usually move, as in chess, to the next square on the board. For the authorities it was a way of solving the unemployment problem by keeping it mobile.

It occurred to Dr. Loa that the hospital's main problem hinged on the fact that, for the hospital, the game had no ground rules. It was also apparent that, since the opposing teams used guns, the hospital was one part of the playing field that was equally important to both sides. Using this fact as a starting point he was gradually able to work out a formula that was remarkable for its simplicity. When bandits and police were hospitalized at the same time they were now segregated into separate wards. It was the hospital's duty to notify police when a bandit was being discharged. A slight alteration to this rule put a twenty-four hour delay on the notification so that a discharged bandit was given a one day head start. It was not the kind of arrangement that met with universal support amongst mission personnel but to Bob McClure it was, if not ethical, at least sporting.

With tacit acceptance by the principal parties of these unwritten ground rules, daily routine in the wards became more secure. It was now possible for the admitting doctor or nurse to demand that a patient surrender his firearms for the duration of his stay, and the patient knew he could comply with safety. The patients also knew that Dr. Loa often carried a .45 revolver of his own. He had only been known to use it on rabid dogs but it was rumoured that he used the weapon with surgical accuracy. Sometimes, when the young surgeon was making ward rounds, a discerning eye could see a bump under the white gown that could be caused by no known medical instrument.

One could debate, and they did, heatedly, the pros and cons of missionary doctors carrying concealed sidearms in the wards, and giving bandits asylum and a head start. The Christian had a duty toward law and order, toward gentle compassion, and non-violence. But there was no law and order here in any conventional Western sense of the term. Even as a student Bob McClure had realized a nurse's duty was to protect the patient from the doctor so there seemed little problem in assuming that a doctor's duty was to protect the patients from each other and from any outside influence, such as broadswords, that would impede recovery. The boy, Pao-pei, had seen enough paradoxes in China for the man, Loa Ming-yuan, not to get hung up now on the niceties of intellectual debate.

The warlords merely added another dimension to the scene.

The warlords of North China became restless with the coming of spring. About the time the spring planting was completed they were usually on the march. By 1925 any area that had any strategic value could count upon an annual war with the same certainty one could count upon the seasons. 'Strategic value' meant the presence of a cotton mill, a railroad, mine, foundry, or an arsenal. A warlord was a general with a private army. The size of his army depended upon the size of his ambition and the extent of his financial success in previous seasons. If he could seize and hold a strategic portion of railway that led from mills and mines he could then levy a freight surcharge upon all the shipments from the mills or mines. He could also tax shipments to and from local merchants. If he captured the mills or the mines themselves he could impose even more direct taxation. The same applied to cities, towns and even big landlords. No warlord was interested in operating or even owning mills and mines, simply in taxing them. Factories, mines and railways, however, carried a special bonus with them in the form of their workshops. There the warlord could have his equipment repaired and could even manufacture crude guns and ammunition. The real prize, of course, was an arsenal. With a good arsenal under his command a warlord was into the really big time. One of the best arsenals was near

Hankow. It was said to be the equivalent of anything to be found in England. And Hankow was strategically situated on the north-south railway line and the east-west Yangtze River. The warlord of Hankow was the boss of Central China. He could extend his influence south almost to Canton and north almost to Peking. The arsenal was capable of producing excellent rifle machine guns as well as anti-aircraft guns. Hankow was worth fighting for and it changed hands frequently.

Some warlords imported German engineers to run their arsenals. One of the North Honan warlords contracted with the Italians for four batteries of 75mm. field artillery, four guns to a battery. He rented them on a monthly basis, it being a short season. Others, less ambitious, formalized the business to the point where it became a war of cheque books. In this version of the game opposing warlords would count armed heads. The general who was outnumbered would surrender on condition that his men's back pay be settled by the conqueror. This would be met by the victor by means of a large cheque on his personal account through the Hong Kong-Shanghai Bank. It was simply the price paid to obtain the local tax concession and the economics of it were not too difficult to calculate. Moreover, an army 'defeated' via cheque book would usually join the victor. In this way an army could grow and eventually graduate to the big league where payment was made in blood.

No matter how he came to power the warlord was the absolute ruler of his area. His word was law. He could judge, condemn and execute. All were economically oppressive because that was the purpose of the exercise, but in other aspects some were benignly paternal. Others would have made Ghenghis Khan look benevolent.

In the Hwaiking area a change of warlords came hard on the heels of the emotional upsurge of nationalism that followed the May 30th Shanghai shooting in 1925. A General Li with a modest force of some 10,000 men fought his way through the area between the coal mine railway and the Yellow River, effectively controlling both. His object was to take control of the transportation facilities, the coal mines, and the city. He achieved these objectives and drove the defeated forces into the foothills. This particular operation was not of the cheque book variety and the defeated forces continued to harass the occupying forces.

Right from the beginning of General Li's advance

wounded soldiers from both sides began to turn up at the mission hospital. The hospital soon found that not only its facilities, but its budget, were being strained beyond the limit. Local merchants rallied around to raise funds so the hospital could buy medical supplies. Some of the missionaries took this as evidence of Christian charity. Dr. Loa interpreted it as evidence that the merchants wanted to be in good favour with whichever general might happen to win. In either case, the financial support of the merchants was important because many mission hospitals had learned from bitter experience that this arbitrary dumping of wounded could seriously impede the hospital's ability to finance its service to the community at large. The defeated general never paid, and it took quick footwork to obtain satisfactory payment from the conqueror.

General Li further complicated matters, even before he had gained complete victory, by sending an officer to invite Dr. Chang Hui-ting to become the army's Chief Medical Officer. It was a losing proposition for Doctor Chang. Here he was, about 35 years old, a fine doctor and a Christian, with a small family, working in a Christian hospital. Attending wounded soldiers was one thing but joining a warlord's army was something else. Dr. Chang, being Chinese, would have no immunity from the General's whims. He would simply be a mercenary among mercenaries.

General Li sent the 'invitation' three times. There was a Chinese custom that the third time of asking could not be refused, particularly when the one asking was a successful warlord. Dr. Reeds arranged for Dr. Chang to be called to a 'conference' in other parts, and sent Dr. Chang's family with him for a 'holiday'. Dr. Chang reluctantly left his friends and associates at the Hwaiking mission station and left for Hankow, where he became involved in Student Medical Health programmes. (He specialized in problems related to tuberculosis. Within ten years he would be recognized as an authority in his field.)

General Li, victorious, entered Hwaiking City with considerable pomp. Soon after he was established, and after Dr. Chang disappeared, several mounted soldiers led by an officer arrived at the mission station. They had with them a spare mount, bridled and saddled, and the officer presented a courteous formal request for Loa Tai-fu to attend an audience with General Li. Young Dr. McClure knew enough not to refuse but it was apparent to him as he rode off, side by side with the officer and followed by the mounted troop, that he was being conducted as an honoured guest and not as a prisoner. As they clattered into the city, along streets where Bob normally pedalled on his bicycle, he was given a great deal of 'face' in the eyes of the bystanders. He had to admit to himself that it was a pleasant sensation.

General Li was most affable. He moved easily through the Confucian courtesies and asked the young doctor to be seated. He offered his guest a choice of cigars. Dr. Loa, who was acquiring a liking for the weed, chose a good one.

The General complimented Dr. Loa on the excellent service the mission hospital was providing in the area in general and for wounded men in particular. Dr. Loa was affable in return but pointed out that attending to so many wounded soldiers was bankrupting the hospital and that it would probably have to close its doors to combatants. The General felt that would be a regrettable course indeed and would incur the hostility of his men. Dr. Loa felt that if the General would be good enough to pay his back bills, and to attend promptly to current ones, that the hospital might see its way clear to continue to function. The General thought there might be a possibility of suitable financial arrangements *if* Dr. Loa would join his army as Chief Medical Officer. Dr. Loa was most touched by the invitation but felt that joining a Chinese army and abandoning his career as a Christian medical missionary was not what he had in mind. General Li was most insistent and showed signs of wanting to extend the invitation at least three times right then and there. Dr. Robert McClure pointed out that he was a Canadian citizen and British subject, and that since Britain still enjoyed extra-territorial rights he still enjoyed His Most Brittanic Majesty's protection. (It was a quaint notion that was 99 percent bluff. This far inland the only armed representatives of His Brittanic Majesty's were thirty Sihks acting as garrison at the Chiaotso mines.) The General, however, was an accommodating man. He pointed out he was merely trying to solve an administrative problem. It would be much easier for his paymaster to divert funds to the hospital through a Chief Medical Officer. Also, there would be much face for a General of his standing to have a Westerner as Chief M.O. Dr. Loa could sympathize with the General's administrative problem and could understand the implications of face.

Bob also realized that these discussions had taken him well

on the way down another path-to-Chinghua and that a certain delicacy was called for in arriving at a suitable destination. After a few moments thought Dr. Loa wondered if the presence in the General's army of an *Honorary* C.M.O. might solve all problems quite nicely.

General Li called in the paymaster and introduced him to Dr. Loa who was to be the army's Honorary C.M.O. with the honorary rank of Colonel. He instructed the paymaster to make an immediate payment of 500 silver dollars to the mission hospital to cover back debts. He further instructed him to honour the itemized bills which would from now on be submitted every Saturday by the Honorary C.M.O. Such weekly bills were to be paid by cash in silver dollars. A body-guard of four men with six ponies were to be put permanently at Colonel Loa's disposal. When Colonel Loa discovered that it was intended he should pay the upkeep for the six ponies and the four men he turned down the offer on the grounds the body-guard was unnecessary and the attendant face was unmerited.

The General was as good as his word.Thus it was that the Hwaiking mission hospital survived a financial crisis and that a twenty-four year old medical missionary sponsored by Toronto's staid Bloor Street United Church became a Colonel and C.M.O. in the army of a Chinese warlord. The arrangement did not receive undue emphasis in reports from the Mission Council Secretary to the Secretary of the Foreign Mission Board in Toronto.

The work of the Menzies Memorial Hospital continued apace. As General Li's C.M.O., McClure seized the opportunity to obtain extra assistance in the hospital and at the same time to disseminate some knowledge. With the co-operation of Dr. Reeds and Head Nurse Janet Brydon he recruited some intelligent young men from General Li's staff as apprentice medical corpsmen. They worked in the hospital alongside the Canadian nurses and the regular medical assistants. The system worked well and planted the seeds of an idea that would come to fruition almost a decade later.

The work escalated. Many of the local bandits were army deserters who had been far-sighted enough to take their weapons, and all the ammunition they could carry, with them when they broke ranks. Wounds inflicted by their steel-jacketed military ammunition made a much cleaner entry and exit than the incredible mess caused by the homemade ammunition used by their companions. If a warlord's army was hard pressed, his men, too, often took to making bullets out of old iron and other junk. And of course there were wounds caused by pistols, machine guns, shotguns, hand-grenades, land-mines, shells, and even swords. Dr. McClure, Dr. Reeds and their colleagues became expert at knowing *what* had caused a wound. *Who* had caused it was no concern of theirs. Even the Good Samaritan of the parable did not try to solve the bandit problem.

A gunshot wound was composed of an entrance, a track and, usually, an exit. It was always infected and one could not simply treat the entrance and the exit. The surgeon had to lay the wound wide open, not only to insert disinfectant but to remove splinters of metal and other foreign objects. The surgeon developed the eye of a connoisseur. If there were bark fragments in the wound the man had probably been poorly concealed behind a tree. Pine fragments with some paint indicated he had probably bought it through a door. Bob got to the point where he could tell the time of year without stepping outside simply by assessing the amount of dirty cotton quilting that had been carried into the wound. He could often tell the type of weapon by the type of wound. Hand-grenades, landmines and exploding shells invariably broke femurs, always with compound fractures.

The discovery of the sulfa drugs and of penicillin was still far off in the future. The surgeon's big battle was against infection. Ingenuity had to be used to win that battle. Little rubber tubes had to be inserted in deep wounds so the wound could be irrigated every few hours with chloride solution. But where to get rubber tubing? Bob went to bicycle shops and rounded up the rubber tubes used to make valve stems for inner tubes. Compound fractures in which the bones broke through causing jagged wounds from inside were a big problem. Setting the bones on the operating table was only the beginning of the problem. The limb could not be confined in a cast because the wounds had to be dressed and re-dressed. Splints would not hold the limb firmly enough. The proper method was to insert special stainless steel wire equipment into the bones and attach it to traction weights. The equipment was manufactured in Kalamazoo, Michigan, and expense and distance put it beyond the reach of the Hwaiking hospital. Again the ubiquitous bicycle provided the answer. Every city in China swarmed with bicycles and they all used stainless steel spokes. Dr. McClure, now rapidly approaching his twenty-fifth birthday, devised a traction system in which he pinned the outer end of a broken bone with a bicycle spoke and attached the traction equipment to the spoke. If necessary both ends could be pinned and traction applied in opposite directions. Once the bone had healed, or at least stuck, the limb could then go into a plaster cast with a window left for the application of dressings, if such were still required. Fifteen years later the technique of bicycle spoke traction developed in Hwaiking hospital was the standard technique used throughout war ravaged China.

In the meantime General Li seemed to be running into financial difficulties. As autumn wore on the paymaster's weekly payments became sporadic, and eventually stopped entirely. It was said the General was laying unusually heavy taxes upon the merchants, a sign that the warlord's coffers were reaching depletion. Once again the hospital was being arbitrarily forced toward bankruptcy. The end of the calendar year was approaching with all its bills and obligatory Christmas bonuses for Chinese staff. If they could survive until February there was hope, because that would bring the Chinese New Year. Dr. Loa knew that according to Chinese custom if he billed General Li before the New Year the General was honour bound to pay his bills or be held up to common ridicule as a bankrupt. The corollary was that if the General was not billed by that time it would be interpreted as an indication that the debt was forgiven and cancelled. There was, of course, no way that Colonel Loa Ming-yuan was going to forget to bill General Li for hospital expenses incurred on behalf of the General's men.

Shortly before the Chinese New Year Dr. Loa received an unexpected but well-known visitor, who arrived in a suitably dignified sedan chair. The visitor was another Li, but no relation to the General. He was Li Hung-ch'ang, a distinguished looking member of the old Chinese Confucian gentry. He was principal of a boys' boarding school the mission had established in Hwaiking City. The fact that the mission had recklessly, or thoughtfully, located the school in the middle of the city's red-light section was no fault of Mr. Li's and is mentioned here only as an irrelevant piece of interesting information.

It was quite unusual to receive a visit from Principal Li. Bob knew some of Mr. Li's students quite well. For that matter he knew some of the students from the government secondary school even better. One of them, Sun, had come first as a patient, but he and Bob had discovered a mutual interest in radio. Sun had come back to borrow Bob's copy of The Amateur Radio Handbook and had made occasional use of the machine shop that Bob and mechanic Chou Teh-kwei were gradually equipping. Sun had built a number of crystal sets and was getting more ambitious. He listened to Peking Radio so much he was developing a Peking Radio accent. It was as though a senior high school student in the Ottawa Valley had started to talk like a B.B.C. announcer. Sun was bright and keen and, in spite of his verbal affectations, Bob quite liked him. But surely the principal of the Mission Secondary School had not come to complain because the young mission doctor was friendly with a student leader from the Government Secondary School? No doubt Principal Li would explain himself in due time.

Dr. Loa received Principal Li Hung-ch'ang in the former's bachelor quarters. They went through the customary Chinese verbal and ritual formalities. They sipped tea and nibbled on cookies. Dr. Loa was consumed with curiosity to know why he was being honoured with a visit from the austere Mr. Li, but it was not for him to ask. Mr. Li had his own problems because what he wanted to discuss was, technically speaking, none of his business. He came to the subject via a casual, circuitous route.

"This most unworthy person is honoured to be in the house of Loa Tai-fu."

"My miserable self is enlarged by the revered presence of learned Principal Li."

"My slight knowledge will grow if watered by the wisdom of Loa Tai-fu."

It was all very pleasant and civilized but the courtesies could go on forever and did nothing to satisfy a red headed Canadian's curiosity. Eventually, however, Mr. Li seemed to be zeroing in on a target.

"I hear that you, Loa Tai-fu, are performing prodigious feats in the operating room. They say the Tai-fu never sleeps."

"They are too kind. It is Reeds Tai-fu who never sleeps and Nurse Brydon, Nurse Brodie, and Nurse Menzies."

"They say the hospital is using mountains of medical supplies that come in from Hankow by rail express."

"What they say is quite correct."

"They also say that such mountains of supplies must be very costly."

"What they say, Principal Li, is remarkably correct."

"My unworthy heart is heavy with concern for the mission. It is to be hoped that General Li is up to date on all payments."

Bob eyed the austere scholarly gentleman opposite and almost laughed. He was willing to bet that Li Hung-ch'ang knew the financial position of both the mission hospital and General Li's army almost to the silver dollar. He sipped his tea, offered his guest another cookie, and gave the required circuitous answer.

"I believe I have heard some of the hospital staff say that there is some delay in payment."

It was apparent that Mr. Li put the correct interpretation on that monstrous piece of understatement. He looked most solemn and nodded sympathetically as one does when one has just heard very bad news.

"My humble home," he said, "is on the street of the wood-carvers. No doubt the Tai-fu is familiar with that street?"

"Yes."

"Only today I was walking past the shop of the Master-Carver. Pausing to admire a cherrywood carving depicting the philosopher Lao Tzu seated reading, with one hand resting on the back of a savage but quiescent panther, I happened to glance toward the back of the shop. There I saw the Master himself working upon a splendid 'bien-tze'."

Ming-yuan did not need to be told what a 'bien-tze' was. As a boy he had watched the craftsmen on the woodcarver's street in Weihwei making the large 'honorific plaques' for presentation to private benefactors or distinguished citizens. The plaques were usually about two feet by four feet in size, with the entire background shining in black or red lacquer. In the centre would be carved, and gilded, a short suitable quotation of a very laudatory nature. Even illiterate folk would identify the quotation. On the right hand side of the plaque, painted in fine gold lettering, would be the name and title of the recipient. On the left, also in gold, would be the name and rank of the donor. The plaque would be hung over the front gate or in the reception hall of the recipient's residence. From there there was a descending order of 'bien-tze' protocol running right down to inside doorways. Bob knew of no book in English that had ever attempted to explain fully the elaborate plaque protocol.

"This beautiful and masterly bien-tze," continued Mr. Li, "bore a most apt quotation to the effect that Hippocrates lives again. I was filled with gladness to see that the recipient's name was Loa Ming-yuan."

There was something about Mr. Li's attitude and tone that suggested he was filled with quite the reverse of gladness. Bob hurriedly checked through his memory to see if he had been of any unusual service to a member of the merchant class. He could think of nothing out of the ordinary. He allowed himself a direct question.

"And the name of the donor?"

"It was not yet there. However, I made discreet inquiries and was reliably informed that the honourable donor is General Li."

Bob glowed inwardly for one brief moment, his ego quite pleasantly warmed at the thought of such an honorific plaque. Then the penny dropped in Ming-yuan's mind and red headed McClure almost erupted out of his chair. That so-and-so General Li, that scheming anal-opening-of-a-Mongolian-mule was on the point of sand-bagging McClure and the whole Hwaiking mission hospital! He paced a moment, fortunately saying nothing, but thinking unmentionable thoughts about generals in general and General Li in particular. To a good Chinese like Ming-yuan the plot was obvious. He, Dr. Loa, was intending to submit a great bill for the army's financial arrears to the General just before the New Year which was almost upon them. General Li would be honour bound to settle before the New Year. On the other hand, General Li was about to present him, Dr. Loa, with a 'bien-tze' before the end of the year. The custom was that, after such a generous and public presentation, after being given such an accumulation of face, no recipient could dream of stooping to ask for money. The presentation of an honorific plaque was an ingenious device for the cancelling of one's debts! It was entrenched in the whole elaborate Confucian behavioural system and neither Dr. Loa nor the mission hospital could afford the ill will of ignoring it.

Bob sat down again, looked at Mr. Li, and came straight to the point. There was no doubt as to why Mr. Li was here, bless him.

"Principal Li, we are talking in terms of two thousand dollars in cold cash. To the best of my knowledge pharmaceutical firms do not accept plaques. You say the bien-tze is not quite finished?"

"That is correct."

"Can we delay the completion of the plaque until the New Year?"

Mr. Li almost twinkled. "It is a thought that occurred to me, Tai-fu. It is, however, a delicate problem. I believe the Master Woodcarver will be sympathetic to our problem—" he hesitated a moment and then qualified his optimism. "But not to the extent of wishing to be shot by General Li."

"May I suggest, Principal Li, that we put our heads together as two Christians and find a Christian solution to this problem?"

They moved their chairs closer together and leaned across the cookie plate in earnest conversation. The dignified gentleman in the long mandarin gown and the young Canadian doctor in khaki breeks and shirt both knew it was serious. It was also a game that delighted their Chinese hearts.

The next day the Master Wood-Carver of Hwaiking came to the mission hospital. He was complaining of a sore right arm and was duly examined by Dr. Loa. Dr. Loa went through the motions of X-raying the offending right arm and clucked sympathetically. A plaster cast was applied to the arm from elbow to wrist and the arm was put up in a sling. As the Master Craftsman walked through the streets of Hwaiking, and down the wood-carver's street to his home, it was abundantly obvious to all who had eyes to see that he would be unable to work for some time.

Shortly before the end of the year General Li paid his bills in full in silver dollars. The next day the Master-Woodcarver again visited the hospital and Dr. Loa removed the plaster cast. They were both pleased to be able to report full recovery.

A few days later there was a ceremony just outside the bell tower gate of the compound. Troops were drawn up, bugles blared, and bullets were fired into the air, not in rifle volleys as in staid Western military tradition but in machine gun burst to simulate the more cheerful Chinese firecrackers. General Li, Warlord of Hwaiking, presented a 'bien-tze' to twenty-five year old Honorary Colonel Dr. Loa Ming-yuan, C.M.O. of the General's own army, Surgeon of the Menzies Memorial Hospital, Missionary of The United Church of Canada.

Something happened at the precise moment of the presentation. It was an action so fleeting that McClure Ming-yuan was never certain of its interpretation. Either General Li had conjunctivitis of the right eye, or he had winked.

14

Moment of Truth

The personnel of the Hwaiking mission station went about their work as usual during the winter of '25-'26. Apart from the complications created by the presence of General Li and his men the 'work' did not change significantly in nature. Dr. McClure, being young and vigorous, worked longer hours in the operating room than could have been tolerated by an older surgeon. He and the whole hospital staff were determined not to let the flood of war wounds stop the work that had to be done for the suffering members of the civilian populace. Daily clinics were still held at the hospital. The two doctors and the nurses went out as often as possible to hold clinics in outlying areas. The great tent was again unfurled from storage and the annual evangelical circus struck off into the frozen countryside.

As time went on Bob was developing ever greater and greater respect for the courage and determination of the evangelistic missionaries. It was only due to the cold of winter and the fact that the radical students were fastened to their books in the city schools that the great seething cauldron of nationalism was reduced to simmering just below the boiling point. Fuel added intentionally or accidentally at any moment could bring it to a full rolling boil and the evangelists had little, or no, protection. For them, sudden forced retirement could take the form of a crucifixion, burning, disembowelment, or a simple beheading. The nationalists made no distinction between a Canadian clergyman, teaching New Testament parables to a literacy class in a tent, and the captain of a British gunboat on the Yangtze River. Students had already been firing cannon at the gunboats. At any misguided moment they could decide on equivalent treatment for some lone missionary.

The Hwaiking doctors worked under a partial protective umbrella. They and the hospital were obviously useful. Young Dr. Loa had negotiated a kind of unwritten constitution that gave them a certain defined place within the pattern of local society. Some of the missionaries took heated exception to McClure's wheeling and dealing with bandits, police and the warlord. They felt he was compromising the mission, allying it with the civil authorities, or the outlaws, or the military. How could they accept payment from General Li when that payment was literally wrung from the peasants? The corollary of course was how could they treat the peasants for kala-azar or typhus or anything else if General Li was permitted to bankrupt the hospital? The Church in Canada had not intended to subsidize a military hospital. But what was one to do when a man turned up at the gate half torn to shreds—turn him away because he wore clothing that bore a resemblance to somebody's quaint idea of a uniform?

The critics were quite right. But so was Dr. McClure. Everybody was right. Everybody was wrong. McClure's position was that those with a philosophical turn of mind could debate right and wrong all they wanted. Somewhere else. He was going to open up wounds, dig out shrapnel, set fractures, remove cataracts, fight diptheria, deliver babies, stop bellyaches, and take out tonsils to the uttermost of his ability. He was running a second practice at the mines and had most of the Moslem community to look after halfway between. It might be lack of sleep but he could become very short tempered when any prolonged philosophical temporizing interfered with getting the job done. Any job.

The winter permitted a few changes in pace. Bob managed to get away for a few days with the tent people. These outings were great fun and, in a way, spiritually stimulating, although in the current political mood a little like camping on the lip of a volcano. He had to make a couple of trips to Hankow to pay pharmaceutical bills and to arrange for more supplies. And there was the annual meeting of Mission Council. It was always great to see the friends from the other stations, to compare news from Canada, and generally to chew the fat. He stayed with Bruce Copland whenever he made it to Weihwei.

Mission Council itself was interesting up to a point, but it could be tedious. Bob began to understand why his father used to abort from a Council Meeting at the earliest opportunity. He would have liked to see his father. The old gentleman was still at Cheloo, still teaching endless medical students and still translating endless medical textbooks. He was in his seventies, and making the finest contribution of his long, useful life.

On a mid-winter trip to Weihwei Bob found that Bruce had fresh news for him of a personal nature. Bob already knew the *big* news, which was that Bruce and Marnie were engaged. That had happened before Marnie had returned to Canada the previous fall. Although the wedding was still somewhere in the future Bob rather envied them. He himself had been thinking of Amy Hislop rather more often than one would think of a casual friend. But Bob could not decide whether or not it was fair to ask a girl to come to China. Bruce had decided. But then Marnie was one of the Weihwei natives, a member of the Language School noble band of "illiterates", and had even been here when Bruce had popped the question. It was different for her. She knew what it was all about.

What would Amy think of that boozy crowd at the mine, of the bandits in the bamboo groves, of General Li and his minions, of public executions before breakfast?

Bruce shook him loose from his ponderings.

"I'm going home this summer. Taking an early furlough."

"Why?" Surely Bruce was not clearing out because of a little political unrest. At least the young bloods should hang on.

"I'm going back to university. Going to take theology. Marnie and I'll get married. We'll both be back."

Bob sighed. Any sane young business administrator who would go home to Canada, deliberately load himself down with a theological degree and the title of "Reverend" and then come back to this country with a pretty slip of a wife was obviously nuts, nuts, nuts!

One had to admit, however, that it was a damned interesting idea and set an excellent precedent.

Not the theology.

The wife.

These were winter thoughts but they flowered.

Before the winter was out, Bob had given Bruce an interesting commission and a sum of money. The money was to be used by Bruce on his way through Shanghai to buy a *lovely* but *inexpensive* diamond ring. Buying it in Shanghai might make it possible to achieve those two admirable qualities. The commission was that he, Bruce, was to make a date with Amy Hislop when he arrived in Toronto, give her the ring and then propose to her for Bob by proxy, or the other way around, depending on how one did these things.

Bruce was intrigued, but confused.

"You mean just give her the ring, don't you? Surely you've already proposed—by letter—haven't you?!" His voice was rising with incredulity.

"Well, we have an understanding." Bob seemed a little vague. "I think you'd better propose."

By the time spring of 1926 arrived Bruce was off on the long Pacific voyage home. He had purchased the ring in Shanghai.

In Hwaiking there was no time for a young man to keep his thoughts lightly turning to thoughts of love. Nor was love uppermost among the thoughts of the young Chinese men of Hwaiking City. In a seasonal rite that was becoming almost as predictable as sunburn, mosquitoes and typhoid, the students closed their books, finished their exams, and went on the riot path. It was an annual ritual that began at Shanghai, spread instantly to Nanking, and then swept into the interior. This year it was given added impetus by the Kuomintang.

The Kuomintang's revolutionary armies under General Chiang Kai-shek came out of winter camp and began to sweep northward from Canton. The Nation's students, uttering nationalist slogans and waving leftist placards, moved out in organized force to bait the foreigners. In Hwaiking the nearest "foreign dogs" were entrenched behind the walls of the compound housing the Canadian mission station.

Everyone knew the storm was coming and knew it would be worse this year than the year before. An almost savage excitement could be felt sweeping through the country. Chiang Kai-shek's armies crashed northward, engulfing minor warlords who had the choice of either hurriedly joining his ranks or of being summarily crushed. The revolutionary armies were obviously aimed at the great triple city of Wuhan, including Hankow. There was a distinct possibility that the students of

Hwaiking might decide in their enthusiasm to raze the mission station as a sign of their support for General Chiang in his siege of the Wuhan cities.

Certain discreet precautions had been taken at the mission station. The married couples and the single ladies had been ordered to the coast for a slightly premature summer vacation. In fact the only people left were the Chinese medical staff, the coolies, and Dr. McClure. It is difficult to reconstruct the real reason McClure was left behind. He has said it was because he was a bachelor and obviously expendable. Others have suggested it was because he was a fire eater anyway and wise heads thought the experience might cool him down. There is some suspicion that he volunteered.

The students that year seemed more organized than usual. They rioted in the city and several hundred of them marched on the mission station. They intimidated the hospital's daily labour staff. Coolies who lived just half a mile or so from the hospital were afraid to come to work. The students prevented the delivery of flour, rice and vegetables to the compound. Patients who were not seriously ill had to be sent home. The demonstrators intimidated non-urgent out-patients so that they stayed away. Many of the veteran medical assistants already lived inside the compound walls, so the bell tower gate was closed and barred and the watchman retreated into his house. Bob and his skeleton staff settled in to attend to the seriously ill patients who were left. The students outside had no idea what a hardy, battle-scarred crew it was who were holding the fort with young Dr. Loa but it would have made no difference to them if they had known.

The main body of demonstrators came in the mornings. They hurled bottles and stones at the walls and chanted slogans of hate. "Foreign—imperialist—dogs! Foreign—imperialist—dogs!" Inside, the only foreigner present had been conceived, though not born, in China. He was a citizen of one of the least imperialistic nations on earth. The epithet of "Dog" was very derogatory but he was willing to debate its suitability on biological grounds.

It was not a time, however, for debate. Even General Li found more interesting concerns elsewhere. He had no margin for profit in interfering in this.

On the second morning of the demonstration, Bob made

his way to a vantage point from where he could assess the numbers and the mood of the demonstrators. It came as something of a shock to him to see that one of the leaders was his amateur radio friend with the Peking accent, Sun. Bob was angry at first, then philosophical. It was probably not easy for Sun. It might even be dangerous for him *not* to be there. On the other hand, he could be there without being front rank centre, and without throwing rocks quite so vigorously, and without shouting "Imperialist dog" quite so vehemently. It was difficult to be philosophical.

Bob was occupying a house about twenty feet inside the west wall of the compound. Since the cooks, houseboys, gardeners and others were no longer coming to work he had the house and much of the compound all to himself. The third night after the serious demonstrations had started in earnest he was sound asleep when suddenly he was awakened by the sound of the bedroom door slowly opening. He almost stopped breathing as he sensed movement coming towards him in the dark. He could just make out the figure of a man cautiously approaching the side of the bed.

Bob rolled from the bed, seizing his flashlight as he went. He switched it on as he hit the floor, hoping the sudden flare of light would momentarily deter the attacker.

The intruder was Sun. He stood, half crouched, looking wild-eyed in the glare.

For a long moment the two young men crouched, separated only by the bed. Sun appeared to be unarmed, but there was a strange look on his face that could be either fear or fanaticism. It was quite possible he had crept in here to make himself a bloodied hero of the revolution. Bob was beginning to sidle closer to the gun in the bedside table drawer when Sun spoke.

"Loa Tai-fu."

"Yes."

"Don't make too much light."

Bob lowered the flashlight. He let the beam bounce up from the floor so he could still watch Sun.

"Tai-fu—my thirteen year old sister is dying. I think she has scarlet fever."

Bob noticed the Peking accent was only partially surviving the strain of Sun's nervousness. He wanted to point out that if

Sun and his friends had not been boycotting and besieging the compound the girl could have been attended to earlier and at more civilized hours. That, however, was academic debate. What was not academic was whether or not Sun was on the level. Was this some kind of a trick? Were they trying to get this imperialist dog away from the compound, to separate him from the staunch corporal's guard of medical assistants?

"I'll talk to some of the men."

"No." There was fear in Sun's voice. "If any know I've come—" there was genuine entreaty in his voice, "I will be killed."

"As a 'running dog'?" Bob could not restrain the sarcasm.

"Tai-fu, my sister has a huge abscess. Here." He put one hand to his neck, just under his chin. "She can hardly breathe."

Bob pulled on his breeks, leather high cuts, and shirt. He gathered up his always present emergency bag and they let themselves out quietly into the dark compound.

Bob trundled his bicycle the twenty feet to the perimeter wall. He stood on the seat and hoisted himself to the top of the eight foot wall. Sun lifted the bike to him and Bob lowered it over the other side. Sun tossed the medical bag up. Bob gave Sun a hand up. In a moment they were both over the wall. Sun retrieved his own bicycle from the shadows.

The two young men rode, quickly and silently, along the lonely dike road some four miles to the village where Sun and his family lived.

It had been no trick. The girl was sick. Very sick. She had an abscess that was truly 'ripe' and very painful. While Sun's mother watched tearfully and while smaller children slept, Bob very carefully gave the girl a whiff of chloroform and incised the abscess. It drained copiously. He dressed the wound, did what he could for the girl's comfort, left some aspirin in a forlorn hope of reducing the fever, and departed quietly into the darkness.

Sun accompanied him back to the compound and helped him hoist the bike back over the wall.

"Loa Tai-fu, how can younger sister and I ever thank you? We are most grateful."

Sun disappeared quietly. It was still an hour before dawn.

Bob crawled back into bed feeling warmly heroic and missionary-like. It had been an adventure straight out of the pages of a Christian biography. Surely he and David Livingstone were blood brothers! Bob had planted seeds of benevolent love and trust. Those seeds had fallen on fertile soil and would now grow like the mustard seed of the parable. He slept the sleep of the just.

At nine o'clock the next morning the demonstrators returned in force. They chanted their slogans and hurled stones, bottles, and dried excrement.

Bob looked from his second storey window. He was stunned to see Sun in the forefront of the mob. He was shouting as angrily as the rest. The large sign he carried read, "Kill the foreign devil!".

McClure was enraged.

He had always had a temper. It was not a savage one and was usually stirred to heat only by the sight of professional incompetence, sloth or carelessness.

This was different.

He was enraged with himself. With Sun. With China. With the whole futile missionary charade. It was a barbaric heathen land and he was wasting his time just as his father had wasted his time. They had all wasted their time right back to the Nestorians. Let the Chinese rot. If they couldn't govern themselves let them rot in their revolutions. If they wouldn't put in public sanitation let them rot in their own sewage. Let them rot of their own typhus and cholera. Let them fester of their own self-inflicted wounds. To blazes with being Loa Ming-yuan Tai-fu and all the rest of it! He was Dr. Robert Baird McClure from Canada and what the hell was he doing here anyway?

It was a good question. What *was* he doing here?

For McClure, that morning in the late spring of 1926 was the 'moment of truth'. He was indeed like the bullfighter, poised between courage and cowardice, between life and death, about to go over the great horns in a supreme moment of self confidence and faith, *or* about to turn tail and run. Instead of a long sword he had a tiny scalpel. Instead of facing a bull he faced the monstrous agony of the Chinese people.

What was it all about!

Why was he here? Why? Why?

There *had* to be a reason. Perhaps he was expecting some kind of a reward. "If so," he asked himself, "what reward?"

He answered himself.

"Public approval?" Certainly that was very pleasant on the rare occasions it was expressed, but it was not essential.

"Gratitude?" He had already helped a great many people who had never shown any gratitude. Many had never had the chance, like soldiers or bandits who were just passing through.

"How about flattery?" Nonsense. Flattery was part of the old Confucian ethic. It was built right into the language and the system.

"Prestige and status?" That was a sticky one. General Li's honorific plaque had been very pleasantly compatible with Bob's ego. Being Tai-fu, Doctor, was a good feeling in any man's language. And there was some glamour to the "Honorary Colonel" bit, and in being C.M.O. But neither prestige nor status was a purpose. They were more like temptations to be guarded against. Occupational hazards. Sins, even.

"Saving souls for Christ?" He was not even sure what it meant! It was a phrase some of the ministers used and he was willing to assume that *they* knew what it meant. He had neither the training nor the inclination for active soul saving. He did have the training for easing pain and even saving life. As for souls, well, he knew he had one, and he was trying to live as a Christian. Whatever that really meant.

He was not doing very well in his search for purpose and was beginning to talk to himself. The demonstrators were still out there chanting for blood, presumably *his* blood, for he was the only foreigner around.

He thought, not of Sun but of Sun's sister, and his anger abated. The poor kid had really been in a bad way. Would still be in a bad way. He had better try to get out there again. It had been difficult to tell at night but if that really was scarlet fever there were hard days ahead.

He thought of the line-up of children at village clinics with little distended bellies and warped limbs and running ears. He thought of women labouring in breech births and of young soldiers, no more than boys, crying on the operating table just before being put to sleep. And it came to him, gently, with no sound of trumpets, no brilliant light on the Damascus road, that there was a very plain reason for him being here. There was nothing philosophical or intellectual about it. It was simply an imperative from the gut. He was *needed*. He was here because it was the *right* thing to do. He was not even going to moralize with himself over what was "right". That feeling in the gut was enough.

Bob suddenly felt very calm and went off to make ward rounds as scheduled. It even sounded as though the noise outside was abating. They had probably passed the peak of this seasonal storm.

It occurred to him as he walked to the hospital that the experience with Sun had amply illustrated something the China watchers had been saying. The mind of China was indeed changing, and the student mind in particular. No longer did the young radicals of China feel bound by traditional Confucian values of courtesy, gratitude, and 'correct' behaviour. It was sad, but he could not blame them. Courteous behaviour should be used to enhance human relationships, not as a chain to bind people to the status quo. In a way he wished them luck, those other young bloods outside the wall, but he hoped they knew what they were doing. He knew what he was doing.

After rounds he went off to the workshop to find Chou Teh-kwei. The producer gas plant was working well. They were already running two hundred electric lights in the compound and Bob and Chou were engineering a hot water system to supply the hospital's thermo-therapy unit. With the hospital almost empty, now would be a great time for them to press forward. Chou was turning out to be alert, skillful, and very reliable.

The Hwaiking demonstrations subsided. The other missionaries returned from their 'vacations'. The hospital resumed normal functions.

By summertime the Kuomintang's revolutionary armies had captured the Wuhan cities. Chiang Kai-shek then turned his armies down the Yangtze toward Nanking and Shanghai. While the right wing of the Kuomintang was providing the armed fist the left wing, the Communists, was providing the propaganda. Communist organizers were moving into the far interior, organizing and agitating. It appeared that the alliance between the Communists and the Kuomintang might at last be putting together the necessary ingredients for a successful Chinese revolution—support from all classes.

15

Wedding Bells

The Georgian Room of Eaton's Queen Street store in Toronto provided an atmosphere for elegant, but not lavish, middle class dining. The room with its pillars, plaster frieze work, crystal chandeliers and discreetly separated tables, could make an ordinary Canadian feel, upon entering, that the forthcoming meal would be an occasion. The tables, with their spotless white cloths, gleaming silver, sparkling glassware and good English china, did nothing to dispel the feeling. The room, however, did not lend itself to the subdued lighting and shadowy nooks required for romantic tête-a-têtes. The Georgian Room, in short, was a most appropriate setting in which a young man could present an engagement ring and formalize a proposal to a young lady without making it too personal. In the late spring of 1926 Bruce Copland chose the Georgian Room in which to carry out the commission received from Bob McClure.

Bruce and Amy had not met before but it was one of those situations where each had heard enough about the other that prior acquaintance was unnecessary. Bruce quite enjoyed the moment when he reached across the table between the candle and the flowers and slipped the diamond on Amy's third finger left hand. It is not every man to whom it is given to propose to one pretty girl while engaged to another.

Bruce had made his own proposal in 1925 and he and Marnie would be married in 1928. Their engagement had had a catalytic action upon Bob. Now that Bob had taken the plunge his marital arrangements were hurtling forward with characteristic McClure impetuosity.

Since Amy's sister Janet and brother-in-law Stan Montgomery were still in Africa it was arranged that Amy's father would accompany her to China and take up residence with the newlyweds in Hwaiking. Mr. Hislop, in his seventies, and having difficulty adjusting to the mechanical contrivance that had replaced his hand, had never been outside of southern Ontario. He sold his house to buy his ticket to China and had his bags packed almost as soon as did Amy. He was a man who husbanded his emotions, but there seemed little doubt he was accepting the move as the adventure of a lifetime. He was to be served a generous portion before the year was out.

Reverend Herbert Boyd, the senior evangelist of the Hwaiking station, was home on furlough with his wife. They were on the point of returning to the North Honan field. Amy and her father were booked on the same ship as the Boyds. It had been Bob's request that the Boyds should take the Hislop's under their wing. The request was based upon a profound knowledge of the vagaries of China.

They sailed from Vancouver in August aboard the American liner, *President Jackson*. The ship was bound for Shanghai via Japanese ports. For Amy it was a journey straight out of a romantic novel. For the first and probably only time in her life she travelled first class. She was twenty-four years old and sailing across the blue Pacific to far Cathay to marry the love of her life. Her young man was to meet the ship in Shanghai, and there was a distinct possibility he might even meet it in Japan, such was the power of love.

Bob did not turn up in Japan. At Shanghai there was no sign of him either. It was little wonder. The Kuomintang armies were battling out of the interior heading straight for Shanghai. Travel routes from the interior, both railroad and river, were cut by the warriors' battle lines. The Boyds told Amy to take heart, Bob was probably just trapped the other side of that 'local' war. It was a normal occurrence and she was not to worry. If Amy had known that for most of the next twenty years Bob would be trapped the other side of a war she might well have taken the next ship back to Canada. As it was, she and her father embarked with the others on a tramp steamer heading up the coast toward Tientsin. It was a miserable old bucket that wallowed in and out of every port on the China coast. The accommodation provided suitable penance for the luxury of the *President Jackson*. The weather was foul and even the veteran travellers were sick. Amy could have died, cheerfully.

The old hulk of rusting iron finally puffed into Chefoo harbour on Shantung peninsula. Amy wondered if she would live for the final run up the Gulf of Chihli. The ship wallowed at anchor while the port doctor made his routine inspection. He was a Dr. Malcolm, a retired missionary and a fellow Canadian. Dr. Malcolm read the passenger list and suddenly left, his inspection tour suspended in mid-air. If he had found the crew and passengers all dead of the plague, he could not have departed more precipitously. Before those on the coaster had decided whether the port doctor was quite mad, or merely an old China hand suffering a temporary derangement, he returned, accompanied by Dr. Robert McClure.

Amy maintained for ever after that her sea-sickness cleared up instantly. (Little did she know she had just been given a preview of the years ahead—a sudden disruption of plans, followed by a period of total uncertainty, ending with the sudden materialization of McClure at an unheralded and unlikely moment.)

When Bob had found he could not travel by a direct route to Shanghai he had diverted north to Tientsin. From there he had been hitch-hiking south by coaster. He joined the wedding party and they all sailed to Tientsin, where Bob and Amy were to be married.

The church wedding had to be Anglican. The British Treaty with China stipulated that British subjects marrying in China could only do so in the Anglican Church. This was quite acceptable. Both Bob and Amy found certain aspects of Anglican services more aesthetically pleasing than the more dour form of their own denomination. The wedding was going to be spartan enough without the service being likewise. But there was a problem. The banns had to be posted three weeks in advance. Bob made a prescribed contribution to the Bishop's Benevolent Fund and the ruling on the banns was waived.

Amy had come expecting a simple Presbyterian-type wedding and had brought a suitably simple, white, street length dress for the occasion, with a flower piece for her hair. The Anglican Church required a hat. A Tientsin milliner made one just in time for her to don it before leaving for the church.

As Amy was driven to the church the sound of a deep throated gong was reverberating forth from the grounds of a nearby Buddhist temple and off in the depths monks were chanting. From the distance came the noise of firecrackers as a cheerful procession escorted a family god for a ceremonial airing. It was all overlaid by the sound of wedding bells pealing forth from the Anglican Church. It seemed as though everybody was happy on that 5th day of October, 1926, and Amy thought the wedding service was very, very beautiful.

The ceremony was followed by a small reception which, for the McClures, was something of a family reunion. Dr. William McClure was there and so was Bob's sister, Margaret. Margaret was not well. She had contracted TB and would soon return to Canada.

After the wedding Bob and Amy literally headed for the hills and spent an all-too-brief honeymoon in a quiet resort hotel. To both of them, the bride from Whitby and the groom from Hwaiking, it was unbelievably idyllic.

The flagship train from Tientsin to the interior was called "The Green Express". It had compartment type coaches in the European style. Amy was certain she had never been on such a beautfiul, such a luxurious train in her life. It far outclassed the Trans-continental back home. The euphoria lasted all the way to North Honan, where the arrival of Dr. and Mrs. Robert McClure on the mission field was a triumph of the unintentional.

Amy knew nothing about Chinese culture or tradition and Bob had not programmed her. The correct bridal costume for China was always red. Amy arrived wearing red. With her fair skin, jet black hair, blue eyes and red dress she looked gorgeous. The Chinese were suitably impressed. At least one was astonished. Amy was a stylish dresser and the Western styles of the period showed a reasonable amount of leg. One elderly Chinese lady gazed at Amy's silk-stockinged legs and muttered, "Is that skin!"

The Chinese were also impressed by Amy's husband, not for the way he looked, but for the way he had gone about getting married.

The Chinese recognized marriage as being a logical result of a biological urge. When the man felt the urge sufficiently powerfully he arranged for a matchmaker to find him a wife. Loa Tai-fu had obviously sent Rev. Herbert Boyd to Canada as a matchmaker. The fact that he had actually sent Bruce Copland was irrelevant. Here was Mr. Boyd back again and here was the bride as ordered. Not only that, the young bride was accompanied by her elderly father. It could not have been more culturally correct had it been planned by Confucius himself. Loa Tai-fu and his bride were off to a good start.

On the surface Amy's new life looked idyllic. Within the eight-foot high walls of the Hwaiking mission compound was a village full of warm, friendly 'family', both Canadians and Chinese. The compound itself was fascinating. Just inside the bell tower gate were the Chinese quarters, then there was the hospital with the chapel attached. There was the Chinese primary school. There were storage sheds, stables, the workshop, the generator shed and all the other appurtenances of a self sufficient community. There were lawns, gardens, and flower beds. Dominating these few walled acres were the residences themselves, the five big square brick buildings engineered by Dr. Menzies.

Four of the houses were identical. They housed the married couples: Dr. & Mrs. Robert Reeds, Rev. and Mrs. Herbert Boyd, Rev. and Mrs. Jack Mathieson, and now Dr. and Mrs. Robert McClure. The fifth house belonged to the single ladies.

As Amy entered *her* house she crossed a broad verandah supported by square brick pillars. The house itself was built on the centre hall plan so popular at home. A large central hallway opened into a living room with a dining room behind that. On the other side of the hallway was a comfortable study for the man of the house. At the back of the house was the kitchen and pantry. Upstairs there were four large bedrooms and a full bathroom complete with running water and flush toilet. One could go from the bedrooms out onto a second storey verandah.

The house was furnished with typical, rather spartan, 'mission furniture'. At some past date that furniture had been made from local wood by local craftsmen following specifications laid down by some departed missionary. Being principally wood with some token upholstery it could accept cushions, afghans or covers. It was a style that always looked as though someday, when times got better, it would like to be corpulent and overstuffed but in the meantime was willing to be spare and functional. The strange thing about that furniture was that it could be found all over the world where, even though built from different woods by different craftsmen from different designs, it always exuded the same atmosphere. It was neither beautiful nor ugly, neither masculine nor feminine. It had been neutered at birth by low budgets.

Amy settled in to try and turn her house into a home. She had a cook, a houseboy, and a gardener, and she could not communicate with any of them. She had by-passed Language School because of the chaos of political events and because, strictly speaking, she was not a missionary but the wife of a missionary. She was to study the language an hour or so every day with a private tutor. It was all rather exotic for Amy and exciting and just a little frightening.

Amy's father could have been forgiven if he had found it all completely overwhelming. There had been no experience in his entire seventy years of life which touched upon this present experience. But the old man was imperturbable. Mr. Hislop set about exploring his new environment with the curiosity of a moonwalker. He had two assets. One was the white hair of age and the other was that artificial hand. The Chinese showed all due courtesy and deference to his age but they were absolutely fascinated by the appliance. The hand was connected to a shoulder harness and by moving his shoulder Mr. Hislop could cause a pincer movement in the thumb and forefinger. Whenever he chose to demonstrate it to a group of admirers, he could count on the same attention as would be paid to a story teller or a juggler.

One day the old gentleman made his way to the city gate of Hwaiking, just a stone's throw from the compound. An unusually large crowd had gathered and his curiosity led him to investigate. The spectators on the outer edges either recognized him or deferred to his white hair. They smiled at him and called to each other to make way. They passed him hand to hand through the press of that crowd so he could be in the front row and have an uninterrupted view of the holiday proceedings. For a retired farmer from Southern Ontario, where even the friendly people are reserved, it was a delightful experience.

He smiled at his new found friends and then, right in front of his eyes, General Li's soldiers chopped off a human head.

The old gentleman tried to move back from the appalling sight. Courteous hands propelled him forward for an even better view. Nineteen other men were kneeling in a row, heads bowed forward, eyes blind-folded, hands tied behind their backs. The line extended almost to where Mr. Hislop was standing. He watched, aghast, while beribboned broadswords rose and fell, heads thudded into the gory dust, and blood spattered his very boots.

After the executions were completed, two boys, realizing that for some strange reason all was not well with the old man, took him to Loa Tai-fu at the hospital. Mr. Hislop was pale and trembling. He was experiencing cultural shock.

The location and the actors had changed, but Mr. Hislop had seen an extreme version of the same scene Bob had witnessed at the age of eight. In between had come the First Chinese Revolution, the overthrow of the Manchu Dynasty, the establishment of the Republic, the rebellion of the generals, the era of the warlords, and the beginning of the Second Revolution. China had made great strides in industrialization and the building of railroads. The old class structure had begun to crumble. Everything was changing. And yet nothing was changing. Poverty, disease, ignorance and oppression were still the lot of the toiling peasant millions. If anything, the poverty and the oppression were getting worse.

16

Exodus

The days and nights of the winter of '26-'27 sped by with exceptional rapidity. Amy, like any new bride in a 'new' home, found more than enough to do to enhance the days and to decorate the hours. The cold Honan winter made for cozy, fire-lit evenings and for snug, lusty nights—a phenomenon not unknown in Canada.

The hospital routine was working nicely now and could absorb the occasional military overload without too much chaos. Bob divided his time and energies, while in the compound, between the patients in surgery, Amy, and the often balky engine in the power house. When the electricity failed he would spend a night shift as a mechanic.

Occasionally there would be an emergency elsewhere with a patient who could not be moved and Bob would peddle off on his bicycle. About every two weeks he would cycle to Chinghua and take the train into the clinic at the Chiaotso mine. Amy accompanied him a few times and admired the exotic path through the bamboo groves. She was unaware of the negotiations that had taken place to make the trip a secure one. At the mine there was some rioting and the occasional strike, evidence that the Kuomintang's left wing organizers were now reaching farther and farther into the interior. At the time, these disturbances did not impinge deeply upon Amy's consciousness.

The Britishers from the mine would drop into the compound when out on weekend duck hunting forays along the river. The hospital staff reciprocated by attending horse races at the mine. Bob, and nurse Coral Brodie, bought a couple of ex-racing ponies which were losers, and therefore cheap. Socializing between the mine and mission communities had been unknown before Bob McClure's arrival at Hwaiking. Now it was all very pleasant.

By the time the little Christian community had celebrated Christmas and the Chinese community at large had greeted the New Year in mid-February, Amy and her father were both nicely settled in. Unfortunately for them, things were afoot down Shanghai way that would soon destroy any illusion they may have had of permanence and of security.

Chiang Kai-shek had captured Hankow the previous summer. There the Kuomintang established a provisional government. During the winter, Chiang had ignored the customary adjournment of warlike activities and had thrust on toward Nanking and Shanghai. Foreign powers sent troops to re-enforce the garrisons of the Shanghai Concessions and sent gunboats with the guns and flags of intimidation. It has been said that, before authorizing reinforcements, the British Prime Minister consulted a map to see where Shanghai was. He was surprised to find that Canton was not near Peking. His Foreign Secretary, studying the same map, was said to have noticed that China was considerably larger than Japan.

Most Western leaders had been told that Chiang's army was a mere Cantonese "rabble" and would never make progress against the more warlike northerners. During February and March of 1927 those Western leaders were busily revising their opinions. In February, as the Kuomintang armies approached Shanghai, the Shanghai workers rose on cue and seized power from the most ruthless of the warlords who had made Shanghai his own private oyster. The workers had been organized by Chou En-lai.

The Kuomintang armies entered Shanghai in triumph. Nationalist soldiers were now confronting foreign soldiers across the walls, wires, and hastily constructed barriers that formed the perimeter of the Shanghai foreign Concessions. Here the Kuomintang forces paused for a long fateful moment of indecision. One more surge and the foreign imperialist dogs would be in Shanghai harbour—and China would probably be at war with the world's major powers. The leash was held firm at Shanghai, but allowed to slip at Nanking. There the revolutionary forces ignored the presence of foreign gunboats on the Yangtze and overran Nanking. There was indiscriminate looting and some killing in the foreign Concessions. Most of the foreigners escaped to the river, saved by a covering barrage from the gunboats and by their own agility at scaling the city walls. Elsewhere British ships were captured and rescuing gunboats were repelled.

It is not surprising that missionaries began to withdraw from the interior. No orders went out to the Canadians in the North Honan field but it was suggested that it might be wise for them to retire to Peking or Tientsin. Once again an early 'vacation' seemed to be in order. There was little hope, however, that this particular spring storm would blow itself out.

There was consternation among old and new Christian congregations of all denominations. If the missionaries left could the struggling congregations survive? As often happens, a threat to survival forced a progressive step forward. Almost a third of the young Protestant churches of China joined in a church union of their own, and hastily formed the infant "Church of Christ in China". Henceforth, as far as the major Western denominations were concerned, the church in China would be indigenous, native Chinese. When and if missionaries returned they would be coming as invited associates to work with the Chinese Church. But before the missionaries could return they had to escape.

The railroad route from Hwaiking to Peking was still open, but with escalating civil war it was doubtful how long that link would last. Married couples, women, children and an elderly father-in-law with an artificial hand were evacuated from Hwaiking. Two ministers stayed behind to complete the handover of the mission property to the new Church of Christ. McClure stayed behind because he had patients to see through their post-operative period before discharging them. There was also his responsibility as Acting M.O. at the mine.

The Canadian missionaries were making a smooth withdrawal, but the British at the mine were hampered by technical difficulties. They were also hampered by a strike, riots, and a siege. The women and children had already been evacuated but a staff of supervisors were trying to remove the pumps before withdrawing. If the pumps were lost in a flooded mine, there would be an incredible waste of time and expense before the mine could ever go back into operation. This skeleton crew was protected by thirty Sikhs armed with Lee Enfield rifles. The Sikhs were there by treaty but such treaties were only an aggravation to the anti-foreign mobs congregating outside the mine fence. Bob knew that if either the mob or the Sikhs lost control, there would be urgent need for a doctor. After he had put Amy and her father on the train with the others, he went to join his compatriots at the Chiaotso mines. If McClure had been a combatant he would have had a problem, because "compatriots" included his Chinese brothers outside the mine and fellow sons of the British Empire within. As a doctor he could follow the dictates of instinct and go to the heart of the action. Reluctantly he completed the closing down of the Hwaiking hospital and withdrew to the confines of the beleaguered mine.

China was in the throes of full-scale civil war. The revolutionary armies in their thrust north from Canton had by now, for all practical purposes, taken the southern half of the vast country. The revolutionary battle line was at the Yangtze River and moving north. In a country of 400 million inhabitants the city streets were always teeming with people and the railways congested. Now, with foreigners fleeing the interior, with refugees fleeing advancing armies, with armies themselves being mustered from various directions as warlords large and small responded to the threat to their self interest, travelling conditions were chaotic indeed. Not only were the railway stations inundated with those seeking to travel but they were also the focal points for nationalist demonstrators wanting to harass the "imperialists", any imperialists—diplomat, merchant, or missionary—of any nationality.

At the Hsin-hsiang junction, Amy and her father and the small Hwaiking group were fortunate to be able to board a train headed for Peking. The one they caught was no "Green Express". To Amy the 'coaches' were more like cattle cars. There were some hard wooden benches and some wooden bunks. The glass in most of the windows had been broken and the weather was still cold. The men tried to hang blankets on the window openings as meagre protection. They managed to find an upper bunk for Mr. Hislop and the old man climbed, uncomplaining, to what was little more than a shelf. The car was crowded with people who were tired, ill, exhausted, frightened, and dirty. There were no toilet facilities. If one had to answer nature, one waited for a rural stop and dashed for the bushes hoping to be able to make it back aboard. The trip that would normally have been completed in about sixteen hours took several days.

During the journey Amy did not feel at all well. She noticed that her ankles were beginning to swell and by the time she reached Peking they were terribly swollen. The scene at the Peking station diverted her mind. It seemed as though everybody either wanted to get on that train or to get off it. Never before in her life had Amy seen so many people in one place at one time. What was worse, there was no order, no method and no discipline.

Some of the men struggled out onto the platform through the gaping windows. The men inside passed the women and children out to them. It was in this fashion, being lifted from strong arms to strong arms like bundles of baggage, that Amy and her father returned to Peking. They were first taken to the Language School, where the residence had become a missionary refugee station, and then on to the port city of Tientsin.

Halfway down the eastern seaboard, at Shanghai, everything hung at a point of extreme tension and most delicate balance. The leaders of the Kuomintang were faced with an intricate problem. All classes, peasant, merchant, and scholar-bureaucrat, wanted to regain China's lost sovereignty and redeem pride and face. All-out war at Shanghai could do that, but it might do much more. The right wing leaders of the Kuomintang knew that a full-scale war with the West would mean they would have to arm the peasants. China would probably lose the coastal cities and, along with them, much of the wealth that was the Kuomintang's power base. For the same reasons such a war would be a bonanza for the left wing.

Both wings of the Kuomintang wanted to regain the foreign Concessions and to nationalize coal mines, banks, and railways. They wanted Chinese principals running all schools and Chinese doctors heading all hospitals. They wanted to liquidate or absorb the myriad warlords. But the right wing had *no* policy for land reform and did *not* want war with the West. The Communists had been tolerated within the Kuomintang as necessary allies but they were already taking over the provisional government at Hankow and were pushing hard for a showdown at Shanghai. It was no part of Chiang Kai-shek's purpose to win *their* revolution.

Chiang turned upon the Communist wing of the Kuomintang and its members were slain, imprisoned, or put to flight. Russians, who had been advising both wings of the Kuomintang, were sent back to Moscow. For better or for worse Chiang had committed himself, and the Kuomintang, to a right wing path that could never lead to a complete social revolution. The Western Powers took note.

It was during this early spring of 1927, with the Nationalist armies still poised at the Concession lines in Shanghai, with the Hankow and Nanking Concessions in ruins, with the Kuomintang organization reeling from the internal haemorrhage of self-inflicted wounds, with foreign gunboats still trying to rescue their nationals up and down the Yangtze, with Chiang's armies beginning to regroup to drive even further north, with Communists running for the hills, it was now that Bob set out to rejoin Amy.

Carrying nothing except a small backpack he caught a freight train running east. That ride took him the hundred miles to the rail junction at Hsin-hsiang. The north-south line to Peking was in chaos. No trains were running and nobody seemed to know when, or whether, they would be. If a train did come it might only get to another city. The mainline cities were decidedly unfriendly to foreigners. It would be one thing to pass through on a train but quite another thing to be marooned. Nor could Bob tarry at the junction. He went to earth for a day at a flour mill run by a Swiss national. Like many Westerners whose lives were tied up in business property, the miller had decided to put property first and to remain. When night came he gave Bob a .45 revolver and let him out the back way. McClure had decided to walk to Tientsin, three hundred miles away.

Bob ignored the railway altogether and struck off more or less along the borders of Shantung and Hopei provinces. En route he fell in with a travelling companion, a fellow refugee whose name was Ma. Ma was a Moslem fur trader from Afghanistan. At first glance one would have thought he was Chinese, but his accent proclaimed otherwise. Ma had decided that the persecution of foreigners included him because he carried a British passport. (He claimed that he had qualified for the passport as a boy by killing a British soldier and acquiring his rifle. In recognition of this act of 'coming of age', the British had awarded him a passport and he was not about to give it up. If it were true, only the British could have done such a thing, and only a Canadian would have believed it.)

The two men travelled together. They headed for Taming and skirted it, as they did all communities of any size. They then struck off, using the Grand Canal as a guide, in the direction of Tientsin. They slept in the daytime and travelled at night.

The Grand Canal made a good guide. At one time it had carried traffic in a great arc looping inland from Shanghai to Tientsin. Now, thanks to the wandering vagaries of the Yellow River, the canal had fallen into disuse. Structures like the Grand Canal always made Bob marvel at the antiquity of the civilization of this his adopted country. The Grand Canal had been built while Europe was still floundering in the Dark Ages.

Loa Ming-yuan and Ma were fortunate that the weather had turned warm. They were able to sleep in the fields, but with the planting season coming that was hazardous. Temples provided better daytime shelter because there were no religious festivals during the heavy work seasons. People were working, not praying, and most temples had no resident priests. Even if a worshipper did come in he, more often she, remained in front of the altar. Ming-yuan and Ma, Christian and Moslem, slept behind the altars at the feet of Buddha and came safely to Tientsin.

Amy, in Tientsin, had had no word of Bob for weeks. She was sure she would never see him again, but there was nothing she could do except wait and pray. One day she realized why her ankles had been swelling and why she was now suffering from morning sickness. She was pregnant. It was not a consolation. It was another wild Chinese aberration of fate. Then Bob McCann, one of Bob's friends from Weihwei days, tracked Amy down at the mission refugee shelter and took her and Mr. Hislop to his home. McCann was the Dodge Motor Car agent for all of North China.

When Bob McClure walked into Tientsin he had no way of knowing what city his wife was in, but he went straight to her. Amy's joy and relief was enormous, but when Bob voiced surprise that she had even questioned the possibility of his survival, her anger blazed. An emotional conflict between anger and relief would become a familiar experience for Amy McClure.

Amy had full details of the situation as far as it concerned the United Church missionaries. The people in West China had been able to sit tight but the North Honan field had been evacuated. Those missionaries who were approaching their furlough time were heading home. Others were lingering at the coast in hopes the whole thing would soon blow over. Much the same was true of the missionaries of other denominations. In general, those on the coastal perimeter and in the far west were holding on while the interior had been evacuated. The Fifth Wave of Christian endeavour in China appeared to be about to break upon the rocks of the Second Revolution. This time, however, the receding waters would leave behind a fragile barque, the Church of Christ in China. Something else would be left behind which was even more fragile and less visible but even more important. It had to do with the hearts of men and was demonstrated in the course of that year of chaos to Bob's father, Dr. William McClure.

The eddies of revolution were swirling around, but not over, the University of Cheloo at Tsinan, away downstream on the Yellow River in the Province of Shantung, when Dr. William McClure received a cable from Canada saying that his daughter Margaret was dying of TB. The Tsinan-Shanghai trains were running at the time but it was a precarious trip for any foreigner, let alone a seventy-three year old man. Dr. McClure set out, hoping to catch a ship from Shanghai to Canada. His students took him to the Tsinan station to see him off. Much to his surprise a former student, a graduate doctor, boarded the train with him. From there on he was never alone. The word had gone out. Other graduates were waiting at other stations all down the line. One Chinese doctor would pay his respects and leave, and another would board. At another time it could have been taken as a mere demonstration of Chinese courtesy but in that year of revolution that token honour-guard of men, who had everything to lose, was a quiet demonstration of Chinese courage and affection. When Dr. McClure arrived at Shanghai another cable awaited him saying that Margaret had died. He turned around and went quietly back to his students at Cheloo.

Shortly after finding Amy, Bob came to the decision that he had no intention of sitting around at the coast twiddling his thumbs. He had even less intention of taking a furlough. He understood there might be something doing on Taiwan, that beautiful island just off the south-east coast of China, that was now occupied by the Japanese. As it turned out he was right. With the recent completion of church union in Canada the Taiwanese field had remained Presbyterian and the Korean field had gone to the United Church. One of the young Canadian doctors in Taiwan had asked to be transferred to Korea, leaving the Presbyterians temporarily understaffed in an area of heavy leprosy work. Bob had never done any leprosy work. It seemed a good idea to transfer for a year to broaden his experience—and to let Amy have the baby in saner surroundings. Surely within a year China would have settled down. He cabled for permission.

As good luck would have it everything was now co-ordinating beautifully. Amy's sister and her husband, Janet and Stan Montgomery, had just returned from Africa and were remaining in Canada. They would make a home for Mr. Hislop. The old gentleman sailed for Canada. He had been away for less than a year, but he had enough stories for the boys at the barbershop to last him the rest of his life.

A cable came through from the Mission Board in Toronto. Arrangements had been made for Dr. Robert McClure to be seconded to the Presbyterians in Taiwan. It was the first of a long line of flexible arrangements the United Church was to make for its peripatetic surgeon.

Bob and Amy sailed for Taiwan.

It was anybody's guess what would happen to China in the next few months. The Kuomintang had regained its equilibrium after purging the Communists and had moved its provisional government from Hankow to Nanking. Chiang Kai-shek was now preparing his armies for a great thrust north toward Peking itself. He would be delayed. Before the summer was out his own Fourth Army, one of his prime fighting units, would mutiny. Not only that, the Fourth would follow its commander, Chu Teh, to the hills to rendezvous with Mao Tse-tung and Chou En-lai, survivors of the bloody purge of March and April. That Fourth Army would soon become the Red Army.

17

Taiwan the Beautiful

Six years before the Boxer Rebellion Bob's parents had experienced a summer of flood, pestilence, and war. In their area the war had consisted mainly of troop movement as China's armies were either moving north toward combat in Manchuria or fleeing south in defeat. The enemy had been the Japanese. In the resulting treaty China lost not only much of Manchuria but also her island province of Taiwan*. The anti-foreign sentiment created by that war subjected Dr. and Mrs. William McClure to a period of danger and insecurity. Now, in 1927, one of the long term results of that same war provided their son and his wife with one of the most secure periods of their life abroad. In Taiwan, Japan had organized an incredibly orderly, paternalistic, colonial society.

The Canadian Presbyterian mission was based in a compound in the capital city of Taipei at the northern end of the island. The city was not walled, and the compound was not walled. There was an exhilarating openness that in a way symbolized the openness of the new life the McClures were now beginning. It was a new life in a new country but Bob and Amy were coming to friends. One was a doctor in the hospital—Dr. Flora Gauld; one a nurse—Gretta Gauld. Both sisters had been studying in Toronto at the same time as Bob. Their brother and Bob had been classmates. The senior evangelist in the mission was Rev. Hugh MacMillan. Bob and Hugh had been in the Student Christian Movement together back in varsity days. Hugh's wife, Donalda, had been a senior nurse at Toronto General when Amy was in training. The Gaulds and the Mac-

---

* It was named Formosa, "the beautiful", by the Portuguese. Taiwan was the native name and it eventually reverted to that. Taiwan is used in this text.

Millans formed a nucleus of old friends, and the McClures were soon to form a broad circle of new friends.

The focal point of the mission station, from Bob's point of view, was the MacKay Memorial Hospital. This hospital had been founded in 1912 and was named in memory of the first Canadian Presbyterian clergyman to venture to Taiwan. He was the Rev. George Leslie MacKay. He had been a big, black-bearded man, with a powerful and not always gentle personality. The Taiwanese had called him "The Black-Bearded Barbarian" and his ghost and his legend still stalked the island.

The widow and children of the Black-Bearded Barbarian were still here. They were "Continuing Presbyterians", the quaint label that had been devised in Canada to designate those who had considered Church Union to be a non-original and unnatural sin and a violation of predestination. With two exceptions the other missionaries were all United Church of Canada and their presence here on a Presbyterian field was considered by some to be evidence of the new denomination's determination to be a "co-operating" church. The two exceptions were the chief of the hospital and his wife, Dr. and Mrs. G. Gushue-Taylor. The Gushue-Taylors were English Methodists. Dr. Gushue-Taylor was a Newfoundlander by birth. He had studied medicine in London and was a gold medalist from the London University Medical College. He was a Fellow of the Royal College of Surgeons. He was a shy, charming man, sincerely interested in the welfare of his associates, deeply religious, and probably the most brilliantly qualified surgeon it had ever been any church's good fortune to send to the Far East.

Dr. Gushue-Taylor had never worked with a surgical colleague before. Dr. Flora Gauld was a medical practitioner, and medicine and surgery simply complemented each other. Now, however, with the arrival of Dr. McClure, Dr. Gushue-Taylor found himself side by side in the operating room with one of his own species. It was something of a shock to both of them. Many buckets of blood had flowed, and much sawdust had been spread around the floor of the Menzies Memorial Hospital back in Hwaiking, since Bob had interned beside Dr. Perfect in Toronto Western. Dr. Perfect had been good, but Dr. Gushue-Taylor was meticulous. And Dr. Gushue-Taylor was not shy in the operating room. He was also the master of the put-down.

He eyed his new associate's first demonstration of Hwaiking surgery and paled visibly at the sight.

"That was an interesting incision, Dr. McClure. What abattoir teaches that technique?"

Not since the days at Toronto Western had Bob been subjected to such sarcasm. It did not help that the O.R. nurse standing within full earshot was his old friend Gretta Gauld. He coiled up inside and paid more attention to the fine points of his craft. He also paid more attention to his Chief. When the latter would mention a particular article in a professional journal, or a chapter in a textbook, Bob would try to read it within the next few hours. And it was just as well. His Chief would question him about it the next day to see if he had read it. Bob began to feel as though he were interning again. He had two ways to go. He could either rebel, or he could settle down to learn. His Chief provided the catalytic put-down.

"You'll never be a Fellow of the Royal College, Dr. McClure." (It was always "Doctor" McClure and "Doctor" Gushue-Taylor.) "But why don't you behave as though you were at least a *student* of the Royal College!"

Dr. McClure decided then and there that he damm well *would* be a Fellow of the Royal College and that the way to get there was indeed to become a student. He enrolled in a correspondence course and began to devote five nights a week to his advanced medical studies. Dr. Gushue-Taylor sensed the drive and continued to use the cattle prod. During rounds or in the O.R. he would get McClure absolutely squirming with mortification. By the end of the day Bob would be feeling incompetent and thoroughly ashamed of himself. As he would be heading for home, and the sanctuary of Amy's calm and reassuring presence, he would hear Dr. Gushue-Taylor's voice summoning him from the depths of the latter's house.

The verandahs were fully screened but Dr. Gushue-Taylor always had his front door yawning wide open like the entrance to a dark cave.

"Dr. McClure, one moment, please."

Bob would go to the Presence in awe and humility.

"You may recall a little chat we had this morning. In these books you will find the opinions of three surgical authors. You might find those opinions instructive."

There seemed to be a never ending supply of Dr. Gushue-

Taylor's books and they were all large. Bob contemplated towing a shopping wagon with him to lug them back and forth across the compound. But he read them. And the next morning during rounds Dr. Gushue-Taylor would never fail to refer to the subject of the previous day, checking to see if McClure had really done his homework. McClure had done it.

It was not easy. Bob was trying to learn a new Chinese language at the same time. That language was Amoy.

At one time the Dutch and the Portuguese had vied for control of the island. The Dutch had triumphed, but only briefly. In the mid-sixteen hundreds, Chinese crossed from the mainland province of Fukien. They expelled the Dutch and drove the native tribes people into the mountains. The tribes people were still there, embedded like the very rock of the mountains they now called home. The Chinese were the only invaders who had truly come to settle and now, almost 300 years later, their descendants were as native to Taiwan as were the descendants of European settlers native to America. But the language they spoke was Amoy, and Amoy was as different from Mandarin as French from English.

There was also the Japanese language.

The Japanese had been here only three decades but they had formed a very efficient colonial administration. In Korea they were being brutal and repressive. In Taiwan they were model colonial administrators. The language of government, upper echelon business, and of all education was Japanese. Bob tried to learn enough Japanese to be polite without diverting his main efforts from the Amoy. Amy studied Amoy, too, but was distracted by the pending arrival of the baby.

The McClure's first child was born under Dr. Gushue-Taylor's care. The date was August 25th, 1927, and the baby was a girl. They called her Norah. Norah was fortunate; she looked like her mother.

An 'amah' was acquired, in keeping with custom, to help look after baby Norah, and Amy settled in to her combined duties of housewife and mother. The presence of servants was a mixed blessing. It was marvellous to have them to do the work but it was frustrating to try to explain to them in Amoy exactly what it was the mistress wished to be done. Amy felt so lost with the language that when Bob was in the room she avoided giving instructions to the servants.

Amy had trained as a nurse and, although she had not graduated, it was tempting to see the hospital right there across the compound and to think that there might be work she could be doing at her husband's side. She was, however, a quietly observant person who seldom rushed headlong into a new situation. Mrs. Gushue-Taylor was a registered nurse, and Amy observed that the husband-wife team created tensions. She took note, and decided to stay clear of the hospital portion of Bob's life. Instead she began to do some of the letter writing.

Missionaries were always writing letters. There was official correspondence with the Field Secretary, with the Foreign Mission Board in Toronto, with the sponsoring church, and with the chairmen of mission committees in Canadian congregations wanting information about ways in which their dollars could be of help. There were letters to friends, relatives, well-wishers and critics. Amy began to set a period aside each day for writing.

The McClures found themselves drawn into an entirely new social life. It came about partly because the hospital had a contract to supply basic medical services to members of the Western business community in the city of Taipei. This contract with the foreigners was for several thousand dollars and was a useful part of the hospital's income. Most of the Westerners were in the tea business. The major crops in Taiwan were sugar and rice. They were grown for the controlled Japanese home market and their production was rigidly dictated and controlled by the Japanese in a system that made the farmers chafe, but that created incredibly stable prices and supplies. Tea was grown for the world markets, and it was a highly competitive business. The Westerners who ran the finishing and marketing end of the tea business were a free-wheeling lot who worked at an intense pitch during the four or five months of the 'buying' season and then threw parties the rest of the year.

Their recreational activities alienated Dr. Gushue-Taylor who was not only shy when outside the O.R. but could not abide smoking and drinking. He turned the foreign practice over to Dr. McClure. It was a happy choice. McClure was certainly not shy. He liked to smoke, and was not averse to the occasional cocktail before dinner. Amy did not smoke because she had tried it and did not like it. What others did was their business. As for drink, she preferred a sherry to a cocktail.

The young doctor and his pretty wife moved happily into the Western social life of Taipei as liaison between the mission, and the foreign 'pagans'. They became familiar with the "tea hongs", or factories, and were given preview samples of exotic blends. They participated in private dinners and large parties amidst the luxury of hand carved rosewood furniture, Peking rugs, solid silver tea service and cutlery, and fine china.

Even Bob had never met such a hard drinking crew in his life. It was common for a man or a woman to consume a quart of whisky a day as a preamble to whatever booze the party of the evening might bring. Bob tried to calculate the amount consumed at a party and failed. It was not unusual to see four men consume a quart of whisky, between them, in the time it took to walk from the host at the front door to the rickshaws at the gate. Very early in this game Bob and Amy realized that moderation was neither understood nor appreciated. They listed themselves as non-alcoholic and joined in the fun with soft drinks. It was something Dr. Gushue-Taylor could not have done. He would have shown, and voiced, disapproval. As for the MacKays or the Gaulds they would not have entered a house where you could even smell liquor, let alone wade in it. It was a tightrope for the McClures. To some of the mission folk they were libertines. To the foreign business community they were puritans, but good company.

In many ways life inside the compound was almost idyllic. The compound was a much more open community than it had been in China. Taiwanese people were coming and going all the time, not as patients but as friends and visitors. As one crossed the compound to the hospital one could hear students practising piano or organ, or hear a full choir in rehearsal. One could see a knot of theological students on a verandah hotly debating the proper translation of a hymn. There was a Chinese scholar ensconced in the Gauld study, busily writing a book. The open atmosphere spilled over into the other homes and permeated the compound. It spilled over into the McClure home in the form of a thick-set, smiling man with a strong Scandinavian accent and acute malaria.

The Scandinavian gentleman turned up in the out-patient

clinic. He was having chills and fever attacks on a recurring pattern of once every two days. A blood smear confirmed that he had malaria. He was a stranger to Taiwan, and alone. There was not much the hospital could do for him, but he was in no condition to live in a second class Taipei hotel. The McClures took him in. It turned out that their guest was Karl Ludvig Reichelt, a Norwegian missionary who was the leading Christian authority on Buddhism.

Reichelt had come to mainland China twenty years before. To become a Buddhist priest in China one studied at a prescribed series of 18 teaching monasteries. Reichelt had gone on pilgrimage. He had completed the prescribed studies, which included reading in classical Chinese the 48 volumes of Buddhist scriptures. Those scriptures were the equivalent of about 24 Bibles. He had then established a monastery of his own which taught Christian scriptures in a surrounding that was completely congenial to, and compatible with, the Buddhist priestly patterns of living and worship. Reichelt's monastery had been included by the Buddhists as number 19 on the prescribed list of pilgrims' 'courses'.

At that time, *all* Christian churches *everywhere* believed that Christianity was the only 'true' religion. Even though Bob had been raised in China it came as a surprise to him to realize that Buddhists could be so open toward a competing religion. Christianity, he now realized, although not holding a monopoly, certainly had a firm hold on the paranoia market. He could just imagine the Buddhists trying to set up a theological college associated with Knox or Emmanuel Colleges back in the good old U. of T.

Whatever Bob's day held for him he invariably migrated by late evening to Reichelt and a conversational course on Buddhism. Again, even though McClure had been raised with Chinese as a mother tongue, never before had he appreciated the problems inherent in two philosophies trying to communicate within one language. Christian metaphors that could be meaningful to some Christians could be truly revolting to a Buddhist. To a Buddhist the four filthiest things in the world were urine, faeces, blood and pus. When a Christian orated about being "washed in the blood of the Lamb" he was being more than revolting, he was being obscene. The concept of religious obscenity gave one pause. It was, fortunately, not all negative. The Buddhists had an almost mystical awareness of words, written or spoken, as being ideas given body. In their contemplative religion an idea was the essence of reality. The first line of the Gospel according to St. John, "In the beginning was the Word", made more sense to most Buddhists than it did to many Christians.

It took Karl Reichelt two months to recuperate from his malaria bout. By the time he was ready to leave Taipei he had made firm friends, not only among the Protestant missionaries, but among the upper echelons of the Buddhist priesthood. His impact among the latter was so strong that, after Reichelt's departure, the top ranking Buddhist priest in Taiwan converted to Christianity. The change was carried out with delicate discretion. It was announced via a Buddhist death notice in one paper, followed by a Christian birth notice in another. As for Bob, never again would he listen to Christian jargon with an uncritical ear; never again would he assume that men of other faiths were automatically antagonistic to his; never again could he rest easy with the idea that the 'essence' of Christianity depended upon Western 'culture'. He reflected upon many imponderables.

No matter what was going on, philosophizing, partying in the tea-hongs, or exploring exotic pathology sections in the lab, Bob always came to earth Saturday morning. Saturday morning was when Dr. Gushue-Taylor held his leprosy clinic.

Bob had had no experience with leprosy. It existed on mainland China but in the warmer south. Taiwan, sitting astride the Tropic of Cancer, had a tropical climate in which leprosy flourished. Dr. Gushue-Taylor was an authority on leprosy, and was trying to organize a colony to house the victims of the disease. This work was progressing slowly, but in the meantime he had established a weekly out-patient clinic that was attracting about 600 lepers every Saturday morning. When McClure arrived on the scene they divided the clinic between them. Dr. Gushue-Taylor took patients over sixteen years of age and Bob took those under sixteen. It worked out approximately evenly. Every Saturday morning Bob was faced with a stream of some 300 children and youths all suffering from what was still one of the world's most dreaded diseases.

The Fourteenth Edition of the Encyclopedia Britannica was published in 1929, while the McClures were in Taiwan. It gave a vivid description of leprosy: "In the nodular form dark red or coppery patches appear on the face, backs of the hands and feet or on the body . . . Thickening of the skin of the face produces a highly characteristic appearance. The tissues of the eye undergo degenerative changes; the mucous membrane of the nose and throat is thickened, impairing the breathing and the voice; the eyebrows fall off; the ears and nose become thickened and enlarged. As the disease progresses the nodules tend to break down and ulcerate, leaving open sores. The patient, whose condition is extremely wretched, gradually becomes weaker and gradually succumbs to exhaustion or is carried off by some intercurrent disease, usually inflammation of the kidneys or tuberculosis. A severe case may end fatally in two years." There was a variation called "smooth or anaesthetic". In this "the discoloured patches became enlarged; sensation is lost, muscular power diminishes, with wasting, contracting of tendons, and all signs of impaired nutrition. The nails become hard and clawed; perforating ulcers of the feet are common; portions of the extremities, including whole fingers and toes, die and drop off. Later paralysis becomes more marked affecting the muscles of the face and limbs. This form of the disease may last 20 or 30 years."

Although Taiwan, with its humid tropical climate, was an ideal spawning ground for the bacteria that caused leprosy the disease there seldom resulted in the more extreme forms that ate away fingers, ears, and nose. That was to be reserved for Bob for other years in another country. But what he saw now was appalling enough. In sheer numbers it was overwhelming. It was also frustrating because modern medicine was still all but helpless in the face of what had been "the greatest disease of mediaeval Christendom".

The leprosy clinic had been established in a separate compound with high brick walls. Inside was an open courtyard and the clinic building itself. The furniture inside the building was painted either white or blue. The staff touched only blue furniture, while the patients sat or lay upon the white. The staff never touched doorknobs or handles. Ingenious devices had been made to permit them to kick doors open and closed with their feet. Dr. Gushue-Taylor never went near the clinic without wearing rubber gloves. The truth was that most of the staff had a deep seated phobia of the disease even though they knew it was less contagious than TB and communicable only in its middle stages of development. The staff phobia was nothing compared to the fear felt by the Japanese. They considered it a venereal disease and shunned it with horror and revulsion.

The clinic was put in readiness every Friday afternoon. On Saturday the hospital shut down entirely so the personnel could devote their energies to the treatment of chronic leprosy cases. A traditional method of soothing the symptoms of leprosy had been to smear the affected parts with chaulmoogra oil, a product obtained from the nuts of the tropical Chaulmoogra tree. Just after World War I it had been discovered that chaulmoogra oil gave more relief if injected into the muscles. It was, unfortunately, a painful treatment, requiring a large bore needle to handle the rather viscous oil. It was a treatment that had to be repeated on a weekly basis over long periods of time. Single injections varied from 5 to 30 c.c. and even here the doctor had problems. Too large a dose caused a reaction, with headache, fever, and a rash of new leprosy nodules. Too small a dose could prolong the treatment endlessly. It had been found that the addition of soluble soap-like derivatives made the injections less painful, but also made them very expensive. The addition of some creosote was found to be a reasonable alternative.

The treatment was painful even for the doctor. Bob soon discovered that forcing the viscous oil through a needle more than 300 times in one day using a syringe that was itself slippery with oil was more than the human hand was meant to bear. He discarded the rubber gloves. He warmed the oil slightly to make it more fluid. He designed and built a syringe holder to improve the doctor's grip on the syringe, and to improve his leverage on the plunger. The syringe holder worked beautifully. Even Dr. Gushue-Taylor was pleased with it.

The staff 'processed' more than six hundred patients every Saturday. At the end of a year of treatment, if they were able to discharge one percent of the patients as "symptom-free" it was considered a sign of success. No one ever referred to a "cure".

Whether it was because he himself was working with the younger victims, or whether it was inherent in the nature of the disease, Bob did not know, but he noticed that the leprosy clinic was an unusually compassionate place. The staff had a fear of the disease but it seemed to increase their empathy for the patients. He realized that no patients had ever moved him the way these patients moved him. He also discovered that although he was self-confident on the outside, his own fear of the disease was deep rooted.

The revelation came to him in the middle of the night. He had been sound asleep curled up beside Amy who was growing comfortably large again with a second pregnancy. He awoke to find that one thigh and part of his lower leg was numb. Anaesthesia was one of the symptoms of "smooth" leprosy. Half-awake, he checked again—still no feeling. Fully awake, his mind raced ahead to the implications. He must not kiss Amy or baby Norah in the morning. Terrible statistics raced through his mind. Of the infections that could be traced, forty percent indicated the victim had been living in the same house as a leper—thirty percent led to a leper's bed. Here he was, his baby daughter in a crib in the next room and his pregnant wife beside him. 'Unclean', he crept out of bed. It was then he discovered that sensation was returning. He had been sleeping in a way that had impaired circulation! A few hours later he told Amy what had happened and they were laughing about it, but brash Dr. McClure had had his moment of terror.

On December 6th, 1928, their second child was born. It was too bad the Chinese of North Honan were not present. They would have thought that the wife of Loa Tai-fu was being very correct indeed, because she presented him with a son. He was named Douglas. It was appropriate that he was born during the season of Yuletide and New Year celebrations.

In some ways Christmas was always more of an occasion on the mission fields, where the Christians were a tiny drop in a non-Christian ocean, than it ever was at home. The meaning of it seemed much closer to the surface and the fellowship of it seemed warmer and more genuine. For some of the men New Year's had an aura it would never have had for them at home. The aura was one of pomp and ceremony and was created by the Japanese. The Japanese loved ceremony. They indulged in it the way one would indulge in a good meal, savouring each of its components. Between New Year's and the Emperor's birthday all male members of the Western community were expected to call upon the Governor General and, through him, to convey their respects to the Emperor. They were also expected to appear properly dressed in top hat, morning coat, and striped trousers. This raised a problem. There was only one morning suit in the compound.

The father of the Gauld sisters had been the proud possessor of the morning suit. He had died but his suit was still active in the service of the Lord, if paying respects to the Emperor of Japan, the Son of Heaven, a deity on earth, could be considered part of that service. The suit fitted some of the men quite well. It fit Bob like a set of maternity clothes. By moving quickly on a ceremonial morning, as many as four missionaries could bow their way in turn into the vice-regal presence, all attired in the same suit. It was a diverting exercise in logistics. It was on a memorable occasion of the wearing-of-the-suit that Bob met Mr. See.

The Japanese were always pleased when anyone else undertook to treat lepers. They themselves found the disease so abhorrent they preferred others to become actively involved. Every year the Empress of Japan made substantial gifts of money to worthy causes. One year the mission found itself upon her financial honours list because of its leprosy work. The thought of a grant of 50,000 Yen filled Dr. Gushue-Taylor with great pleasure. It brought his dream of establishing a leper colony much closer. He preferred the dream, however, to the thought of the public ceremony. He detailed Dr. McClure off, in plug hat and baggy morning suit, to go through the acceptance ritual.

There were six beneficiaries. They were lined up in an ante-room and were thoroughly inspected and briefed. The ceremony, although not elaborate, was formal and rigid. There was a little Taiwanese gentleman in the line ahead of Bob who, although he was wearing a suit even more Chaplinesque than McClure's, seemed to know exactly what he was doing. His name was Mr. See. They stepped out of the ante-room and found themselves in a large ornate room and confronted by a strip of red carpet. The carpet led some forty feet in a straight line, then took an abrupt right turn and ran another forty feet to a low dais, where the Governor General of Taiwan, resplendent in full civil uniform, stood at rigid attention. When his turn came Bob made the journey with dignity, accompanied by the suit, and came to attention in front of the representative of the Empress. A secretary stepped forward and read the mission's citation which was phrased in the highest style of Japanese language. Bob stepped forward and bowed low three times, finding, as he did so, that the trousers provided more than ample room for the exercise. He accepted the proffered cheque with both hands and bowed low once again. He then went into reverse, as protocol demanded, and backed away down the rug, around the right angle turn, and backward into the ante-room. Not once did he so much as step on a loose cuff, and little Mr. See congratulated him on a sterling performance.

The two men began to talk.

Mr. See said he ran a small home for beggars.

Bob had never heard of him, but he did not say so.

Mr. See said four of his beggars were lepers who attended the mission clinic every Saturday morning. He would appreciate the doctor's advice concerning building some housing for lepers. Bob agreed to pay him a visit that afternoon. There was something about the little gentleman that aroused his curiosity.

Bob found the beggars' home to consist of several rows of little, well-painted, wooden cottages. Most were quite new. One was still under construction. He found Mr. See up on the beams nailing rafters. Mr. See was wearing overalls that were cut on as nondescript lines as his suit of the morning. It was apparent that Mr. See was not a man of large pretensions.

As Bob came to know Mr. See he came to know a most unusual man. Mr. See was a Buddhist. He had been born wealthy. He had been a devoted playboy until he had inherited his father's fleet of trading junks. There had been more than 100 ships complete with crews. He had confounded his competition and expanded the fleet and made the business thrive. One day he happened to give some money to a beggar and found that it made him feel, as he put it, "very good under the vest". He tried the experiment a second and third time. The feeling under the vest continued, and he took a beggar home for a meal. Much to Mr. See's delight his wife, although she did not wear a vest, developed the same warm sensation. Mr. See and his wife agreed that it was pointless to give a man money but leave him in the street. It was just as pointless to give a man a meal but turn him back into the street. They began to build the beggars' colony and to find work for its residents. Mr. See finally gave up the shipping business and he and his wife took on their own private mission as a full-time job. He finally ran out of money and so went and canvassed from the Taipei business men who had been his competitors. Since he had removed beggars from their streets and himself from their business, they could not find it in their hearts to refuse him. And now he was building a cottage for lepers.

Young Dr. McClure gave some clinical advice but had the humility to refrain from offering any other counsel to Mr. See.

Leprosy had a strange habit of making an appearance at moments, and in places, when one least expected it. Bob encountered it one day when he had been totally off guard. He and three other missionaries had met for a holiday break at Taichung, halfway down the island. They had then struck across the island on a walking tour. It was only about 80 miles to a crow, but much of it was almost straight up. It took about one day to cross the beautiful western plain and another three days up jungle and forest paths until they were above the treeline. Here, at about 9000 feet of elevation, their route led along cold and rocky paths with mountain peaks soaring to 14,000 feet on either side. This was the homeland of the aboriginal tribes of Taiwan. Up until the mid-eighteenth century they had been head hunters. One tribe had been cured of the habit by a Chinese governor, a Confucian scholar called Wu-feng, whom they had learned to love. At a time of famine and resurgence of head hunting fervour he had quenched their thirst by donning a disguise and letting them lop off his own head. Appalled by what they had done the tribe had gathered together and had sworn a mighty vow to take no more heads "until charcoal turns white". The vow still held.

The hikers passed through tribal country, fording mountain streams, and crossing great canyons on wildly-swinging suspension bridges. They descended the steep eastern slopes to the coastal town of Hwalien. From Hwalien there was a choice of train to the south, or boat to the north. Both choices led through the office of a Japanese ticket agent.

The Japanese agent asked Dr. McClure if he would look at two patients in the Japanese community. Dr. McClure would.

Bob found himself in a small shed about eight feet square. The only opening was the door. There was no window. It was almost totally dark and equally airless. Inside were two Japanese men about twenty years old. They had leprosy, and had been locked away with their shame for more than six months. The disease was moving quickly and making harrowing inroads. Late every night they were allowed out of their prison for an hour's walk. They were also fed. Other than that nothing was being done for them.

Bob explained to the agent that it was really up to the Japanese community to get the two men from Hwalien north to Taipei. Once in Taipei at least some attempt could be made at treatment. The agent explained that it was unthinkable that lepers should be permitted on either a boat or a train. Bob explained that that was a Japanese problem. The treatment was at Taipei. He and his friends completed their holiday journey. Bob told of the incident a few times after returning to Taipei and then forgot about it.

A month or so later he received a request from Mr. See to go to the beggars' colony to examine two patients. A new cottage had been built and inside were the two Japanese boys from Hwalien. From them Bob learned how they now came to be in Taipei. Mr. See had heard about them through McClure's casual report and had gone after them himself. He had taken the boat to Hwalien but had been refused transportation for the lepers. The three of them had then elected to hike out of Hwalien by the same mountainous route that Bob and his friends had entered. It had been a gruelling trip and the emaciated young men were not only weak but had ulcerated feet. Mr. See had been greatly worried lest he set too fast a pace. He had solved the problem by taking off his shoes and coming barefoot through the mountains.

The young Christian doctor went home that day from the Buddhist's beggar colony in a very pensive mood.

The summer of 1929 was a memorable one. Good news came from the Mission Secretary. It was news that sent Amy scurrying around seeing that the house was in order, that there was food in the larder and flowers in the vases. She then sped to the seaport of Keelung, not far from Taipei, in time to greet an ocean liner nosing its way in from Japan. At the rail of that liner stood a couple in their mid-twenties just completing a long 'honeymoon'. It was Bruce and Marnie, now Rev. and Mrs. Copland.

Bruce and Marnie knew that Bob and Amy were in Taiwan and were hoping against hope that they would all have time for a visit. They did not expect to spot Amy on the pier before they had even landed. They were swept off to the McClure home, were installed in the guest room, and each couple settled in to catch up on the other's news.

Bruce had taken his theology at McGill and had been ordained in The United Church of Canada. He and Marnie had been married and they headed for Scotland for post-graduate work. They had both studied theology at Edinburgh. At the same time, Bruce had been corresponding with the mission in North Honan. Things were settling down again and the church there said they wanted him. He had corresponded with the United Church Foreign Mission Board in Toronto, and had been told they had no money to send him. He then talked to the Presbyterian Church in England. They said they could use him teaching English language in Taiwan. Taiwan was at least a stepping stone to Honan. Bruce agreed to take the job for two years. So here they were and here were the McClures, all refugees biding their time to get back to Honan. There was one catch. The English Presbyterians functioned in the southern half of the island, so the McClures and the Coplands would not be close neighbours. They managed to make that first visit a good one. It lasted more than a week.

That same summer of 1929 Dr. Gushue-Taylor departed on furlough and left Dr. McClure in charge of the MacKay Memorial Hospital. It was a different Dr. McClure from the young man who had arrived at the hospital in the late spring of 1927. That McClure had been enthusiastic, full of energy, brash, and reckless. He still was enthusiastic and full of energy but some of the brashness had gone when faced with those endless lines of lepers every Saturday morning, and much of the recklessness had disappeared in O.R. under the withering fire of Gushue-Taylor's sarcasm. McClure was now a much more fully rounded individual. He was a married man with two children. He and his wife were having an enormously enjoyable social life. He was being challenged to the utmost in his work. His medical education had been improving by leaps and bounds thanks to the correspondence course and to Dr. Gushue-Taylor's prescribed readings. His theological understanding had been enriched by Karl Reichelt. He had learned about humility and service from Mr. See. McClure was finally ready to take on the responsibility as Chief Administrator and Surgeon of a modern hospital. He was determined that he would hand the hospital back at the end of a year in even better shape than he received it.

Bob had been impressed by MacKay Memorial Hospital right from the start. The whole of the hospital, both medical and surgical, was employing the latest in nursing techniques. The O.R. was well equipped and was using modern anaesthetics. There were excellent recovery facilities and a well equipped pathology lab with well trained personnel. It was a perfect situation for a young Chief to try out some of the things that had been catching his interest. One was the use of spinal anaesthetics. It had been known for years that one could induce complete loss of sensation in the lower half of the body by injecting a cocaine derivative into the spinal sheath near the lower ribs. The technique had been well written up but not generally adopted. (Back in Toronto Western Hospital Bob's old mentor, Dr. Abe Willinsky, had introduced spinals to Canada just as Bob and Amy were fleeing the Second Revolution.) McClure was attracted by various aspects of spinal anaesthetic, not the least of which were the reduction of surgical shock and the elimination of post-operative nausea. He began to use spinals with considerable success. He increased the laboratory work and began to make use of the hospital as a teaching institution. They began to make wider use of the X-ray fluoroscope in routine TB survey work. Since many leprosy patients suffered from TB lungs he arranged for X-ray screening of all the leprosy patients. Many of the leprosy patients also had syphilis as a complication. This could be detected in the lab but the tests were cumbersome. The Kahn Test for syphilis had been developed but was not being used in Taiwan. McClure introduced it. Soon about one quarter of his time was being spent in the laboratory studying pathology sections, teaching, and trying to find the most efficient methods and the least expensive equipment to do important jobs.

By the time summer of 1930 rolled around Bob felt ready to tackle the one project that Dr. Gushue-Taylor had said Dr. McClure could never manage. He was ready to make the great attempt—to try to qualify as a Fellow of the Royal College of Surgeons!

18

Assault on Edinburgh

It was late Spring of 1930 as Bob and Amy set out for Europe accompanied by Norah, approaching her third birthday, and Douglas, one and a half years old. Their principal baggage consisted of many happy memories of Taiwan the beautiful. They sailed via Japan to Korea and travelled the South Manchurian Railway to Harbin. There they caught the Trans-Siberian train just as William McClure and his family had done twenty years earlier. They had an enjoyable week in Paris followed by a brief English holiday. The holiday over, Amy and the children sailed for Canada and a small rented house in Whitby, Ontario, while Bob set sail on an arduous journey toward the distant goal of earning the coveted degree of F.R.C.S. There were rocks ahead.

Bob had decided to take his specialist's studies in gynaecology. He began in London at the Chelsea Hospital for Women. Back in Hwaiking he had begun to be interested in the problems, techniques, and philosophy of family planning. Now, studying gynaecology in London, what had been an almost casual interest became a major one. The depression years were beginning and Chelsea Hospital for Women was doing a great deal of free gynaecological work. To the working women of a depressed area in a depressed time the question of family planning was of more than academic interest.

Family planning ran the gamut from overcoming sterility on the one hand to sterilization, contraception and abortion on the other. It was not a subject that found wide popularity among churchmen. Canadians were even more conservative than the English and Bob already knew that many of his associates, older and younger, considered family planning to be the work of the Devil. But by now, at the age of twenty-nine, he had already decided that too many people too easily confused God's work with the Devil's.

There was a large family planning clinic in London called the Cromer Clinic. Bob's day at the Chelsea Hospital was finished by 2 o'clock in the afternoon. He worked in the Cromer Clinic from 2 to 7. What he saw and learned in the clinic was to have as great an impact upon him as the more formal learning experience in the hospital.

Late in November he headed for Edinburgh and the climax of his studies—the examinations. The F.R.C.S. examinations were to begin on January 4th. The customary routine was for a candidate to undergo an intensive study period in Edinburgh for about six weeks before the exams. Bob arrived and arranged an interview with one of the examiners. He received the shock of his life.

The examiner was a woman. There was no shock in that. Bob had been accustomed to lady doctors since he was a child. Back in Weihwei Mary Grant's mother was a doctor, and so was Bill Mitchell's, although neither had actually practised much. He had recently been associated with Dr. Flora Gauld in Taipei, and he could think of half a dozen others on the mission fields of China. He could not actually think of any lady surgeons but that was not the point. Or was it? The examiner discussed Bob's gynaecological aspirations with him and then came to the point.

"Dr. McClure," she said, "if you have not heard already you soon will. I have a reputation for being very rough with male candidates."

Bob had not heard but he was intrigued to hear it now and from the mare's mouth.

"I want you to realize, Dr. McClure, that there is no animosity in this. I only do it because the male examiners seem to have established a pattern of being very tough with the female candidates."

Bob appreciated her truthfulness. He asked if she had any specific advice for him. She had.

"Don't take gynaecology. You have a fifty-fifty chance of getting me as your examiner and believe me, Dr. McClure, I

will plough you. If I were you I think I would change to operative surgery and surgical pathology."

There was something about her that conjured up for Bob
an image of the ultimate Head Nurse. He changed academic
horses in mid-stream.

Thanks to the five nights a week for three years that he had
been studying in Taiwan, his grounding was good. He obtained a tutor. Tutors were very expensive, costing a guinea
(about $5.00 Canadian) an hour. In those depression times it
was a large sum and Bob was financing his own post-graduate
education. He skimped on the tutorials.

There were about one hundred candidates who tried the
exams that January of 1931. Seven of them passed. Dr.
McClure was among the top dozen but not among the lucky
seven.

Bob was discouraged but his tutor was not. "Come back
before the next exams. Give me a month with two hours a day
to tutor you. I can get you through." The next exams were six
months away.

Bob went home to Canada and to Amy.

As usual Amy was good for his morale. She never saw the
world in black and white, the way Bob did. She was already
developing a gentle yet firm skill in controlling his excesses,
whether up or down. Bob decided the world still had a place
for him. He lined up a course of studies in Toronto that would
lead to a Master of Surgery. They bought themselves a Model
A Ford, and Bob commuted from Whitby to Toronto, Monday
to Friday. His studies were at Toronto General Hospital.

The Master of Surgery studies dovetailed very nicely with
what Bob had been studying in Edinburgh. Some of the professors, sympathetic to his missionary endeavours, gave him
what amounted to free tutorials. The exams came up in the
spring.

McClure failed.

There was still the tantalizing gleam of those F.R.C.S.
exams in Edinburgh in July. But the whole thing was taking on
the dimensions of a quest for the holy grail, and looked as
though it was going to be about as fruitful. Nevertheless, Bob
returned to England the middle of May and gave his tutor six
weeks to work on him.

This time McClure was not only paying his own room,

board, fees, and tuition, but was also paying his own fare. The Mission Board was prepared to help, because a missionary's first furlough was intended to be devoted to study. (Subsequent furlough years were divided, with half being for holiday and half for deputation work—that endless journeying from congregation to congregation giving talks about the good work of the Lord in heathen lands.) Bob and Amy had decided that the church's money should not go into his education. They had seen others complete their education, and before long leave the church. Besides, Bob did not appear to be a good academic bet. If he were a racehorse at the Chiaotso mine he would not have encouraged anyone to put money on his nose.

In July, 1931, Dr. Robert McClure was again among the long list of hopefuls aspiring to become a Fellow of the Royal College of Surgeons.

Bob made it. After his name he could now write "F.R.C.S. (Edin.)". McClure had assaulted Edinburgh, the surgery citadel of the English speaking world, and in the final assault had managed to scale the battlements. He found himself hoping news of the triumph would seep back to Taiwan and to Dr. Gushue-Taylor, who was now finally building the Happy Mount Leper Colony outside Taipei. Dr. Gushue-Taylor's achievements were proving to be varied.

That year of study had been a horrendous experience for Bob. Not only had it put him under severe academic pressure and heavy financial strain, but it had defeated him twice in one of the most precise ways society offers a defeat—as a result of examinations conducted by his peers. The fact that he had won in the end was important. What was even more important was that in the course of the whole affair he had questioned himself concerning his own long-term objectives. And he had received answers.

McClure had decided that he was going to be a good surgeon. A really good one. Now, that was obviously an attainable goal. But it was not an end in itself. It had been demonstrated to him, however, that he was not the academic type. He knew he would never head for a university, as had his father, and become a professor. Nor was he an innovator who would develop entirely new operations. He was not analytical enough for that. He was not sufficiently self-critical. Nor was he cut out for research; he did not have the patience to do painstaking statistical analysis of thousands of case histories. None of this was for Bob McClure.

But he was part of China. He was a son of the third world. He already knew, intimately, some of the real needs of millions of people. It was going to be his job, he decided, to take established techniques and apply them to the needs of those third world sufferers. It was going to be up to him to see that he knew the latest in techniques. It was also going to be up to him to be able to tell which techniques could be applied and which could not. He would adopt and adapt. That would be his mission.

It was a humble enough decision to make at the age of thirty.

He began to implement his decision before the end of furlough. He had been interested in X-ray ever since the days, and the nights, at Toronto Western. His interest was not only in X-ray as a visual probe but as a therapy for attacking deep-seated tumors. In Taiwan he had reactivated the cancer equipment in the pathology lab. In his F.R.C.S. studies gynaecological malignancies had interested him and he had paid more than usual attention to the progress that was being made in radium therapy. Radium was grossly expensive. The world's total production was measured in grams and one gram cost about 15,000 pounds sterling. Bob and Amy dug into their already debilitated savings and added contributions from well wishers. They managed to buy an infinitesimal amount of radium. It was hardly enough to do anything with. It was, literally and metaphorically, a mere seed—but McClure was the second missionary doctor in the world to equip himself with radium.*

In the late summer of 1931 Bob, Amy, and the two children took the trans-continental train to Vancouver and sailed for the Orient. They were returning to China; to North Honan; to Hwaiking.

This time Loa Ming-yuan Tai-fu was returning as Superintendent and Chief Surgeon of the Menzies Memorial Hospital.

---

* The first was probably Dr. Wanless of Miraj Medical Centre, India.

19

Return to Hwaiking

There were other Canadians on the ship, that late summer of 1931, as Bob McClure and his little family sailed for China. They were all friendly folk but one group in particular were not only friendly but were more than casually interested in Dr. McClure and his background of Chinese experience. The principal member of this group was a Mr. Vincent Massey. He was a one-time lecturer in history at U. of T., the ex-President of the Massey-Harris Company (the largest manufacturer of farm implements in the British Empire), a failed politician and, until very recently, Canada's Ambassador to Washington. Mr. Massey had left this last post rather abruptly when the Canadian people in August had removed the Liberal Government of Mr. Mackenzie King from office and had installed some others. Much to Mr. Massey's amazement, for he was under the illusion like all good Liberals that his tenure was secure, the new boys replaced him in Washington with one of their own. Being suddenly liberated, Mr. Massey was now sailing to the Orient for a meeting of the Institute of Pacific Relations. The presence back in second class of a knowledgeable 'old China hand' was too good to be missed. Mr. Massey and his group needed a good interpreter for their meetings in Shanghai. The McClures were invited for a visit to first class.

Mr. Massey and his friends were so captivated by the extrovert doctor and his charming wife that the invitations became frequent and the visits became lengthy. McClure regaled them with stories of bandits and warlords, adding only the embellishments expected of any good story teller. He told them of lepers in Taiwan and of children with kala-azar in North Honan. He described the Hwaiking Mission Hospital and told how Dr. Menzies was murdered going to rescue the ladies. He described how the Chinese municipalities still refused to accept responsibility for public sanitation, while in Taiwan the Japanese went to the other extreme and once a year turned everybody out of their houses, lock stock and barrel, to fumigate and inspect. He talked of cataract operations, and of laparotomies for stomach removals and, at their request, he brought his little treasure of radium forward to first class for inspection.

The McClures arrived in Shanghai accompanied by Mr. Vincent Massey and party.

It was the second time Bob had returned to China in the aftermath of a revolution. Much had happened since 1927. The Second Republic was now in place with Chiang Kai-shek, now referred to as "Generalissimo", as its first President.

Bob and Amy had left for Taiwan in 1927 as the Fourth Army was defecting and re-grouping around Mao Tse-tung and Chu Teh in the southern mountains, and as the Kuomintang's armies were re-grouping, having spared Shanghai, for a major drive north. Early in 1928 the Japanese had interfered by inserting a military roadblock in the form of a small army at Tsinan, where Bob's father was still teaching, but Chiang Kai-shek had gone around them and almost effortlessly captured Peking itself. The incumbent warlord of Peking, a Japanese puppet, had fled north into Manchuria where the Japanese had obligingly blown him up in a private railway car. The era of the warlords was said to have come to an end.

It was difficult to know whether the warlord period had really ended (a few were still in power, keeping a low profile, away off in the west) or whether the ultimate Warlord had finally made it to power in the person of the Generalissimo. The Kuomintang had staged the revolution in order to draw the entire power of the state into its own hands, the theory being that only when that was accomplished could there by any possibility of reform. It was an age-old political theory faithfully followed in every country in the world. Now, in 1931, the prospects for China looked almost hopeful. The Generalissimo had certainly made great strides toward unifying the country. There were, of course, the troublesome Communists down in the south, but Chiang Kai-shek had plans for them. In the meantime the capital had been officially moved from Peking to Nanking and the Western Powers had recognized the Kuomintang Government of the Second Republic. The Powers were appreciative of the fact the Generalissimo had had the good sense to abort the revolution's major thrust in '27 and save the Shanghai foreign settlements.

Other important things had been happening, some of which had been under way long before Bob and Amy had left for Taiwan. One thing had been the Chinese migration into Manchuria. Manchuria had been a kind of no-man's land. The Manchu Emperors had seen it mainly as a buffer zone between civilization and the 'hordes' from Outer Mongolia and had forbidden settlement in much of the area. The Russians had been interested in it mainly as a transportation corridor to the seaports of Port Arthur and Vladivostok. The Japanese had their own plans for it but a treaty in 1905 had ceded it all back to China, leaving the Japanese some coastal territory and control of the South Manchurian Railway. China's First Republic had opened the gates for Chinese immigration into Manchuria with amazing results. Since then about thirty million Chinese had emigrated north out of the Provinces of Shantung, Hopei, and Honan. Those settlers were aggressive, hardworking types, as keen to make a new life for themselves as had been the pioneers in North America. Manchuria had begun to flourish. But almost as Bob and Amy came ashore in Shanghai the Japanese seized key points in Manchuria. They claimed "provocation" as their excuse.

In a strange roundabout way all these things—the new "incident" up in Manchuria, the establishment of the Second Republic under Chiang, the forming of the Communist Red Army in the southern hills—all were to bear directly upon the lives of the McClures. But for the time being, mission life was almost tranquil.

Physically the mission compound was almost the same as when the McClures had left. Some of the personnel had changed, but the population of a mission station was always in a state of flux with people going on furlough or returning from furlough, or vanishing for a few months to relieve someone else at another station. The biggest change was not just at Hwaiking but in China in general. The role of the foreigner had completely altered. As the logical outcome of a nationalist revolution the Chinese were now taking over. Chinese Protestants had already formed the Church of Christ in China and now missionaries like Bob were here as a result of having been "invited" to participate as "fraternal delegates". The Hwaiking mission schools were now all headed by Chinese. Evangelistic work was under a senior Chinese pastor. Soon after Bob arrived he re-organized the hospital as a "Co-operative Society", and the head of that society was Chinese. Theoretically, the missionaries were now present as respected advisors only. In practice, they were still doing a great deal of work. When it came right down to it, there was no doubt as to who was running the hospital. A Co-operative Society and fraternalism were all very well but there was only one Chief Surgeon. The United Church of Canada was, of course, still being permitted to pay the shot for all the Westerners at Hwaiking who were participating in this fraternalism. (The Chinese did not lose their innate sense of practicality simply by becoming nationalistic republicans.)

The hospital was Bob's domain. It had changed very little. Dr. Reeds had returned in 1928 to get it functioning again. He had now been posted to Changte, leaving the Hwaiking hospital in good condition. Some of the medical assistants were still here. Others had set up their own practices in competition with the hospital. Head Nurse Janet Brydon had returned. Bob was relieved and delighted to see her. She had been recruiting on her own and had some new girls in training as nurses. It appeared that China had at last become stable enough under the Second Republic to make it practical to have more female nurses. In the bloodier, more violent days, it had been best to have male nurses prowling the wards. But General Li and his men had departed, and were now going straight as part of a Kuomintang army. The police had become more efficient. Most of the wounded now were bandits.

One of Janet Brydon's recruits was a girl of nineteen called Ai-lian. It was a musical name that lost none of its melody in translation—"Loving Lotus". The lotus flower was a symbol much treasured by the Chinese because it is rooted in mud and raises its white beauty towards heaven. Although Loving Lotus did not spring from mud she had certainly been raised in rugged soil. Her father was a landowner with a ranch in the foothills, some twenty-five miles from Hwaiking. Loving Lotus had been raised on horseback. While still a youngster she had manned the ranch house walls with a rifle, to fend off bandits. She had been betrothed at sixteen, married shortly afterwards, and then separated. Although her father was wealthy, Loving Lotus was 'only' a girl and consequently had received no formal education. She was totally illiterate. But Janet Brydon had spotted her as a potential nurse's aid. Janet also saw something about the girl that suggested she might make a good scrub nurse in the operating theatre. Dr. McClure had learned to have great respect for Nurse Brydon's instinct. Loving Lotus was apprenticed to the O.R.

Bob soon discovered that Loving Lotus was swift to learn and had an incredible memory. Once she had been rehearsed on an operation she never forgot the procedure. The O.R. team practised intestinal repair and stomach re-sections on dogs. By the time a dog had been reassembled, sewn up, and was in recovery, Loving Lotus would have memorized all the detail. She would know what instruments were to be sterilized for that operation and the order in which they were to be used. The O.R. group developed into a smoothly functioning team and Loving Lotus became Dr. Loa's number one scrub nurse. She was with him for the vast majority of operations performed during the next six years and during that time the surgeon never asked for a clamp, a suture, scissors, a needle, or any other instrument. When he extended his hand the correct instrument was always slapped firmly into it. For a surgeon whose major outbursts of temper were always reserved for the slow, the slovenly, or the incompetent, it was an exhilarating experience.

Loving Lotus had other traits that appealed to McClure. She was quite unflappable and not the least disturbed by either the sight of blood or the thought of violence. And Loving Lotus, for all her delicate name, was quite prepared to look after herself. This came home to Bob one very hot day in late Fall when Loving Lotus appeared wearing a clinging sheath dress. While eyeing her approvingly Bob was alarmed to notice a slight lump in the region of her appendix. He questioned her about it. Loving Lotus moved smoothly but quickly and, as though as a result of sleight-of-hand, the lump disappeared and a little .38 Walther automatic materialized in her hand. Dr. Loa took her out to the back of the compound to see if she knew how to use it. She did. She was even better with a heavy Colt .45 revolver that McClure had acquired. Nurse Loving Lotus was an unusual angel of mercy, but then so was her Chief. He gave her a wrist-watch as a token of his respect.

Chou Teh-kwei was still employed by the mission when Bob returned to Hwaiking, and their small producer gas plant was still functioning and generating electricity—aided occasionally by the Delco system. Even back in '27 Bob and Chou had been working on steam sterilization units and other devices in the hospital, and Chou had managed to keep such units functioning. Chou had also learned to run the dispensary and to make up simple prescriptions. He had learned some accounting. Bob moved him off the mechanical work and into the hospital and began to give him some systematic training. He did the same for some other likely fellows. It was the opening stage of a move that had been at the back of McClure's mind for several years. In the meantime, however, he needed another mechanic.

An apprentice mechanic turned up in the shape of a young teenager. His family name was Yang and his given names were Yung-lo—"Eternal Happiness". Yung-lo learned to run the Delco, then graduated to producer gas. Bob had re-established his medical work at the mine, and this time the management was more appreciative. Money earned for medical services at the mine was ploughed into improving the mission's electrical system. McClure and Yang Yung-lo increased their producer gas output and Bob was able to get a bigger engine. Soon he was ordering electrically driven pumps and they were beginning to install hot and cold running water in all the compound houses.

Amy had returned to Hwaiking in some trepidation as to what China might have in store for her this time; but everything was going surprisingly well. Marguerite Mathieson, the wife of one of the evangelistic missionaries, had been a teacher. She organized a nursery school for her own two children and for Norah and little Doug. The Mathiesons were Winnipeg folk, and friendly. And there was Margaret Brown, one of the single lady missionaries. She taught school in the city of Hwaiking. She was a vivacious person, well groomed both in her person and in her mind, and Amy found her extremely compatible. And it seemed no time at all before Bruce and Marnie Copland were back on the North Honan Field. They were not at Hwaiking but were at the little one family satellite station of Hsiu-wu, about forty miles east of Hwaiking, and turned up every now and then for a visit. Bruce and Marnie were working as a team conducting literacy classes in the villages. They were enjoying it greatly. Amy found it was a treat just to hear Marnie describe some fifteen year old village youth sitting "face like a mask and eyes like marbles" uttering the phonetic sounds for a written symbol, and making no connection between those sounds and a real word. Then suddenly the light in his brain would click on as he made the connection. The mask would dissolve into smiles and the eyes would glow with the sudden excitement of discovery. Listening to her enthusiastic friends, Amy had the distinct feeling the world was beginning to function as it should.

Bob was in no doubt of it. Around Christmas time he received a message from Vincent Massey. Mr. Massey and his friends had rounded up several thousand dollars for Dr. McClure to use to purchase more radium!

There were other assets turning up besides money and they were not just assets for Hwaiking, they were for China. They came in the form of people. They were refugees from the new Japanese regime that was being established in Manchuria. Millions of Chinese had migrated to Manchuria and now thousands of them were returning. The ones coming back were the bright ones, the aggressive ones, the independent and venturesome ones, who wanted to carve a life for themselves without the interference of a regime that tried to control every facet of that life. These were the ones who had gone to the new land and had built modern communities from the foundations up. There they had installed sanitation systems, built power stations, strung 'phone lines, and graded roads. They looked now at old China and were appalled.

One of these ex-Manchurians was the local postman who had the Hwaiking mission on his route. In the course of a day he would meet merchants and farmers. He was a one-man walking stimulant.

"Why are you using that wooden plough that just scratches the earth?" the postman would ask across a ditch.

"We always use this plough in China."

"No we don't. Up in Manchuria we Chinese used a wider

plough. It went deeper and rolled the earth back. Made farming a better business."

Or he would stomp into a merchant's shop on a wet day scattering both mud and good advice.

"Why do we put up with streets so deep in mud you can't walk?"

"Some of our streets are cobbled."

"Yes, and so rough they'd break the bones of an ox!"

"That's the way streets have always been in China."

"No they're not. Up in Manchuria we graded the streets and put drains at the side of them. And there were bus lines. And telephone service. It was very, very good for business."

The "good for business" line was an appealing one to many Chinese. They listened. They listened to the postman and they listened to the others. It seemed to Bob that he could see the impetus from the Manchurian refugees spreading through the country. He felt it was a phenomenon to which historians never paid proper attention.

There had been efforts underway to get rudimentary telephone systems into rural China but there had been an almost total lack of trained labour. Many lines had been strung without insulators. When the rains came and the posts got wet the telephones stopped working. But with the return of the Manchurian emigrés even this began to change. The pressure was now upon the local Chinese officials to have things done *correctly*. This pressure put McClure and his mechanical staff into the telephone business.

Bob had installed a telephone system within the compound and was extending it to the homes of Chinese staff beyond the walls. He and his little mechanical staff were beginning to put telephones into the neighbouring Christian village. The county officials wanted to put in long distance lines linking all their borough offices. They started coming to Dr. Loa at the mission asking to borrow his men. And they knew that Dr. Loa had found a place to buy telephones, so would he please obtain them for the county?

Dr. Loa had indeed found a good source of telephones. Shanghai was beginning to convert from the old crank-handle magneto phones to the automatic cradle 'phones. Dr. Loa purchased the old ones in lots of twenty at a time on behalf of the county offices. With psychological pressure from the returning emigrés, and with active assistance from Dr. Loa, the Hwaiking area was going 'modern'.

And now, in much the same manner as the telephone was beginning to reach out to remote areas, McClure expanded the outreach of the hospital. It was in answer to an old problem to which he had been giving deep thought.

In 1924, when Bob had first arrived at Hwaiking, there was a phenomenon that had worried him then and continued to worry him now. It was the disaffection of Chinese medical assistants. Every so often one who had been with the hospital for many years would decide to leave. He would set up shop on his own, and go into practice in direct competition with the hospital. There was no uniform licensing system in China. Anyone could call himself a "doctor", hang up a shingle, and give his "clinic" a name resembling that of the mission. The new "doctor's" source of medical supplies was often questionable. It was sometimes found that members of the hospital staff were bootlegging supplies. All in all it made for bad blood between the hospital and the former employee, and for an unhealthy state of competition. It was not a phenomenon restricted to Hwaiking. Other missions all over the country ran into the same problem. Within a few blocks of every mission hospital there blossomed a forest of medical shingles.

It was a thorny problem for a highly qualified surgeon who wanted to improve standards. Many doctors would simply have declared open warfare against the unqualified practitioners, and some did. McClure found himself in strong sympathy with young men who had aspirations of their own. He also wanted his own hospital to extend its services far beyond its own walls. The solution, he decided, lay in co-operation rather than in competition. In many Western medical circles the idea of co-operating with those self-styled doctors would have been heresy indeed. At first glance it might have appeared that Dr. Loa was being very simple minded; but Dr. Loa was not. He had decided to design the 'competition' so it would be to everyone's advantage to be co-operative. In his plan the big winner was to be the public.

When McClure moved Chou Teh-kwei from the machine shop to the hospital he was beginning to implement the plan. He would give Chou, and other apprentices, experience in the lab and the pharmacy. Then he would teach them some medicine, and even some surgery. He saw ahead to the time when each of his men might be a 'specialist' in a handful of particular ailments and would go out to set up a private practice—with the expertise and the facilities of the hospital to back him up. Dr. Loa knew that one of the major specialties to be acquired would be the good sense to refer serious cases to the hospital.

It was an audacious plan and it was destined to grow and to flourish and to become part of China's 'forgotten' history.

In the meantime another kind of history was being written and would not be forgotten. Ever since the "Manchurian incident" in the fall of '31 the Chinese had stepped up a boycott against Japanese goods. In response, the Japanese had completed the subjugation of Manchuria, claiming "provocation". Now, early in 1932, the same excuse was used to send 70,000 Japanese troops into Shanghai. The Kuomintang's Nineteenth Route Army was driven away from the vicinity of the International Settlement. The Republic was forced to accept a demilitarized zone around the Shanghai settlement, and to stop the boycott.

The bandits were not all on the borders. Hwaiking still had its quota. The Menzies Memorial Hospital still had an exclusive bandit ward, and was still using the twenty-four hour head start rule for discharged patients. It was still standard admission procedures for firearms and ammunition to be checked with the superintendent or the head nurse. Most of the outlaws conformed with this requirement, having learned through experience that Dr. Loa protected his own regardless of their trade. There was, however, the occasional hardened customer who liked heavy hand guns with hair triggers, and who trusted no one.

One day word filtered through to Dr. Loa that such a customer was occupying bed number five in the bandit ward, and that he had a loaded gun under his pillow. Dr. Loa pondered the situation and then called for his scrub nurse, Loving Lotus.

20

Loving Lotus and Others

The bandit ward contained twenty low wooden beds. From sunset until 10:30 p.m. the ward was lighted by two bare electric bulbs. At 10:30 the electric lights were turned out and a small kerosene lamp provided a night light. Dr. Loa and Loving Lotus decided to stage a raid just before lights out, when everyone would be drowsy.

Loving Lotus was not a stranger to the ward. Although her major duty was scrub nurse in the O.R. she would fill slack periods by wheeling the surgical dressing cart through the wards. In those days even surgical wounds infected easily. Dressings had to be changed frequently. Not many of the female nurses could cope with the rough language and manners of the all male bandit ward, except for Loving Lotus. Her repartee could make even a bandit blush. And it was not unusual for Dr. Loa to come to the ward, although he and his scrub nurse seldom came together.

There were two doors into the ward. Just before 10:30 p.m. Loving Lotus, wearing her rather voluminous padded blue gown, stepped through one doorway and stated in a loud voice that she had an announcement to make and would appreciate the patients' attention. Attention was easily achieved because the men found themselves staring at the business end of the Colt .45. Loving Lotus had produced it with the same sleight-of-hand with which she had impressed her Chief with the Walther automatic. He and she had decided that the Colt carried a bigger message for this occasion than did the Walther.

Dr. Loa then stepped through the other doorway and explained in a very fatherly fashion how much he and the rest of the staff appreciated everybody's co-operation in the matter of personal weapons, and that he was now going to conduct a routine search.

Loving Lotus recommended that everyone who had two hands should place them, nicely folded, above the covers. The big Colt had a tendency to beam toward bed No. 5 which was halfway down the ward. Loving Lotus suggested that if the men could refrain from moving there would be no need to plunge anyone's wife into a sudden state of widowhood.

Dr. Loa proceeded to make a "routine" check. From under the pillow of bed No. 5 he extracted a Mauser, loaded and ready. Looking suitably surprised he unloaded the weapon, and told the patient it would be returned to him when he left the hospital. So the man should not feel too deprived of affection, Dr. Loa sat by his bedside for a few moments and gave him some thoughts about brotherly love. Dr. Loa and Loving Lotus then left the ward and the incident was closed.

It was easy to talk about brotherly love. It was not always so easy to put it into practice. One major test came along in the form of a refugee from Manchuria. He turned up in Bob's office one day looking worn and haggard. It was Dr. George Washington Wang—Kuo-pao, the "Treasure of the Nation"—blood brother to Loa Ming-yuan McClure. George had quite a story to tell.

He had emigrated to Manchuria back in the mid-twenties and had started a private hospital in a major city. The hospital had grown to about forty beds, and finally represented an investment of more than one hundred thousand dollars. In just a few years Dr. Wang and his hospital had achieved quite a reputation. All this Bob already knew. With the Japanese take-over in '31, however, everything changed and George had left.

"But George, why? Surely even under the Japanese your hospital was still needed?"

"Of course, Ming-yuan. And the Japanese government would have paid me."

"Well then—"

"But that would have made me an official of the government. Every time a Japanese dignitary arrived I would have been expected to be on hand with all the others to meet him and to entertain him and to wave friendly farewell at his departure."

"Oh. Mandatory, eh?"

"Mandatory! And they would expect me on many occasions to get up in public and say how much we all owed to the Japanese for having helped us gain independence!"

Wang Kuo-pao laughed and there was no mirth in it. "There was no way to win. Play that game and before long you're assassinated by some nationalist."

"What did you do?"

"Refused to co-operate."

"How'd it go?"

"Not well. If there was a death in the hospital I was brought before the coroner. They brought false tax charges against me. I could not get supplies. You know how these things are done."

"What then?"

"I left."

"Just like that?"

"Yes. I gave my hospital to the employees. Everything. Walked to the railway station and caught a freight train south. I think it is what you call 'riding the rods'."

"Where is your wife?"

"With friends. She and the children."

It was a dilemma for Bob. The hospital had just taken on a Chinese doctor and had no budget for another. However, he managed to get a telegram through to Mrs. Wang. Within a few days she and their two children were also in Hwaiking. Amy moved in with Norah, Bob moved in with Doug, and the Wang family moved into the other two bedrooms of the McClure residence. It was at a time when Amy was again pregnant.

Dr. Wang was well known in North China. After graduation he had served for a while as a health officer, giving instruction to new magistrates. Many of his former pupils were in the Hwaiking area. George liked entertaining and would invite as many as twelve guests at a time. Amy not only had to plan these occasions with the cook, but had to make the family budget cover all the additional expenses that had come along with the sudden doubling of her household. These were depression years and the Mission Board at home had already cut their salary by 25 percent and reduced the children's allowance by 50 percent. In addition, Bob and Amy were insurance conscious, seeing it as one way to guarantee their children's education. They were putting 55 percent of their total annual income into life insurance. Nevertheless, brotherly love was able to embrace the refugee Wangs until Bob found enough budget to hire George part time at the hospital. George found additional medical work with the Province of Honan. George and his family then moved into Hwaiking City.

In the meantime Bob was making progress with the training of Chou Teh-kwei and the others who formed the little nucleus of medical trainees. He was spending at least a half-hour every day in the laboratory, going over work with them, helping them read difficult slides, and quizzing them on what they had learned. The more advanced were moving beyond the lab and beginning to scrub up to assist in the O.R. Bob hoped that eventually each of the better men would have a 'repertoire' of about twenty simple operations he could perform, such as tonsils, adenoids, haemorrhoids, circumcisions, draining of abscesses, and even eye operations. Trachoma was an eye ailment so common as to be a scourge. In trachoma the eyelashes turn inward and rub the eyeball, eventually causing blindness. The remedy was a delicate but simple operation nicking the cartilege under the eyelid. It was an operation for which the men showed considerable aptitude. Bob was becoming increasingly optimistic about his plans. He would teach them the use of ether and chloroform and perhaps how to use spinal anaesthetic. He began to think of them, affectionately, as his "quack" doctors. A Fellow of the Royal College of Surgeons who was deliberately creating quacks would have been drummed out of any right-thinking medical association back home. It was an amusing thought.

Fortunately Dr. McClure did not have to deal with medical associations. He had to deal with very few officials of any kind. The Board in Toronto seemed remote and co-operative, willing to endorse whatever the local Mission Council recommended. The Mission Council was a democratic affair. The members seldom opposed each other's projects, as long as those projects seemed to make sense. Official approval was easily come by. Approval, unfortunately, was not always followed by money— but that was another problem.

There was, of course, the occasional church luminary from Toronto who would visit the 'field'. Such visits were like those of a commanding officer inspecting the troops and could generate more havoc than enlightenment. A memorable tour of inspection was carried out by the Rev. A. E. Armstrong, a rather intimidating Secretary of the Foreign Mission Board of The United Church of Canada. He would have been nonplussed at the time to know that the focal point of his visit to North Honan was not himself but a ham.

The problem was that in those depression years it was not easy to entertain a V.I.P. The cost of entertainment did not come from the mission budget but from the family budgets. The women put their heads together and pooled their resources. The McClure's contribution from the family budget came to almost a week's food money. A huge ham was ordered all the way from Tientsin. A. E. Armstrong was served baked ham one night and the ham then preceded him across the compound to another home where he had it grilled. It went to Hsui-wu ahead of him where Marnie served it with sauce. Dwindling in size and increasing in portability it managed to outpace him at all times and undoubtedly wound up being diced and creamed and then finally served as croquettes padded out with breadcrumbs and potatoes. Whether or not he finally had ham soup was not recorded, but he was reported to have arrived back in Canada to say that the missionaries were living it up. They had ham at the table practically every night!

McClure always claimed it was after that visit their salaries were cut and he blamed it on the ham, but no one gave much credence to that. Bob was developing a reputation for cheerful exaggeration.

There was a certain amount of official going and coming between the mission stations of the North Honan field. Most of it was on a relaxed basis. Mission Council rotated its gatherings between Changte, Weihwei and Hwaiking. Sometimes there would be meetings involving an influx of seventy to eighty people, both Westerners and Chinese, and the host station would be crowded to the walls trying to accommodate everyone. At such times there was always a bustle of preparation among the housewives. These were occasions that Amy enjoyed. She did not get away from Hwaiking nearly as often as did Bob.

Bob had itchy feet.

That does not mean that McClure sloped off for other parts and shirked his duties. Far from it. But if duty called him to the mine, or to Weihwei to confer with Dr. Struthers, or to Hankow for surgical supplies, or to Shanghai for telephones and spare parts for the generator, then duty often received a favourable answer. But the scales maintained an even balance. For every pleasurable business trip there was usually an arduous one. Sometimes they were physically arduous, sometimes emotionally, sometimes both. One urgent invitation to travel came by 'phone, shortly after midnight. The caller was Bruce Copland.

Bruce was 'phoning from the little railway station at Hsiu-wu and was greatly agitated. Marnie had had a miscarriage and was haemorrhaging, badly. Bob gave Bruce some terse instructions and told him to stay calm, that he would be right down. Bruce went back to Marnie knowing the doctor could not possibly "be right down". There was no train before morning and it was now just after midnight on a dark night. It was more than forty miles from Hwaiking to Hsiu-wu. The mission did not yet own automobiles, and anyway the roads were almost impassable.

Up in Hwaiking, Bob seized his emergency bag, awakened Amy to tell her where he was going, and struck off on his bicycle. He headed for the railroad and when he reached it rode off down the footpath that always followed the base of a railway embankment. It was a dangerous time of night to be travelling. If he happened onto prowling bandits it could be all over before anyone exchanged the courtesies of mutual introductions. In the darkness he could easily hit the open culverts that pedestrians merely stepped across. People broke their necks going over the handlebars of bicycles. On the other hand, there was a certain air of primitive adventure to both those dangers and there was certainly an urgent purpose to his trip. Bob began to suspect that it was probably 'purpose' that gave 'adventure' its zing.

He arrived at Hsiu-wu two and a half hours after Bruce had 'phoned. He found the Copland home a bit of a shambles, and Marnie white and weak from loss of blood. Her husband, too, was white and weak, a situation that doctors came to expect. Bob administered a needle to stop the haemorrhaging and generally took command. In the morning he and Bruce rigged a stretcher from a cot and got Marnie down to the train and off to Hwaiking. She was taken into the McClure home for a brief period of observation and recuperation and soon all was again well. Marnie had received a swifter house call than would have been the case has she been in rural Canada.

Dr. McClure's practice was far larger than would appear at first glance. He was responsible for much of the Hwaiking area, up to and including the Chiaotso mines. But he was also surgeon to the North Honan mission field. There were other fine doctors at the other hospitals, but McClure was *the* surgeon. Cases would be referred to him at Hwaiking, or he would journey to the cases. Bill Mitchell and his wife (Bill had married Helen Craw, a doctor) brought their infant son to McClure from Changte, for corrective surgery on a cleft palate. Some Westerners came to him all the way from Hankow. Other 'family' patients were already at his elbow. One was Loving Lotus.

Loving Lotus had been developing symptoms of gastric ulcers. A fluoroscopic X-ray examination showed severe scarring and obstruction. Dr. Loa was keeping an eye on her. Both of them knew her condition was getting worse and that there was really only one remedy. Gastric ulcers were a common condition in China. It was not surprising that one day they had two laparotomies in a row, each for the purpose of removal of portions of stomach. In the medical dictionary "laparotomy" is defined simply and tidily as "an abdominal incision". In the operating room when that incision leads to the stomach and bowels, and to the removal of portions thereof, there is nothing very tidy about it. Surgeons take it for granted that their scrub nurses are not unduly squeamish but they do not expect them to assist in the partial removal of two stomachs and then ask to get on the table themselves. Loving Lotus did. As the second patient was being wheeled off to recovery, Loving Lotus spoke up.

"Loa Tai-fu—" she was still cleaning instruments and disposing of remains—"I would be so humbly grateful if you would perform same great service for me."

A few days later Loving Lotus underwent a laparotomy and partial removal of her stomach. Before a month was out she had taken a fifty mile round trip on horseback to visit home and had returned to full duty. From then on whenever a female patient required a laparotomy, and needed reassurance, one could count on Loving Lotus to be quick to display her own scar. She would thump it loudly with her fist to reassure the nervous one that full strength returned after Loa Tai-fu's surgery.

Time moved quickly that winter of '33. On February 20th Amy gave birth to their third child. It was a daughter and she was baptized "Patricia". Amy thought she would probably be called "Patsy", or "Triss", or, hopefully, even "Patricia". Bob was more direct. The baby was "Pat".

In the spring Bruce and Marnie were posted to Hwaiking. They moved into one of the big square mission homes. Their principal work was still out in the villages conducting literacy classes, which would take them away for weeks at a time, but Amy was delighted to have such good friends living next door. She also found it frustrating. Marnie had a natural flair for making even a barn of a mission house look attractive, with a delicate picture here, a colourful cushion there, and a vase of flowers in just the right place. Amy was getting a reputation as a most gracious hostess but she felt her home always seemed a bit too spartan and functional. With McClure for a husband, and three small children, she had little alternative.

And then, late in the summer, she realized she was again pregnant.

The McClures always maintained that theirs was a 'planned family'. This was a reasonable contention with Bob being a pioneer in family planning in China. He had been an advocate back in the '20s, and was even more of an advocate since his post-graduate studies in London. He always emphasized that family planning meant having children as well as not having them. He would go to great lengths to help overcome sterility in a childless couple. He did not care for abortion, except as the aftermath of rape. The core of his doctrine centred around contraception. In a country like China it was not easy to teach contraception, although in those years it would have been even more difficult in Canada.

Chinese men considered that contraception was really the women's problem, not theirs. Anything that depended upon high motivation was not much use. The condom was available in the coastal cities, but not in the interior, and anyway the men had low motivation. For the women there were jellies

available but they were of indifferent quality and again depended upon good motivation. Diaphragms were completely
effective but of use only to a highly intelligent woman. When
he had returned to China in '31 Bob had brought with him an
intra-uterine device, later known as "the loop"*, which had
been invented in 1927. It was a small ring made of a filament of
sterling silver. He brought the first ones with him at his own
expense, having obtained them from Holland. Following the
precedent set by Dr. Menzies with the McClary furnace, Bob
took the rings to a silversmith in Peking and had him produce
them in quantity. He promoted the intra-uterine device among
other doctors, weathering as he did so the occasional violent
blast from a member of the old school who held that all tamper-
ing with procreation was a sin against God. During this decade
he himself had about three hundred of the rings in use among
the Chinese peasant women around Hwaiking.

The other family planning method was sterilization—tubal
ligation for the woman or a vasectomy for the man. Sterilization was not popular but, in some ways, it was what Bob really
preferred. There was much to be said for a couple simply having a planned number of children and then tying off the tubes.
It was simple, efficient, and final.

Against this specialized background it was difficult to pretend that Amy was happy being pregnant again a mere five
months after having her third child. There was, for awhile, a
certain tenseness in the McClure household.

Norah was six years old. Douglas was four and a half. That
Fall they went off to Weihwei to attend school. They were
taught by a Miss Buchanan, whom they loved, and they lived
with a missionary couple, "Aunt Mary" and "Uncle Bill" Roul-
ston, who were friends of the McClures. Norah and Doug
found the Roulstons to be even more strict disciplinarians than
father, and father was not noted as a softy.

Shortly after the children went off to boarding school Bob
was at the Canadian Anglican Mission Hospital of Kweiteh
doing consultation and surgery. While there he had a vasectomy performed upon himself. From now on, when he
preached sterilization as part of family planning, he had scars
to show a hesitant candidate. This was just as well because

*Originally called the Graefenberg Ring, after its inventor.

there was a brief period at Menzies Memorial Hospital when Loving Lotus confused the issue and disturbed the patients by preaching castration.

It came about because some misguided bandits had the audacity to rob Loving Lotus as she rode her pony back to the mission one Sunday evening after a weekend at home. They took a ring that she treasured, and Dr. Loa's wrist-watch, which she treasured even more. She came into work Monday morning and she was still furious with the indignity of it all. She had lost possessions, true, but even worse, she had lost face. Dr. Loa tried to calm her, and even promised to have another watch brought out from Canada. There was no consolation for loss of face. She was particularly incensed when she thought of all the bandits they had had on the O.R. table and of what damage she could have caused during laparotomies, etcetera, and yet she never had. Dr. Loa was somewhat alarmed to hear his scrub nurse even voice such sentiments and tried to convince her there was really nothing one could do about ingratitude. He thought ruefully of his experience with young Sun when the hospital was under siege.

Loving Lotus did not agree with her Chief's philosophy. She suggested there was a great deal could be done about ingratitude. She requested permission to visit the bandit ward. She said she wanted to talk to the patients.

Dr. Loa thought this could be interesting and suggested that he had better go along.

Loving Lotus said it would be much too formal with him present but that she would be happy to have a male orderly go with her. Dr. Loa assigned the senior Chinese male orderly to the project, and had the forethought to ask him to give a confidential report when the lecture was over.

The orderly returned looking somewhat amazed. It had turned into a family planning lecture—the most interesting one he had ever heard in a mission hospital or anywhere else. There had been an attentive audience composed of bandit patients and their visitors. Loving Lotus had explained how sad it was that any Chinese should lift a hand against anyone associated with a Christian hospital. She suggested that the word should go out that her ring and watch were to be returned to her by Thursday morning. If they were not returned, she explained, she would personally take action in the O.R. against the reproductive organs of any and every bandit who entered it from then on. She had elaborated with such fury, and in such clinical detail, that one of the patients had vomited his breakfast. Even the orderly did not look too well as he now relived the scene.

Although that Monday morning lecture probably set family planning in the Hwaiking area back several decades, it had its desired result. By Tuesday evening Loving Lotus was again wearing her watch and her ring.

There were some among the evangelistic missionaries who considered Loving Lotus to be more of a cross than a God-fearing mission station should be asked to bear. They occasionally thought the same about the Chief Surgeon. Certainly he was willing to tolerate a great deal of non-conformity in anyone who was also extremely competent in their job.

One who was competent, but restless, was George Wang. George was still associated with the hospital and with the provincial government but he dropped in on Bob one day to announce that he was done with both.

"Ming-yuan, I have made a decision. I am going to build another hospital."

"Oh?" Ming-yuan was a little alarmed at the prospect. Was his brother going into competition across the street? "Where?"

"At Hsin-hsiang."

Hsin-hsiang was the railway junction not far from Weih-wei where the coal mine branch line met the Peking-Hankow main line. It was a good location. That was George's home territory and a hospital at Hsin-hsiang would in fact complement the Weihwei hospital. There were, of course, some major problems.

"How about the money!" George had walked away from his previous project and now had nothing but a meagre salary. "How will you finance it?"

"The merchants in Hsin-hsiang all know me. They will lend me some. The magistrates and county administrators all know me and will help raise money."

"Can they raise enough?"

"No. But you will help me. We are brothers." There was a direct simplicity to the statement.

George was quite right, his brother would help him, and

did. Bob and Amy had some securities back in Canada, including some of the Pennsylvania Railroad stock inherited from Bob's mother. They cashed most of their securities, only refusing to invade the sacred precincts of life insurance. George went off to build his hospital. No ground rules were established for paying back the McClure loan, but about 20 percent of it was repaid before the Sino-Japanese War put an end to mundane commercial transactions. George paid back in another way—he built a thirty-four bed hospital that was a model private institution, the first of its kind in that area of China to be staffed with a fully qualified medical staff.

Bob's own medical staff received a transfusion of quality in the late Fall of 1933 in the person of a tall, good looking lady doctor. It was Dr. Mary Grant, one of the old Weihwei gang, a member of the "illiterates", a graduate of the U. of T. Dr. Mary was a medical doctor, not a surgeon, and she and McClure worked in easy, comfortable association. For a brief period now the Hwaiking compound housed Marnie, Mary, and Bob, all three of whom had swum in the Wei River, drifting along with the current and clambering out at the water gate steps. There was something reassuring about their presence here together, as though the Lord's labourers were self-propagating.

Dr. Mary was on hand to deliver the fourth and last McClure child. The baby was born in March of 1934 and was christened "Josephine". Once again Amy had been a party to the wrong name. Her husband settled immediately for the abbreviation, "Jo"—with or without an "e" it sounded the same. The family was now complete—Norah, Doug, Pat and Jo.

After Mary Grant's arrival at Hwaiking Bob had begun to concentrate on two areas of the work that concerned him the most. One was the training of his "quack" doctors. The other was the detection and treatment of cancer. He was particularly concerned about gynaecological cancer. He knew from the literature that progress was being made in the use of so-called radium bombs and he was familiar with deep X-ray. The radium bomb treatment was prohibitively expensive, and deep X-ray required very sophisticated monitoring equipment and a reliable source of electricity. He and Yang Yung-lo, and a growing team of mechanics, were still not guaranteeing reliability in the electrical energy department. Bob read that the system of treatment being developed in Sweden and Paris centred

around the use of radium needles. It was the direction he had
been progressing with his own minute radium supply. It was a
system that promised to be thoroughly adaptable to the conditions of interior China. Bob had promised himself to "adopt
and adapt". In the late Spring of 1934 he left the hospital in the
capable hands of Dr. Mary Grant and departed for Sweden.

Amy and the children were to spend the summer at the
coastal summer resort of Peitaiho. For some of the time she
would be accompanied by Bob's sister, Janet. Dr. Janet
McClure had married Dr. Leslie Kilborn and they were now
stationed at the sister mission field of West China.

Bob was away about five months. During that time he
studied a month in Paris and three months in Sweden. In Sweden he sat under one of the world's foremost gynaecological
radiologists. He studied the use of the radium needle in cancer
of the lip, tongue, cheek and uterine cervix. The "needle" technique involved the surgical implantation of a radium sliver, encased in platinum, directly into the cancerous tissue. Bob's
studies were carried out at his own expense, plus a $500.00
grant, from the Rockefeller Foundation, for travel. Travel took
a month and his route lay around the world. He stepped back
across the border of China with 25¢ in his pocket and a wealth
of new information in his brain.

21

The Hwaiking Rural Medical System

During 1934 some rapid moves began to be executed on the political chessboard of China. Ever since 1927 it had appeared that the Kuomintang's main pre-occupation was with the Communists within China, rather than with the aggressive foreigners on the edges. The Communist forces in the southern mountains had been harried constantly by the Kuomintang armies, while the Kuomintang leaders had compromised and negotiated with the Japanese.

The Communists had not been idle. They had been learning. In adherence to Marxist doctrine, their Russian advisors had advocated the seizure of cities. It was in the cities where the "workers" were, and Marxist theory held that the workers were the only possible base for a true socialist revolution. The Chinese Communists had followed their advisors' advice with disastrous results. They had managed to bring down upon themselves the fury of the Republican government and of its armies. After the bloody purge of 1927 the Russian advisors had left. It was then that Mao Tse-tung began putting into practice his theory that Chinese Communism must rest on the peasant masses, and that the struggle must be won by guerrilla warfare. "The people are the sea," went Mao's doctrine, "we are the fish, as long as we can swim in that sea we will survive." In order to win peasant support the Communists had begun to harass landlords and Kuomintang officials. Harassment took the form of burning, killing, and torture. At the same time they took a staunch pro-nationalist stand, proclaimed that Chinese did not fight Chinese, and declared war against the Japanese—who were mostly out of their reach. Their ultra-nationalist stance and their hatred of the Japanese began to attract merchants and intelligentsia to the Communist side.

The Kuomintang increased its efforts to dislodge Mao and the Communist military leader Chu Teh from their southern mountain retreats. Mao, Chu Teh and their followers pulled up stakes and departed upon what was to become famous as "the Long March". They started out in 1934 and there were about 100,000 of them as they broke out of the Kuomintang blockade and struck south-west. Then, in a great arc, the "marchers" moved west and north through the incredibly rugged country of West China. The Republic's armies followed but could not catch them. Those same armies could not intercept because there appeared to be no logical destination. The soldiers and ci-vilians—men, women and children—of the Long March crossed the upper reaches of the Yangtze River, defying can-yons and currents. They skirted the very borders of remote Tibet. Finally, in 1935, after a journey of some 7,000 miles, they came to rest near the steppes of Mongolia in the Province of Shensi. There were only about 10,000 of them left, but those survivors included Mao Tse-tung, Chou En-lai and Chu Teh. In Shensi they could defend themselves. Here, too, they were near the Japanese of Manchuria and near the historic military route of the Yellow River. It was of no concern to the Commu-nists but they were also next door to the Canadian mission field of North Honan and they could almost breathe down onto Hwaiking and Bob McClure.

Bob's experience with his "quack" doctors was blossom-ing. There were eight counties in the area that comprised the hospital's sphere of influence. Before long eight of his "gradu-ates" had each established a clinic, one in each county. The clinics had anywhere from six to ten beds apiece. These clinics worked in co-operation with the mission hospital. Each man had served an apprenticeship in the pharmacy and the lab. Each had been sent off to Hankow and had earned a certificate from the inter-mission Institute of Hospital Technology that had been set up in the Union Hospital in Hankow. Each man had learned to handle X-ray and to diagnose and treat certain common diseases. Each man also had acquired a repertoire of minor operations. One of the men was former mechanic, Chou Teh-kwei.

Dr. Loa visited each clinic once every two weeks to consult and to assist. The nearest clinic was about 15 miles away and the farthest 35. The mission acquired a "Baby" Austin touring car. In the dry season the peasants of eight counties became accustomed to the sight of Dr. Loa jolting along in the tiny machine with its top down. The roads were usually occupied by pedestrians, wheelbarrows, and carts, and everyone ignored the sound of the Austin horn. The Honanese enjoyed watching Dr. Loa half stand at the helm, his short-cropped red hair like a beacon, as he shouted across the windshield at ambling roadblocks.

Dr. Loa worked out a fairly elaborate code of procedure between the clinics and the hospital. Difficult cases were to be sent to the hospital, but as soon as possible the patient would return to the clinic to recuperate. This was to everybody's benefit. The clinics sent specimens to the hospital lab and a routine was established that put the results back into their hands in about 48 hours. The hospital acquired a tablet machine and made up its own tablets and capsules. Each of the clinics was given a rotating credit account of $300 to be used against drugs. The clinic received the drugs at hospital cost, plus 10 percent. Occasionally a clinic would go over the $300 and not be making payments, and Bob would find on a visit that the owner's personal standard of living was increasing rapidly. The time for the next visit might well find Dr. Loa "indisposed" and unable to make his bi-weekly call. The clinic operator would suddenly feel lonely and naked in the face of complicated ailments. He would realize how much more comfortable it was to have the hospital backing him up and taking the major risks. He would attend to his drug accounts. Dr. Mary Grant, watching from the institutional sidelines, felt that only a magnetic and forceful personality like McClure could have kept the restless and energetic clinic operators in line.

Finding a suitable terminology for those same operators was more difficult. Dr. McClure, F.R.C.S. (Edin.), aware of what an affront his system would be to the hide-bound medical organizations of his homeland, thought of the men affectionately as his "quacks". It was not a term for official use. There was really no name for them. They called themselves "doctors". They were practitioners.

The practitioners were allowed to hang out a shingle stating their association with the Menzies Memorial Hospital. It was a coveted and much envied privilege. It was also a privilege that caused concern among some of the missionaries. At one memorable meeting of the Mission Council, Rev. Harvey Grant of Weihwei, now getting on in years, rose to question the "affiliation" of a doctor in the Weihwei area in whose clinic it was said that wealthy patients gambled. (To say that a Chinese businessman gambled was about as newsworthy as saying that Englishmen bet on dogs.) Mr. Grant dropped his glasses to the end of his nose and peered over them, tucking one chin into his clerical collar as he did so.

"May I ask what assurance we have that this—uh, 'doctor'," he used the word reluctantly, "is indeed a Christian?"

McClure was on his feet before the reverend gentleman had a chance to subside.

"I regret to report, although we have a highly reliable lab test for syphilis, we as yet have no lab test for Christianity."

The question was dropped.

The other missionaries always appreciated McClure's honesty and bore with his flippancy. (He had once been overheard describing the chapel, which doubled as the hospital waiting room, as "the place where patients get their Christianity immunization shots".)

McClure's quacks, his "practitioners", were Christian. So were most of the trained hospital staff. It had not come about as policy but more as a result of frustrating trial and error throughout many years. The Christians were more reliable, had a sense of purpose, and stuck to their work. But still, it was a condition of the mind and not of the blood. There was indeed no lab test for it. (Chiang Kai-shek had become a Christian not long after the blood purge of the Communists back in '27. But then Apostle Paul had been no saint when he was still Saul of Tarsus.) It was an area of judgement where Bob preferred to tread very softly.

McClure structured a "planetary" system around the practitioners and these men were mostly non-Christians. There were half a dozen or so of them out in the villages orbiting each clinic. They had no laboratory, pharmaceutical, or X-ray training but they knew how to lance boils, and how to place a temporary splint on a fracture, or a sterile dressing on a gunshot wound. They referred their patients to the nearest clinic, never to the hospital. The route to the hospital lay through the practitioner. It was a system that was beginning to permit the hospital to function at a high level of efficiency where it could do the most good while at the same time having an outreach that would have dazzled the imagination of the young medical student on the pentacycle.

Again, there was really no name for the men of the outer fringes of the planetary system. In the irreverent and somewhat paternal mind of McClure they were his "idiots". In later years the members of a remarkably similar system would be given the happier title of "barefoot doctors".

Up near Peking there was a city called Tinghsien. The mission there had been established by Americans—Congregationalists and Presbyterians. Now, in the mid '30s, there was a vigorous agricultural reconstruction programme underway and the hospital was experimenting with ideas similar to McClure's. The doctor in charge was a Dr. Mou. Dr. Mou had been born and raised in China but had taken post-graduate work at Iowa State University. Dr. Loa and Dr. Mou exchanged ideas and experiences. Both rural medical systems began to move in harmony.

That his system was gaining a considerable reputation was impressed upon McClure one day when he found one of the practitioners had taken on an assistant. The assistant was a graduate doctor from one of the provincial medical schools. He was willing to work with the Hwaiking practitioner because that practitioner had had a better training under Dr. Loa than the graduate had had at the accredited institution. This was a twist. Dr. Loa had always told his quacks they must never compete with a graduate. If a graduate came to their town they were to co-operate or, close the clinic—and now a graduate was joining up as an assistant. The same pleasant thing happened to one of his other lads over in another county. The work was surely going very well.

In the official report of the Menzies Memorial Hospital, 1935, McClure touched with forgiveable pride upon a variety of subjects: "Probably the most satisfying work in the hospital is on tuberculosis of the spine. We operate and do bone grafts on all the adult cases that we can get hold of, and with very high degree of success up to now. We have also gone to other hospitals in North China to help them get started on this work and to show them the method that we have employed." He was not so pleased with the progress being made in training nurses for the wards (not to be confused with O.R. nursing) and yet was clearly aware of the challenge: "We feel very strongly that modern nursing in China has started off on the wrong lines. It has copied the trade-unionism of Western countries, without the spirit of service and self-sacrifice that brought nursing into the high place it holds in those countries." He was quite pleased with the progress being made in equipping the hospital: "One of the most important is our surgical diathermy unit or 'bloodless knife', which is much used for cancer operations. We have also added a modern traction apparatus for our fractures, for with the tremendous number of gunshot wounds there is a high proportion of fractures. We are now in the process of adding part by part a bronchoscopic outfit for retrieving foreign bodies from the gullet or windpipe of patients. The program for replacing our instruments in all stainless steel is practically complete; our instrument cabinet is something of which we are quite proud." He mentioned that medical journals were reporting that the Hwaiking hospital was treating more cases of venereal disease than any other hospital in China. In addition: "In the medical journals during the year there have been published statistics to show that we have the highest proportion of cancer work of any hospital in China, having nearly a third more than our nearest runner-up. This, we feel, is due entirely to the co-operation of other hospitals in sending their cancer cases to this center. Our radium supply, though small, is in continuous use, and we hope within the year to get some much needed additions to it."

In that report McClure showed no hesitation in attributing the efficiency of the base hospital at Hwaiking to the system of branch hospitals.

Bob's time was not entirely devoted to developing a rural medical system. There were normal temporary distractions such as the occasional flood or other disaster. After one flood he ran into his first cholera epidemic and was amazed to see how quickly people died of it. Bob was equally amazed to see how easy it was to save them, if given the tools and the opportunity. And missionaries were not immune to disease. Over the years they and their children had caught malaria, or dip- theria, or TB. Adults and children alike had died of everything from smallpox to typhus and most compounds had a cemetery tucked away in one corner. Typhus had been the big scourge. It was carried by body lice which could be acquired in the vil- lages, on trains, in Chinese inns, even in the hospital, and it was usually fatal. In the mid-thirties a vaccine had come along for typhus and everybody had breathed a little more easily.

And then Norah took sick.

It was the Fall of '36. She had just returned to school at Weihwei when she came down with a high fever. Dr. Gordon Struthers examined her and could reach no satisfactory diag- nosis. He 'phoned Dr. McClure. Bob caught the train to Weih- wei and he, too, was stymied. Bob took Norah home to Hwaik- ing where the hospital had more complete laboratory facilities. He could not reach a diagnosis and eight year old Norah was very, very ill. They rigged a stretcher, made the child as com- fortable as possible, and Amy took Norah by train to Peking. By now the whole North Honan field knew of Norah's plight. Prayer sessions were held on her behalf.

At Peking, Norah was taken for diagnosis to the Union Medical College Hospital.* The first diagnosis there indicated a desperate need for surgery. One doctor left a note to another attached to the patient's chart and young Norah, weak and with high fever, struggled to reach her own chart, and suc- ceeded. She read that there was no hope for her and that it was only a matter of time. Dr. Ernest Struthers, a brother of Gordon of Weihwei, came up from Cheloo where he was teaching with Grandfather McClure. Norah was already scheduled for sur- gery when Dr. Ernest Struthers diagnosed Malta Fever.

He was right.

There was no swift cure but the condition was not fatal. Amy and Norah returned to Hwaiking. On the way Norah caught the measles and they seemed to dislodge the Malta Fever.

Dr. Bob McClure was a profoundly affected man. When asked to what he ascribed his daughter's recovery, the practi- cal, self-confident surgeon did not cite pathology labs, or even

---

*Founded by American missions. Taken over by the Rockefeller Foundation.

the diagnostic skill of a colleague, but said, "The prayers of the missionaries", and left it simply at that.

Within a matter of days Norah's sister, two year old "Jo", had caught the measles and as a complication of that Bob found himself doing a mastoid operation on Jo's ear. He hated treating his own family—it was almost an ethical sin—but Dr. Mary Grant had gone home on furlough and he had little alternative. The family struggled through that period, although Norah's school term was a loss.

It seemed for awhile as though it was time for everybody's holiday except the McClures. Even Bruce and Marnie had gone home on furlough. Not that Bob wanted a furlough. He had plenty to do. Even the routine visits to the practitioners' clinics were incredibly time-consuming. Some visits could stretch alarmingly.

One day he dropped into a clinic run by a practitioner with the very common name of Li. Dr. Loa was alarmed to find that "Dr." Li had booked the little clinic O.R. for TB glands of the neck that afternoon at 4 o'clock.

"Forgive me, Dr. Li, but do you not think that operation should be done in the hospital?"

"You are kind to suggest it, Dr. Loa, but it is very simple and we can do it here."

"Forgive me, Dr. Li, but I have not always found it simple."

"Dr." Li looked a trifle taken back but insisted that the operation had to be done in the clinic. It became apparent to Dr. Loa that there was face involved. Reluctantly he agreed to stay and assist.

TB glands of the neck feel like little pellets about the size of a pea, and they feel as though one might simply shell them out like a pea. Unfortunately they are connected to the large veins of the neck and each pellet tends to lead to another one below.

"Dr." Li, assisted by Dr. Loa, began about 4 o'clock. An hour and a half later they were still at it. The patient was still under anaesthetic but the "surgeon" was getting deeper and deeper into the neck. Dr. Loa took over but the light was beginning to fade and the clinic O.R. was not equipped for efficient night time work. Finally, however, they completed the operation. Dr. Loa, standing in the midst of a shambles he would never have tolerated in Hwaiking, was tense and angry. The two men stood for a moment in the deepening darkness, and then the practitioner bowed a little formal bow.

"Dr. Loa," he said, "I wish to give you strong assurance and fervid hope that this humble doctor will never again attempt to remove TB glands in the clinic."

Dr. Loa bowed in return. He had been trying to teach that lesson for five years. For just a moment he found himself wondering if the whole scheme had overstepped the bounds of reason.

Fortunately, life had its lighter moments. They might have appeared grim to others but they were light to McClure. There was one moment he would have loved to have witnessed, but had to take it second hand from two of the single ladies who returned breathless from an adventure up in the foothills. They had been jolting along in their covered Peking cart, the mule driver perched on a shaft dragging one toe idly in the road dust, when they had been held up at gunpoint by three bandits. The bandit leader relieved the two ladies of all their valuables and then caught sight of a peasant girl cowering in the back of the cart. He ordered her forward. She complied in obvious terror, whining that she was merely catching a ride home. The bandit leader did not know he had just made the acquaintance of Dr. Loa's scrub nurse, but he quickly identified the little Walther automatic. It was presented to him suddenly, and so close he could almost read the serial number. Loving Lotus removed the bolts from the rifles and gave the men a little lecture on the shamefulness of stealing from the Jesus people. The bandits, suitably mortified, returned all the valuables. Loving Lotus demonstrated Christian charity by depositing the rifle bolts at the base of a tree some distance down the road. She explained to the ladies that she did not think it right to deprive the men of the only means they had to make a living.

The bandits were not the only ones staging ambushes in the Yellow River valley. In December, 1936, Generalissimo Chiang Kai-shek came up the valley following the same route travelled by Confucius, except that the General travelled by air. And his destination was not Loyang, where Confucius had met Lao Tzu, but Sian, where the inscribed stone had survived as the only vestige of Nestorian-Christianity. The Generalissimo had his staff with him and was planning a final drive against the Communists. It was to be a "final" drive because he planned to exterminate them. At Sian, Chiang was ambushed by some of his own troops who were ex-Manchurians and who sympathized with the Communists. They held him prisoner. They argued for a truce with the Communists and for a more aggressive response toward Japan. The rebels invited Chou En-lai to speak to the Generalissimo. Chou, a master of the reasonable argument, convinced Chiang that he could either co-operate with the Communists or die at the hands of the rebels. On their part the Communists were willing to accept Chiang as head of state *if* he would get on with the job of opposing Japan. The Generalissimo accepted. The Kuomintang and the Communists declared peace between themselves, and promised a united front to meet any further Japanese aggression. The Communists agreed to stop calling Commander Chu Teh's force the "Red Army" and to call it instead the "Eighth Route Army", in line with Kuomintang terminology.

Downriver at Hwaiking it all sounded like very good news indeed. China was becoming more and more stable and united. Everyone was making progress.

Bob wrote a pamphlet outlining the progress being made by "The Hwaiking Rural Medical System" that was evolving around him. He was able to report on a system that was now reaching into most corners of the North Honan field, an area of some five thousand square miles. It revolved around the three mission "base" hospitals. There were "Direct Branch" hospitals fully staffed by the base hospitals on a salary basis. There were "Co-operating Branch Hospitals". There were "Grade A Associates" who were university graduates from Grade A Medical Schools. There were "Grade B Branch Hospitals". These were the clinics run by his beloved quacks. Orbiting them were smaller "Grade C Clinics" and out on the periphery the numerous and homespun "Grade D Practitioners", the lads without shoes.

He wrote the pamphlet at night by the strong light of his own electrical system which was functioning with a generator driven by his own producer gasworks. On his desk was a 'phone connecting him with other hospitals, other doctors, and with the clinics. It was an incredibly satisfying feeling to be able to write, "We now have an 'A', 'B' or 'C' man within 20 miles of any populated portion of this field and a 'D' grade practitioner

representing us within 8 miles of any man in the territory."
That territory embraced one and a half million people. He continued to write enthusiastically, sketching in plans for the future that called for more sophisticated rural clinics, with better
facilities and more highly trained staff, but always thrusting
farther and farther into the remote areas. It was an exciting vision of a medical system in which every part, from the humb-
lest practitioners to the great base hospitals right on up to Provincial Medical Schools would all interlock in a state of
co-operative inter-dependence. It was a vision, but McClure
was more than half-way there!

Before turning out the light and heading to bed Bob permitted himself an even more long term projection. "This whole
system", he wrote, "is a make-shift until State Medicine can
come in China." He wondered idly whether his peers in the
Canadian Medical Association would read that and send out a
lynch party.

22

Quicksand

By 1937 McClure not only had the Hwaiking Rural Medical System functioning in high gear, he was also running an informal school for mechanics within the compound walls. He and Yang Yung-lo had been far from idle out in the workshop. The producer gas plant was running one heavy engine and one small one. The "power house" was producing reliable electricity. It was driving water pumps in the mission, and was lighting the compound and much of the adjoining Christian village. The machine shop was complete with a shaper, a planer, a milling machine, and a lathe. They were manufacturing small producer gas plants for village use, and there were four Fairbanks Morse 10 hp gas engines also being prepared for village use. They were having castings made in the city and at the mine, and were milling them in their own shop. China had a tremendous need for mechanics and there was no shortage of youths wanting to apprentice under Dr. Loa and his 'master mechanic', Yang Yung-lo. The apprentice lads would begin by simply breaking large lumps of coal into smaller lumps for the gas producer; then they would be put to cleaning the engine and mopping up; then to being charge-man to sit and monitor the gauges; then to oiling and mechanical maintenance. They would finally graduate to good jobs in Hwaiking and other cities.

Bob's clinic practitioners were as restlessly aggressive as anyone. They had already acquired a small portable X-ray and generator. The whole unit could be towed on a little trailer behind a bicycle. It went from clinic to clinic and it was towed out to villages where, during the evenings, its little fluoroscope screen glowed with pictures of the peasants' chests.

The practitioners were not satisfied. They came to Dr. Loa one day in the spring of 1937 and said they wanted to buy an ambulance. They had noticed that the roads had improved to the point that the little Austin was now functioning almost ten months of the year.

"We were thinking, Loa Tai-fu, that it would make for very happy good work if Mr. Austin were to send us a car large enough to bring our sadly sick ones here to the hospital."

"It will probably have to come from Mr. Chevrolet and will cost much money."

"We are most pleasantly certain we can afford it. We will, of course, need some help."

"Could you men find 50 percent of the capital cost and pay the rest off over, say, three years?"

"Yes, Tai-fu."

There was an American Baptist Mission Station at the big railway junction of Chengchow on the south bank of the Yellow River. Word filtered through that one of the missionaries was returning home and would like to sell a large station wagon. It was, indeed, one of "Mr. Chevrolet's" units, and was selling for about $600.00 (U.S.). The practitioners were delighted—provided Dr. Loa would bring the vehicle from Chengchow.

There was no road bridge across the Yellow River. The only way to transport motor vehicles across was to put them on a railway flatcar and have them taken across by train. This was expensive. McClure, accompanied by mechanic Yung-lo, drove the "ambulance" west along the south shore of the Yellow River until they came to a ferry crossing about 17 miles from Hwaiking. The ferries were simply open boats that hauled men, mules, rickshaws, coal, garden produce, and pack donkeys, but usually nothing larger than a Peking cart. As far as Bob knew no one had ever tried taking an automobile across.

They found a sampan that was as wide as the car and considerably longer. Bob recruited coolies and found some planks, and after much manoeuvering they managed to get the vehicle aboard. Its wheels sat on the eight-inch gunwales on the boat. The whole thing was very top heavy.

There was a crew of six and a captain. Normally they

would have hoisted a sail to help fight the powerful current. With the load already top heavy a sail would have been suicidal. The crew manned long poles and pushed off.

They poled almost a mile upstream, parallel to shore, before finally swinging out and committing themselves to the current. Then, poling furiously, they headed for the other shore, three quarters of a mile away. Although wide the river was shallow, which made for strong currents and shifting sandbars. The sampan hit several sandbars. Each time, it appeared that the car was going to heave off into the river. Each time, the load settled, rocking on its springs and creaking on the wooden gunwales.

The captain and his men got the cargo across and, now professionals at this particular job, offloaded the car with relative ease. At the ferry landing there was a temporary coolie community of several hundred people living in huts made of reed mats. (Huts and warehouses were all expendable. In the rainy season they would all be swept away.) The residents of this community watched with awe and great interest as the car arrived. Loa Tai-fu and Yung-lo were heroes of the hour as they climbed into their vehicle and drove off across the Yellow River mud flats.

Ahead, on a cart track, lay a little pool of water not more than twenty-five feet across. Bob put the car in low and eased through it. He got halfway, and stuck. The car began to sink. They were in quicksand.

Dr. Loa and Yung-lo leaped to safety and watched in horror as the practitioners' ambulance slowly sank from sight. Within twenty minutes there was nothing to be seen except some acid bubbling on the surface and a slick of cylinder oil and gasoline.

It was, temporarily and to that date, the single greatest disappointment of Bob McClure's life. It was as though that second-hand station wagon symbolized the aspirations of the Hwaiking Rural Medical System, and China had swallowed it—literally.

One of McClure's major strengths was the ability to face reality. If something happened that he could do nothing to remedy, he never sat around brooding. If there was action that could be taken, he would ponder and then act. Sometimes he would eliminate the pondering, which could be unfortunate.

This time, however, he pondered and then conferred with some of the coolies.

He hired about thirty men. They brought planks and drove them into the sand to form a cofferdam around the sunken vehicle. They then brought buckets, shovels, woven baskets and anything else that came to hand, and they bailed and excavated. They uncovered the station wagon, which had come to rest with its wheels about eight feet below the surface. They borrowed the masts from three boats and rigged a giant tripod over the hole. Using blocks and tackle, and a great deal of the coolies' "bitter strength", they raised the machine from its grave. A mighty concerted heave on a rope attached to the top of the tripod toppled the whole rig sideways. The station wagon landed on firm ground.

Bob and Yung-lo removed the wheels and cleaned the sand out of the bearings, then replaced the wheels, hired three teams of oxen, and were towed off to Hwaiking. It was not a high moment in Loa Ming-yuan's life to be hauled into the compound in that incredible mess of machine behind half-starved oxen. He was relieved to see that none of the practitioners were on hand to witness the event.

Dr. Loa and Yung-lo took the automobile apart. School had just finished for the summer and they commandeered a schoolroom. They found that under the enormous pressure of the quicksand the grit had invaded everywhere. They removed the body and left it out in the yard. The frame was deposited on the school verandah. Bob would work until five o'clock in the hospital and then join Yung-lo until midnight in the schoolroom. They took the clutch apart and poured a pyramid of sand eighteen inches high onto the schoolroom floor. They found sand packed into the transmission and mixed with the oil in the differential. The ignition system came off and went into one pile. The carburetor was taken apart and put into a paper bag. The head was removed from the engine block and off came the valve lifters and out came everything else. They took that machine apart down to the last spring, clip, nut, and bolt. They cleaned, groomed, and polished all moving parts and repainted the frame.

They reassembled everything except the engine. Bob found this was beyond him. He had never realized a Chev engine had so many pieces!

It was summertime and the family was due to go to the coast for a holiday. McClure 'phoned his old friend Bob McCann, the Dodge Agent in Tientsin, and said he wanted to work for a couple of weeks at the Chevrolet agency. McCann arranged it.

The beginning of summer, 1937, found Amy and the children at the coast, and found Dr. Robert McClure, F.R.C.S. (Edin.) in overalls in a large Chinese garage in Tientsin. He was learning the mysteries of a Chevrolet engine. There were other mysteries thrown in as a bonus. There were a number of Russians working in the garage and Bob got the feeling they were no more mechanics than he was. It gradually dawned on Bob that they were secret agents. He was intrigued to find they were using the Chevrolet parts catalogue as their code book. "Mr. Chevrolet" was all things to all people.

At the end of the first week of July, just as Bob had almost completed his 'course', fighting broke out between Japanese troops and Kuomintang troops just south of Peking. The Peking-Hankow railway was cut.

To Bob it looked like another summer war. He expected that the fighting would continue awhile. There would then be a truce, and the Japanese would make demands. The Republic would object, but eventually would yield. It was an old pattern. He decided Amy and the children were in a safe place for the time being. He, however, should be back at the hospital.

McClure met some merchants who were upset because the railroad had been cut south of Peking. They wanted to buy a truck and drive around the perimeter of the fighting to connect with the railroad in the interior. Loa Ming-yuan struck a bargain. If the merchants would buy the truck he would act as driver-mechanic. They agreed.

They bought a truck from the Chevrolet agency. The merchants loaded it with merchandise and loaded themselves on top. It was grossly overloaded and Ming-yuan objected, but they insisted. To the merchants the philosophy was quite plain. If it were a truck rated one ton, and they put on two, they were getting one ton carried free. If the tires were overloaded, they were putting one over on Mr. Goodyear. If the springs were inverted and the frame hit bottom on every hole, they were putting one over on Mr. Chevrolet. They were cheerfully unconcerned by the fact that there was no rural motor traffic in the area through which they were headed; that in fact it was more than likely that no motor driven vehicle had ever made the journey before; that through the centuries cart roads had been worn six feet deep into the ground, and were just about the same width as the truck; that bridges came and went with the seasons and were not rated for tonnage; that there were, of course, no road maps. They put their confidence in the Big Nose with the Chinese name, who knew about these things. The Big Nose was not nearly so optimistic, but figured it was worth a try.

It was a moderately mad group on a somewhat insane journey but they struck south and then west, keeping the sound of heavy gunfire always to their right. Eventually they made it to the railroad south of the battle area.

Bob arrived back in Hwaiking in time to hear that the Japanese had seized Peking and Tientsin. He and Yung-lo feverishly set to work to complete the assembly of the ambulance. The two weeks in Tientsin paid off. There were no parts left over and the machine worked beautifully.

Early in August the Japanese began an all-out campaign against Shanghai. The Japanese, alarmed at the progress being made in China and at the united front apparently being built between the Communists and the Kuomintang, had decided to add China to the Japanese Empire while there was still time.

The Sino-Japanese War had begun in earnest.

It was only a matter of weeks before Bob received a telegram from Hankow. It came from Dr. James L. Maxwell, the Secretary of the Christian Medical Association in China, and asked Dr. McClure to attend a meeting in Hankow. Bob attended and found that it was a meeting of missionaries, merchants, and industrialists who had established an International Red Cross Committee for China Relief. Dr. Maxwell explained that they expected the Japanese to overrun China north of the Yellow River. The Yellow River would probably become the battle line. They expected the Japanese to bomb the civilian populace all along the Yellow River and they wanted Dr. McClure to become Field Director for the International Red Cross in North and Central China. His duties would be the organizing and co-ordinating of relief work among civilians along the battle front. Chengchow would probably be the strategic centre. Relief work would radiate from key Chengchow missions—those of the American Southern Baptists, the American Free Methodists, and the Italian Roman Catholics. It was doubtful how long the Canadian stations of Changte and Weihwei and Hwaiking would remain out of Japanese hands. All three were north of the Yellow River.

Bob's wife and children were at the coast, refugees inside Japanese-held territory. They were Canadians, however, and not at war with Japan, so probably were in no danger. The people who were in danger were the Honanese of the Yellow River valley. They, too, were his people.

McClure agreed to become Field Director for the International Red Cross in North and Central China.

Bob returned to Hwaiking and put the hospital, and the supervision of his beloved Hwaiking Rural Medical System, into the hands of two Chinese doctors who had recently joined the staff.

Mission Council approved of Dr. McClure's switch to a new function. Confirmation returned from Toronto to the effect that the United Church would continue to pay the McClure salary and family allowances; their surgeon was now seconded to the International Red Cross.

23

Times of a Red Cross Man

By the end of August, 1937, the Japanese had established a naval blockade of virtually the entire coast of China and had invaded Shanghai. The Chinese had shown unexpected determination to resist. The Japanese landed a whole army at Shanghai but it was November before they managed to batter their way out and begin to move inland along the Yangtze valley. (A British garrison in the International Settlement remained neutral during this time, and the only active help China received was from Russia, in the form of arms and aircraft.)

Late in the autumn, in the face of the Japanese advance, the Chinese capital was moved from Nanking. The executive authority, meaning Generalissimo Chiang Kai-shek and his staff, came to rest at Hankow. In December, Nanking fell and Japanese bombers attacked British and American ships far inland on the Yangtze River. Both the British and Americans made noises of protest but fired no missiles heavier than diplomatic notes.

Up in the north the Japanese began to move south from Peking. By Christmas time they had taken Tsinan where Bob's father, 81 years old, was still teaching medicine.

In January of 1938 the Japanese began to move down along the north-south railway that led through North Honan. It was the same route that Loa Ming-yuan had travelled after Language School, and it would take the Japanese directly into the heart of his territory. By the end of January they were down to Changte, the northernmost of the large mission stations of The United Church of Canada's Honan triangle.

Long before the Japanese arrived at Changte their pattern of attack had become very clear. Days, even weeks ahead of the army, there would be sudden ruthlessly devastating bomber attacks on cities and large towns. The attacks were designed to cause complete civilian panic and mass evacuations. When the roads were crowded with refugees the 'planes could then bomb and strafe at will. The crowded roads also hampered the movements of the Chinese military. To begin with that movement in this northern area was half-hearted at best, the major opposition coming not from the Republican armies but from guerrillas.

The Communists moved in force into the mountains paralleling the north-south railway line, and established a military district. From there they reached out to organize the bands of guerrillas, (many of them already with experience in bandit groups and warlord armies) and gave them leadership, motivation, and drive. The term "guerrilla" gradually came to be synonymous with "Communist" and, more specifically, with Chu Teh's Eighth Route Army. While the Kuomintang armies were occupied mainly in the Yangtze valley the guerrillas were impeding the Japanese advance from the north.

Such was the unfolding tapestry of the war and those were the weavers at work in the autumn of 1937 as Bob McClure plunged into his duties as Field Director for the International Red Cross, the I.R.C. There were several problems to be faced. The most immediate would be the handling of civilians wounded in the first massive air raids. Then would come the problems of feeding and housing refugees. And then there would be orphans. And wounded soldiers from both sides.

McClure set off at once to visit communities up and down the Yellow River valley. He knew the mission hospitals would have to be the centres around which the work would orbit but he had learned from experience that most people refused to think that they, or their area, would be bombed. Relief committees had to be organized in every major centre. Everybody's help had to be enlisted, including merchants, industrialists, and the Red Swastika Society.

The Red Swastika Society was a Buddhist version of the Red Cross. Their swastika turned counter clockwise and was not to be confused with the version turning the other way, which was becoming more and more dominant in Europe. The

Red Swastikas had a habit of lying dormant for years, even decades, then re-surfacing only when human needs, in Chinese terms, became desperate. They re-surfaced now, and McClure found their help invaluable.

The preparations in Chengchow were typical of many centres. The cloth merchants handed over an inventory of all their warehouses and gave the I.R.C. carte blanche to take piece goods for bandages. The I.R.C. took it by the wagon load. Other merchants turned over tons of bleaching powder and people were set to work extracting the chlorine from it. This was cotton growing country and the cotton mills were asked to step up production of absorbent gauze. The hospital staffs had to be taught to hide major supplies outside the cities so they would not be destroyed in air raids. Portable generators and portable X-ray equipment were brought in from Hong Kong. It was all cached outside target areas. A coolie system had to be organized to get supplies into the hospitals immediately after air raids. The Red Swastika Society commandeered outlying Buddhist temples as supply dumps. For the next decade Buddhist temples would become almost as familiar to McClure as were mission hospitals. The Red Swastikas also gathered in corn meal, wheat, millet and rice so refugees could be fed. Chinese movie theatres, which were huge, holding several thousand people, were commandeered to shelter refugees. Mission hospitals had to be able to expand, quickly. Nearby schools were commandeered for wards. In enlarging a hospital it was essential to keep the nucleus of the staff together under one roof. With the staff doctor, the head nurse, the pharmacists, the lab and X-ray technicians, and the business administrator all centralized it was much easier to plug in additional migratory staff. As refugees began to flow down from the north, and in from the east, non-medical missionary staff went to the railway stations and raised signs asking for nurses, doctors, anyone with medical training of any kind. The volunteers thus gathered were directed to areas where their skills could be put to use.

McClure was at the heart of it. He already knew many of the hospitals. He had been on barnstorming surgical trips to most of them. For him, and for many others, organizational edges became blurred. He drew on anyone and everyone to co-operate with the I.R.C. Right from the start he had little patience with the religious fundamentalists who still tried to quarantine themselves behind the insular walls of doctrine. The principal mission of Chengchow was run by the American Southern Baptists, a breed that McClure considered to be the most unbending of all fundamentalists. "They were," he said later, "a very sticky crowd. Very sticky. Very hard to tell a Southern Baptist very much about anything." For McClure, who liked to tell everybody very much about everything, it was, as Canadians would say, tough sledding. He could not resist his own attempts at ecumenical proselytizing. He convened a meeting of Buddhists, Roman Catholics, and Protestants in the Southern Baptist compound—then asked the Catholic Bishop to open with a word of prayer. The Baptists could not have been more appalled had the Devil himself risen from brimstone to burn incense in their presence.

Although the Papists had entered the compound some of the Baptists were sure bombs never would. After all they were not only Baptist, but *Americans.* They covered an entire spread of tennis courts with the Stars and Stripes, a fetish to deflect bombs.

On the other side of the ledger was Dr. Sanford Ayers, the American Southern Baptist doctor who headed up the hospital in that same Chengchow compound.

Dr. Ayers had been born and raised in Shantung Province. His Chinese background had instilled in him some of the same liberal tendencies that afflicted McClure. Some of his staff were his former Chinese schoolmates. They had migrated with him into Honan to the Chengchow hospital as the Japanese overran Shantung Province. The nucleus of the hospital staff was like a Chinese family with Dr. Ayers as the patriarch. A Japanese army had not broken that family, nor would Japanese air raids.

The first air raids were always disasters. In most communities there had been so many trial alerts that when the real thing came no one believed the warnings. In the early days, even if they did believe the siren, the warnings came only a matter of minutes before the bombers. When Chengchow was first hit the raid lasted not much more than a quarter of an hour. It left 2,000 people dead (no one ever knew exactly) and about 3,000 wounded (no one ever counted). It was Bob's first major air raid and was every bit as appalling as he had expected it would be. But Dr. Ayers' hospital expanded as planned. Soon, what had been a forty bed hospital became a six hundred bed hospital, and the staff nucleus of five professionals was surrounded by several hundred others with varying degrees of skill and training.

Eventually, the Japanese 'planes, flying in low and unhampered by anti-aircraft fire (because there was none), were able to pinpoint the American flag. They used it for target practice and blew a wing off the hospital.

The pattern of Japanese air raids became quite predictable. It was possible to mark on a map where the next strike would come and to predict its timing within a few days. McClure scuttled back and forth along the Yellow River trying to precede the bombers, to strengthen the relief organizations, to see that the committees were functioning and that supplies were safely cached in temples or caves. He would then try to be on hand for the first attack. After it was over he would set to work in the nearest O.R.

Trains still ran, but once the 'planes started coming most of them ran only at night. Bob took to his bicycle. Even when he hopped a train he carried his bike with him. If the train stopped because of a blown track, or uncoupled to break up the target, he would simply toss out his bike and keep going. He still wore his breeks, leather boots, khaki shirt, and leather jacket. On his back he now carried a pack that contained a blanket, shaving gear, a small typewriter, pictures of Amy and the kids, and a New Testament. He put in almost as much mileage on top of boxcars as inside. He found that driving snow combined with the smoke and sparks from a wood burning engine made for unpleasant travel conditions. His area centred on Chengchow but extended south to Hankow, east to Kaifeng, and west to Sian.*

It soon became an almost routine day for McClure to cycle a hundred miles, hold some meetings, inspect some stores, and end up doing surgery in a mission O.R.

Very soon after accepting the I.R.C. job, McClure recruited Dr. Richard F. Brown as a travelling companion and headed up into Shensi province, into Communist territory. "Dick" Brown and Bob were both Canadians and had overlapped at the U. of

*See map on front end paper.

T. Both were fluent in Chinese. Both were surgeons. Both were missionaries. Brown was in China under the auspices of the Anglican Church in Canada. He was working at their hospital at Kweiteh, about 150 miles east of Chengchow.

McClure and Brown crossed the Yellow River and made their way north on a trip that eventually took them to Communist Headquarters at Yenan. Here they introduced themselves as Canadian missionary doctors come on behalf of the International Red Cross to discuss the problems of getting medical supplies to guerrilla fighters and to the population in general. They were met with courtesy. They were shown maps of supply routes, camps, and caches. They met Mao Tse-tung, Chou En-lai, and Chu Teh, but the discussions were carried on with lower echelons. Although the doctors emphasized they were Christian missionaries there seemed to be a smiling belief that they were Communists—like another Canadian doctor who was expected to arrive fairly soon.

After they returned, McClure arranged to have the I.R.C. ship supplies to the guerrillas. Communications were poor. The Eighth Route Army seemed to make no effort to keep in touch with him. More than a year would pass before McClure realized the Nationalists were in fact impeding the delivery of Red Cross supplies to the Communists. Later on he would confess, ruefully, that he had been very naive about the depth of the gulf between the Kuomintang and the Communists. He, and other members of the I.R.C., had taken it for granted that everyone would be co-operating for the good of China.

Hwaiking, being north of the river, was difficult to reach, but Bob was there often in the autumn of '37. The Hwaiking hospital worried him. He was terrified of seeing everything to which he had given impetus gradually coming to a halt. He heard that Bruce Copland might be coming back. It was good news. If only Bruce could go to Hwaiking and take over as Hospital Administrator everything might still work out all right.

Bob was also worrying about Amy. She and the children had stayed on at the coastal summer resort long after any semblance of summer weather had departed. He knew from snippets of information that they were having an uncomfortable time of it. Many other mission families were in the same predicament. The fact that they were in Japanese occupied territory did not put them in immediate danger because as far as

Japan was concerned all the Westerners were still neutrals. There was no such thing, however, as good communication with his family. Bob would write to Amy but send the letter to a friend in Canada, who would then re-route it in another envelope with a Canadian return address. The Japanese would have intercepted anything that looked like a letter from McClure of the I.R.C. Amy's letters went around the coast by ship and came in via neutral Hong Kong.

Bob kept hoping to be able to get out for a brief respite. He thought he might make his way to the coast. There, they could at least make some family plans. Amy kept holding on, not applying to the Japanese for exit, wanting to be there if and when Bob made it. By December of '37 she was still holding on and Bob was writing: "The more it goes the more we all wish it would finish soon. Our hope of being together for Christmas is all off, that is for sure."

He was also reporting that he thought he had an American doctor lined up who would tackle Hwaiking, and that Hankow area was coping with 19,000 wounded. Many of them were soldiers, coming from the Nationalist struggle being waged farther east down the Yangtze valley.

The military wounded were a tremendous problem. Bob learned very early that a visit to a military hospital was invariably a visit to a den of horrors. Military hospitals came under the Chinese Red Cross, which was organizing with agonizing slowness, and the military seemed not only ill-equipped to handle casualties but almost indifferent. The mission hospitals were taking in as many military wounded as they could. The big Union Hospital at Hankow was inundated. And there was a problem. A big one. When the military received orders to move on they never knew whether or not to leave wounded in mission hospital or to take them with them. The fear was that the Japanese would consider wounded in a civilian hospital to be guerrillas and would shoot them. It was a prospect that did not appeal to the wounded, the missionaries, nor to the International Red Cross.

Just after New Year's Day, 1938, McClure decided there was one way to solve the problem. By now the Japanese were in Changte. He decided to go to Weihwei, which still had train service, then bicycle north to Changte, cross Japanese lines, and ask the Japanese their policy, face to face. As an I.R.C. man he should be able to do it. Besides, as an I.R.C. man he wanted to find out what medical problems the Japanese had. It was all very straight forward.

He soon learned not to be so naive about trying to pass through outposts.

It was Sunday morning as he pedalled away from Weih-wei. This was a route he had never cycled before. It was the only area of the Honan triangle where Dr. Loa on a bicycle was not a well known sight. He made it almost to Changte without mishap, arriving within distant sight of the town by about 4 p.m. He could hear train whistles from the railway station and knew that Japanese traffic was moving down from the north. He argued his way past a Chinese military outpost whose officer was reluctant to let him through, fearing McClure would be shot before he could get close enough to the Japanese to talk to them. McClure agreed to wait until dark before chancing it.

He finally mounted his bicycle and headed out into what he thought was no-man's land. There was a tiny village just before Changte. Here he was accosted by a sentry. It was a Chinese military outpost. One hardy little group of soldiers were holding down the village, and even the outpost Bob had just left had been in ignorance of their presence.

They were not at all pleased by the arrival of a Big Nose. The sentry took him in for questioning.

"I am a mission doctor," McClure explained. "I am also Field Director for the International Red Cross. I am trying to get through to talk to the Japanese about the treatment of wounded."

"Then you should have credentials from the Generalissimo."

"I do. But not on me. Why would I carry Chinese credentials to the Japanese?"

"You are a Russian spy."

"Do I sound like a Russian?"

"You sound like a Honan farmer. The Russians must have trained you for many years."

"That's nonsense. My name is Loa Ming-yuan. I am Tai-fu, a doctor. I am a missionary."

"Missionaries do not wear high leather boots and leather jackets. You're a spy."

Ming-yuan was feeling just a little desperate. "Ask your people at Weihwei."

"We don't have any people at Weihwei."

"Then the post I just came through. They believed me."

But nobody here believed him. They marched him away to a small room and put him under armed guard. The guard seemed somewhat excessive, being composed of four riflemen with grenades on their belts. Late in the evening the guard was changed to two men carrying automatic pistols and the ubiquitous grenades. These two informed him, casually, that he was to be shot. Every Chinese fibre of him, from Pao-pei to Ming-yuan, knew it was quite possible. It was the most natural thing in the world for a Chinese military unit to be totally out of touch with its senior officers. The only thing more natural would be for that same unit to execute a Russian spy, any spy, without giving him a second thought.

McClure sat on the floor and tried to be philosophical. When he wearied of philosophy he eyed the two guards and calculated their weight and wondered what his chances would be against them and the automatics.

A big chap came in who seemed to be a plain clothes intelligence officer. He was a huge, pock-marked man, a good six feet two inches in height. Once seen he was not easily forgotten. McClure had seen him.

"You are an agricultural engineer," said Ming-yuan. "You worked on rural reconstruction."

"Yes," said Pock-mark, peering at McClure. "And we've met somewhere."

"Yes. At a committee meeting on irrigation. My name is Dr. Loa and I am from Hwaiking."

"Well, you know, Tai-fu," he smiled a little pock-marked smile that looked somehow sinister, "these people here do not believe your story."

"You're telling me!"

"You've had a very close call. I can't turn you free, but I'll see if I can get you transferred back to a senior officer."

Pock-mark left the room and nothing more happened. The day came and passed. Bob was fed some watery noodles. It was after dark when other men entered the room and he was blindfolded and tied. "This is it," he thought. "Pock-mark was just keeping me quiet." They took him from the room and out into the yard. He could smell the night air and hear dogs barking in Changte. There were fellow Canadians little more than a mile away and Bob Ming-yuan McClure was about to be shot by his own Chinese people. It all seemed somewhat pointless. And then he found himself being loaded into the back of a rickety truck.

They drove for what seemed like hours. Eventually the truck stopped and he was hauled from the back. "This is really it, this time," he decided. "Just in case they've made a mistake they're shooting me somewhere out of the way. Maybe even inside Japanese territory." He could not tell from the sounds where he was, except that the air had the somewhat swampy smell of a Chinese river. He thought he could hear the lapping of water.

The men untied his hands and left him standing, blindfolded. Then he heard the truck drive away. He tore off the blindfold. It was still dark, but he knew where he was. He was by a river and it was the Wei River. He was just by the bend where Pao-pei, Wolfboy, and the rest of the gang used to swim. He was just outside the walls of the old Weihwei compound. His bicycle was lying on the ground beside him. Pockmark had indeed had him transferred, right back to his childhood.

His next letter to "Dear old Ame" simply chronicled arriving near Changte by 4:00 p.m. Sunday, but said he "could not get through the lines on this side and so had to turn back". He said he returned to Weihwei well after midnight Tuesday morning. Amy may have wondered what had happened to Sunday night and all day Monday, but there was no clue in the letter.

Bob never did get to ask the Japanese, point blank, what their policy would be toward military wounded found in a civilian hospital. He did not have to. They answered it themselves. Their policy was to take them out of the wards and shoot them. The I.R.C. was soon advising all mission hospitals to evacuate their military wounded before Japanese troops arrived.

It was about this time that Bruce Copland returned to the Honan field. He entered "free China" at the same point Bob had tried to exit, just south of Changte.

Bruce had not stepped off a ship from Canada and simply asked the Japanese for travel papers. He had taken a C.P.R. Empress boat to Japan, and then a Japanese ship to Korea, which was a Japanese protectorate. He had travelled by train up Korea and into Manchuria, a more recent Japanese "protectorate". He had looped down into occupied China, getting extensions to his travel permits as he went, until he arrived at Tientsin. At Tientsin he saw many of the 'exiled' missionaries, including Amy and the children, and brought himself up to date on the situation, as far as anyone there knew the situation. He then took the train down to the 'lines' at Changte. He spent four days there familiarizing himself with the positions of Japanese outposts and then one night he and another Canadian, Rev. Don Faris, took bicycles and made a dash for it. They made it. If they had been a few days earlier they would have collided with McClure on the edge of no-man's land.

Bob was back in Chengchow by the time he heard that Bruce had returned to Hwaiking. It was great news. The Menzies Memorial Hospital was, in Bob's own words, "a mess". The doctor who had come in to take over had vanished. (There was a strong feeling he had felt 'the call' to go farther south.) McClure was witnessing the gradual disintegration of almost fifteen years of his own efforts. But Bruce Copland was back. With Bruce taking over the administrative duties at the Hwaiking hospital Bob felt that the work there might still survive. His elation was short-lived.

On the boat between Vancouver and Japan Bruce had met Bishop Lindel Tseng of the Anglican Church in China. He was the first Chinese Bishop to succeed the Canadian Anglican Bishop at Kaifeng. He had convinced Bruce of the great need for someone to organize an International Relief Committee at Kaifeng, to help look after refugees in transit. Much to Bob's consternation, Bruce applied to the mission for release from Hwaiking. The other Hwaiking mission folk opposed the application, but before long Bob found himself supporting it!

McClure had had to back off in order to take a look at the work of the past at Hwaiking, and a look at the needs of the present along the Yellow River valley. In a letter to Amy he stated his reasons for supporting Bruce's application for transfer: "There is a very obvious need for a chap like him in

Kaifeng, so that to me is where he belongs. I get terribly impatient with narrow minded people in times like these."

Bruce was given leave of absence to go to Kaifeng. The Hwaiking hospital was again rudderless.

Bob began to think in terms of inveigling Anglican Dick Brown into taking over the Hwaiking hospital. He had tremendous respect for Dr. Brown's surgical skills. But Bob was worried about his friend's nerves; Dick seemed to be getting morose and edgy. McClure held off. It was about this time that Dr. Donald Hankey joined the Chengchow Baptist Hospital.

Dr. Hankey was, so Bob informed Amy, "a tall, handsome bird, with polished manners". He was in his late twenties and only recently had completed his training at Guy's Hospital in London. He had a British accent that was a bit much for a colonial's taste. He found everything "perfectly topping". He talked about "playing the game", and wanting a chance "to see the enemy at close quarters, don't you know". McClure thought that six feet four inches of burlesque Englishman was almost more than he was called upon to bear—until he found that Hankey had come at his own expense to give a hand to China. He also found that Hankey and a friend had started out in a small, private, single-engined airplane. The 'plane had given up on them; the friend had headed for home; Hankey had hitch-hiked by air, boat, train and road across Europe and Asia and into the heart of besieged China. Under that tall, impeccable, unflappable, impossible exterior McClure spotted a fellow adventurer. He became Hankey's surgical tutor and came to look forward to any time they could spend together in the O.R. of the Chengchow Baptist Mission Hospital.

Dr. Ayers' hospital was having chronic generator and X-ray problems and Bob spent much of his spare time working on the Diesel engine. It was an occupational hazard. Everywhere he went as the I.R.C. man everyone also knew that he was a mechanic as well as a surgeon. Hospitals would have both surgery and maintenance lined up for him. Fortunately, his physical and mental energies were immense.

He wrote a letter to "Dear old Ame" at the end of February, 1938, which was unusual in that it included a day to day diary, but what it chronicled was, for McClure, quite normal activity. It was set against a background in which a Japanese elite division under General Doihara had finally driven south to the Yellow River, and was beginning to head westward toward Hwaiking. As usual McClure was organizing one jump ahead of the action:

Feb. 11th. (Near Wen-hsien)* Took my bike and got a boat to cross the river. The crossing takes two hours. Just as we got off the boat—I had a light pack on my back and started off at once across the soft sand—an airplane came over at 2000 feet on a scouting trip. I lay down in the sand as it passed, much to the amusement of the Chinese around. It circled back and again made me lie down. Again much amusement. Suddenly I heard its motor note change and looking up saw it in a dive. It looked as though it was going to machine gun the crowd so I took out my pistol and, yelling at those near me to lie down, I put a couple of pistol shots over their heads and they lay down promptly. Just then 4 huge clouds of dust and 4 explosions in quick even succession smashed into the crowd from our boat who were still at the river bank. Quite a mess.

Feb. 12th. (at Hwaiking) We worked from 2 p.m. today until 10.30 p.m. on gunshot wounds and bomb wounds and at night had operated on every case in the hospital that required it. Saturday night so tired one could hardly stand. Soaked to the hide with perspiration but too tired to bathe.

Feb. 13th. Bicycled to Chiaotso. Halfway home the daylight gave out and the rest was done by moonlight. There are few bandits now and night travel is really quite safe . . . Rather interesting news that the airplane that bombed us on Friday had half-an-hour previous to the bombing alighted in a wheat field to the west of the main motor road and stopping its motor the men had gone over to the village, obtained water for their radiator and then started up and gone off to bomb. There were probably 50 to 100 rifles in that village and no one knew what to do! I ask you!

Monday, Feb. 14th: Started at 11 a.m. for Loyang by bike. Had to put on a new chain and a stronger luggage carrier for now I carry a blanket and my raincoat is too heavy to carry in these warm days. My pack on my back is heavy with some 50 doses of diptheria antitoxin for Shensi and some smallpox vaccine for 20,000 people . . . Got into Catholic Mission Loyang and had the usual cordial welcome. Made the trip in 5 hours and 15

*17 miles from Hwaiking, where the ambulance went into quicksand.

minutes for 55 miles and a Yellow River crossing. Was soaking with perspiration and rather tired. My pack had rubbed a sore on my back. Had a good stiff peg of brandy but couldn't drink it neat so put it in my coffee. My bike is handed over to a brother here who was a professional bike builder and who serves the Lord by fixing and building bikes for the Lord's servants. Night I did a removal of a "housemaids knee" on one of the Catholic padres under spinal. His came from kneeling of course and he was glad to get rid of it . . .

Tuesday, Feb. 15th: Spent the day getting to Tungkwan and it was cold and windy. Met China Travel Service man here who is from Wen-hsien in a little village I often pass through going to clinic and we sat up half the night talking Wen-hsien news.

Wednesday, Feb. 16th: Terrific north west wind bitterly cold and as thick with dust as a heavy London fog . . . Everyone said ferry crossings were impossible but finally at noon one boat got permitted to cross and I was on it . . . At 3 p.m. the "toonerville trolley" sort of Shansi railway started and as we got going the wind died down. It was a beautiful trip along the higher Shansi plains with prospects of excellent crops*. Trains average 10 miles per hour by their usual schedule. Tonight weather was only 10 above zero (Fahrenheit) and we all suffered terribly from cold sitting up 4 per seat and too cold to sleep. Really it is lonesome in times like these and nights are terribly long. Early morning held up for 4 hours for troop trains to overtake us. All kinds of exercise still left me shivering all over as soon as I stood still . . . This is no blooming excursion believe me . . .

Friday, Feb. 18th: (At Linfen) Conference today with local people about war work. In afternoon biked 20 miles on a borrowed bike to C.I.M. station at Hungtung. Roads were deep in dust but did it in under 2 hours. Talked war work and refugee problems. Got back after dark on strange roads but actually no trouble.

Saturday, 19th of Feb: Stopped over today to operate on a small breast cancer recurrence. Also met the C.I.M. Shansi superintendent . . . They are ill prepared, ill informed and rather lack all insight into war problems. Sort of 'babes in the woods' who hope for a Santa Claus to come and show them out of all their troubles. Saturday evening got in a box car on a military train—

---

*Bob is at this point travelling due north into what is Communist territory.

unheated of course but reserved for a Communist propaganda corps on their way to Hankow. They were a cheery crowd like kids at home visiting another town for a football match . . . The night was again very cold, only room to sit straight up or stand so stood most of the night . . .

Sunday, Feb. 20th: Nice warm day. An easy river crossing. A good Chinese meal when we got to Tungkwan. Got a green express to Sian . . .

Monday, Feb. 21st: Got around Sian working with the German anti-epidemic commission who are efficient, cordial and capable men all young and all know their job well . . . The English Baptist people here are a very competent crowd.

Tuesday, Feb. 22nd: Worked on X-ray and engines for Chinese Red Cross . . . Went to visit the Nestorian tablet . . . With latest Russian fighting planes practising overhead and us reading ancient tablets did seem to be a bit queer all in all. Midnight got a train east-bound for Chengchow.

Wednesday, Feb. 23rd: All day on a train and at Loyang could hear the guns firing.* Here refugees from Hwaiking told of the capture of Chinghua and Hwaiking . . . (Nationalist) troops retreating to the west. The policy of "resist and retreat" seems to be all retreat and little or no resist. At least 60 li** per day for retreat is something like a stampede. Decided that this railway line may not last long so made right for Kaifeng and up all night got in at 5 a.m.

Thursday, Feb. 24th: Woke up in Kaifeng Anglican Mission W.M.S. house on chesterfield. What a life it is to be Field Director for Int. Red Cross! Went to see Bruce. He is executive-secretary for the International Refugee Relief Committee of Kaifeng. They have done very good work in preparing for refugee inrush. Got a train out at 2 a.m. and got to Chengchow at 5 a.m. All trains run through this area at this time for fear of air raids.

Friday, Feb. 25th: Chengchow is terrible. The city has been awfully banged about by the big air raid here on the 14th just after I left. There were some 1,200 civilians killed—Baptist Hospital alone got some 200 civilian wounded in 8 hours. Ayers . . . had a narrow escape . . . (He was) crouching under the window sill

---

*The Japanese advance is now just across the river from him. They are advancing west, north of the river. He is travelling east, south of the river.
**60 li = about 22 miles

and bomb fragments went through backs of chairs at the desk and a foot deep into books in the filing cabinet. Everyone in hospital did well. 3 bombs landed in hospital compound and only two wounded. One big hotel where we used to stay got a direct hit by a huge bomb and crashed to pieces like a movie set piece with 200 employees and 300 guests in it. Three days later people could be heard still groaning inside the ruins that they cannot clear away in a month . . . The Chinese Red Cross X-ray man has left and so there were 30 X-ray operating cases waiting for me . . . I'm taking Rev. Floyd Pannabecker on as X-ray pupil and he is going to be the technician pro tem.

As usual, Amy received much of the news but not all of it. There was an incident on February 23rd that did not get recorded. Bob either forgot to mention it because it was too trivial, or he refrained because it had embarrassed him. At any rate, the twenty-nine hours between leaving Sian at "midnight" and arriving in Kaifeng were not spent entirely on the train. At Tungkwan station, McClure had been met by harried officials who regretted to report the disappearance of a Canadian doctor. The doctor's name was Norman Bethune.

Bob knew of Bethune by reputation as a famous thoracic surgeon, and indeed had sometimes used Bethune-designed rib sheers in the O.R. He also knew that the doctor was expected up in Communist country, in Shansi. Bethune was to take the same "toonerville trolley" route that Bob had taken one week before. There had been a delay waiting for the Yellow River crossing and Bethune had vanished. Bob was told that his countryman had been drinking heavily, had been annoyed at the delay, and had been very restless. McClure of the I.R.C. left the train, changed hats, as it were, to Loa Ming-yuan, took his bicycle, and went bird-dogging out into the adjacent villages asking questions as he went. He soon struck the trail of a Big Nose who apparently spoke no Chinese but who had a tremendous thirst. It was a good spoor. Before long he found Bethune, well advanced in a rural Chinese pub-crawl. McClure was relieved, and somewhat surprised, to find him still functioning. The Chinese liquor he was drinking was the same stuff Bob was using in O.R. as a hand rinse after scrub up.

The two men returned to Tungkwan together to continue their separate journeys. It had not been a pleasant meeting. Dr.

McClure had found Dr. Bethune to be very anti-Canadian, paranoic about his thoracic work, too militantly communist, and bitter. Gregarious thirty-seven year old McClure had met a forty-eight year old fellow Canadian surgeon in the boondocks of wartime China and had found no single point of contact. In retrospect one knows it was a golden moment for Bethune to establish an invaluable contact. He was momentarily with the one man in China who had the drive, the initiative, the knowledge, and the ability to cut out red tape, to ignore Kuomintang-Communist politics, and to divert (smuggle, if necessary) more medical supplies into Communist territory *if* he were kept reliably informed of the true situation. That golden moment went by, never to return. Bethune and McClure went their separate ways.

March started strong. "This place (Chengchow) is bombed almost daily now," Bob wrote to Amy. "Air-raid warnings are on and off almost all the time while there is daylight. Our hospitals are filled with bomb victims, all civilians. There is a very high proportion of instant death with these shrapnel bombs . . . Trains are hit quite often and tracks are blown up every day . . . Coming back from Loyang two days ago I pedalled all night and got here at 6 a.m. then did four operations . . . I never get caught up with my work. I spent all the time I could on the big X-ray here which is still out of order and then I have still their old Diesel engine to get working aside from operations and the Red Cross Work. We work like horses, eat ravenously and sleep like logs. It is now 11 p.m. and I was operating all morning and then X-ray all afternoon and then I had to go two miles on my bike to the Catholic Hospital. They always make the trip out there worthwhile however!"

Before long he was "almost fed up enough to quit this work . . . I really think I shall have to try and get out soon. This pace is about getting me and I sometimes feel that I've about done my share." And again, "I feel as if valuable days that ought to be spent with the kids are slipping away into oblivion."

But he kept going. The only thing that almost had him defeated was trying to get the Christian missions to co-operate among themselves. "Few if any of them care two bits about any people other than their own converts. Each of the Protestant missions thinks of their folks and each of the Catholic missions thinks of theirs. Altogether it is not always a nice picture. Of course if anything is to be done at all it has to be done in a union sort of way. So far luck has been with me and the results in most cases have been good. Just now I am working on a job to get the C.I.M. and the Seventh Day Adventists and the Catholics to work together and frankly it seems to about have me stuck."

He found himself becoming partial to the Catholics. They laughed more, and told him jokes, and would pour him a beer to relax the tensions of impossible days. Some of his ancestors were probably turning in their graves, but then his father had made them restless with the same heretical discovery decades ago.

By mid-March he had adopted a pair of roving English journalist-poets who were making a tour of the front. Their names were W.H. Auden and Christopher Isherwood. They accompanied McClure for more than a week and found him to have "the energy of a whirlwind and the high spirits of a six-teen-year-old boy". They chronicled their travels with him in a breathless fourteen pages of a book entitled *Journey to a War*.

By the end of March McClure was on top of the world again. He had been bitten by a dog, had a right hand the size of a grapefruit, had cycled forty miles with it hurting "like hades", but was still operating and apparently unconcerned. The American Baptist Hospital at Chengchow still tended to be his main base. When he was there he was himself attending to about twenty-five beds, doing consultation with the other doctors, and helping clean up the backlog in O.R. By this time, in that one hospital, all the Chinese male doctors had left. A Chinese lady doctor had just arrived but McClure was afraid she would not "stick through the dangers of occupation". A young volunteer doctor from New Zealand was also newly arrived but he had just graduated and was untried. The only regular doctors were Dr. Ayers and Dr. Hankey. Dr. Ayers was the only American still on staff and the only representative of his mission. The nursing was in the hands of a Miss Reid, one of a pair of Canadian girls who were working in the American Free Methodist Mission. "They take life much too seriously," Bob confided to Amy, "and are rather 'salvation sisters' in their own way. The kind who never joke and never see any fun in anything. There is a saintly gloom around them all the time.

Under such circumstances my sense of humour cannot blossom to its full flower."

The war was bringing McClure into close contact with missionaries of all stripes. It was a revealing experience. Air raids, he noted somewhat cynically, had a way of sending some of the more noisily 'devout' heading for friendlier climes. He was, however, willing to accept any of his fellow Christians at face value without questioning the validity or sincerity of their beliefs. But there was little doubt that he was more impressed by deeds than by words, and he had an extremely low level of tolerance for those whose religion was a thing of gloom and restrictions. Simple faith was quite another matter. He met a lady doctor at a tiny remote mission and reported: "Dr. Mary King, a lady doctor of the old, old school, has run a little dispensary down there for years. She was having her 69th birthday that night and we had quite a party. She is a kind old soul who has never read a medical book or journal since she graduated, and that was some time ago, but she has prayers with her patients and most of them get better."

The kind of person who impressed McClure the most was typified by Dr. Donald Hankey, the unflappable Englishman who had come out "to give a spot of help". Hankey had demonstrated from the beginning that he was a fine medical man and that he had good potential as a surgeon. He was keen and alert in O.R. and learned swiftly. He had hardly arrived, before Chengchow was being hammered by air raids, sometimes three a day, and the hospital itself was being hit. Zig-zag slit trenches had been dug in the yard and the staff had orders that they, and all patients who could move, must take refuge during attacks. It was Hankey who arrived late one day, after the bombing and strafing had already begun. He came trotting across a wide open space of lawn carrying a patient on his back, a boy who had lost both feet. It was Hankey who could be found out on the hillside behind the hospital at night. When the hospital was already filled to overflow with those who could be helped, those who were dying were placed on the hillside. It was terrible but it was war. After the rest of the staff had dropped to sleep, senseless with fatigue, Dr. Hankey could be found out in the darkness going from patient to patient, turning them, easing them, talking to them. There was nothing he could do, except *be* there. And it was Hankey who was in charge of the fracture ward the day the hospital area took eighteen bombs. Most of the patients had fractured femurs and many of them were in the now famous McClure bicycle-spoke traction and could not be moved. Sudden movement on their part could cause a fresh dislocation. It was regrettable but such patients had to be left alone during the height of an air raid. Except that that particular day Dr. Hankey never turned up in the slit trench. When the 'planes had gone, and the worried staff had hurried to the fracture ward, they found that the wing had been hit. The windows were broken and splinters of glass were embedded in the walls and pillars. The end wall of the ward was split. The plaster had all come down from the ceiling, landing indiscriminately upon floor and patients. In the middle of the floor stood Donald Hankey. He had plaster on his head and plaster on his shoulders and he was still chatting to the patients as calmly as an Oxford don. He spoke no Chinese and the patients spoke no English, but he had been there all through the raid and his manner and tone had told them there was really nothing to worry about, that the Japs were terrible marksmen, and that everything would be quite tickety-boo old chaps. And he was quite right. Not one patient had moved. There had not been a single dislocation in the entire fracture ward. The Chinese gave him a name which meant "Noble Soul". Donald Hankey was one of those rare men who not only talked about "doing the decent thing", but actually did it. McClure's admiration knew no bounds.

Donald Hankey joined Bob on a foray behind Japanese lines. McClure noted that Hankey was as unflappable in the field as he was in the hospital.

Bob crossed the Yellow River several times in the spring of 1938. Travel was mostly under cover of darkness. The Japanese never occupied the countryside. Their armies passed through it and their 'planes flew over it but all they actually occupied were the cities and towns. At nightfall they withdrew behind town walls, leaving only a few outposts extended, and the countryside then belonged to the guerrillas. One could travel at night with relative impunity, the only hazards being the sudden breaking of one's neck in a culvert or shell crater, being fired upon by nervous peasants, being shot on sight by a guerrilla band, or being impaled on the bayonet of a startled Japanese sentry.

McClure made one trip in the naive hope of arranging a local truce between the guerrillas and the Japanese so both sides could move stretcher cases to base hospitals. He was shown through a Japanese field hospital. He saw no broken femurs and few abdominal wounds and deduced that the Japanese were shooting those casualties in the field. He also discovered that neither the Japanese nor the guerrillas were in any frame of mind to agree to any kind of a truce, for any purpose.

Bob made an uneventful trip to visit Hwaiking. He had given up thinking of asking Dick Brown to take over the Hwaiking hospital. He had found the explanation for Dick's moodiness. Dick had plans of his own. He was chafing at being cooped up in a hospital treating air raid victims when most of the fighting that was delaying the Japanese drive from the north was being done across the river by the Communists. Dr. Brown hankered for some front line surgery. Before long he joined Bethune for three tremendously active months with the Eighth Route Army.

McClure made a third crossing of the river that spring, in another forlorn attempt to talk some sense into the guerrillas and the Japanese. He used the Hwaiking area again because at least one side there knew him. It was just as well he did. He was at a guerrilla outpost, pondering whether it might be best to wait until morning and approach the Japanese in daylight, when the guerrilla in charge told him it was not safe for him to go at all, at any time. McClure was not convinced.

"But Loa Tai-fu, the Japanese want you dead."

"That's nonsense. I'm a missionary. A doctor. I represent the International Red Cross. I am as concerned about their wounded as about ours."

"They do not think so, Tai-fu. We will show you."

The guerrilla leader spoke quietly for a moment to a young man of the area, who then moved off into the darkness. He was unarmed. After what seemed like endless hours of darkness the young man returned. He looked flushed and nervous and was carrying a sheet of paper. His leader spoke sharply to him for taking so long. Dr. Loa overheard the answer.

"It was posted beside the city gate and there were two sentries pacing there. I had to strangle them quietly with their rifle straps and I am only learning." The apology was accepted at face value and the roll of paper was handed to Bob. The corners were missing. It had obviously been torn from a wall. It was a poster with a crude sketch of a Big Nose on a bicycle. He wore leather high cuts, and breeks, and a leather jacket. The poster offered $50,000.00 (U.S.) for Loa Tai-fu, Doctor Robert McClure, "dead or alive". Apparently the Japanese had decided that his excursions were for the purpose of spying. It did not give a nice feeling.

By the end of April McClure was signing himself to Amy, "Your lonesome old man, Bob". He also had malaria, and a left index finger infected from a cut received operating without rubber gloves—but he was still on the go.

24

Number One Hankow Lady

Free China was being governed from Hankow. Hankow
was not the capital, but it was the centre of executive authority.
McClure was in Hankow frequently to make more contacts, to
wheedle more supplies, and to report to the executive of the
I.R.C. Central China Committee. It was on one such trip, in
early spring of 1938, that he received an official looking message requesting that he make himself available the following afternoon. The only other information was the name of a street
corner where he should wait.

McClure kept the appointment. He had no sooner arrived
at the designated corner than a green Chevrolet drove up, the
back door swung open, and the driver gestured to him to step
inside. He was driven along what appeared to be a random
route and was transferred to a truck. The random ramblings
and sudden transfers continued for the better part of an hour,
until he found himself being escorted inside the perimeter wall
of a Chinese surburban home. Here he was greeted by a small,
exquisitely dressed Chinese lady who spoke faultless English
with a trace of an American accent. It was Madame Chiang Kai-
shek.

Bob had been in communication with Madame Chiang before, but they had never met. She was interested in all aspects
of relief work but had been particularly concerned about the
plight of war orphans. Right from the beginning she had managed to funnel government funds into orphan relief. McClure
had been involved in putting her wishes into action. By spring
of 1938 there were at least 30,000 orphans being cared for in the

Yellow River area. The logistical problems were enormous, involving shelter, medical supplies, food, and clothing.

Bob was amazed to discover how much Madame Chiang understood in detail. He discovered that she had an encyclopedic memory, and the brain of an engineer. Reports she had received concerning per capita rice requirements, storage facilities, and problems of distribution, once read were never forgotten. (The poet-journalists, Auden and Isherwood, had been so impressed by Madame Chiang that they almost exhausted the English language of adjectives. In one short paragraph they used: vivacious, cultivated, simple, affectionate, terrible, gracious, ruthless, and clinging. They were also impressed by her perfume.) McClure, susceptible to both a fine mind and fine perfume, was enraptured. He had never met anyone like Madame Chiang.

The Generalissimo joined them and they had supper together. He was a much more gentle man than Bob had expected, slight, bald, and almost shy. He was wearing his uniform, but without giving the impression of ramrod starchiness that appeared in newsreels. The Generalissimo preceded the meal with a simple grace. The food itself was unpretentious and was served in just sufficient quantity for adequate nourishment. The couple apologized for the cloak-and-dagger way in which McClure had been brought to see them, but explained that the Japanese had the idea that if the Generalissimo and his wife could be eliminated the war would be over. It was a naive assumption on the part of the Japanese, but nevertheless one that made it necessary for the General and his wife to keep constantly on the move. As a rule they never slept twice in the same house. The alternative would have been to go to earth in a heavily guarded military establishment and to lose touch with their people.

An air raid alert sounded after dinner and his hosts invited Bob into the garden for a stroll. He would much rather have been invited into a dugout. Although it was now dark the Japanese had finally taken to night time bombing. Soon the sound of bombers could be heard.

"There are some missing," said Madame Chiang. "I hear twenty."

"There should be twenty-four," said the General. He told McClure that their spies had reported that twenty-four bombers had taken off from Nanking. Before the evening was gone a messenger reported that four 'planes had had to turn back.

Soon they could see bomb flashes and fires in another area of the triple city.

"They are one day late," said Madame Chiang, and explained that the 'planes were bombing the area in which she and the General had spent the previous night.

Madame Chiang continued to make personal contact with McClure. Always she displayed an insatiable thirst for information and a remarkable ability to assimilate facts and figures. In the interests of security Bob referred to Madame in his letters to Amy, not by name, but simply as his "number one Hankow lady".

Madame Chiang began to turn up in Chengchow. She would suddenly appear, disguised as a working woman, or a Chinese grandmother, and have Bob take her on a whirlwind tour of orphanages or hospitals. Then she would vanish again, with a security man close in her wake. One day in Hankow she insisted on being escorted, incognito and unannounced, to an orphanage in a large Roman Catholic mission. She went just as "a friend" of Dr. McClure's. The Mother Superior, who thought the worst of all Protestant missionaries, was mightily miffed at Dr. McClure having the effrontery to visit her orphanage accompanied by his loose woman, but she was impressed when that same woman eyed a bin of rice, took some of it in her hand to see if it was husked or unhusked, and then told her to within a day how long that much rice would feed the orphans. Even so, Bob could feel the cold waves of disapproval as he and his tart were shown around. Just before they left he was permitted to make a proper introduction. The Mother Superior's confusion, and guilty embarrassment over the thoughts she had harboured, were so enormous that McClure was still laughing forty years later.

Madame Chiang and her husband incorporated in their persons all the ingredients that appealed to McClure: they were courageous, unflappable, and enormously good at their jobs. He disliked their politics and was worried by their lack of willingness to compromise with the Communists, but he recognized the size of the achievement that had moved China forward out of the warlord era. He was concerned, however, by the quality, or lack of it, of some of the men who surrounded the Generalissimo. Once, taking the liberty of a 'neutral', he warned Chiang Kai-shek that a certain general in charge of a provincial administration was a very bad number indeed. The Generalissimo chided him gently.

"You think I should get rid of him?" he said. "But tell me, how many examples can you give me of a leader in a Western democracy who has climbed the ladder of his organization, gained a firm hold at the top, and has then kicked the ladder out from under?"

McClure racked his brains but could come up with no examples. He continued to think, however, that the Generalissimo had some very poor advisors.

By late spring it looked as though Bob was finally going to get away for a brief rendezvous with Amy and the children. Exactly where or how they were to meet was not clear but recurring bouts with malaria had shaken him. "This confirms me in my decision," he wrote, referring to the latest boneshaking chills and fever, "to definitely take a holiday if at all possible in about two weeks' time . . . It just has to be or I shan't be able to hang on."

McClure was on the verge of heading out for his much needed reunion with his family, when he received a telegram asking him to report quickly to Hankow.

A few hours later Bob sat down at a small table in the Lutheran mission in Hankow and took out his portable typewriter. He stared gloomily at it for many minutes. He was about to write one of the most difficult letters to Amy that he had ever written. Finally he slipped in a sheet of flimsy paper. He usually used whatever paper came to hand. This was the first time he had used the International Red Cross Committee letter head for a letter to Amy. The Chinese lettering above the English, and the small cross in stark red, may have bolstered his sagging morale. The motto underneath may have given him courage: "To provide succor to the poor and helpless."

"My dear old Girl," he typed, "This is going to be a black letter."

The summons to Hankow had been from Number One Hankow Lady herself. She and the I.R.C. Committee wanted McClure to go to England, for a World Red Cross Conference in June, to speak for the Central China Committee. They wanted him then to go on a tour of England, Europe and, eventually, Canada to raise funds for the I.R.C. Bob tried to squirm out of it. Everyone insisted that it was an important task and that he was best qualified. He even heard rumours that his own mission was trying to get him out because of alarm over his frequent forays into occupied territory. Whether the alarm was for him, or the mission, the rumours did not clarify. As for the I.R.C. Central China Committee, the 'request' from its Patron, Madame Chiang, and from Dr. Maxwell, the General Secretary, was as close to being an order as anyone had ever given Bob McClure. He was writing to Amy to tell her he was going out, but to England, and that "the letter ought to have a black border around it."

There were so many things he had wanted to tell her and so much to talk about and discuss, not least of which was the family future. So far the major decisions had all been postponed until he and Amy could be together. Should the family head for Canada? Or come around and enter Free China, and even come up to Hankow? Now it all had to be rushed into a letter. "I don't care for my kids to be near bombings. I've carried in kids out of the mess. I've tried to keep them alive and I've seen them die in a way I don't want my kids to die. I saw a whole family roasted alive in a dugout last Thursday. There is nothing cute about those things and our natures are more coarse after even seeing those things. There is a lot more yet to come. For China the war is only beginning. 'Peace in East Asia' is a good long way off." He urged Amy to catch the first sailing possible to Canada and hoped she would be able to convince his father to go along. They would rendezvous in Toronto in the Fall. "I shall have half of September and half of October with you folks then come out here and do another little job of work. Beyond that neither you nor I can plan very much. Let's take it step by step."

By this point in the letter he had stated what he had to state. He was doing what he had to do, but still felt terrible. He hammered out another paragraph on his little packsack typewriter. "Well that is that and I feel all in having told you this. . . . I feel as though I had left you with all the reasons for a divorce on the grounds of 'desertion'. You cannot bring alienation of affections into it though, for those were never more nor were they ever more concentrated on one person. I'm much more of a 'one woman man' than I ever was in my life before. I'm more of a family man than ever. That is one of the parts that hurts most. Love to you simply cannot go on paper."

It was too bad they had not been able to talk the whole thing over together. That "black letter" was the best news Amy had received for months! At last her husband was being sent out of the war zone, if only for a few months. She did not care a pin which direction it was they were sending him. At that precise moment almost anywhere in the world was safer than the Hankow-Chengchow region of Central China. As Bob had said, "step by step", and at least now it was clear that the next step for her and the children was home to Canada. She applied for their exit and travel permits and hoped it would not be too long before the local puppet bureaucracy was able to comply.

As for Bob, no sooner did he inform Number One Hankow Lady of his decision, than he was gone. She had arranged air passage for him and was paying his fare. He travelled to Hong Kong, where he found himself on board one of the great Empire Flying Boats. Five days later he was in London, England.

Bob carried with him vivid, living memories of the charnal-house that was Chengchow; nightmare O.R. memories of dismembered, disembowelled victims that he and Hankey and Dick Brown and Ayers and the others had been trying to reassemble; stalking-abroad-memories of his Chinese brothers buried under tons of rubble, their cries rising muffled from the sudden tomb; chaotic memories of thousands of refugees fleeing in panic; haunting memories of wide-eyed orphans waiting trustingly to do whatever the adult world decreed they should do; memories of typhus, gangrene, and death. And he carried, too, the memory of a farewell party given for him by the cheerful Italian Catholics of the Order of St. Francis of Parma. Each of the padres had concocted a dish, and no questions were asked as to contents. They had two courses before even getting around to the soup. The unusual banquet was presided over by the Bishop himself and they all, Chinese, Americans, Italians, and Canadians, devoted one and a half hours to demolishing it. It was a jovial testimonial to the indestructibility of both the intestinal tract and the spirit.

Just as Bob left China the Japanese broke through the Nationalist forces that had been valiantly barring the approach up the Yellow River valley. Early in June they captured Kweiteh, where Dick Brown had been before he went off to join Bethune. Then the Japanese divisions hammered on toward Kaifeng.

Bruce Copland's organizational efforts in Kaifeng came to a head as wounded soldiers began to pour out from those same great battles downriver. The pivotal point of assistance was the C.I.M. hospital in Kaifeng. In a period of about ten days upwards of 40,000 wounded soldiers moved through the hands of the co-operating missions. A military hospital, just across the tracks from the Kaifeng railway station, stood by in stunned immobility. Bishop Tseng had been right. Pre-planning had paid off. Bruce, his leave of absence expired, left just before the Japanese reached Kaifeng. He was not running from the Japanese tiger, but going into its jaws, because he was returning to Hwaiking.

The river crossings had been tightened enormously and Bruce took a roundabout route, finally travelling 2,500 miles to progress the necessary 150. By mid-July he made it to Hwaiking, formally submitted his credentials to the commander of the Japanese garrison, and settled in as Chairman of the Mission and Superintendent of the Menzies Memorial Hospital. When that news reached Bob in far off Europe it gave him some hope that his work in Hwaiking might yet survive. As it turned out the real news was too depressing to send.

The strain upon medical personnel in all occupied areas was tremendous. In the daytime they were under Japanese surveillance. At night they were called upon to slip out and administer to the guerrillas. Both sides played very rough and took swift measures against anyone they felt was not completely with them. At Hwaiking the eight practitioners, Dr. Loa's treasured quacks, were in the most precarious position of all. One by one, over a period of a few months, seven of the eight were taken out by the Japanese and shot. Only Chou Teh-kwei, the ex-mechanic survived. There were, fortunately, too many of the Grade D practitioners, the more humble, barefoot ones, who functioned in the most rural areas. Even the Japanese could not eliminate all of them.

They could, however, seize Loving Lotus. Her family farm up in the foothills had already been raided by both guerrillas and Japanese searching for arms and food. The family had eventually all been killed, except for one brother who escaped to Hong Kong and, years later, to Canada. The Japanese charged Loving Lotus with aiding guerrilla wounded. It was a charge that was undoubtedly true. They tortured Loving Lotus for days, and finally killed her.

It was just as well that Loa Ming-yuan was far away. That final news would have been more than he could have borne.

In the meantime, the Japanese armies were moving toward Chengchow. Away down on the south coast they had already captured Amoy, the major city just across the straits from Taiwan. Early in October they captured Canton, which had been bombed mercilessly for months. With the fall of Canton, Free China was cut off from Hong Kong which had been the one remaining major port of entry. There was now only the tortuous rail route up from Haiphong in French Indo-China,* and an unfinished overland route from Burma. A great noose was tightening around China.

On October 25, 1938, Hankow itself fell to the Japanese. But Number One Hankow Lady and her shy husband, the Generalissimo, had already quietly moved the government, and the army centre of command, another 600 miles up the Yangtze River to Chungking.

Britain and the United States, with France occasionally joining in, were still protesting Japanese actions and Tokyo was still not listening.

*Vietnam

25

On Tour

For McClure the last six months of 1938 were so active, and yet so singularly unmarked by personal adventure, that they tended to blend into a miasma of travel, meetings, and public speeches, with little islands of personal contacts rising out of the sea to offer temporary havens.

The Red Cross Conference in London went very well. Bob enjoyed some limelight as being not only a delegate from one of the hottest battle fronts of the moment, but as being a Westerner who had actually been handpicked by Madame Chiang herself to represent the I.R.C. Central China Committee. It was also apparent at the conference that as a result of the conflicts in Ethiopia, Spain, and now China, the I.R.C. people were beginning to get the idea that another major war would not follow the pattern of 1914-1918. Next time there would be no dividing line between civilians and military. They all would share the battle wounds. It seemed strange that laymen were getting the picture more quickly than were governments.

After the conference McClure went on a speaking tour in Britain to raise money for the Lord Mayor's Fund. The Lord Mayor's Fund had already performed tremendous service in raising relief money for Spain. Its efforts were now being turned toward China. McClure dove into what seemed like an interminable session of talks in church basements, town halls, and lecture rooms. He found himself speaking to groups that ranged all the way from packed Rotary Club luncheons to six millionaires in a Sheffield board room. It was the millionaires who boggled him. He had never met such a stuffy crowd in his life.

Sheffield, as is well known, was the centre of the stainless steel industry. Bob had a contact there, the uncle of an English Methodist missionary he had come to know in Hankow. "Uncle" Fred Osborn introduced McClure to the Sheffield Manufacturers' Association. It was to that tiny group that Bob spoke at a boardroom table. It was them he assessed as being, without doubt, the stuffiest crowd of stuffed shirts he had ever had the misfortune to meet. After McClure had said his piece the president, a very British type with the teutonic name of Kaiser, rose from his chair and said, in a very British accent, "Well, Robert," (a colossal unbending to use his first name, but then McClure had been brought in under the wing of one of their own) "Well, Robert, the Stainless Steel people will have to do their stuff, eh, what? Ha, ha." Mr. Kaiser had then walked out. But the real mind boggler for Bob came when the Stainless Steel people began to do exactly what that one sentence had said they would do, their "stuff". From then on they raised hundreds of thousands of pounds for China Relief. Before McClure returned to China the Sheffield research people had come up with the answer to a surgeon's prayer. More precisely, it was in answer to McClure's prayer, and it became known all over China as the "Sheffield Dressing". It came in a cellophane wrapper. One simply tore open the wrapper, moistened the dressing, applied it to the wound, and bandaged it in place. It was an antiseptic dressing that gradually liberated chlorine, thus carrying on a running battle against infection. McClure was particularly delighted to find it had been designed with no right side up or upside down. Even a surgeon could not apply it incorrectly.

In mid-summer he received word that the bureaucratic wheels in occupied China had finally ground out exit visas for Amy, the four children, and old Doctor McClure. They were all sailing for home. It was a huge relief. There had been no escape from the nagging fear that if the Japanese wanted Bob badly enough to post a reward, they might hang on to his family. He sometimes wondered if Madame Chiang had shipped him out of the country to forestall that very action. It would have been quite like her. Bob caught the first ship that was heading in the right direction and arrived in Toronto a week ahead of the family.

With a little time on his hands McClure seized the opportunity to do some recruiting for China. He dropped in on Miss Gunn, the Head of the Nurses' Training School at Toronto General Hospital. She was just as austere and terrifying as she had been when Amy trained under her, and was still positively oriented toward missionaries. This missionary, however, had come to suggest that some of the nurses from the graduating class might like to serve in Central China, and Miss Gunn was not about to permit any glib doctor to sell her girls a bill of goods.

"May I enquire, Doctor," she asked coolly, "what the terms of employment are? What salary? What benefits? What working hours?"

Working hours was a tough one. Bob had never really calculated the working hours during an air raid. He doubted that Miss Gunn had even seen a movie of an air raid. While he was wondering how to explain, she continued.

"Dr. McClure, let us suppose that one of the girls volunteers to go and, by some chance, is wounded."

If that was a question, Dr. McClure did not care for it. He figured there was a 50 percent chance she would be wounded and there was a 25 percent chance she would never come home! Again he was saved from giving an answer.

"What would be the compensation, Doctor? What accident insurance is on their lives?"

Hanging on the wall behind Miss Gunn's desk was a picture of Florence Nightingale. McClure pointed to the picture and said, "They will have precisely the same terms of employment as the little lady up there."

The interview terminated inconclusively, but some months later a number of Miss Gunn's nurses went to China.

Bob was on hand at Toronto's Union Station, familiar haunt of his student days, to greet his family. It was a grand reunion, but not an outwardly emotional one. The McClures were not given to outpourings of deep emotion in public. A casual observer could have been forgiven for not realizing the family had been separated from the head of the household for more than a year.

They stayed with friends for about two weeks and then Bob was whisked away on a fund raising tour across Canada and into the western United States. Amy shouldered the task of house-hunting. Her father-in-law, now in his mid-eighties, and still alert and active, was to live with them.

Bob made it back from the States in time to join Amy in a small rented bungalow on Linsmore Crescent off Danforth Avenue in Toronto. He arrived on the evening of their twelfth wedding anniversary. They were together for about ten days before he was away again. He was heading for Europe—on a major I.R.C. fund raising campaign; then to India—for a world missionary conference; and on to China—to resume field work for the I.R.C. Before leaving Canada he was commissioned by the Canadian Red Cross. From then on he wore a Red Cross "Canada" flash on his shoulder.

In England, Holland, Germany, Sweden, Denmark, and Belgium, McClure spoke on behalf of China's suffering millions. He also observed the European scene in that autumn of 1938. As he left Europe he wrote to Amy, his only true confidante: "Tension in Europe is very high. England is in a bad way and her people make no bones about it. France is even worse off. To think that so much of the fear is of the (possibility of) bombings and to think that years ago when all nations could have agreed to scrub the bomber that Britain stuck out for it being retained so that she could bomb the civilians on the Northwest Frontier (of India). Certainly these things have come home to roost in a most alarming manner."

During his last few days, and even hours, in England Bob was harassed by the Oxford Group. Members of this enthusiastic non-organization for spiritual rebuilding, which had been founded in the United States and had swept through Canada in the mid-thirties, seemed determined to add Dr. Robert McClure to their supposedly non-existent membership rolls. It was a movement that would become known later as "Moral Rearmament". Such was their persistence that Bob was still fuming as he wrote a letter to Amy while sailing down the Mediterranean en route to India via the Suez Canal. "They think that if they got me that I could perhaps get Madame Chiang. Now she is definitely Christian, and strongly so, but not Oxford Group. As I see the Group in the past ten days in England I am deeply disappointed in it. The idea that God has to be sold to people by such high-pressure methods is ridiculous in the extreme. The idea that one small group of people have the one and only method of getting in touch with God is a reversion to an old doctrine that I cannot accept. I am afraid that what I said to some of them might have been almost impolite but they did irritate me so. I think between ourselves, though I am not sure, that they may have had a tip-off from A.E. Armstrong* to get going on me because I was sympathetic and sort of half done already. They have undone me completely now, I can assure you."

McClure did not let the memory of the Oxford Group spoil the trip. He was spellbound by the Suez canal in the moonlight, and there, in the daytime, he watched British Gladiator fighter planes doing aerobatics overhead while, off to the east, riders of a camel corps swept long-shadowed across the sands of Egypt.

He was amazed to find that it took three days to sail the Red Sea. It had always looked so insignificant on a map. It was not only large, but it was beautiful, too. There were purple hills on the southern shore, desert beyond, and sunsets too marvellous to describe.

He learned to dance the Palais Glide, perfected the Lambeth Walk, and came dancing into Karachi harbour. It was early December, 1938, and McClure was in time for the world missionary conference being held in Madras, India.

Bob found the conference fascinating. There were delegates from Finland, Africa, Mexico and all points in between. There were other United Church of Canada missionaries there, including Tucker of Angola and Outerbridge from Japan. There were people he knew, and people who knew people he knew. The Chief of Dr. Ayers' Board was on hand. Of him Bob wrote an amazing summation. He found him to be "quite a good scout," and then, with fine McClure disregard for paradox, went on to say that he was "a good routine chap for running a mission I should say, without any too much Christianity and no ideals at all. Hardboiled." It was a recipe that would have paralyzed the good folk of Bloor Street United Church.

Bob found himself comparing the Indian Christians with the Chinese. He passed his findings on to Amy: "The Indians

*The United Church of Canada Board Secretary who ate of the Honan ham.

are born theologians, they love to argue and talk about theories of this and that and then they never do anything about it. They are quite different from the Chinese in that respect, particularly the modern Chinese. The modern Chinese, after almost every session in which theory has come into it a great deal, come out terribly worked up and wonder how people can spend so much time over the unimportant things . . ."

He also took a fresh look at missions: "There is one big challenge has come out of this for me and that is while we all admit that mission policy is to work in a place, make Christians, establish a Christian Church and then move on into new and more difficult fields, yet there is no mission in the world that has yet done that."

McClure may not have been moving into a more difficult "field" but he was certainly about to move into more difficult terrain. Before the conference was over he received two communications from China. One was from the Secretary of the North Honan Mission, telling him to keep away from that area. It did not explain whether it was the Japanese or his fellow missionaries who were feeling unfriendly. Bob hoped it was only the Japanese. The other message was from Madame Chiang, suggesting that on his way into China he should acquaint himself with the Burma Road. It was an interesting suggestion.

The Burma Road was still officially secret. It would become known as the greatest military road ever built, but at the moment many people were skeptical as to whether it really had been built. McClure had heard of it from the Generalissimo, upon whose orders construction had begun, secretly, back in 1937. It was known in some circles that hundreds of thousands of coolies—men, women, and children—had been 'recruited' from many areas of China, and sent into the western mountains to claw a highway through and over those same mountains into the British territory of Burma. It was also known that the task was being carried out without Western implements, in other words with hoe, hammer, pick, shovel, basket and bare hands. Somehow it had all seemed rather mythical. Now, however, that road and the rail line from French Indo-China were the only supply routes into Free China, and Bob was being asked to explore the Burma Road for himself.

The instructions from Number One Hankow Lady gave McClure permission to travel the road with companions. It seemed a good idea, particularly as there were a handful of others at the Madras conference who would be interested in moving relief materials into China. One was Bishop Ralph Ward of the American Methodist Mission. The Bishop and some others arranged to finance the trip—on condition McClure would obtain and service vehicles. The party crossed from Calcutta to Rangoon, Burma, where Bob found a Dodge station wagon and also a Dodge pick-up truck with a jitney body that had been designed for local light bus service. Engines and chassis were the same, and parts were interchangeable. It was an incredible stroke of luck. McClure managed to buy them on the black market, acquiring the jitney just ahead of the bus company. They bought enough spare parts to build another car, and enough gasoline in drums to last about 1,200 miles.

Bob was exhilarated to find in Rangoon that the British had at last caught fire. The Japanese had closed the Yangtze River to all shipping, including British, and the British were retaliating by preparing to let war munitions, and anything else, flow through Burma into China. His spirits high, Bob reported to Amy, "This means Britain has at last decided whom she is backing and it looks good for China".

His spirits were not quite so high as the two car convoy left Rangoon. The Bishop had taken on more passengers, assigning eight people to the jitney, which Bob was driving—three more than Bob felt made sense. It meant that additional baggage and gas drums were loaded on a trailer, which the jitney now had to haul. As far as they could discover in Rangoon, only one vehicle had yet travelled the handmade Burma Road from the border of China the 700 miles to Kunming. It was driven by Dr. Gordon Seagrave, who would become famous as the "Burma Surgeon". Another vehicle had started out but had not yet returned. It was a taxi in the hire of a British salesman supposedly pushing flavouring extract but probably dealing in war chemicals. The third and fourth vehicles to travel the Burma Road would be, if they made it, the jitney driven by Bob McClure and the station wagon driven by Bishop Ward.

26

The Burma Road
With a Bishop

The first part of the journey led from Rangoon to the city of Lashio*, more than 600 miles north-east through the interior of Burma. In the southern regions the roads were congested with people, donkeys, bullock carts and all the usual parambulating paraphernalia typical of Asia. In the less heavily populated regions of the interior the road climbed into mountain country. The travellers reached Lashio, after only two days of hard driving, and were much elated. At Lashio they abandoned the trailer. It was a menace. Bob took time to dash off an enthusiastic note to Amy: "Lashio is a booming frontier town. Everyone is busy as can be. Everyone is prosperous. Everyone is cordial. . . It is going to be fun."

The next filling station was 650 miles beyond Lashio. McClure departed from Lashio carrying passengers, medical supplies, baggage, and a ton of gasoline in the jitney. More luggage, including bedrolls and extra clothing, was on top of the Bishop's station wagon. On top of that again was a new Raleigh bicycle belonging to Bob. It was the finest bicycle he had ever owned.

The road within Burma had been built by the British and Burmese, and was still under construction. Along the 116 miles between Lashio and the China border steamrollers were still at work. They were the last signs of mechanization the travellers would see for hundreds of miles.

The Burma-China border ran through mountainous country which was the domain of small tribal kingdoms. These

*From now on refer to map on *back* end paper.

states were called the "Shan", or Mountain States. The chief-
tains of the larger tribes were autocrats who still considered
taxation to be a personal prerogative. The people spoke tribal
languages, but Mandarin was the lingua franca. Most of the
tribes had a head-hunting tradition lightly buried in the not-
too-distant past.

The actual border crossing was a disappointment. One
hardly knew one had crossed into China. The road dipped
slightly, making a short descent to a small stream. Before
reaching the stream the road was surfaced with crushed gravel.
After crossing the stream it was surfaced with round pebbles.
Beside the stream were the charred ruins of a shack that had
apparently been carelessly burned. It was only because the
road construction technique changed that the travellers could
tell that they had crossed into China. Twenty-five miles farther
on, with nightfall approaching, they found a passport control
office. Here they were told that the charred ruins at the border
were all that remained of a Chinese customs station after the
local Cochin tribal boys had decided the Chinese Government
did not have taxation rights in that area. The tribesmen had
burned the customs post and had massacred the officials. The
customs office was now a discreet 65 miles inside the border.

The passport official told them that before reaching the
customs post they would have to pass through the village of
the "Shwabu"—the Shan chieftain of the entire area. It was essential that they stop and pay their humble respects to the
Shwabu. It was a courtesy that might help them get through
alive.

The approach to the Shwabu's village was via a temporary
wooden bridge that had low overhead structural supports. The
Bishop was in the lead with the station wagon. McClure was
following with the jitney. Bob had a front row spectator's seat
as the Bishop charged the bridge. The baggage on the station
wagon roof struck the overhead. The impact tore the baggage
rack off and simultaneously wrecked Bob's new bicycle. The
Raleigh's frame was bent and the rear wheel mangled. It
looked like a write-off. Bob dismantled the bike and tied the
pieces back on board as salvage.

As luck would have it, the Shwabu's mother had died and
funeral festivities were underway. Instead of hostility they en-
counted hospitality. It was four hours before they were able to

free themselves and proceed. Bob's jitney, being slower and more heavily loaded, left first.

It was almost nightfall as McClure's party arrived at Lungling, a community nestling at 6,000 feet. Here, at last, was the Chinese customs station. The drive had been a weary one, spent grinding along mostly in low gear. But Bob was worried; in spite of their lumbering slowness the Bishop had not overtaken them. In those days, the traveller always carried his own bedding. All their bedding was with the Bishop. Their extra clothing was also with the Bishop. The Bishop, too, had the expedition's funds. Bob and his passengers rented some skimpy bug-infested blankets and bedded down, shivering with the cold. They went to sleep picturing their friends marooned by a breakdown or—terrifying thought—lying broken at the bottom of some Himalayan precipice. It was even possible that the Shwabu had turned unfriendly.

The next morning there was still no Bishop. Bob was already beginning to unload the jitney, in preparation to retrace the route, when the station wagon arrived. At the last moment the Shwabu had invited the Bishop and his passengers to stay overnight. They had decided—not unanimously—that it was too good an invitation to miss. They had greatly enjoyed the remains of the funeral feast, and had been warmly and comfortably bedded. Bob confided his thoughts, as usual, to Amy: "The Bishop is rather careless at times about how much trouble he causes others. With the worry over them, the lack of our bedding, the lack of funds and the wreck of my bike of the day before I was definitely not feeling fraternal towards the Bishop. I guess he noticed it, too." The chill was not all from the January weather at 6,000 feet.

The Chinese customs official moderated the climate. He graciously allowed their vehicles to enter duty free because they were destined for Red Cross use.

The next day's journey took the travellers into spectacular country. Bob had never seen anything like it. The road spiralled snakelike through mountain passes; it clung leachlike to the sides of towering precipices; it hung stringlike across canyons so deep their bottoms were lost in darkness. The vehicles climbed to 8,000 feet and then almost plunged to 2,500 where a steel suspension bridge thrust across the Salween River gorge. Here they were stopped by a ragamuffin group of soldiers under the command of an illiterate officer who demanded to see their passports. McClure, whose practiced eye spotted the officer as an opium addict and his men as would-be-bandits, was carrying a Chinese military pass. He gave the officer and his men a tongue lashing in Mandarin they were not likely to forget. The demands for passports were dropped.

At that same Salween bridge they met the Rangoon taxi conveying the English 'flavouring extract salesman' on his return journey. McClure helped expedite him past the soldiers. The Rangoon taxi-driver had, understandably, become alarmed when he discovered his client's route lay along the Burma Road, but his passenger had solved the problem by buying the vehicle from him and keeping the Burmese on as driver. Bob thought the driver had the right to claim a record-breaking taxi run.

There was still overhead scaffolding at one end of the Salween River bridge and the Bishop managed to complete the wrecking of Bob's bicycle. Thanks to the soldiers, and the Bishop, Bob's mood was like the Salween River, sulphurous green, as the jitney ground its way in second gear on a continuous 4,000 foot climb, eventually arriving at the town of Pao-shan, "Precious Mountain". Paoshan was the first genuine Chinese community of any size to be encountered on the Burma Road. To most of the group it was fascinatingly strange. To McClure, the city wall, the narrow cobble-stone streets with water gutters down both sides, the smells, the hucksters, and the crowds were all so familiar it was like coming home. He had no way of knowing at the time but before the war was finished he would have adventures at Precious Mountain. Now, however, Paoshan was merely an overnight transit point.

On their fifth day in China the road led into even more tortuous conditions and to even more dizzying heights. Hill gradients increased to 15 percent, and more. The road itself climbed to 9,500 feet of elevation. Someone had told Bob that travelling the Burma Road would be "like an ant climbing over corrugated iron". It had been an apt description.

They crossed the Mekong River on another newly completed suspension bridge. McClure, always curious about man-the-builder, eyed the suspension bridges with appreciation. He also eyed them with a view to running Red Cross trucks across them. The bridges were rated for seven and a half tons, enough for four tons of truck with three tons of load, plus a safety margin. He was already convinced in his mind that the I.R.C. should buy charcoal-burning trucks for this run. He had initiated enquiries while still in Rangoon. He was seeing nothing now to change his mind.

In the Mekong area the jitney itself had difficulty. It could not make the grades. Several times everybody had to climb out and help push the labouring vehicle over a crest.

They passed numerous work gangs. Those gangs would be part of the Burma Road scene for many years to come. Patient re-building was the only answer to the landslides that wiped out huge sections of highway after torrential rains. Bob talked to a group of coolies who had been 'recruited' from Honan. They said they had started on the project with 20,000 others from home. There were now 100 of that group left, the rest having succumbed to malaria, dysentery, accidents, and overwork. He was told that although the forced labour was paid, the principal payment had been in opium. The Westerners new to China could not believe it. McClure could believe it. (He eventually met some knowledgeable engineers who had statistics on the death toll among the Burma Road construction force. They calculated that if one laid the victims' bodies end to end they would form a curb on both sides of the road from the Burma border to Kunming. At least two workers died for every six feet of road built over a distance of about 700 miles.)

There was an inscription painted in towering Chinese characters on the face of a cliff. McClure deciphered it: "This road was built by the natives of this district without the aid of foreign implements."

China was truly fighting her war with flesh and blood.

The sixth day they moved out of mountain country and began crossing wide fertile plains, dotted with lakes and under intensive cultivation by Chinese farmers. The road would leave one plain to climb a thousand feet or so across a ridge of hills and then plunge down onto another plain. For long stretches the road surface was hardpacked mud that was almost like asphalt. They were able to purr along at an exhilarating 35 miles per hour. The Burma-China Railway was under construction and here it skirted the highway. Thousands of coolies were at work.

The travellers began to see airfields. They passed one that

had fifty fighter 'planes sitting on the tarmac. They were American 'planes. American volunteer pilots were now actively training Chinese pilots. The American people and their government were, like the British, slowly discovering what the missionaries had known for years—China needed help.

Another range of mountains again forced the road to heights of some 9,000 feet, this time without the steep gradients of the earlier passes. About mid-day the travellers passed out of a beautiful river gorge to find themselves looking down onto an industrial valley with smoking chimneys and roads bustling with traffic. They had come to an area where new salt wells were being developed to supply the needs of Central China, now cut off from coastal sources.

They approached Kunming in much the same way they had approached the salt plains. They came through a pass in the hills to find a beautiful plain revealed below. The focal point was a lake some three miles wide by ten miles long. Its waters were dark blue and it lay like a sapphire gem on a green rug. There were boats on the lake. Stern-wheelers beat their way along in romantic splendour like the Yukon riverboats of goldrush days. At the far, or eastern, end of the lake lay the city of Kunming, until recently merely the capital of a most provincial province, Yunnan, but now one of the three principal cities of Free China.

As the jitney and the station wagon skirted the lake their occupants saw more railway construction. They saw railway work shops and factories going up alongside the roadbed before tracks had even been laid. They drove from the new industrial area through the old city gateway. There were no gates here, just the towering three-portalled entrance with its soaring Chinese roofs, the main portal flanked by two guardian lion-dogs. Over this portal, and under the central roof, hung a large sign with Chinese characters announcing to all who could read that "The Heavens are open, the clouds are auspicious".

It would have been an appropriate sign to have read back at the border because the clouds must have been most auspicious. McClure and the Bishop had brought their two-vehicle convoy fifteen hundred miles from Rangoon, including the entire length of the new Burma Road, without damaging anything other than a bicycle, a luggage rack, and tempers.

Kunming was a transportation centre. From here roads

went on to Kweiyang and to the capital of Free China, Chung-king. Other roads branched north. A narrow-gauge rail line ran from here right down to Hanoi in French Indo-China and on to the harbour at Haiphong. At Kunming, the group broke up to scatter to their various posts. McClure, however, was not yet at his destination. That lay another 350 miles further on at the city of Kweiyang, where the I.R.C. had its principal China office.

It was a three day journey from Kunming to Kweiyang. Bob drove the jitney into Kweiyang late on a Saturday night, just after Japanese bombers had been and gone. "The whole sky was red with the flames of the city," he wrote several days later, ". . . the whole central portion of the city was a blazing furnace . . . there were 600 wounded and heaven only knows how many killed . . . We saw one man digging in the ruins of a house where 22 people were killed by the falling building and, while we were looking, he came across the remains of his wife. The debris had completely covered the remains and he had been pulling on what he thought was a bundle of clothing, when he realized, as the dust shook off, that it was his wife's face. The body had been completely bisected between the thorax and the pelvis and was in entirely two parts. The sights in the morgue as people tried to recognize the bodies laid out in cheap pine coffins were equally distressing."

It was a brutal message, but it was telling Amy that he had returned to an area where he did not wish his wife and his children to follow. The letter continued: "They did not need my medical help for there are three medical schools here with their staffs and several big hospitals from Nanking and other places. They did need, and immediately got issued to them, such of our supplies as were already here and such as we had brought with us in our truck."

It was February, 1939. McClure was back in the war and about to play a new role, which would soon be defined.

27

Trucking Along

In Kweiyang McClure met with the International Red Cross committee. They confirmed what he had suspected—the challenge now facing the I.R.C. was to expedite the shipment of relief supplies into Free China. It was, basically, a transportation job. It seemed like strange work to be asking of a surgeon and Bob admitted as much in his next letter to Amy.

"It seems funny for a surgeon to be doing this work in war time," he wrote, "but it also involves a lot of medical supervision in the field just as the other job in the north did, and as I go about delivering supplies I shall have to supervise and help the hospitals as well. Also . . . they have not a single medical man on their central committee here to take care of purely medical matters, so all that will be with me, too. There is absolutely no one else out here who seems to be able to move on this transportation scheme, for while all recognize it as a problem none seem to know how to go about it."

McClure knew how to go about it. Before the end of that first meeting, the committee had agreed to order two Dodge two-ton trucks immediately. They already had the Burma jitney and the station wagon. In addition they authorized McClure to order four four-ton charcoal burning trucks from England. (He had very nearly ordered them on his own while coming through Rangoon.)

McClure also suggested to the committee that they ask the Canadian Red Cross to send out a man to take charge of maintenance for the fledgling trucking fleet. The committee agreed, unaware of the fact that a letter had already gone off to Amy asking her to broach the subject to A.E. Armstrong. Bob had named the man he thought could do the job and had suggested that the United Church should co-operate with the Canadian Red Cross in making it possible for him to come. This was not an unusual request to go through Amy. More and more Amy was functioning as an informal clearing house for Bob's 'suggestions'.

Although McClure had made a survey trip of the Burma Road it was clear now, as he took stock of the situation, that the Burma route would be held in reserve. The best route for relief supplies was through Haiphong harbour in French Indo-China (Vietnam). From there supplies could come by rail through Hanoi and up to Kunming. For the time being the French were allowing the I.R.C. one boxcar free each month on the train from Hanoi to Kunming.

The most urgent problem was to get the supplies moving out of Kunming. To do that McClure would have to develop a trucking system, beginning with almost nothing. There were no service stations. Gasoline depots had to be established. Hostels had to be set up for the drivers. Bob had already learned from experience that in the mountains between Kunming and Kweiyang the hotels were insect-infested opium dens, and he felt his drivers deserved better.

To begin with, his drivers did not exist. He would have to recruit them, and then he would have to train them. The problem of trained drivers was worth a study in itself. The current estimate was that for every five trucks actually on the road in Free China there was only one *qualified* driver. This led to hair-raising accidents, and put trained drivers in high demand. Unscrupulous drivers boot-legged gasoline out of their own tanks and sold parts off their own trucks.

Partly on a quest for drivers and partly to follow through on an idea for a co-operative trucking system involving the I.R.C. and the missions, Bob took the jitney and hauled a load of supplies through Chungking and on to Chengtu. Here he had the pleasure of staying with his sister Janet, and her husband, Dr. Leslie Kilborn, while he got acquainted with three nieces and a nephew.

This was McClure's first visit to West China, the sister to his own field of North Honan. There were, of course, other missions in the area that had been working for years around

Chengtu. They had been co-founders with the Canadian Methodists (almost thirty years earlier) of the great West China
Union University. There were also refugee universities here
that had been forced back to the hills by the floods of war. For
that matter, there were universities refugeeing all over western
and south-western China. The Japanese considered schools to
be strategic targets. Thousands of students, with their professors, had simply walked west. Bob almost ran down one class
whose teacher was using the dust of the road as a chalkboard.
They were on the last lap of a 1,500 mile trek. From students
Bob learned that when on a journey of unknown destination
one could never stop in indecision at a crossroad. Such hesitation was a sure invitation to aerial attack. "Never stop at a
crossroad," struck McClure as good advice for life's journey.

In the course of his first brief visit to Chengtu, McClure
met with community and university leaders. He was preaching
an old I.R.C. sermon. Like many sermons, it fell upon deaf
ears. "Had a good chance to talk about Air Raid Precautions
with them," he told Amy. "They are simply not interested in
air-raids. There is not a single X-ray in the city that could work
if the city power supply was to close down. They have had no
special lectures in war surgery. They have no emergency dressings and no regular air-raid practice and no first-aid squads on
the campus. They kid themselves that the Japanese would not
hit them. Such faith is seldom seen in Israel! I did my best to
stir them up."

McClure broached the idea of the I.R.C. and the United
Church mission co-operating in transport. He found that the
Chengtu people were quite satisfied with the three trucks
which they were currently running. The three vehicles were of
different makes. There was no supply of spare parts and no
maintenance man. At that very moment two of the trucks were
broken down somewhere near Chungking. These minor details
seemed to be of little concern and there was no great urge to get
involved with an I.R.C. scheme. Bob was disappointed, and
frustrated. The Chengtu folk did promise, however, to look for
apprentice drivers from among senior high school boys (prefer-
ably destined for theology). This, at least, was good news because, as had happened so often in Hwaiking, McClure was
being faced with the fact that if he wanted apprentices who
would dedicate themselves to the ideal of service rather than of

graft he would have to employ Christians. He returned to Kweiyang, hoping it would not be too long before the first recruits would follow.

That first trip to Chengtu made him homesick. He confided in Amy: "It is a bit hard to go over to these places where people live in homes instead of houses. Where there are kids, where things around show that there is a mother around and where people go to bed two by two . . . However, we'll not turn back now but plan for the end of the year." It was early March. The end of the year was more than nine months away.

He was homesick, too, for Hwaiking: "How often I think back to Hwaiking just two years ago with the good times we had. Possibly they may come again, or is that a closed chapter? Perhaps we have to move on through the rest of the book."

Wherever he went McClure listened avidly for any news from Honan. The Canadian missionaries were still in North Honan and still, ostensibly, neutrals. They could still send letters to Canada and after much delay those letters would come into Free China via Burma or Indo-China. Bruce Copland found a shorter mail route from Hwaiking. He had letters smuggled across the Yellow River at Wen-hsien. They came down to Bob without even passing through the Chinese censor.

Things were tough in Honan and getting tougher. The Japanese had started out a year and a half ago by pretending respect for the missionaries. Initially, they had sent liaison officers who spoke faultless English, and who liked music and literature. Now they were sending bully boys whose main objective was to harass the missionaries into 'voluntary' withdrawal.

Bob received word of Dr. Dick Brown. When Dick's leave of absence had expired he had come out of guerrilla country, had circled south of the Yellow River, and then had crossed through Japanese lines and made his way to his old hospital of Kweiteh. He was there now, trying to keep the hospital functioning in spite of the hazards and frustrations of Japanese occupation. The word-of-mouth report was that Dr. Brown's nerves were in very bad shape. The experiences he had shared with Bethune and the Eighth Route Army had left him "dissatisfied and confused in his mind".

Dick was not the only one to be confused. A doctor down

in McClure's area was in the process of transferring to another hospital when he suddenly changed his mind and went home on furlough. He had not been home more than two weeks before he committed suicide. There were elderly China veterans around who were going to the other extreme and, instead of yielding ground to the war, were hanging on and quietly going senile on the job. On balance, McClure figured that he was holding out rather well, although his letters were soon showing more signs of testiness than they ever had during the Chengchow period. He was referring to drivers in general as "a dirty bunch of crooks" and was irritated by a cross-eyed Western nurse who had not had the sense to have her eyes uncrossed as an infant. Even his own mission folk up at Chengtu irritated him as being too individualistic and requiring kid glove treatment. There was an acidity in some of his comments that was new to McClure's letters. In the past he had been forthright in his comments but there was usually more humour than acid.

McClure had reached a psychological plateau. He was lonesome, homesick, and overworked. It was just possible that China, and the war, might break him.

He suggested to Amy that they agree on a given time every day and try to communicate by telepathy. It did not work out. His time was mid-morning and he usually seemed to be negotiating hairpin turns beside yawning chasms when he was supposed to be concentrating on his wife. If the distraction was not driving it was bound to be something else. As medical advisor to the I.R.C. committee he examined requisitions that came in from about fifty civilian hospitals, and he helped to draw up drug orders. He was made Special Commissioner for Highway Health. He was a member of a cholera sub-committee responsible for an area as big as Ontario, with a population five times that of Canada. He was commandeered by the Yunnan Goitre Prevention Committee. He helped draw up a submission to the Rockefeller Foundation proposing a scheme to provide medical and technical training for the local Miao tribal people who would still be in the area long after wartime refugees had moved on. All these responsibilities were in addition to the main job, which was that of moving relief supplies.

The I.R.C.'s gasoline trucks arrived. Fortunately an able volunteer driver also arrived in the person of a twenty year old

American college student, Ed Taylor. Ed had been raised in China. He helped McClure get the trucking business through the crucial period while the doctor was training Chengtu high school boys as truck drivers. Bob tried some refugees from Germany but only two were good drivers and all were unreliable. A Ceylonese professor, by the name of Aras, turned up during a leave of absence and volunteered. Aras was no mechanic, but a good driver and a thorough gentleman. He raised Bob's spirits.

McClure was a hard taskmaster. The first of the Chengtu student volunteers he described as being "a lazy slut" who was afraid of dirt, hard work, and early rising. Within two months the same boy, who had probably never ridden in a motor vehicle before joining McClure, was piloting an I.R.C. truck, loaded with medical supplies, several thousand miles into guerrilla country toward Shanghai. More lads arrived from Chengtu and generated a similar initial reaction: "Some of these Chengtu boys are the dumbest things in the use of their hands with tools. They are below the average standard of country lads thanks to their higher education. This is something that is sadly lacking in all government curriculum schools but why it should be so conspicuous a lack in a mission school is rather disturbing." But after a few months under the McClure lash six of the lads had not only "learned enough to be sure to hit something", but had vowed to stick with the I.R.C. right through to the end.

The roads and the driving combined to create a perpetual nightmare. The nearest gasoline pump was 800 miles away across three mountain ranges and over two days of bad roads that were bombed and machine gunned at all hours of the day. The nearest spare parts depot was 400 miles away. The roads were the most winding motor roads in existence. Any that once had surfaces had lost them due to heavy rains and heavier traffic. Grades of 22 percent were common. One of the I.R.C. gas depots could only be reached after grinding in low gear up a 28 percent incline.

Month after month McClure kept hounding the United Church offices in Toronto to get together with the Canadian Red Cross and send a maintenance man out to him. They seemed unable to produce. Time after time he would find himself lying in the mud in pouring rain, changing broken leaf springs on overloaded trucks.

Month after month he kept hoping to hear that the charcoal burners had arrived at Hong Kong. They, too, seemed fated never to come. Nevertheless, McClure, young Taylor, Aras, the high school boys, and passing volunteers, gradually built up an I.R.C. trucking centre. It was a truly international operation. It was not unusual to find as many as eight nationalities represented among the men working on vehicles in the I.R.C. garage at Kweiyang. But Bob found it difficult to make lasting friendships in a community where everyone was mobile, everyone was temporary, everyone was, in a way, a refugee.

The Executive Secretary of the I.R.C. took sick and was invalided out to Hong Kong. He was replaced by an American seconded from the government Salt Administration. The new man's name was Joseph Spencer. Joe was a congenial type about Bob's own age and he, too, was "doctor". He was a Doctor of Philosophy, having a Ph.D. in Geology from the University of California in Los Angeles. Dr. Spencer had the foresight to bring a good Chinese cook along with him. McClure and Spencer shared a room together in spartan conditions in a small house on the outskirts of Kweiyang. The house was on a hillside with a cemetery above it containing a 'funk-hole' where one sheltered during air raids. There was something bizarre about sheltering from death in a cemetery. It appealed to McClure's sense of humour.

The McClure-Spencer establishment was like a rural mission station; it was always full of travellers. The transients borrowed their hosts' clothing, bedding, and beds. When Bob returned from a trip, he never knew who would be wearing his shirts or occupying his quarters. After a few months of it he confessed to Amy, "It would be nice to be less of a communist some day".

Communal living was not new to McClure. What *was* new, was to be working in an all-male environment.

"The lack of any attractive ladies out here and the arduousness of the work has made me completely asexual," he told Amy with straightforward honesty,". . . I never thought I could ever arrive at that stage myself but here I am. Seem to be able to sleep eat and work and never think of women at all. The ideal monk. It must be partly the war atmosphere at least or we should not be this way. I know when I get home it will not be this way."

The same spartan and monkish existence was not endured by all his colleagues. McClure had a counterpart in the League of Nations, a French doctor about ten years his junior, by the name of Mauclaire. (To the Chinese, McClure and Mauclaire were pronounced the same.) He, too, was trying to build a trucking fleet. Dr. Mauclaire liked to stay in bed until ten, to move slowly until twelve, and to have a siesta after lunch. He went to Hanoi as often as possible for female consolation. He managed, in short, a style of living that was remarkable under prevailing conditions. He was appallled to hear that Dr. McClure was actually driving a truck himself. Mauclaire intended to accompany the occasional convoy, but in a sedan equipped with commodious food hampers, select wines, and other necessities. Among the I.R.C. gang the words, "I weel take zee sedan," became a catch phrase of infinite use. And Dr. Mauclaire contributed another phrase. Once, in a moment of clinical reflection, he calculated that a former Parisian girl friend, who had been much-married and much-escorted, must have accepted a total of male organ equivalent in length to four times the Eiffel Tower. It was an interesting calculation and put "Eiffel Tower!" into the I.R.C. vocabulary as a defiant exclamation.

McClure liked Mauclaire but would torment him intentionally by barbaric acts. Acts such as tramping into the League man's bedroom at the ungodly hour of 10 a.m., dressed in mud-spattered leather boots and breeks and a dilapidated leather jacket, and tearing off the bedclothes, upsetting the breakfast tray, and then demanding action on some problem of mutual responsibility. Mauclaire would counter-attack by being infuriatingly soothing and reassuring, explaining that most things lost some of their apparent urgency if one thought about them for awhile. He could, however, be ruthlessly direct when the chips were down, as was demonstrated in the face of a cholera epidemic.

The heart of the epidemic was in Japanese-occupied territory in the south-east. The League of Nations anti-epidemic people, under a Dr. Pollitzer, were much alarmed. The I.R.C. went into action to obtain anti-cholera vaccine to prevent the epidemic from spreading through Free China. The nearest source of supply was French Indo-China, but the French did not seem inclined to 'meddle' in the affairs of Free China. Bob took the problem to Mauclaire. Mauclaire demonstrated a better knowledge of politics than he had of trucks. He contacted the Governor General of Indo-China and explained that the epidemic would undoubtedly sweep down into the colony. By stopping it in China they would in effect be placing a *cordon sanitaire* around French territory. It was a telling argument, but when it was not followed by sufficiently swift action Mauclaire sent another message to His Excellency the French Governor. The message was so terse and to the point, so direct and abrupt, so totally lacking in the customary official courtesies that even forthright McClure was amazed. He could never have signed his name, or that of the Red Cross, to such a missive. But Mauclaire's technique was flawless. The vaccine began to flow.

Three tons of vaccine was shipped by rail to Kunming and trucked by the I.R.C. into cholera territory. A handful of medical staff dispersed into strategically located villages. They taught vaccination technique to high school students, armed them with needles and vaccine, and sent them forth. The students vaccinated six million people and the epidemic was stopped in its tracks.

When the accounts came in, it was found that the French had donated the vaccine.

The French had come through in style. But McClure still had had no word of his charcoal burners from England, and was getting discouraged by the lack of positive response from Canada concerning a maintenance man. He felt for a while that he was getting better co-operation from other churches than he was from his own. In transportation he and Mauclaire now had the League and I.R.C. sharing each other's garage facilities and hauling on a co-operative basis. The Seventh Day Adventist mission was joining in enthusiastically but the United Church people at Chengtu were still muddling along on their own.

The lack of a maintenance man really bothered McClure. He sounded off to Amy knowing she would relay the message to the right ears: "I cannot understand the hold up. Is it that (a maintenance man) does not want to come or that there is no one to send him? . . . Really Canada is not much of a show compared to Sweden or Britain in these things. When one remembers the hot air that was shot off at Rotary and all the other dinners, and then this muddling along, they seem to leave a very confused and discouraging picture." He rattled right on into another paragraph that told a great deal about McClure—about the kind of men he admired and about an amazing lack of awareness of his own accomplishments: "The Swedish doctor* whom I brought up last time is going to be a second Hankey. He is a marvel. Within a week of his coming here he was on his way to the front with Chinese Red Cross units and though he does not speak the language he is with them, sleeping on boards, eating Chinese food and working where they work. Swedish stocks are rated very high indeed, I don't mind telling you. He can ride horseback excellently, drive a car or truck and, which is more, maintain the old thing. He can ride a bike well, can do surgery or medicine and is no mean hound at bacteriology. . . . I do wish that we could turn out some chap like that in some sphere of this war work who could show them what Canada can do."

There were some who might have been forgiven for thinking that doctors Robert McClure, Richard Brown, Norman Bethune, and numerous others were not doing too badly as Canada's standard bearers.

As an I.R.C. man McClure was supposed to be neutral, but there was always something intensely personal about the war. It was *his* China and it was *his* war. He had little but scorn for anyone who did not take it seriously or who participated half-heartedly. He could forgive Dr. Mauclaire because Mauclaire "took zee sedan" with such stylish flair, but anyone else who took zee sedan, heaven help them. McClure went to Hanoi several times for trucks and supplies and admired the French colonial society for being unstratified and without colour prejudice, but the French customs officers he described as "swines to the very last", because they impeded the flow of his relief supplies. But when heavy July rains caused landslides on the Burma Road and the British closed it at their end, the French not only let relief supplies through but also arms and munitions—then McClure's estimate of the French soared.

Many British, including Canadians, were being forced out of occupied China. The Japanese threw hand-grenades over the Canadian mission gate at Changte, and burned the gates. These and other unfriendly acts finally caused the United

*Dr. Holm

Church to recall all the Canadians from the North Honan field. Bob heard this from Bruce, and others, who had no alternative but to leave. All British subjects were having the same problems. But Britain entered into 'negotiations' with the Japanese and, while doing so, kept the Burma Road closed. McClure was outraged. "It is little wonder," he wrote, "that that French adjective sticks so closely to England—'perfidious'."

But all was not gloom. A great shipment of Sheffield dressings and stainless steel surgical equipment came in from 'Uncle' Fred Osborn's people. The shipment was composed of small packages with the signatures of the English donors on them—names of shopkeepers, farmers, truckers, children, widows—and McClure found himself almost in tears as he trans-shipped them to front line hospitals. And then a Chinese youth walked in one day with a smile on his face and asked if Loa Tai-fu could use a humble mechanic. He was met with a McClure bearhug; he was one of Bob's boys from the Hwaiking mission power plant.

There were moments of happy, relaxed comradeship. Young Ed Taylor, Bob's mainstay driver, had his twenty-first birthday and Dr. Pollitzer found a fat goose and a bottle of red wine for Joe Spencer's cook to create with. A good time was had by all.

There were even little luxuries. Although there was a shortage of imported tobacco, McClure found a Kweiyang cigar maker who made him little custom cheroots from the local leaf. Life began to look almost sunny.

There was also the occasional exhilarating trip which offered a combination of pleasures. On one such journey Bob had a brush with bandits, his truck dropped to its axles in mud, and he negotiated mountain hairpins with a steering mechanism that was reluctant to make a right hand turn. McClure always felt better after the adrenalin had been made to flow, and he seldom failed to learn from every adventure. After that one trip he ordered tire chains from Canada and installed a revolver in the toolbox of each truck.

After slogging away for seven months, however, he still had not received the shipment of charcoal trucks and still had no chief maintenance man. The war was showing few signs of progress in any direction and the philosophical side of him was feeling rather low: "One gets rather depressed about this war at times. When one is drumming along the road with a truck load of medicines to relieve suffering and then to think that by this very relief one is making the war last longer! The more intense the suffering on both sides the earlier will one or the other give up . . . How crazy this world really is. It gets one down a bit . . ."

It *did* get him down. It *was* depressing. His weight dropped—146 lbs—142—140. He again expressed sentiments concerning his Chengtu compatriots which were, for McClure, vitriolic: "One is much impressed by the slow and sluggish mental reactions of our West China crowd. They are very self-centred and *so slow*. I think the climate is much too salubrious and they become like lotus eaters in West China. What they need is a bit of cold North China winter to jolt them into action." The fact that his own sister and her husband were among the lotus eaters was no deterrent and besides, in the same letter, McClure took himself to task: "All the things I start seem to be such one-man shows. Maybe there is something wrong with me. Everyone says it is such marvelous work and all that but the work seems to be one-man type . . . If I leave, after getting five gasoline trucks and four charcoal ones, and leave the whole show in suspense—really it would hardly seem sporting." In almost the same breath he said, "I have made up my mind to come home at the end of this year." He began counting the days. He counted them all through a weary fall and into winter.

McClure was on the road with a convoy when World War II broke out in Europe. He heard about it two days later when he pulled into Kunming after dark, having towed a bus the last twenty miles over mountain roads. The news had about the same impact as though he had been told the Japanese had once again bombed Chungking. His immediate reaction was mainly of annoyance with the fact that some Jewish refugees who were working with him should suddenly become enemy aliens because their passports were German. As he had already noted, it was a silly world.

It got sillier.

The Chinese government banned the import of gasoline! They were out to get the big oil companies and wanted to establish a monopoly of their own. The monopolistic move, combined with a great capacity for graft and corruption, ensured that very little gasoline flowed at all. It was just at this time that McClure received word that two of the charcoal burning trucks had arrived in Hong Kong. The timing could not have been more opportune.

Bob had high hopes for charcoal burners. They had been running in areas of France and in Scotland for years. There they ran on charcoal but the trucks ordered for the I.R.C. were to be adapted for coal, which China had in abundance. Bob's calculations indicated that $1.00 worth of coal in Kweiyang would be the equivalent of $135.00 worth of imported gasoline.

He headed for Hong Kong, via Hanoi. He could hardly wait to see those trucks. It was exciting just to think of their simple 90 h.p. engines with cylinders the size of water-buckets.

In Hanoi, much to his consternation, he was kissed effusively on both cheeks by a French passport officer who seemed determined to show his friendship for his Canadian allies. In Hong Kong harbour he got a great lump in his throat when he saw the CPR *Empress of Russia* setting sail for Canada. She looked beautiful even in her warpaint. And on the Hong Kong docks the trucks were awaiting him. They were beautiful, too, in spite of the fact that they were hulking four-ton brutes that looked as though they had locomotive blood in their tubes.

McClure had one of the Chengtu lads with him and the two of them spent several days checking out the trucks and test driving them. The first day, Bob turned a valve the wrong way and received a back blast that singed his eye-brows, hair, and moustache. It was a gentle reminder that there were things to learn about the beasts.

The trucks worked on much the same simple principle as did Bob's producer gas plant in Hwaiking. The methane gas produced by the combustion of the coal was fed into the truck carburation system and exploded in the cylinders. It was only the principle that was simple. The driver had to stoke the fire, get it going, and keep it going. He had to regulate the flow of oxygen through the fire. The engine had to be started on gasoline, and then be gradually weaned over to the gas. Once it was running on straight gas it created its own draft through the fire-box—until one coasted down a long incline, making no power demands. Then the fire might even go out. On a very heavy climb the driver had to beef up the gas with a little gasoline. All the adjustments governing the flow of oxygen, gas, and gasoline, could be made from inside the cab by opening and closing valves. It was a little like driving a mobile pipe organ.

Throughout all the trial runs Bob found the British to be interested and helpful. They seemed to be less stuffy than normal. War was an amazing alchemist.

Everything was looking up. A bundle of letters from Amy reached him in Hong Kong. In them were two pieces of family news. Norah had cleared the 'Entrance' hurdle and was now entering high school. It was good news that hurt. Norah in high school! His family was growing up, he was growing older, and he was still away from home. "Finished by Dec. 31st," was his response and he continued, literally, to number off the days. The other news was that the family had moved. They had left the rented bungalow for a house of their own, on Glengrove Avenue in Toronto. They took 83 year old Dr. Wm. McClure with them. It was a three-storey house with a guest room and a third-floor mess-around area for the kids. Bob had no idea where Glengrove Avenue was, but it all sounded great. He began to bubble with enthusiasm for the world in general.

McClure and the Chengtu lad put the two charcoal burners onto a ship bound for Haiphong. Bob found that the same ship was carrying tetanus antitoxin from the Canadian Red Cross worth $2,000.00 (Cdn). He promised himself the antitoxin would be the first cargo on the new trucks.

He was horrified, upon reaching Haiphong, to find that the French had issued a list of goods that were not to be conveyed through Indo-China. It was a list that included everything in which the I.R.C. might ever be interested, including cars, trucks, parts and drugs. The last item on the drug list was a real loophole-plugger. It was No. 00318: "All chemicals not named above." And here was McClure steaming into port with two monster trucks and two thousand dollars worth of drugs. It made his old Shanghai box-of-human-parts problem look insignificant. He thought of Dr. Mauclaire and wondered how *he* would attack the problem. It was certainly not a time to take zee sedan. Somehow those regulations had to be Eiffel Towered, and thoroughly.

McClure attacked head on. He explained to the French authorities that the two I.R.C. trucks were hauling a shipment of vital drugs that were a gift from the people of Canada. He then crossed his fingers and said that if the shipment was blocked it would cause a terrible anti-French backlash in Canada and the reverberations would split the Allied ranks in Europe. It was an interesting argument. The customs papers went across four- teen separate desks before they were finally approved. As it turned out, the officials were not above applying a bit of the Eiffel Tower to their own regulations—the trucks left for China carrying the Canadian tetanus antitoxin; spare tires for I.R.C. vehicles in Kweiyang; a group of Finnish missionaries with two tons of groceries; two Swedish missionaries with another ton of supplies; forty-eight French bicycles for the Chinese Red Cross mobile public health units; and two tons of coal for truck fuel all nicely packaged in 90 kg. bags. There was also an Anglican missionary from New Zealand and she, too, had medical sup- plies with her.

Amy learned of the New Zealand lady in a letter Bob mailed from Haiphong: "There is a rather interesting lady going in with me, a Miss Hall. Vintage 50 years or so. She has been working up in the Wu Tai Shan area of the 8th Route Army and has been working with Dr. Bethune up there. She has resigned from her mission and is going back for one year's work supported by a group of left wingers in Hong Kong. She herself is much too elevated to know anything about politics at all but she is keen on doing her stuff. She is a former S.P.G.* missionary . . . She thinks rather well of Dr. Bethune and evi- dently once he gets away from his alcoholic beverages he does a good job of work and is not a bit afraid of hardship. I am glad the reports I had of him before have not proven to be true when he gets out at work . . . You may at times meet people who know of him in Canada and it might be as well to give him full marks for what he has been doing. I was rather frank in telling what I knew of him before but I should not like to give a wrong impression about him now that he is doing his stuff."

McClure had made the road trip from Hanoi to Kweiyang several times before. It was a long haul, more than eight hundred miles, most of it in China and most of it on mountain roads. The route lay through Nanning, a city toward which the

---

*"Society for the Propagation of the Gospel"—a missionary arm of the High Church of England, (Great Britain).

Japanese armies were now heading. The road had been bombed and strafed for months. On a previous trip Bob had found the hillsides at the border crossing lined with citizens of Indo-China sitting, like football fans in a stadium, to watch Japanese 'planes machine-gun convoys as they moved into Chinese territory. Now the run from the border would be made mostly after dark, and the daylight hours would be spent with the trucks hidden under the spreading shelter of trees.

Before they got out of Indo-China the new trucks began to act up. Both developed fire-box trouble. The dynamo gave up on one. The speedometer cable broke on the other. As they pulled into the border station the Chengtu lad's gear shift lever sheered off near the floor. It took Bob four hours of greasy, hand-scarring work to remove the broken part, and twenty-four hours to get it repaired. They made a night run to Nanning and lay up for the day. The next night, well out of Nanning, the gearshift lever snapped again. Bob again wrestled it out. He left the driver with the truck, took all the passengers with him, and headed back to Nanning. En route his clutch and brake pedals began to jam, making night driving in hill country more than usually interesting. Before he reached Nanning the hand brake had given out. There was another forty-eight hour delay for repairs. They were all set to go again, and Bob's truck was sitting with the engine idling, when a big cast-aluminum valve casing broke and poured the engine oil into the street. There was a thirty-hour delay for welding, while the second truck still sat up country by the roadside, protected by a worried youth from Chengtu.

As they gradually put distance between themselves and Nanning they decided to risk some daylight travel. It was a rash move. "We got right into the middle of a raid," Bob reported to Amy later on. "You could hear the big fellows grinding away somewhere but could not see them. Over to the right about two miles away a village was in flames. It had just been bombed in the last 30 minutes. We were on an open stretch of dusty road in broad noon daylight and no cover for miles and we with our 4-tonners raised an awful dust. They are big trucks and easy to spot. The 'planes were so near that coolies along the road had put down their baskets and had taken to the long grass. However, so long as we could not see them coming for us, the best thing was to keep moving. We were driving towards the hills where things would be more safe. I never had such nervous tension for an hour or two in my life before . . . the best thing was to make a joke of the whole thing to keep the passengers from being nervous and to keep ploughing ahead." Most of the passengers had had little air-raid experience and were frightened. McClure had had a great deal of experience and was *very* frightened. He had once seen a traveller emerge from this same run with forty bullet holes in his suitcase. It was a high moment in McClure's career when they reached the hills and pulled off under shelter with trucks, passengers, and cargo all intact.

Fifty miles from Kweiyang, in the midst of cold drizzling rain and on one of the worst hills in the area, the firebox on Bob's truck burned through, knocking the gas apparatus out for good. He had to switch to gasoline. From there on he had to stop every few miles to fill the truck's little one gallon reserve tank. Ten miles from Kweiyang the other truck blew a gasket and took water into a cylinder. It was a battered, weary, two-truck convoy that limped into Kweiyang. The run from Haiphong harbour had taken fifteen days instead of five.

They arrived in Kweiyang in time for Miss Hall to receive the unhappy news that Dr. Bethune had died, after one year and nine months of Herculean endeavour with the Eighth Route Army. Miss Hall decided to push on anyway.

News came through that Nanning had fallen to the Japanese.

Everything was turning sour, including the trucks. McClure was frustrated but not defeated. He was enraged by the poor workmanship that would permit trucks to be shipped with sub-standard parts but he was philosophical about problems caused by his own lack of experience. "The firebox can be welded," he wrote. "I think that the fuel was not suited and got much too hot. We are now going to get them in order and try them on local charcoal . . . I'll know a lot about these things by the time it is my turn to hand over." And a week or so later: "We had a marvelous run yesterday in the charcoal trucks. When no one is looking they behave like children do. They do the cutest things and are excellent, but let some famous engineer come up and see them and they think up the wildest ways of disappointing one."

He still had no maintenance man and no one to whom to

'hand over'. He received a letter from Dr. Pidgeon urging him to come home. There was also a letter from a medical friend in Toronto, Dr. George Young, with much the same message. There was even a letter from Bruce telling him to pull out and take a furlough, that someone would turn up. If Bruce had been doing some calculations he had realized that McClure had not had a genuine holiday furlough since he went to China in 1923. Amy's letters, too, were beginning to get rather insistent.

McClure was caught in the middle. In Chungking and Kunming and Kweiyang associates were telling him he had to stay on. "I'm having a terrible time with critics now that my show has come near the time to be handed over," he complained to Amy. "They are jumping on me so badly. The whole thing boils down to the same as the Hwaiking Medical System that it was all right for R.B. to handle a thing like that but no one else can do it. It gets me so fed up. Any old fool can come and do this thing if they do not mind eating the odd bit of bitterness. Surely our entire nation has not gone so soft that the fear of being wet with the rain and cold at nights—surely some are still made who are not entirely upset by such things. Anyway the criticism right here in the room is so bad just now that I cannot collect my thoughts to continue this letter but I do want to let you know that . . . I'm coming home in the rather near future." It was then early November.

The United Church had no intention of sending in "any old fool" to replace McClure. They seconded one of the old Weihwei gang to the I.R.C. It was Rev. Bill Mitchell, himself a man of varied experience and dedicated to relief work. McClure was delighted. He could hardly wait for Bill to arrive.

And then a wire came in from Sian saying they had a Chinese mechanic there who was refugeeing from Hwaiking. He wanted to know where he could be of most use. His name was Yang Yung-lo. A return telegram went back so fast the wires almost melted. It was now mid-December. Bill Mitchell had made it as far as Kunming. Yang Yung-lo was on his way south from Sian. All Bob had to do was to hang on long enough to work them into their jobs and then be off. He could not be away by December 31st but it was going to be close. Then word came telling him he was to fly home! He would be ahead of schedule.

All he needed now was a monkey. The kids had been pestering him by mail for a monkey and everywhere he went he had been on the lookout. There had been no suitable monkeys in Hong Kong. If he did find a monkey now, would it be permitted to fly on a clipper? Anyway, he was headed for home! But he knew he would return. There was so much to be done in China. His head was fairly bursting with ideas. He had already unloaded some thoughts in reports to A.E. Armstrong and, less formally, in his regular letters to Amy.

To Amy he gave an uninhibited assessment of the mission work in the south-western provinces: "Missions here have been, up to now, run along very conservative lines both as regards their doctrinal teaching but more particularly as regards their actual technique of mission work. Many of the mission hospitals are not much more than baiting dispensaries to get a chance to reach the people with preaching, and the medical work that many of them do is far inferior to what is being done by purely philanthropic agencies of Chinese origin in the same city. A little forward policy is badly needed."

He saw an opportunity for the missionaries driven out of North China to re-group in the south-west: "The urgent mission field now is . . . in the southern half of Yunnan province, particularly along the Burma Highway . . . They could use easily right now one complete mission station of a doctor, a nurse, a married couple for evangelistic work and a single lady or two . . . the Highway Bureau has offered every assistance, such as building the hospital."

He had some fairly clear ideas of how, and where, he himself wanted to serve: "If we are going to work up country in China then I do feel that I should like to work on rural medicine once more, and that everlasting problem of how people in rural areas can get some of the benefits of modern medicine given to them."

For McClure, "up country" did not include Chengtu: "Chengtu is rather badly eaten through with cliques and factions and it does not make for smooth running . . . we can definitely mark off Chengtu from our list."

The idea of opening a United Church hospital on the Burma Road appealed to him. Perhaps at Lungling, up in the Shan States: "We could live there as a family with the older kids going to school in Burma."

On December 18th Bob signed off a long newsy letter to Amy, "I'm so excited now I can't think straight so excuse the jumble. Heaps of love and the kisses will come soon."

Two days later he was in the garage yard organizing a departing truck convoy that, on its return, was to bring Bill Mitchell from Kunming. He was standing beside one of his own trucks, his back toward it, watching a student driver manoeuvre for position. The lad swung at too sharp an angle and was backing in toward McClure and the parked truck. Bob shouted at him. The boy swung the wheel but hit the accelerator instead of the brake. The big truck lurched backward, angling in against the other machine.

Bob was caught between the trucks. He was pinned, arms at his side. He was rolled, helplessly, like a log into a pulp grinder, into an ever decreasing gap between the two four-ton monsters. One shoulder was dislocated. Neck muscles began to tear. Both collar bones were forced out of location at the breast bone and in a monstrous blur of pain McClure became unconscious. One final slow turn between the relentless weights fractured his ribs in eighteen different places.

The I.R.C. yard was only a hundred paces from the Provincial hospital, a rambling affair with little wards in thatched huts, pretending to look like a Chinese village. The young drivers tenderly carried McClure into the hospital where a big Chinese doctor, Dr. Yang, took charge. Dr. Yang was soon assisted by a Dr. Shen who rushed over from the Chinese Red Cross. (Dr. Shen had been one of the interns at Rockefeller Hospital whom Bob and George Wang had tutored through the language problems fifteen years before.)

The accident happened about 11 a.m. Joe Spencer arrived and sat with Bob the rest of that day and all night. Next day a nurse, Miss Grace Feng, volunteered to take over the vigil. She was an excellent nurse and it turned out that she had trained under nurse Coral Brodie at Cheloo. Coral had been "set apart" with Bob at Bloor Street Church those many years ago. Joe returned for the night watch. Miss Feng took over again the next day. A special nurse was brought in that third night while a weary Joe Spencer sat down to write a letter to Amy. Joe had taken no course in this kind of communication: "I feel like a man making his first public speech, not just in the fact of writing you the first time, but in the way of what must be written . . . Can't avoid it much longer . . ." He gave Amy a cursory description of the accident and then, to quieten her anxiety and to keep the letter to a manageable length, he told her what was *right* with her husband. "Heart entirely normal in pulse and pressure, temperature quite normal, lungs in good shape and working properly . . ." and then, the next morning, a P.S. "Very good night. (Bob) sat up this morning for a bit."

The very next day McClure managed to write a one paragraph letter to Amy.

The day after that was Christmas Day and McClure struggled out of bed. Using Joe Spencer as a crutch and wearing Joe's coat he walked the quarter mile to the I.R.C. house, with numerous pauses for breath. He refrained from coughing because the pain of a cough put him into shock.

For once the communal house was absolutely empty. Joe propped him up in the sun for an hour and then they had Christmas dinner—a box of Shanghai Bakerite biscuits and a tin of Del Monte peaches.

The next day Bob again laboriously wrote to Amy: "I look like a guy about 85 with lumbago who has recently had a stroke! My feet and legs and pelvis are all okay, however. Both my sternomastoid muscles were ruptured so it is painful to move my head and one has a downcast expression . . . I suppose in some 40,000 kms. of driving over these roads with volunteer and student drivers something like this now and then is a matter of averages. That it happened 25 yards from the hospital door is a matter of vital good fortune . . . I'm so glad to be alive, don't worry about my ever taking any chances with any of my remaining 8 lives. They're all being saved for Toronto and our meeting there . . . Your old crock, Bob."

It was, at last, time for McClure to take zee sedan, but flying by clipper was out. If they had to fly higher than 10,000 feet he would find it impossible to breathe. The journey home would have to be by a slow boat from China.

Bill Mitchell arrived on New Year's Eve. As of January 1st, 1940, the I.R.C's Chief Trucker was Rev. William Mitchell.

Yang Yung-lo arrived to head up maintenance. Bob spent his period of recuperation briefing Bill and Yung-lo.

Early in February McClure was well enough to take the train trip to Haiphong. En route he adopted a war-orphaned monkey. Everything was turning out just fine. His spirits were soaring.

He caught a freighter headed for California.

28

Oh Canada!

It was late one evening in the early spring of 1940 when Bob arrived in Toronto and was met by his family. He was ushered home to the house he had never seen at 228 Glengrove Avenue. It was the first home that he and Amy had ever owned. Detailed memories of that homecoming were to vanish in the following years but Bob was delighted to find Amy looking well, the children flourishing, and his eighty-four year old father still very mobile and mentally keen. Dr. William McClure's only complaint was that a new set of books he had purchased tended to be too heavy for bedtime reading. Bob diagnosed that as a sign of deterioration, until he discovered the books were the Encyclopedia Brittanica.

Even Amy forgot the details of that homecoming, she was so relieved to see her husband in good shape after that terrible accident—although his shape had changed. He had been quite broad in the chest. Now, after that tremendous crushing, he was a little deeper in the chest, almost pigeon-breasted.

For the children, the really memorable part of that homecoming was not that their father had returned from a close brush with death, but that he had brought a monkey. They were delirious with joy. During the following months Bob McClure was known in the Glengrove area not as the missionary surgeon from China, but as the "monkey-man". And since the animal was clever at escaping and liked to take to the roof, where Bob would follow in his sock feet, the neighbours had frequent opportunity to observe the monkey-man in action.

This was McClure's first furlough since the study furlough

of 1930. It was supposed to follow the standard pattern of being half holiday and half deputation work. Since he was convalescing from a serious accident it seemed only logical that the holiday portion should come first. In letters to Amy, Bob had commented that he longed for nothing more than the privilege of "being a cabbage" for a time, and now was his chance.

He had a strange way of vegetating. It never occurred to him to refuse invitations to speak to various groups at Bloor Street Church, or to Toronto Rotary clubs, or to local schools. To him that was all merely friendliness, not deputation work. Deputation speaking was where one had to travel away from home. He talked informally about China, her war effort, the International Red Cross, mission work before the war, and about the new challenge he saw for missions in south-west China. He also kept close contact with Walter Judd, an American missionary who had returned from China, had been elected to Congress, and was now active in the 'China lobby' in the States. Judd and his friends were trying to stop the export of strategic materials from North America to Japan. They provided McClure with interesting figures on Canada's shipments of scrap iron, steel, and nickel. Armed with this information McClure stopped being informal and fired public salvoes at the Liberal government of Mackenzie King. He prophesied that Canadians were not going to like it when the nickel they were now shipping to Japan would eventually have to be dug out of the bodies of Canadian soldiers.

It was difficult to get his countrymen in Canada to get worked up about the war in China. Everybody's attention was focused across the Atlantic. It seemed that Bob had no sooner arrived home than the "phoney war" period in Europe had ended. Just as he arrived in Toronto the Germans hurled themselves upon Norway. While he was settling in and beginning to make his first public appearances on behalf of his beleaguered brothers in China, the Nazi armies were overrunning Holland and Belgium. While McClure was beginning his protestations that Canadian nickel would soon be fired from Japanese guns aimed at Canadians, the Allies were in the trauma of the Dunkirk evacuation. While Bob described Japanese bombing tactics, and urged more generous relief for China, Hitler's minions were marching down the Champs Elysée in Paris. France fell and Canadian boys were among the sons of the Empire who were rallying in England for a last ditch stand against an all-too-probable Nazi invasion of Britain. Very few people were thinking of China—even though Japanese warships arrived like vultures in French Indo-China seaports demanding the right to land troops.

By now, all Bob knew about his own future was that when furlough was finished he would return to China. He had no idea in what capacity. He decided to improve his personal assets by acquiring a new skill. McClure signed up for flying lessons.

The Toronto Flying Club had a contract to train, as pilots, Norwegians who had escaped from Norway. It seemed as though Hitler had invaded Norway and the Norwegians had invaded Toronto. They were all billeted on Toronto Island and most of them were being trained under R.C.A.F. auspices at the Toronto Island Airport. The Island establishment became affectionately known as "Little Norway". Those not being trained there were being trained by the Flying Club up at Downsview Airport just north of Toronto. The Club's contract permitted it to accept two civilians with each batch of trainees. Dr. Robert McClure, F.R.C.S. (Edin.) was accepted as one of them. While the Norwegians went into training in Toronto with their hearts in Europe, McClure donned the aviator's cap and goggles with his heart in China.

Bob had to pass a physical examination in order to qualify. That was a tense quarter hour, what with calisthenics, running on the spot, deep breathing and all the rest of it. When he passed the medical he knew that the episode of the fractured ribs was all behind him. It was just as well. Wartime pilot training included parachute jumping.

The day of his solo flight was, to that date, the second most exciting moment of McClure's life. The most exciting had been in Toronto in 1922, the day he learned he had graduated in medicine. But even graduating did not have the sheer exhilaration and glamour that flying had. The remembered joy of his first solo flight—of flying the required circuits and of making several quite respectable landings—was to remain with him for years. It was before the noisy pug-nosed Harvards and the sleek Cornells had taken over Canada's training skies. Bob was flying a bi-plane, a Tiger Moth, with no 'greenhouse' on top, just an open cockpit; it was helmet, goggles, and gung-ho all the way.

The day of McClure's first parachute jump was not as pleasurably memorable as the day of his first solo flight, but it had a certain claim to distinction in the face department. The students had been given some ground training. They had learned how to pack their parachutes, and it was impressed upon them that the parachute with which they jumped would be the parachute they themselves had packed. The drill for the actual jump was simple. A batch of them were to go aloft in a DC 3 and, on order, would step out of the side door, one after the other. There would be no safety cord and each man would simply release his own chute by pulling the metal ring attached to the release cord. It was only necessary to pull the ring an inch or so but experience had shown that most students were so excited on their first jump that they would rip the ring right off and throw it away. There was a prize for any man who could report afterwards with the ring still attached, or even in his hand.

McClure decided that after all the varied experiences he had had—and being now at the ripe old age of thirty-nine—that he would give the boys a demonstration of sophisticated sang froid and retain the ring. The DC 3 lumbered up to its specified height, the door was opened, commands were barked, and the Norwegian boys tumbled out into the clear Ontario sky. Bob McClure tumbled with them. His parachute opened and his body absorbed the great surge of the harness with no more than the expected pain. He landed safely, somersaulted to a stop, and recovered his chute. But he never found the ring. He could not even remember pulling it, let alone hanging onto it. Ming-yuan, who had faced bombs, bandits, pestilence, and warlords, joined the rest of the fellows in a cursory search of the field for any stray rings that might help save face at check-in time, but to no avail.

During the summer the British again closed the Burma Road, while engaged in further discussions with Japan, and they kept it closed until mid-October. In the meantime British garrisons were withdrawn from the International Settlement areas of Shanghai and other northern cities. While this was going on the Japanese were, in return, supposed to be talking peace with China. Instead, they occupied Indo-China, and struck upward into the southern underbelly of Free China. Japan then joined with Italy and Germany in a friendly treaty "for the creation of conditions which would promote the prosperity of their peoples". The British were involved by this time in fighting the Battle of Britain, but the Americans seemed to get a message from Japanese activities because they placed an embargo on the export of iron and steel scrap to all countries (with the exception of Great Britain) outside the Western Hemisphere. The Japanese considered this American embargo to be "an unfriendly act". However, according to McClure's contacts, the friendly Canadians were still permitting their nickel to find its way to Japan. McClure was enraged at Canada and continued to sound off.

Early in December he made his charges in a speech in Toronto. He was called to Ottawa to explain himself.

It was Saturday morning, December 7, 1940, when McClure made his way onto Parliament Hill in Ottawa, and through the portals of the East Block. The beautiful old East Block building housed the Prime Minister's Office and the Department of External Affairs. McClure's appointment was with O.D. Skelton, the highly respected Under-secretary of State for External Affairs, and with Skelton's right-hand man, Norman Robertson. Many years later McClure described that meeting, and it appears to have gone like this:

The meeting began affably enough. Skelton was courteous, and appreciative of McClure's willingness to come to Ottawa. After the opening affabilities Skelton withdrew, leaving Robertson and McClure to lock horns.

Norman Robertson was a senior civil servant—so senior that within two months time he would succeed O.D. Skelton as Under-secretary of State. Robertson's colleague in the Department, Mike Pearson, considered him to be "erudite and wise".* Bob and Norman had met several times, through the Masseys, because of their common interest in the Institute of Pacific Relations. But any friendship there may have been between the two men was now about to dissolve.

McClure's position had been spelled out by him in a telegram to Skelton on December 5th: "I believe it would be in the best interest of Canada and the Empire if you would unequivocally state that in addition to no permits being granted for the direct export from Canada to Japan of nickel that every precau-

*Mike The Memoirs of Lester B. Pearson, Volume 1

tion has been taken to ensure that no Canadian nickel, in any form whatsoever, is finding its way, even circuitously, to Japan . . ." McClure's information indicated that Canadian nickel *was* taking the "circuitous route" and was being trans-shipped from other countries.

Robertson denied the allegation completely. He was, according to McClure, adamant and hostile. After a lengthy and somewhat heated discussion, Robertson ushered McClure in for a brief confrontation with Prime Minister Mackenzie King.

In contrast to Robertson, the Prime Minister did not deny McClure's allegations. On the contrary, he asked McClure how much Canadian strategic material he thought was being exported in the general direction of Japan.

McClure told him.

The Prime Minister did not deny it. He tugged a moment at his forelock, slipped his round dark-rimmed glasses on, then took them off again, and looked at McClure.

"Ten times that amount would be more accurate," said Mr. King. He followed the statement with a question. "Dr. McClure, have you heard of the Defence of Canada Regulations? Or the War Measures Act?"

McClure had heard of them.

"Well then, Doctor, I recommend that you cease these public statements about the trans-shipment of materials to Japan. You have, of course, a choice. I don't want to coerce you in any way."

"A choice, Prime Minister?"

"You can make a public apology for your error, or go to jail."

There was no doubt in McClure's mind that his "error" as the Prime Minister saw it, was not in the essence of his information, but in his public airing of that same information.

Bob looked at the roly-poly, oily politician in front of him, and thought he had never seen anything so spineless in his life. He compared him in his mind's eye to the dignified Chiang Kai-shek who, for all his ruthlessness, McClure considered to be a man of great personal courage and integrity. There was a flaw in the McClure character which made him intemperate in his dislikes. When he despised a man, which was rarely, he despised him thoroughly. He realized now just how completely he despised Mackenzie King.

The meeting with the Prime Minister was over. It had been of such little importance to Mr. King that he made no reference to it in his diary. It was, however, of great importance to Bob McClure.

The meeting with Norman Robertson continued. Bob could hardly bring himself to speak to him. King was at least a politician working at the politician's trade but Robertson, as a senior civil servant, was supposed to be above the muck of the moment. But here he was acting as a political 'yes-man' to Mackenzie King. Worse. He had denied what King had admitted. McClure went into a slow burn that remained with him. Talking about it thirty-six years later there was still anger in his voice: "I was disgusted to see a man of Norman Robertson's achievements prostitute himself in doing a lackey job for Mackenzie King. I was really disgusted, nauseated. I'm afraid it's one of the things I don't excuse, a gutless, gutless political lackey."

Regardless of what he thought of the principal players, McClure had been given two clear alternatives by the Prime Minister. Apologize or go to jail. Bob's principal goal was to assist China. He could be of no help to China in jail. A secondary objective was to keep Canadian nickel and steel out of the bodies of Canadian soldiers, but that was trying to protect people against themselves—a thankless chore.

McClure decided to make the required apology. He and Robertson settled down to write a press release acceptable to both of them—an almost impossible task. However, at 1:15 that Saturday afternoon McClure issued a written statement to the Canadian Press: ". . . I am now satisfied that the Canadian government is taking every possible precaution to prevent Canadian nickel reaching Japan . . . I am, therefore, desirous of expressing my apology to the Prime Minister and his Government . . . I do not agree with the Prime Minister that an apology from me is owing the British government or other governments of the British Commonwealth of Nations . . ."

In Robertson's opinion, McClure was "less than candid in his efforts to wiggle out of a complete recantation".* In McClure's own opinion, he had gone too far. He was plunged into temporary despondency.

---

*Stated in a memo to the Prime Minister.

McClure's disposition was not helped by the appearance of an editorial in the Ottawa Journal. Bob assumed that it was written by the editor, Gratton O'Leary. The editorial, referring to McClure's initial charges, said: "This sort of criticism, hearsay tittle-tattle, Pullman smoker stuff, broadcast to the nation by supposedly responsible people, is bad enough at anytime. It is vicious in wartime. We are not sure it should not be punished . . . It is precisely the sort of talk that serves the purpose of Hitler."

The next day, as a follow-up to Bob's press release, the same paper launched another editorial attack: "People who go about in wartime mouthing irresponsible charges . . . are as dangerous as Fifth Columnists. They are especially dangerous when they carry with them such high-sounding titles as 'international Red Cross director for China' . . . There should be no patience with gossip-mongers and notoriety seekers who neither know nor take the trouble to find out what they are talking about."

Bob McClure contemplated changing his citizenship. If his Canada had come to the point where it was dominated by such men, then it was just possible he had better give up on the whole country and put his citizenship elsewhere. He debated with himself as to what his choice should be; the United States or Britain? As his anger subsided he reflected, sadly, that none of them were pure—he may as well stick with the corruption that was native. "Canada and China," he thought, "what a pair of homelands!"

January, 1941, brought the end of the first half of furlough. Deputation work began in earnest. But once again the United Church refrained from monopolizing the colourful McClure personality on behalf of its own mission enterprises. Instead, the church kept him on full salary but again loaned him to the International Red Cross to help raise funds for China Relief.

McClure rather enjoyed platform speaking. He was developing a style that would stay with him through the years. It was a somewhat unorthodox combination of an easy-going attitude and a staccato delivery. He liked anecdotes and believed that a good story would get a point across better than a lecture. He never had been above embellishing an incident because he knew, with the instincts of the true raconteur, that exaggeration often revealed the truth. He did not like the stereotype image of the pious missionary, and would sometimes over-compensate with a statement or phrase just a little too grossly forthright. To most North American audiences that was more of an asset than a liability.

McClure knew China, loved China, sympathized with her entire twentieth century struggle, and cared passionately about her survival. During the first few months of 1941 he carried his plea for China Relief down to Buffalo, Washington, Miami, Fort Myers, St. Petersburgh, Tallahassee, Philadelphia, New York, Albany, Richmond and points in between.

The speaking engagement that made him the most nervous was at a special Anglican dinner. "It is with the most posh Anglican group here in New York," he explained to Amy, "and only the big bugs are attending. One has to be so careful in a bunch like that for the people here are scared green of anything that might be the least bit pink in what I say about China." It was an interesting problem because McClure had a great deal of respect for the Chinese Communists. He recognized their achievements and had little quarrel with their objectives. Many of their methods were bloody and ruthless but as one who had lived through the warlord era he was not inclined to pass judgement upon either the Communists or the Nationalists. If the Americans wanted to view it all in absolute terms of good and bad that was their problem. McClure was at that very time trying to formulate a plan whereby he might link up with Bruce Copland (who was now in West China) and go as a team into North Honan guerrilla country. That would look very pink indeed. However, the Anglican "big bugs" were more broad-minded than he thought. China Relief collected a thousand dollars that evening.

By the time McClure returned to Toronto in April the United Church was urging him to go to a small outpost station in the West China field with a poorly equipped hospital that had been running downhill for the past several years. It was not a place he wanted to take his family, but at least it offered some prospects of a return to rural medicine. He said if the Church would guarantee him some good X-ray equipment, and a power plant, he would consider going in for a maximum two year period. But the prospect did not fill him with joy. Before accepting, he made one last all-out attempt to sell the Foreign Mission Board on the idea of him linking up with Bruce and moving into guerrilla country. He was convinced that a mobile team headed by Copland and McClure, one carrying on teaching and evangelical work and the other concentrating on surgery and medicine, would make quite an impact. It was an audacious plan that captured the imagination of some of the younger people. There were others who were not necessarily old in age but, as Bob put it in a letter to Fred Osborn in Sheffield, they were "elderly in mind". The proposition was voted down as being not "safe".

McClure was not enraged, he was simply depressed. It had never occurred to him that being safe was one of the job specifications for a medical missionary. He was incapable of understanding that those voting him down might also have been motivated by a feeling that Bob McClure had already done more than his share and that perhaps he should now be preserved, in spite of himself, for his family and friends.

The day his project was rejected was an abysmally low point for McClure. It looked as though he would have to go to that backwater on the West China field.

The very next morning a telegram arrived from England. It was from a Dr. H. Gordon Thompson, General Secretary of the British Fund for the Relief of Distress in China, which had grown out of the Lord Mayor's Fund, and was now co-operating with the International Red Cross Committee for Central China. The telegram asked Dr. McClure if he would consider going to China to take command of a Quaker outfit called the "Friends Ambulance Unit".

It was a quaint name but there was nothing quaint about the F.A.U's proposed area of operation. The Friends Ambulance Unit was headed for the Burma Road. It hoped to haul medical supplies, to transport wounded, and to provide mobile surgical teams. McClure could hardly believe the offer was genuine. It was too good to be true. He rushed to Philadelphia for a conference with the Society of Friends. The Quakers there assured him it was all quite true. He hurried back to Toronto and conferred with the United Church. He asked for, and was granted, leave of absence. McClure wired to England, accepting command of the FAU in China.

Before the end of June, 1941, Ming-yuan McClure was on his way back to China to take command of an ambulance unit completely staffed by pacifists. Ming-yuan thought of himself as a pacifist but it was reported that, when they heard the news, all the missionaries in China were convulsed with laughter. It would be a show worth watching.

As usual the United Church went the second mile with its untamed surgeon, and paid his passage back to China.

29

The China Convoy

Back in the days of World War I many an Allied soldier—gassed, mangled, wire-torn, broken, or psychologically dismembered—found himself being transported from front line aid station to base hospital in one of the high-wheeled, high-topped, ambulances that had become as much a part of the battle scene as had the artillery, trenches, and primitive tanks of the warring armies. Many soldiers owed their lives to the young unarmed madmen who piloted those ambulances around smoking shell craters, and through the artillery barrages that caused the craters. Few were the injured occupants who were concerned by the fact that the youth driving the truck was often a conscientious objector. Out there on the brink of hell it was abundantly clear that, although the driver might be determined not to kill for his country, he was obviously willing to die for his comrades.

Conscientious objectors came from a variety of ethnic, economic, and religious backgrounds, but a great many of them came from the religious organization called the Society of Friends, those people of friendly persuasion, known colloquially and with little accuracy as "Quakers". Many of the ambulances transporting wounded away from the front line carnage belonged to one organization, the Friends Ambulance Unit, known simply as the F.A.U. The F.A.U. was not an official arm of the Society of Friends nor was membership in it restricted to Quakers. Under British law a man who registered as a conscientious objector, and who was so accepted by his tribunal, could elect to serve in the F.A.U. During World War I the tribunal could also direct a conscientious objector to join the Unit.

With the outbreak of war in Europe in 1939 some British Quakers, who were F.A.U. alumni from World War I, managed to revive the Unit. A convoy of F.A.U. ambulances went to Finland, then to Norway, and many of its members were soon interned in Sweden. Back in England the organizers looked for new areas of service. Paradoxically, the Nazi blitz on London made them aware of China. China's cities had been bombed since 1937. McClure had seen the aftermath of the first raids on Chengchow in 1938 and by 1939 the Chinese were counting as many as 20,000 made homeless after one raid, with 3,000 wounded and 5,000 killed. But in 1940, after the Nazi bombers had winged repeatedly over London, out of the smoke and the ruins of China came a gift of relief money from the people of China to help the people of London. The organizers of the F.A.U. paused to think of China. The whole country was a battle front, with civilian and military medical needs often intertwined and indistinguishable. Any organization that hoped to be able to contribute to the alleviation of suffering, in the vast geographical expanses and amid the incredible confusion of China, would have to be highly mobile, very adaptable, and full of vitality. It was a prescription that could have been written for the F.A.U.

The most ardent supporter of the resurrected F.A.U. was Peter Tennant, the son of an affluent member of Parliament from Scotland. Tennant was a man who combined an easygoing charm, and somewhat aristocratic sophistication, with great enthusiasm, idealism, and drive. He became the chief recruiting officer, and was soon the leader of the F.A.U. "China Convoy".

Now, in World War II, the rules had changed. No longer was a tribunal able to direct a conscientious objector to join the F.A.U. This time around membership was completely voluntary. Almost incredibly, Tennant was swamped with volunteers. He whittled the British contingent down to a selected 40 members. All that was lacking was funding.

A member of the F.A.U. headed for the States to confer with the Friends Service Committee in Philadelphia. By this time there were seven American organizations co-operating in raising funds for China Relief and one of these groups was the American Friends Service Committee. The Friends conferred with their associates in this joint China Committee and all came to the same conclusion. The F.A.U. China Convoy could be, and should be, supported. But it lacked a leader who had China experience. The Committee conferred via telegram and letter with their opposites in England. The end result was the cable from Dr. H. G. Thompson to Dr. Bob McClure asking him to take command of the F.A.U. China Convoy.

When McClure accepted, he did not know about the other "commandant", Peter Tennant. Tennant was already on his way to China with a handful of the first contingent, and did not know about McClure.

When Bob left Canada in June, 1941, the opinion makers in Ottawa were still keeping their eyes firmly shut. "If Japan doesn't want war with the United States," pontificated the Ottawa Journal in response to rumours Japan was trying for a non-aggression pact with the U.S., "all it has to do is to act decently in the Orient". Since there had been no decent act by Japan since the Manchurian incident in 1931 the editorial's hope was optimism carried to the point of stupidity. The same paper, Conservative to the bone and usually keen to belabour the Liberal Government, was miffed by the fact that some Canadians objected to Canada still shipping wheat to Japan for use by its armies in China. "It is only the part of fairness that this wheat, contracted before permits were prohibited, should be shipped . . .", wrote Grattan O'Leary, or an editorial twin, "the amount of wheat involved can make very little difference to the Japanese or anybody else—the likelihood of it reaching Germany is remote."

Bob flew into Chungking from Hong Kong just as Peter Tennant flew in from Rangoon, and the wheat-fed Japanese pilots flew in from points east. For five days and nights, while McClure and Tennant tried to sort out their own positions with regard to each other, and the F.A.U. relationship with other agencies, the Japanese bombers came in squadrons. There were seventeen raids in those five days with one of them lasting more than eight hours. The world had marvelled at London and the Londoners but hardly knew of Chungking, by now probably the most-bombed city on earth. The Chinese were now so used to it, so adapted to dugouts, bomb shelters, and hillside refuge that, although property damage was almost total, the loss of life was incredibly low.

The political scene in Chungking had not improved. It was still difficult to understand who was co-operating with whom. It was almost impossible to get action out of the bureaucracy, and difficult to divert aid from the channels that led to private pockets into channels that led to the suffering populace. It was even more difficult when, in the midst of every meeting, one had to call for an abrupt adjournment and run for a bomb shelter. It was difficult to *find* agencies and offices in the first place. Many had decided it was more efficient to take permanent refuge on the slopes of the skirting hills.

And of course there were internal political problems for the new China Convoy—such as that little matter of just who was in command.

It would have taken a particularly obtuse man not to recognize in McClure a man with impressive qualifications for the leadership, and Tennant was far from obtuse. He knew, however, that not only was McClure not a Quaker he was not, strictly speaking, a conscientious objector. McClure had turned down no military draft and had been heard by no tribunal. He claimed to be a pacifist, and his missionary calling would have tended to support that claim, were it not for the large Colt .45 that seemed to be part of his wearing apparel. At this stage Tennant and his associates knew very little about the Burma Road, about bandits, opium-smoking soldiers, and other interesting features of the Chinese landscape. Their judgements had to be based solely upon what their eyes, and their intuition, told them. As for McClure, he was acutely aware of the fact that the volunteers now beginning to arrive in China and in Rangoon, Burma, had joined the China Convoy to serve under Peter Tennant. In his telegram of acceptance McClure had said he was willing "to command or assist". He had meant it. Fortunately Tennant and his fellows brought with them the Quaker tradition of democratic meetings based on open and frank discussion. The question of leadership was thrashed out in open forum. Dr. Bob McClure, F.R.C.S., was confirmed as Commandant of the China Convoy, with Peter Tennant as Second in Command.

One of Tennant's first tasks was to ask the Commandant,

politely, to put away the Colt .45. The Commandant was a little surprised to find that the sight of the hardware upset his men, but he complied willingly. The men assumed McClure had put the weapon into storage, but the man who *did* know about bandits and broadswords and straggling soldiers and all the rest of it sold his side-arm and quietly used the money to help two homeless children. For Bob it was the beginning of a post-graduate course in pacifism. He was to be taught by experts.

Many of the newcomers had already read Auden and Isherwood's book and had stumbled upon the description of McClure as having "the energy of a whirlwind and the high spirits of a sixteen-year-old boy". They were, perhaps, not unprepared. But McClure, even though he had associated with a cross-section of humanity, had never had to deal with any group quite like these young men who were now arriving on his doorstep. Some of them seemed more like Cambridge and Oxford dons than rough and ready frontiersmen ready to tackle the boondocks of China. Bob was alarmed by a certain arrogance, and a slight aristocratic tendency on the part of some to expect things to be done for them. He was also handicapped by the Scottish-Canadian's ingrained prejudice—a mistrust, bordering on a dislike, of the cultivated Englishman. Fortunately there were Scots and Welsh volunteers as well, and there were to be New Zealanders, Americans, Canadians and Chinese. In the meantime Bob held stern conversations with himself about prejudice—and remembered Donald Hankey.

The core of the China Convoy had arrived in Chungking and some of the men were soon establishing a depot in Kweiyang. The days and weeks dragged on waiting for word that the main body of the 40 had arrived in Rangoon, and while the days dragged so did the discussions concerning policy. Bob had never been exposed to anything like it. He had sat through meetings of Mission Council. He thought he had heard every non-practical idealistic idea that had ever been conceived, and every philosophical argument that had ever been devised to take the place of action. He decided now that no Mission Council could hold a candle to the boys of the F.A.U. Most of the hang-ups revolved around the fact that the men were conscientious objectors, and meant it. They would in no way assist to wage a war, but they would assist in every way possible to alleviate suffering. The crunch came in deciding what actions would do the one without doing the other. With which agencies could they co-operate, and with which would they not co-operate? Were they to provide medical services, as their name implied, or were they to haul relief supplies? If they hauled supplies what constituted "relief"? Was medicine and food for a wounded soldier the same as medicine and food for a civilian? Was there a problem in the fact that most "civilian" hospitals were in fact mission hospitals? All the discussions went on in the Quaker tradition, with no real chairman of the meeting, no Roberts Rules of procedure, no counting of hands or ballots in a final once-and-for-all vote to reach a decision. Instead, they groped through to a consensus that was felt rather than counted. McClure would take as much of this as he could and then would finally announce, "Let's cut the cackle!" It was an announcement that would usually bring silence, more often from shocked disbelief than from any feeling of acquiescence. "Let's cut the crackle!" was in danger of becoming a McClure slogan, and McClure was in danger of abandoning the F.A.U.

Bob escaped when he could to the operating room of The United Church of Canada's Chungking hospital on the south shore of the Yangtze. One day an air raid coincided with an emergency appendectomy. It was exhilarating. He confided to Amy: "That bit in an operating room almost started me off again. Combined with hours of conferences, and political yip-yap about our future work, it made me feel I wanted to chuck this and get back to some war surgery."

The political yip-yap, however, finally resulted in agreement. The first priority of the China Convoy would be the transportation of medical and other vital relief supplies. The Unit would have close liaison with the International Red Cross and with the Chinese Red Cross and British Red Cross Societies. They would also work closely with the New Life Movement, an organization not unlike the Y.M.C.A., that had been founded by the Generalissimo and his Lady back in the mid-thirties and was now active in front line relief and medical work.

No sooner was the F.A.U. role defined than McClure was hauled on the carpet by Generalissimo and Madame Chiang Kai-shek. He had seen the Lady from Hankow and her husband only occasionally during the two years since the government had moved from Hankow up river to Chungking. He had always found them friendly, although each time looking older and somehow wearier. But who was not? This time, however, they were angry. They were not angry with Loa Tai-fu, their old friend from Honan, nor with the Commandant of the China Convoy, but they were very angry with some of Loa Tai-fu's missionary associates.

"It has come to my attention," said the Generalissimo, "that many Christian missions are buying trucks abroad and bringing them in through Burma with Red Cross markings."

"I can understand that," said Dr. Loa. "Many missions do indeed co-operate with the Red Cross. I myself while Field Director for the I.R.C. tried to encourage that co-operation. We have talked of this before."

"That is true," admitted the Generalissimo, "but I am also informed many of those trucks as they cross the border carry what appears to be mainly mission supplies."

Dr. Loa was still not particularly impressed. "That is a problem of definition. A mission's main requirements are food, clothing and drugs. Those are also relief supplies."

"The real problem, Tai-fu," interrupted the Lady from Hankow, "is that by bringing those trucks in under Red Cross markings the missions pay no duty upon them, and not long afterwards they sell those trucks in China."

McClure got the message and suddenly he, too, was angry. Here, in this room, the Christian missions were losing incredible face. And then the Lady from Hankow inserted another knife.

"The biggest offender is your own West China Mission at Chengtu."

McClure was tempted to point out that he was not at the moment representing *any* mission—that he was commandant of a volunteer ambulance unit—that his men were, in fact, being eyed suspiciously by many missionaries because they had no conscientious objection to hard liquor, strong cigars, and pretty women. He refrained, however, and took the blast. It was not a pleasant session. After it was over, he saw to it that the word went out to the concerned parties that the Generalissimo and his Lady were not amused. Neither was McClure. He decided, however, that he could forgive the folk in Ottawa for not knowing there was a war on in China when some of his own people in Chengtu were still unaware of that fact.

He might have felt better had he known that about this same time the Ottawa Journal had suddenly become very hostile toward Japan. The hostility came after Japan finally committed a most indecent act. She froze all U.S. assets in Japanese territory. "Obviously," roared Ottawa's editorial lion, "this would-be colossus of the Pacific has to be stopped."

Bob fled down to his old stamping ground of Kweiyang where some of his men were establishing the nucleus of an F.A.U. hostel. Suddenly the atmosphere changed. In Kweiyang everybody was working and co-operating. Bill Mitchell was in great form with the I.R.C. transport going full bore. The charcoal trucks were working well and running at a tenth of the operating cost of conventional trucks. Many other organizations and companies were now using charcoal burners. Yang Yung-lo was considered to be the expert on the maintenance of some big Sentinel charcoal burners, the flagship trucks of the I.R.C.'s fleet. Yang Yung-lo and Loa Tai-fu had a good old chat about their struggles with the gas producing plant in Hwaiking away back in another era, in another world.

Bob stayed at first with the Evans brothers, a couple of cheerful Welshmen who were in the process of moving over from Bill Mitchell's I.R.C. unit to join Bob's China Convoy. They were establishing an F.A.U. hostel in an I.R.C. godown which had formerly been a temple. The resulting atmosphere was unique. Bob found it a cozy, truly communist style of life, not unlike that practised by groups of Christians in the first century. Everyone ate out of the common pot, as it were, and pooled all their pocket money. Even clothing was bought from the common pool.

Kweiyang in general seemed to have come to realistic terms with the war. The various organizations—mission, relief, and government—were all co-operating for the general good. The Province had brought in rigid alcohol prohibition and freed enough grain to feed 600,000 people. Even the Governor had gone dry. The price of grain had dropped 25 percent in the last month. Alcohol for motor fuel was cheaper now than when Bob had left. He was impressed, and pleased. Kweiyang was more like it.

Word came through that members of the Unit were arriving in Rangoon. Ambulances for the China Convoy were being unloaded on the Rangoon docks. McClure hitch-hiked to Rangoon.

The message about the trucks having arrived had been correct, but their clearance papers were not with them. While the red tape was being untangled, Bob assessed his new men. These were not the 'dons'. These were the craftsmen type and men of a mechanical bent. They were aliens in an alien land, but Bob liked them. They would shape up well, he thought, and took comfort from the knowledge there were more like them on the way. There were also two doctors with the group. Dr. Henry Louderbough, American, and Dr. Quentin Boyd, British. The plan, for the time being, was that Dr. Louderbough would join a New Life medical team in the interior and that Dr. Boyd would join the Canadian hospital in Chungking, for a period of three months. It would be a good break-in period for the doctors while the Unit got on with transport.

Transport was so much in demand that the Chinese Red Cross (C.R.C.) office in Rangoon was in a panic. They had just taken delivery of 20 new Studebaker trucks and were receiving frantic wires from Chungking saying they were desperately needed on the Changsha front, where a major battle of resistance was raging south of Hankow. But the C.R.C. in Rangoon had no drivers.

McClure undertook to get those trucks to Lashio, from where the Chinese could take over. It would be an excellent way to break the men in gently, not only to driving on Asian roads, but to Asian food, climate, and living conditions. He himself led the first convoy and everybody drove, including the doctors. It was a break-in all right. They had the usual trouble with the trucks, and everyone, including McClure, caught dengue fever. They shivered and sweated their way to Lashio, where they delivered the trucks, and hitch-hiked back to Rangoon. All the time McClure was telling them that the roads in Burma were A-1 compared to the roads in China.

In Rangoon, Bob ran into Dr. Dick Brown. Dick was in good health. He had been having almost as many adventures as had Bob. At the moment his wife and three children were in a Japanese occupied city on the east coast of China and Dick was hoping they might catch a ship for either Canada or Australia. It was all complicated by the fact that his wife was German. Dick himself was now in the British Army, in the Medical

Corps. He was refusing, however, to wear a uniform. He did not even own one. His Colonel was struggling manfully to be broad-minded, but was finding the sight of an un-uniformed colonial in the officer's mess almost too much to bear. Dick was being sent to Chungking to attend to the ailments of the British legation and hoped to be able to work at the Canadian hospital. Dick was depressed because he was very short of instruments, particularly eye instruments, and had just broken his ophthalmascope. Bob had some new instruments that had been given to him just before leaving home. He handed them over to Dick, leaving himself with nothing but a good blood pressure apparatus and a stethoscope. He felt naked.

The ambulances came out of customs. Each one was designed to carry ten stretchers. They were a uniform fleet all mounted on Chevrolet chassis with Chevrolet engines. They were beautiful. In addition to the ambulances there was a repair truck complete with a metal lathe, welding and valve grinding equipment, and other items designed to delight the heart of a motor mechanic. There were also two operating theatre trucks. They were a unit, one containing the generator, the sterilizer, lab equipment, and water supply. The other was the operating room itself, complete with table, overhead fluorescent shadowless light, X-ray, and other amenities that would have graced any hospital in China.

There was only one catch to the whole fleet. Every last one of the vehicles was six inches too wide to cross the bridges of the Burma Road.

McClure went into action. Soon he had convinced the British Army that they wanted the magnificent machines for Burma. He arranged to trade the twelve vehicles for twenty-four identical Chevrolet chassis, without bodies. He put his men to work stripping the equipment from the two O.R. trucks. The men were appalled. They had come out to join an ambulance unit and here was their new C.O. ordering all this desecration. They had only his word for it that the vehicles were no good for the Burma Road. They settled into the work, however, unaware of the fact that the sight of a contingent of white men all setting to in overalls was a unique experience for the Burmese.

McClure then tackled the industrial segment of Rangoon that built truck bodies. He found it was largely in the hands of

Chinese who spoke Amoy. He unleashed his Amoy from Taiwan days and soon had twenty-four new truck bodies in production. He then rallied his men and they headed out with another convoy of trucks for the Chinese Red Cross. This convoy they took as far as Kunming.

They came back from that trip with the men having survived the tropical heat of the Burmese lowlands and the icy cold of the Himalayas. They had slept in Chinese inns, and in the trucks, and under the trucks. They were becoming as hard as nails.

Back in Rangoon there were twenty-seven new volunteers waiting for them—along with the news of Pearl Harbour and the Japanese invasions of Singapore and Hong Kong. It was heart-rending news, but not one word of it was any surprise to McClure. He wrote to Amy: "Isn't it ironical that Canadian soldiers in Hong Kong got their first dose of Canadian nickel-coated bullets and propelled by powder made from Canadian cellulose just exactly, to the date, one year after I had been to Ottawa for talking on that subject! It gives one a chance to say 'I told you so'. One must not however. It is much too tragic for that."

It was more than tragic. The Canadian Government had agreed only recently to send two battalions of troops to help reinforce the Hong Kong garrison. There had apparently been some feeling among the Mackenzie King cabinet that it would be a worthwhile gesture. It would demonstrate Commonwealth solidarity, would deter Japan, and would encourage Chiang Kai-shek and his Chinese Nationalists. The two Canadian battalions, the Royal Rifles and the Winnipeg Grenadiers, had been trained without ammunition for mortars, anti-tank rifles, or machine carbines. Even their hand grenade practice had had to be carried out by throwing wooden dummies. The Canadians arrived in Hong Kong, almost two thousand of them, at the end of November, just in time to carry out Mackenzie King's political gesture by taking into their bodies those "nickel-coated bullets". McClure could have wept with frustration. Canadians, like the Chinese, seemed destined to suffer from the political follies of their own leaders.

With Hong Kong and Singapore under siege the pressure to get trucks and supplies out of Burma became enormous. The F.A.U. trucks were still being remodelled. In the meantime the

Chinese Red Cross had more trucks and supplies it wanted delivered. McClure threw all the new arrivals into the task. Before
they would finish they would get 200 trucks out of Burma for
the C.R.C.

McClure added to the F.A.U. fleet any way he could. A
mission wanted to ship in 16 tons of Bibles. McClure agreed to
handle them, *if* the mission would provide a truck. The drivers
assigned to shuttle that 16 tons protested that they had not
joined the F.A.U. to haul Bibles. But when the huge shipment
of the Word finally reached the end of the journey the men
found that what they had really been hauling was the *truck*.
McClure had made a deal with the mission that the F.A.U. was
to keep the medium in exchange for the safe arrival of the message.

Bob took time out between one of the shuttle trips to con-
fide in Amy: "I never associated with chaps who have more
mental vigour or more spiritual dynamic. There are one or two
among them—strange to say—who are not even Christians in
their views. They are all vigorous pacifists and it is very interesting indeed to see them trying to get things in order between
their ideals and their practical necessity."

More doctors arrived, including Handley Laycock, an
F.R.C.S. The doctors had never met anything in the medical or
surgical line quite like their new Commandant. They would
have been flattered if they had known that his intuition told
him there might well be several "Hankeys" among them.

On Christmas Day, 1941, while Bob was 'somewhere on
the Burma Road', Hong Kong surrendered to the Japanese.
More than 25 percent of the Canadian garrison troops would
never see home again, and even the China Convoy had suffered its first loss. Owen Evans had been in Hong Kong on
F.A.U. business and was trapped. He had not been killed but
was a prisoner of war.

In the meantime the F.A.U. members at the China base,
now centred in Kweiyang, had been getting more and more
restless. A lot of disillusionment had settled in. It had not taken
the intelligent minds of the China Convoy principals very long
to realize that the Chiang Kai-shek regime, which had been
sold so enthusiastically by the Western press as the champion
of Christian democracy, fell far short of the claims that were
being made for it. Some of the corruption around Chungking

was monumental. And life in China was not heroic. It was cruel and squalid. As for the China Convoy itself, strange things had been happening. Red Cross trucks had been flowing in from Burma but no China Convoy ambulances. They heard the ambulances had arrived and been dismembered. They heard all kinds of things. Bibles had arrived by the ton, as well as other assorted gear, some of it perilously close to being war material. The Commandant had been reported several times to be as close as Kunming, but had then vanished back along the Burma Road into some sort of Oriental limbo. Some of the members were still uneasy about diving whole-heartedly into a transport role, but the big worry was that *any* role might suddenly and arbitrarily be changed overnight. The Commandant was obviously willing to make decisions on his own. The democratic fervor that had continued to smoulder in the Unit now flared into full flame. They sent out a patrol, and snared McClure somewhere near Lashio. As it turned out, he was already en route for Kweiyang anyway.

The Quaker meeting that followed promised to be a verbal dust-up of major magnitude, so many were the grievances, both real and imagined, that had to be aired. McClure had a few grievances of his own, not the least of them being with the idea that any group of men could debate their way through the brutal realities of the present war. But it was all aired, every last shred of it, and the Quaker method triumphed. The China Convoy stuck with McClure and McClure stuck with the China Convoy, still as Commandant. An administration was set up with an Executive Committee empowered to act during Chairman McClure's absence. Some observers had maintained that a debating society of rather gentle people could never harness the 'whirlwind' but before long Bob was writing a letter to London: "There is a great desire in the Unit, easily understood, too, in a group of thinking men, for 'democratic control'. I'm all for it. I believe in it myself. It is a fine line indeed, however, dividing from 'lack of firm leadership'! It just cannot be had both ways. Now with the boys hard at work there is less discontent and in fact considerable control does have to be kept in the hands of a few people for the sake of efficiency. We seem to have struck a happy medium now."

Knowledgeable observers felt that if the members of the China Convoy had really managed to adjust to Bob McClure, and he to them, from here on a mere war in China should hold no terrors for any of them.

Japanese pressure on Burma increased and the fall of Rangoon appeared to be inevitable. Word came through that the F.A.U. trucks were almost ready for the road. Peter Tennant headed for Rangoon to take delivery, leaving McClure, who by now had driven the whole Burma Road twelve times, to come to grips with mundane administrative problems. There were 69 volunteers on hand now, with more to come. Their numbers would soon be augmented by Chinese volunteers (nurses, doctors, assistant drivers) and by paid Chinese staff (cooks, houseboys, and office staff). Before long there would be 83 F.A.U. members, 3 associates, and 60 employees. Administration could not be ignored.

The fighting in Burma, however, had altered the Unit's priorities. McClure began to organize two mobile surgical teams. Each team was to consist of an anaesthetist, a scrub nurse, an X-ray technician, an O.R. nurse, a mechanic, and a surgeon. All were male. All but the surgeons had to be trained. McClure was Chief Instructor.

In Rangoon, Peter Tennant and his men found the city almost deserted. They had made the whole journey in record time, travelling the final 606 miles from Lashio to Rangoon in 26 hours. The men already there had been putting in some feverish weeks. Every organization was trying to get everything it owned, that was useful and movable, out of Rangoon before the city fell. Soon after Tennant and his boys arrived, the city was cut off. It was declared "open", which meant that anybody could take anything. Instead of despairing, they raided the dockyard. They found Chevrolet trucks, partially broken down in packing cases. In two days they reassembled four new Chevrolet trucks to add to the fleet.

One of the lads, "Tiger" Rowlands from Bristol, liberated a huge Bedford Diesel truck from a dealer's showroom. Without breaking any law, he had the ineffable pleasure of driving the Bedford into the street straight through a plate glass window.

Tennant and his men loaded all their trucks with anything they could find resembling medical supplies, and headed for China. They were able to head for China because British tanks punched a narrow rescue corridor, just a few hundred yards wide, into Rangoon. Tennant and his men were among the last to squeeze through it.

During those last feverish weeks the F.A.U. greenhorns had not only taken all their trucks out of Rangoon, plus a few they commandeered, but they had loaded them with more than a half million dollars worth of supplies and had hauled 1,400 drums of gasoline to keep the China Convoy rolling. Even as they fled up the route to Lashio they paused to salvage parts and supplies from wrecked and abandoned trucks. The idealists were turning out to have a practical streak of as formidable dimensions as their courage. When word reached Kweiyang of the escape from Rangoon their Commandant almost burst with pride.

Tennant made it back to Kweiyang long enough to convince McClure that half the Unit should be sent to concentrate on work on the 'front' in northern Burma. Tennant left for Lashio and Bob had a row with a dyseptic Bill Mitchell who felt the trucks would have been more useful hauling for the I.R.C.

Bob was worrying about Bill these days. Mitchell's nerves finally seemed to be getting the better of him. Bill's language and manner had become quite sulphurous and the I.R.C. office staff was threatening to quit en masse. Fortunately Bill was showing signs of taking furlough.

On April 20th, 1942, the Japanese captured Lashio, cutting the Burma Road. Tennant and his men were caught up in General Stilwell's famous retreat to Imphal, India. They lost eleven trucks, but Tennant and six other F.A.U. men entered history as part of the indomitable group of 114 people who walked out of Burma with Stilwell through the swamps, jungles, and mountains that divided Burma from India. An important part of that group was the American Baptist doctor, Gordon Seagrave, and his Burmese nurses. Dr. Seagrave was impressed by the F.A.U. men, who could pick up blood-drenched patients as though they were "sweet and lovely", and he wrote about them with admiration and affection.

Not only had the F.A.U. China Convoy been cut in half, the Burma Road had been closed, this time by the Japanese fist rather than the British political finger. Free China was completely cut off. Her only connection with the rest of the world lay by air over "the Hump", that stretch of the Himalayas that lay between Assam in India, and Kunming in China. It was an air route that was said to lead through "stuffed clouds". As many a pilot would soon find out, they were stuffed with granite.

In Kweiyang, McClure was temporarily tied to the area by administrative commitments. He was reading reports, and writing reports. It was driving him wild.

One of the reports came from a Hong Kong escapee. He reported that the F.A.U's Owen Evans, by some miracle, had managed to get himself assigned to the job of driving a rice truck to prison camps. He had been offered an opportunity to escape and had turned it down on the grounds that he could be of service right where he was. And then word came in from India that Dr. Handley Laycock, the English F.R.C.S. who had been off on the Burma campaign with Tennant, had written a private codicil to the whole incredible retreat to India. He had turned up in Imphal, India, still driving one of the F.A.U. Chevrolet trucks! The British engineers went and checked the area he had emerged from but there was no road. It is said that to this day no one knows how Laycock drove from Lashio to Imphal.

It all only served to remind McClure once more of the fact that he was in charge of a remarkable group of men. Not that he needed reminding. Not long after the first forty volunteers had arrived, McClure had been approached by the Reader's Digest to write one of their "Most Unforgettable Character" articles. Even then the men thought the Reader's Digest had made a mistake—the article should surely be *about* McClure. And even then McClure's response to the Digest people had been, "I can write you an article about *forty* of the most unforgettable characters I've ever met". Bob had solved the problem by writing about Donald Hankey. But away off in London and Ottawa some people had indeed been writing about McClure—privately.

On February 11, 1942, a coded telegram was dispatched from the London office of the High Commissioner for Canada in Great Britain, Vincent Massey. It was addressed to the Under-secretary of State for External Affairs in Ottawa, Norman Robertson.

"I do not know whether any decision has been arrived at as regards selection of Canadian Minister to China," cabled Mr.

Massey. "If not, it occurs to me that consideration might be given to Dr. Robert McClure." His Excellency the High Commissioner went on to enumerate McClure's many qualifications, including the fact that he was a personal friend of the Generalissimo and Madame Chiang Kai-shek, and ended by affirming Mr. Massey's own personal acquaintance with McClure.

When the Under-secretary replied to that telegram he referred to the year-old confrontation: "McClure's experience and Chinese connections should make him a useful man, but unfortunately his only previous contact with the Department was a thoroughly unsatisfactory business. . . personal impression left on us by incident was disappointing and at variance with impression of McClure held by his many friends and admirers."

Robertson sent a memorandum to Prime Minister King, enclosing Mr. Massey's cable and his own reply. The memorandum came back carrying a scribbled comment in Mackenzie King's handwriting and initialled by him. The comment was short and to the point.

"I wouldn't consider him."

The F.A.U. men were right. McClure was indeed an unforgettable character.

30

Precious Mountain

Militarily those first six months of 1942 had been almost universally depressing. Not only had Hong Kong fallen and the British and Chinese armies been driven out of Burma, but the Philippines had fallen, the Battle of the Java Sea had been disastrous for the Allies, and Java had fallen along with most of the Netherlands East Indies. By June the Japanese were landing on the Aleutian Islands. Their appearance in the Aleutians, the back doorstep of America, was sparking the frantic construction of the Alaska Highway, North America's version of the Burma Road, but that was of small comfort to anyone in the summer of '42.

There had been two boosts to Allied morale. One was the Battle of the Coral Sea, which for the time being appeared to have kept the Japanese out of Australia. The other was a Nationalist victory in the Province of Kiangsi, which at least served to remind the Chinese that they could cope with the Japanese when they put their minds to it.

A big problem on the China scene appeared to be that the Chinese were having great difficulty deciding *where* to put their minds. Some Westerners were getting the distinct impression that the Generalissimo was reluctant to fight an Oriental enemy who was also fighting the Western 'barbarians'. Or was it that he did not wish to exhaust his Nationalist forces now, when they would still have to take care of the Communists later on? Much the same state of mind seemed to apply to the Chinese Communists. In fact, back in 1937, Mao Tse-tung had analysed the party's prospects and had decided that whether the Nationalists should win, draw, or lose in the coming war, the Communists would stand to gain. Part of his premise was based upon the assumption that the Nationalists would be exhausted—the obvious corollary being that the Communists would have to take care not to become exhausted themselves. The Generalissimo was astute enough to come to the same conclusion. It seemed all too evident that he had no intention of becoming exhausted. He also had very little intention of letting much American lend-lease material get into Communist hands. He was virtually blockading the Eighth Route Army in Shensi. Now, in '42, the Nationalist-Communist united front had all but crumbled. On the other hand, the British and Americans, who were now firmly enmeshed in all this, had to encourage the Chinese to keep going—if only to divert Japanese strength from more interesting targets such as Australia, India, and the underbelly of Russia. The politics of the war in China was thus becoming enough to drive rational men mad. It was fortunate for the men of the F.A.U. that they were dedicated to the relief of suffering, regardless of who was doing what to whom. As for McClure, although he could be thrown into a rage by politics in Canada, he could take that of China in his stride.

Now, in July of 1942, the F.A.U.'s Kunming garage was happily putting Diesel engines into two Ford trucks and the Kutsing garage was converting Chevrolets to charcoal. The men were becoming quite sentimental over the tempermental charcoal burners and the China Convoy, with the highest percentage of non-gasoline vehicles, was already considered to be one of the most efficient transport units in the country. The Burma Road was closed but supplies were being air-lifted from India, over the Himalayan Hump, and into Kunming and Chunking. The F.A.U. was trucking airlifted medical supplies to hospitals as far north as Sian and as far east as the guerrilla country around Shanghai. But all this was not really what McClure had come to China for. He had wound up with the trucking business on the previous stint. The men themselves were unhappy with too heavy an involvement in transport. The most restless of all was their Commandant. When Peter Tennant flew in from India early in July McClure almost erupted out into the field.

He headed for the 'front', for Paoshan, "Precious Mountain".

After capturing Burma, the Japanese had followed up their

triumph by thrusting into China along the Burma Road. They penetrated as far as the Salween River where the Chinese, assisted by British and American special combat groups, managed to hold them. The Japanese spread out through several hundreds of square miles of jungle and mountain on either side of the road, but never managed to cross the Salween in force. Much farther south, where the Salween was well inside Burma, the Japanese penetrated to the Mekong River. Both these remote jungle fronts became scenes of intense activity for China Convoy mobile surgical units.

On the Free China side of the Salween, the road climbed steeply to the mountain town of Paoshan. Bob remembered it as the first genuine Chinese community that he and the Bishop had encountered on their journey after the Madras Conference. Now the city itself was in ruins, the walls rubble, and much of the housing destroyed. Japanese 'planes, flying from a base that was only ten minutes away by air, had been able to do their task thoroughly and at leisure. Outside Paoshan, and nestled in a valley, was a small airfield big enough for reconnaisance 'planes and not much more. Here, too, was a Chinese military hospital, and the headquarters for the Chinese division that was holding the Salween front. McClure had dispatched two surgical units to this area several weeks before. He found his men cozily entrenched in a couple of recently built structures in a sheltering valley about 2 miles from town.

The two surgical teams were headed by the American doctor, "Hank" Louderbough, and by Dr. Terry Darling, an enormously tall and disarmingly youthful Irishman. The head nurse, to begin with, was a young Englishman who had joined the F.A.U. at the age of seventeen. He had gone to Finland with that ill-fated convoy. He had escaped from Europe in time to work in the London blitz before volunteering for the China Convoy. His name was Michael Harris, and he doubled in brass as the business manager.

The Precious Mountain surgical teams were attached to the Chinese army's Seventy-first Field Hospital. All Chinese military hospitals had one thing in common—squalor. It was common to find a military hospital with as many as 1,500 beds, all full, and no surgeon to remove bullets or to set fractures, no X-ray machine, no drugs, no plaster of paris for casts. Often the only treatment patients received was to have their dressings changed periodically. A great majority of patients were chronic cases, still carrying shrapnel and suffering from un-healed wounds that were often more than two years old. The Seventy-first Field Hospital was no exception.

Drs. Louderbough and Darling had set up shop following a drill laid down by McClure. They took charge of forty beds as a surgical ward and established their own O.R. Then, using their own supervised forty beds as an intensive care unit, the two surgeons tried to catch up on the backlog of surgery. (McClure calculated that each six-man team should be able to average six operations per day.) Any member of the team who was not actually busy full time in the O.R. occupied himself im-proving the hospital's housing, water system, electrical sys-tem, and latrines.

The Chinese Red Cross had two medical teams functioning in the Precious Mountain area, and the New Life Movement had a medical team that also did light surgery. The New Life surgeon was Dr. Wesley May, a Chinese educated at John Hopkins in the States. The medical men had their hands full with cholera, small-pox, dysentery, malaria, meningitis and typhus. During the rainy season as many as 70 percent of the troops could be out of action with disease. The F.A.U. teams did medical work as conditions dictated, but their prime func-tion was heavy surgery. Just as mission hospitals had done for years up in North Honan, F.A.U. teams saved their really heavy surgery for McClure.

McClure did three operations the first day he was at Pao-shan, and then the pace picked up. The three doctors and the two teams worked at an intense pitch to catch up on the accu-mulated cases.

Soon the rainy season was upon them, and Hank Louder-bough and McClure went on a survey trip down through the jungles of the Salween gorge to see what problems the guerril-las were having. They found, not unexpectedly, malaria, dys-entery, trachoma, beri-beri, scabies, and a woeful lack of knowledge on the part of the so-called medical corpsmen. Tra-choma was a surgical problem, but the others were more a mat-ter of proper diet and of protection from fleas, lice, mosquitoes and contaminated drinking water. Hank and Bob came back and launched a series of lectures for medical corpsmen. One third of the entire Chinese medical military staff from the entire front was brought in for a one month exposure to higher learning. The other two thirds would come later.

Bob and Hank also came back to find that Dr. Terry Darling had been making a name for himself while they were gone. An officer had come in with his thigh bone shattered by a machine gun bullet. These fractured femurs were always a problem. A bullet, or a tiny piece of shrapnel from a landmine, travelled at such high velocity that when it hit bone the bone would shatter, for an area of two inches or so, into nothing much more than powder. Since a soldier is usually a muscular man, the muscles pull the bone ends to overlap by several inches. It was nothing for such a wound to leave a man with one leg permanently three inches shorter than the other, along with the tilted pelvis and all the other complications that went with it. This particular victim reached Terry Darling's O.R. table within twenty-four hours of receiving his wound, which gave the doctor a chance to fight infection. He had lost almost two inches of bone, completely shot away. Terry had cleaned the mess up and had installed a Stienmanns pin that the F.A.U. mechanic made for him in the local shop. By the time Bob and Hank were back from the Salween survey, Terry had the leg in a Hwaiking bicycle spoke traction with no sign of infection. It was already apparent that not only had the leg been saved, but the patient would come out of it without so much as a half inch difference in length between limbs. Chinese officers had been in to inspect Terry's handiwork. The word had gone out that if the junior surgeon of a team was this good then how good the seniors must be! Young Dr. Darling had gained enough face to match his six foot three inch frame and Dr. McClure was very proud of him. In the weeks and months that followed, the teams proved that the acquisition of face had been no accident. Their reputation spread. People began carting in fractured femurs from far down the Burma Road. Patients who had the choice, would have themselves taken 200 miles to Paoshan instead of 100 miles to one of the many hospitals in Kunming. At one time the Paoshan F.A.U. ward overflowed to seventy-two beds of fractured femurs.

McClure was at Precious Mountain for a full six weeks, while the two surgical units became fully established, and while he and Hank Louderbough and Dr. May from the New Life team put the first batch of medical corpsmen through their one month course. Bob enjoyed teaching this group. As budding anaesthetists they were, in his own words, "a menace to the nation", but they reminded him of Chou Teh-kwei and the other men who had been through the Hwaiking system. Even at Hwaiking he had had to defend the patients with alacrity, having once had to do three resuscitations in one day in the wake of an enthusiastic student. Now, face to face with these men drawn in from all along the Sino-Burmese front, he drew upon the wealth of experience accumulated in those few short years while he was establishing the Hwaiking Rural Medical System. He wrote to Amy about it with his customary candor: "That stuff we did at Hwaiking did not seem very important at the time, but it is the very dope for this work now, I tell you. Say what you will, I suppose that work for what seems like such a short time in Hwaiking was the most constructive bit of medical work I shall ever have a chance to do." At the same time he knew he could not capitalize for ever on past achievements: "When this blinking war is over it will be very late to start on a new type of work and yet much of what we did before will have become so out of date." But he spent little time worrying about the future, there was quite enough happening in the present.

The Precious Mountain military hospital was built to look like a Chinese village. The wards were small huts with thatched roofs. They were clustered around a typical open village square that doubled in harvest season as a threshing floor. In order to create an air of authenticity animals were kept around—goats, pigs, and even a water buffalo called "Daisy". It was a typical set-up for Chinese wartime hospitals. Here at Precious Mountain, with the 'village' sheltering in a tree-cloaked valley within a ring of protective hills, the ruse was very successful. 'Village' life was suitably spartan. The F.A.U. men ate the basic 20 oz. daily rice diet of the soldiers, but encouraged their tribal cook to supplement it with whatever her native ingenuity suggested. They slept on boards with no mattresses of any kind. The latrine was an open air affair with a flimsy wall, with a space between it and the roof. The walls were built to Chinese specifications, which posed problems for towering Terry Darling. Daisy the water buffalo used the latrine one day, and found it something like a lobster trap—easy to enter and impossible to leave. To extract Daisy the F.A.U.

had to take hammer and saw and do a Caesarian on the latrine. It was a surgical 'first'.

The unit's O.R. was in a building which nestled into a bay carved into the hillside. A window, covered only with a cotton gauze screen, looked out into the naked earth. One day McClure was in the midst of a delicate operation when he thought the Japanese bombers had finally found him. The whole earth shook and the wall of the O.R. seemed to billow inward. There was a noise of roof tiles falling and of the heavens collapsing, and Bob came closer to being thrown off stride than he ever had been before. In spite of himself he raised his eyes from the patient for a quick glance at the window and saw Daisy's horns tangling in the gauze screen. Daisy had walked into some loosely stacked building materials up on the hillside and had fallen onto the O.R. That, too, was a surgical first.

At the other end of the surgical spectrum were several brain operations made necessary by bone being forced into the brain. McClure followed procedures that Dr. Wilder Penfield had been developing in Montreal, and which still were considered by many surgeons to be too radical and unorthodox. In each case McClure reported exceptionally good results.

The days and weeks went by in kaleidoscopic fashion. The teams rose at 6:30 a.m. Bob always shaved but most of the men were growing beards. They washed in cold well water, held silent grace before meals, went ward rounds, held seminars in everything from trachoma to ignition systems, spent hours in the O.R., went on salvage expeditions for parts to improve hospital facilities, and held regular X-ray sessions in the wards using the portable generator. They lived tense moments of O.R. drama, told bawdy stories in the mess, played bridge in the evening, and once a week would fire up the generator and burn precious gasoline for an even more precious fifteen minutes of listening as the American Armed Forces Radio Service broadcast news from home. In his scraps of spare time McClure was writing letters, and reading Tolstoy's essays on *Life and Religion,* which he found "good stuff". He was also reading Tolstoy's *Anna Karenina.* Bob enjoyed every minute of every hour.

When the day came to wind up the final session with the first batch of medical corpsmen, McClure was deeply touched by an unexpected speech. It happened at the end of the final seminar when the routine question was put, "Have you any more questions?" One of the young men rose, not to ask a question, but to make a speech. He was a political activist sent in from one of the co-operating guerrilla units. Until now he had had almost no contact with Westerners of any kind, nor even with Chinese Christians like Dr. May. The young man's speech was more like a harangue and it was not aimed at the teachers but at his own group. McClure found it almost startling in its forthright candour.

"Comrades," so started the speech, "we have been given a lot of teaching, much of which is over our heads." (That was true enough.) "We have heard all along of many places where the front-line medical men have fallen down on the job." (That, too, was quite true. It was one of the reasons for getting them in here.) "We have seen what can be done when the front-line men and the back men all do their work properly." (That was good news, but Bob wished the young fellow would moderate his tone somewhat. He was using a very stormy voice.) "As for many of these things we have heard about, these are not new to us! We have not heard a single new thing really!" (Bob, with memories in the back of his mind of Gushue-Taylor and of the female examiner at Edinburgh, had to admire the kid's guts, but was not happy at what sounded like the demolition of a month's hard teaching.) "The trouble was that we knew it, but did not put it into practice! Comrades, we do not so much need new knowledge to go back to our work, neither is it necessary to carry back many new patent medicines. You know as well as I do that what we need to take back to make the difference is the spirit of these teachers of ours who are Christians. If we did dressings ourselves and saw the cases more regularly instead of leaving it to our subordinates—if we really had the Christian spirit of service—we could get these results. We could save this suffering. We could save all this waste of manpower and medicines. Let us resolve right here, at our last clinical conference, to take back this essential spirit of service!"

The young Chinese guerrilla medic from the fever-ridden jungles of the Salween gorge had put his finger on something that McClure had long suspected—that it was more effective to live the spirit of Christianity than it was to preach the doctrine of it.

Living the spirit of Christianity was not easy. Off near

Kweiyang two of the China Convoy men were walking to fill water buckets to replenish the truck radiator, when they were confronted by a group of men. They brazened it out and walked through the group, only to hear the sudden rush of bare feet from behind. They turned to find themselves the object of a sword attack, which they fended off as well as they could with the water buckets. The attack left one of the men, Tom Thompson (who had hoped to become a physical education instructor), with his left arm badly carved up, both bones of the forearm broken and the ulna nerves severed beyond repair. The wound reminded Bob of the descriptions of the Boxer wound suffered in 1900 by Bruce Copland's uncle, Dr. Percy Leslie. The question was immediately raised as to whether the China Convoy men should start carrying guns, but was dropped after a discussion in which the victims both spoke against it. In the months that followed, Thompson underwent several operations, with the Commandant himself trying to effect some repairs. During this time the bandits' trial came up. Thompson took a three day journey in order to attend that trial. He entered his plea that the guilty men should not be executed.

In Kutsing there had been a chronic problem of parts being stolen from the F.A.U. garage, and a wall had been built around the garage enclosure. They had even hired night watchmen, but the thefts had continued. Finally the authorities had the watchmen jailed for assisting the thieves. But the F.A.U. men depleted their precious pocket money 'pool' to send extra food to the incarcerated watchmen. "That is inconsistent as anything," Bob wrote to Amy, "but so help me, it is more Christlike than any behaviour I have seen before in China. I do think now that to live a Christlike life in these times is a much rougher road than many of our Christians at home realize."

One of the Convoy men, John Briggs, had written of a concern that was troubling most of them. It was the problem of the straggling soldier left to die by the roadside. Most of the drivers had pathetic stories of trying to pick up dying men and of being politely but firmly prevented by officers, on the grounds, often very true, that there was nowhere the men could be taken. The F.A.U. men established a small sick bay of their own at Kutsing in order to accommodate at least a few such victims. The number they could help was miniscule, but at least it provided a training ground for new F.A.U. members. But what really moved McClure was the fact that when John Briggs was writing of this shared concern, Briggs himself was dying of typhus fever. He was the first member of the China Convoy to die.

Living the Christlike life was a trial-by-fire for most of them. Not only were they pacifists in the midst of a rapidly deteriorating society in which violence on the civil scene was escalating, but they were functioning close to the lines of actual combat and were becoming more and more aware of the nature of the Japanese enemy. Every now and then one of the boys would decide to pack it in and go 'active' by joining the R.A.F. or the British Army or the American Forces. Not many did so, but enough to make all the rest of them re-assess their own positions. McClure never seriously entertained the thought of joining the military. He felt he was more useful with the F.A.U. than he would be with a military medical unit. He quite frankly admitted that no one would really think of putting a rifle into a surgeon's hands and telling him to enter combat. Even so, he was finally provoked to the point of unarmed combat, but it was a Chinese bandit who did it, and not the Japanese.

It was on the road in the mountains near Paoshan. McClure, Dr. Wesley May, and a high ranking Chinese army officer were rounding a corner in a truck when they were stopped by a small group of 'soldier-bandits'. Bob pulled the truck to a halt and climbed out. They were on the edge of a typical chasm, an easy place for an illegal roadblock. It might have been another one of the usual verbal conflicts, if one of the ruffians had not come forward and ostentatiously loaded his rifle (which was already complete with bayonet) and aimed it at McClure. Bob had had loaded rifles aimed at him before, but they had always been in the hands of sentries, sometimes Japanese, who were doing their duty. There was something about it this time, however, that was too much for the fledgling pacifist's patience. It may have been the bayonet that was the last straw to the surgeon because, in a strangely irrational move, McClure seized the rifle, tore the bayonet off it, and sent the blade whirling into the canyon. The owner objected. The disarmament conference proceeded for a few moments with fists, after which McClure emptied the shells from the rifle and removed the bolt. It all happened very quickly but by this time the other bandits were loading their rifles and Dr. May and the officer were climbing from the truck. The sight of high ranking Chinese military insignia turned the scales, and the bandits backed off from further opposition. McClure, perhaps in memory of Loving Lotus, returned the empty rifle. Those men were fortunate that they had stopped a pacifist. The next truck along had armed American soldiers in the cab who were accustomed to deal with armed opposition just as swiftly, but on a more permanent basis.

McClure was in and out of the Precious Mountain area many times. His sojourns varied from swift visits to lengthy surgical sessions. The length of stay depended primarily on the amount of action in the Salween combat zone. If there was no surgery for him, there was usually some other problem that caught his attention. One such problem involved the survival of crashed airmen.

Paoshan itself was under the eastern end of the main part of the Hump, that air route full of stuffed clouds. It was strategically located for rescue work.

McClure found himself involved in several 'walk-in' missions in which a military team with a doctor would walk into the area of a crash in the hope of finding survivors. The U.S. Tenth Air Force asked McClure to write a little booklet of survival advice. He did. It was not just a first aid manual. The booklet explained that each tribe tended to occupy one valley and had little to do with the people in the next valley. The airmen were told that if they could follow a mountain river downstream they would invariably come to the junction with another river, and there they would find a village. The farther down they went the bigger the villages until they would finally come to the village of the Shwabu, or 'King'. The men were given some guidance on the culture, so they would not be too disoriented by finding themselves in a matriarchal society where not only did the women do most of the work, but where the 'Queen' wielded the real power. She let the Shwabu live on opium, and kept him around mainly for reproductive purposes. The airmen were warned not to leap to the conclusion that because female clothing was loose and scanty that female morals were the same.

The survival problem, however, seemed to call for something more practical than good advice. The F.A.U. started bringing in representatives of the tribal people to the Paoshan hospital for some first aid instruction. If the person needed some medical treatment himself, it was given to him as a bonus. McClure hoped eventually to have a tribal 'ambassador' in every valley. But even this did not seem to be tackling the problem head on. And then someone made the suggestion that what was really needed were some medics who could be parachuted into crash sites as soon as air surveillance had verified that there were survivors. But even swift medical attention was only part of the problem. The rescuer should also be able to speak Chinese, should be reasonably familiar with the terrain, and must be able to organize the villagers as stretcher bearers to bring injured flyers out to the Burma Road. Somehow, as qualifications were listed, all eyes turned to Bob McClure.

McClure found himself pioneering air-to-ground rescue work in the Himalayan mountains.

It was an exhilarating activity, about which Bob wrote not a word to Amy. Although he could at times be strangely insensitive to other people's feelings, apparently this time he recognized that there were worries to which a loving wife should not be subjected. There were also censors. Amy learned about the parachute period in later, more tranquil times.

McClure began with some solo rescues. The pilot would circle and drop a walkie-talkie so they could get some feedback from the ground to prepare the doctor for the type of medical problem he might literally fall into. One of the first tries with the walkie-talkie brought back a description from the injured pilot telling in detail how one strap of his parachute harness had broken and had ruptured his urethra, the canal from the bladder. When McClure queried the fact that he was hearing 'doctor talk' and not 'pilot talk' he found he had an ex-medical student down below. McClure parachuted down to find a composed young American aviator who was able and willing to participate in his own first aid. After they had passed a catheter and made him comfortable, it was then McClure's job to get to the nearest village and arrange for stretcher bearers.

As the drops continued, Bob devised a standard procedure. Usually four native bearers were required for each injured man, two to carry while the other two rested. They would also carry several days food ration with them. Their destination was simply 'the Burma Road'.

As they neared the road, McClure would use the walkie-talkie to pin-point their probable time, and point of arrival. The Americans would meet them with a truck, as well as with payment for the bearers.

The problem of payment was solved neatly. The tribal people scorned paper money (with good reason). They liked silver and gold. In fact, the Japanese were offering rewards in silver and gold for any downed airmen who were turned over to them. But there was a more precious commodity—salt. The Japanese had cut off the traditional salt routes into the mountains. McClure struck a bargain to pay carriers in salt, pound for pound, the weight of any man they escorted out; twice his weight if they carried him out.

When McClure and his little safari would arrive at the Burma Road there would be a weapons carrier there with a load of salt, and a teeter-totter would be set up by the roadside. The rescued airman would go on one end of the teeter-totter and his weight in salt would be measured out on the other end. They weighed him complete—parachute, pack, pistol, and all. It was a simple system and it worked. The other part that worked was the system of unofficial tribal ambassadors that had been created via the Paoshan hospital. Although a Japanese reward would have been enough gold to let the population of an entire village retire for life, McClure never heard of any case of a downed airman being turned over to the Japanese.

At the end of one five day walk-out McClure had a brief but fascinating conversation. This time the usual crew of rather patched-up, well-worn, Americans was augmented by a major who was a Public Relations Officer fresh out from the States. As the four weary little tribesmen were about to depart into the woods with their salt, the U.S.A.F. major asked McClure to hold them a moment, that he wanted to speak to them.

"Well, okay," said McClure, "but they're tired. They've been carrying your man for five days and they want to get home—make it short."

"They'll want to hear what I have to say," said the Major. "If you can handle the translation for me just tell them that the Great White Chief is very appreciative of what they've done."

"Who the hell is the Great White Chief?"

"President Roosevelt!"

"That's what you want me to tell them?"

"That's the way you talk to these people. They talk in pictures."

McClure turned to a wizened, wiry little man who was the leader of the four and who spoke a functional Mandarin without Chinese ornamentation. "Look," said McClure, apologetically, "this is the way this fellow talks and he wants me to translate for you. So here's the translation."

McClure made his way through the Great White Chief bit and then found himself describing how tomorrow morning millions of Americans would hear of the heroic rescue of the heroic aviator, and how the four carriers would be rewarded with much publicity. It was a strange speech. Bob knew while he was delivering it that the tribesman had no idea what it was all about and that he had no interest in publicity, which could neither be eaten nor worn. He thought, however, that the little man was listening with unusual attention, his eyes riveted upon the immaculate officer. The speech finished with a summary dismissal, but the carriers did not leave. Instead, the little man spoke to Bob.

"Major Loa," he said, "if you will translate I have a message for the man in the funny brown clothes. Tell the man in the funny brown clothes that in our country we don't go by what a man says. In our country we go by the look in his eyes. Tell the man in the funny brown clothes I don't like the look in his eyes."

Loa Ming-yuan translated every last word of it with impeccable precision, and the four wiry little men made a dignified exit into the jungle.

After the first few drops proved the system worked, McClure began training others to go with him and, eventually, to take over. American Air Force doctors, who had been studying the language, began taking the plunge. Some of the other F.A.U. men also took to the silk. Young Michael Harris was one of the first to accompany McClure out the door of a DC 3 on a rescue mission. Although McClure did not know it, it was the first time Harris had ever jumped. Although the members of the China Convoy could grouse about the niceties of democratic leadership, some of them seemed more than willing to follow the Commandant anywhere.

By the end of 1942 the composition of the F.A.U. teams associated with the Chinese Army's Seventy-first Field Hospital at Paoshan had changed. Some of the members had been transferred to other China Convoy units and new people had arrived. Another doctor was on the scene, Arthur Barr, from Philadelphia. Trained female nurses had by now been incorporated in the F.A.U. and were with the teams at Precious Mountain.

The introduction of women had upset the all-male domain—until the girls had proven they could take the spartan life as ruggedly as the men. Here and there throughout the China Convoy there was, as Bob put it to Amy, "some trouble with hormones," and he found himself playing the role of father confessor. But there was no doubt that the presence of female nurses at Precious Mountain had a positive, civilizing effect.

The presence of Chinese army officers was not necessarily civilizing. And at Christmas time, 1942, the temporary addition of McClure, three American army officers, and a British Colonel, created a leaven of formidable potency.

Just before that memorable Christmas, the C.O. of the area, General Sung Hsi-lin, made a surprise inspection of the hospital and seemed to be pleased with what he saw. When he discovered that the China Convoy units and the New Life team were each contributing heavily toward a Christmas dinner for the patients he immediately doubled the kitty. He also invited the medical teams to join with himself and his officers in a Christmas dinner at 3 o'clock in the afternoon of Christmas Day. It was an invitation that sounded too good to miss.

When they arrived for the General's 3:00 p.m. dinner they found that a 9:30 a.m. feast was just beginning. This was a banquet in which local gentry were feasting the General. With much cordiality the medical teams were pressed into place at the table, being assured that the next banquet would be a little delayed. It was.

After this first feast, with everyone as stuffed as any turkey had ever been back home, they lumbered out onto the basketball court where the foreigners agreed to play against any or all. Much to their surprise they found themselves playing General Sung himself. Much to their delight, they found that he was very good at the game. Onlookers, however, had a great deal of difficulty coping with the problem of face inherent in anyone checking a Chinese general.

Then the British and American officers arrived and started in to drink. That was a major tactical error. Chinese officers who could watch with aplomb as their armies perished and dynasties crumbled had never been known to be defeated by a bottle. General Sung's feast finally got underway, with remarkable informality, and was interrupted at intervals by unannounced barbershop harmonies emanating from the three Americans and the British Colonel.

Toasts were drunk in a wine called Mao-tai, which has gained much favour since World War II but which was almost unknown in civilized China prior to that time. It was a brew concocted by the tribal people of the south-west and hid a mule's kick under a slight raspberry flavour. General Chennault's American Volunteers, who understood such things, called it "Tiger Piss". Just as a Westerner likes to sip a little wine from the first glass before giving it his stamp of approval, the Chinese liked to touch a match to a little Mao-tai. If it burst into flames that was approval enough.

General Sung's feast went through many toasts while the military stewards burned a little wine from each new bottle, like uniformed acolytes burning offerings to the gods of war. It all came to a head as one of the F.A.U. boys was on his feet announcing a toast. He stopped in the middle of a sentence and did not so much collapse as simply melt, from the feet upward, slowly dissolving under the table. A hush fell upon the assembly as they watched his disappearance with interest. The hush lasted until broken by the voice of General Sung.

"Be so good," said the General, concentrating his mind as he composed a saying that was destined to make the rounds of several Chinese armies, "be so good as to call in the driver who drives the ambulance for the ambulance driver."

It was at this point that McClure took the pledge. "This," he thought, "is no way to run a Quaker ambulance unit," and he turned his glass over. He singled out a particularly rednosed Chinese officer near him and said, "Tsai-li". It was a Buddhist phrase meaning, "I have taken my vows", and it was an invitation to the other man to be his deputy. Chinese officers had been known to shoot men who refused hospitable drinks and they were incapable of understanding temperance, but they could understand abstinence if it was of the 'tsai-li' variety. They also considered it a great honour to be singled out as a deputy-drinker. Bob hoped the man he had just honoured was a relative of the general. Where the Chinese army was concerned he would keep 'tsai-li' in force for the remainder of the war.

General Sung's party ended late that night beneath a starlit sky as Ming-yuan McClure drove a truckload of the quick and the dead, of Quakers, Buddhists, and non-conformists, back to their barracks within the shelter of the protecting hills. On the road behind them strode a British Colonel, singing lustily and pushing manfully on the tailgate. There may not have been peace on earth, but that night at Precious Mountain there was a great deal of goodwill toward men.

31

Raid on Chengchow

McClure was back at the administration base (which was now in Kutsing) for the first weeks of 1943. He managed to avoid his desk as much as possible in favour of the operating room at the little Church Missionary Society hospital where the F.A.U. sick bay had been established. He repaired a ruptured gastric ulcer for a Chinese Fifth Army man. It was the first gastric ulcer he had worked on for several years and it was good for his morale to find he had not lost his touch. It also reminded him of the phenomenon that he observed in common with other doctors in other theatres of the war—gastric ulcers were less common in wartime than in peace time. He himself had had some ulcer problems back in the pre-war years (if one can use the term 'pre-war' with reference to twentieth century China) but never a sign of ulcers now. He also repaired a badly crushed ankle, and put a youth back into circulation who had been broken in a traffic accident. He removed tonsils from an adult, and had a depressingly messy time of it. He removed the appendix from one of his own F.A.U. lads, an American college boy, who, since it was being done under spinal anaesthetic, insisted on watching with a mirror. He performed a hysterectomy on a lady who had travelled from a mission so remote it had taken her three weeks to get to the nearest road. It was the most ambitious operation the little hospital had ever witnessed. It was made more dramatic by the sudden arrival of a mother who was in the third day of labour with her first child. McClure had to take a few moments away from the hysterectomy to execute a low forceps delivery. There was something strangely satisfying about being able to deliver a fine baby while in the midst of a radical hysterectomy.

The McClure enthusiasm was in top form these days. It could be disconcerting. The staff of small mission hospitals, who were always pleased and relieved to have one of the best surgeons in China cleaning up their backlog of cases, were not always prepared to find afterwards that their O.R. log book showed that what they had thought was a hysterectomy was actually a "crown gear and pinion job". Bowel and rectal surgery would be entered in the small, but very legible, McClure handwriting as "muffler and exhaust pipe repair". These unorthodox log book entries moved one of the China Convoy members, Bernard Llewellyn, to take refuge in verse:

> I do not think we could endure
> Another Robert B. McClure.
> One is about all we can handle
> Another one would be a scandal;
> For in the hospital theatres
> They'd take out ladies' carburetors.

The trucking business and surgery were finally coming together in a most unique blend.

McClure was unorthodox in more than his log book entries. He had a chronic clothing problem. None of the men were immaculately uniformed but all the Old Country men were accredited to the British Red Cross Society and wore B.R.C.S. uniforms, or portions thereof. The China Convoy was working in liaison with British, American, and Chinese army units and used a few military ranks out of deference to the military liking for pigeon-holes. But Major McClure had no B.R.C.S. affiliation, and his more civilized jackets and trousers seemed to be in a perpetual state of just having been lost, stolen, or worn out. Thus the Commandant of the China Convoy, Major Chairman McClure, was usually seen in the leather high cuts and the breeks (or shorts) of pre-war days, topped by a decaying windbreaker and an Australian bush hat. On one occasion he did manage to 'dress up' by borrowing a pair of long trousers in order to have dinner with the British Ambassador in Chungking. When Bob arrived at the Embassy, he found the ambassador wearing shorts out of deference to him.

A well-established scene in the vast south-west was the sight of McClure arriving in, or on, a truck at some outpost hospital. He would hit the ground already running and would start calling to the nearest staff people to get the operating room ready. The conditions never seemed to bother him. Whether the O.R. was in a hospital, a Buddhist temple, a go-down, or a thatched hut made no difference to him as long as the equipment was functioning, the staff was alert, and the conditions were as sterile as possible under prevailing conditions.

The only things that really irked him were still the old bug-bears of slowness and incompetence and, in the case of some of the mission hospitals, piousness. Incompetence, he would not tolerate. Slowness, on the part of a new nurse or a junior surgeon, he could manage to put up with. He knew that speed and deftness only came with practice and that surgery was an art juniors had to learn from seniors. (It made him think of all the Chinese doctors he had worked with, and of his Hwaiking practitioners, and of the men who had studied under his father at Cheloo.) Piousness, however, was another matter. That it could irritate him was amply illustrated on at least one memorable occasion.

McClure arrived one day at a fundamentalist mission hospital—after making a considerable journey out of his way because he knew they had surgery they were holding until he could get there—and was less than pleased to be advised, as his feet hit the ground, that there must be no smoking inside the compound. The request came from the senior evangelist and it was not so much the request that bothered McClure as the look of abhorrence that the man cast upon the precious cheroot that was clamped between the McClure teeth. The man had then turned to McClure's F.A.U. companion, Michael Harris, and told him there could be no drinking inside the compound either, as though they were planning to organize an instant orgy. McClure and Harris complied docilely enough with both these requests. They had long ago reconciled themselves to the knowledge that many of the missionaries considered the China Convoy to be a "sub-Christian organization".

It was one of those sweltering hot days when there seemed to be barely enough oxygen in the air to go around, and it helped to make McClure's temper even more volatile than usual. When he found that the O.R. nurse was a missionary lady even more pious than the evangelist, it was too much for him. He scrubbed up in that oppressive heat and then headed for the operating table clad only in his underwear shorts. The staff had to capture him and con him into donning at least an oilcloth apron in order to preserve O.R. decorum. The staff then started in to pray.

Bob himself had been accustomed to begin every day in the Hwaiking O.R. with a few words of prayer, but this particular hospital seemed to have everything out of balance. When they called for prayer he made a loud announcement of his own. "I may not be very good but there's no need to call on the Almighty before I even start!" It was a statement calculated to make the staff pray even more fervently than they had intended. When the Amen finally sounded, the surgeon announced, with evident relief, "Now that we've cut the cackle let's cut the patient".

They operated all that afternoon and far into the evening. It was after midnight when the weary surgeon and his assistant finally made their way to their room in the mission residence. There, in the privacy of his room with his feet up, McClure smoked a cigar. When he had finished he flicked the butt through the open window into the courtyard below, and prepared for bed. Five minutes later there was a knock at his door. Upon opening the door he found himself confronted by the evangelist, who was holding the cigar butt gingerly between two sticks, as one might hold a lab specimen from Sodom and Gomorrah. A few minutes later McClure and Harris found themselves and their few belongings out in the dark on the street, and McClure was recalling more dockyard phrases in two languages than he had used since the day he wrestled the goat to a first fall on the Weihwei station platform.

That had been one of the bad days and was remarkable because it was rare. It was seldom that McClure could not get along with any individual or group. Just as in his college days, he was still adept at fitting into any surroundings—although the process had altered, significantly. Now it was not so much that he could fit into any particular context as it was that he was his own context. He could gate-crash an embassy party in Chungking in his baggy shorts and open necked shirt and make everyone else feel overdressed. He could come in from the boondocks for a meeting with the Generalissimo and prepare for the solemnity of the occasion by bouncing up and down on Madame's chesterfield in sheer delight at the unexpected sensation of comfort. He could talk flying and air rescue work with General Chennault of Flying Tiger fame, and warm to a man as unorthodox as himself. He met with men of as disparate backgrounds as Lord Louis Mountbatten, General "Vinegar Joe" Stilwell, and Chou En-lai without ever being aware that there were cultural differences. People who worked with him for any length of time usually found themselves trying to conform to him. They would be exhausted after he had moved on, but on appraisal they would find that he had generated more action and filled them with more fervour to be up and doing than they (or certainly their friends) had thought was possible. In the process he often stepped, metaphorically, on people's toes and sometimes, usually unintentionally, he hurt their feelings. But he made people think, make decisions, and act. It was a triple process that he felt was often sadly lacking among mission folk. But the missionaries had their own opinions of him, and of his unbounded energy. One of them put it gently, as befitted a man of the cloth. "I love Bob McClure," he said. "He can produce forty new ideas in twenty minutes, and two of them are good." At which point someone else said, "Ah yes, but which two?"

One idea which McClure had was of making a personal raid on Chengchow or, more precisely, on the American Southern Baptist hospital at Chengchow which had been the domain of Dr. Ayers and Donald Hankey. The fact that Chengchow was a thousand miles away, and alternated frequently between Japanese and Chinese occupation, did not deter him. He knew that the hospital was no longer functioning but he also knew that Dr. Ayers' big X-ray machine was nestled in storage. How long it would remain there he did not know but he did know it was one of the best and biggest X-rays in the country and the Baptists had announced that anyone who could get it could have it. Bob himself had helped assemble it. He proposed to liberate that X-ray machine and install it somewhere farther west, perhaps near Sian, where it could again perform the humanitarian functions for which it was designed.

Bob left for the north in February, 1943, just as the Chinese

New Year was being celebrated with the biggest blow-out in more than five years. The celebrations were in honour of the abolition of all the special treaties that had been in effect over the years with foreign countries. Gone at last were the "foreign settlements", the "concession territories", the privileges which allowed foreigners to maintain "garrison troops" and to answer only to their own courts. The symbols that reminded the Chinese of a whole interminable century of foreign intervention and exploitation had now, finally, in the midst of a life and death war, been officially terminated. Away back in 1912 Bob's father, while on deputation work in Canada, had denounced those same foreign "rights" so vehemently that at least one youthful listener still remembered that speech sixty-five years later. Bob himself was pleased and relieved to see those hated special treaties finally laid to rest. He hoped that now brotherhood and the spirit of co-operation might make more progress. He moved quickly to put the F.A.U. China Convoy under the higher command of the Chinese Red Cross, and he attended a celebration hosted by a Chinese Colonel. During the proceedings a young Chinese officer, who had imbibed rather freely, swayed up to McClure's chair and put his arms around McClure's neck. "Brother Loa," he said, "I can really call you 'brother' now, can't I?"

"Yes, brother," came the answer. "And as a brother I am going to make demands on you that I have never made in my life before."

After the dinner a very pukka British Colonel, aptly nicknamed "Poona Pete", came to McClure and said, "Major McClure, I never was so embarrassed in my life. Think of a yellow man daring to embrace you in public like that!"

McClure answered Poona Pete as solemnly as he could. "Colonel, I think I shall recover. In fact, I am sure I will, for this is the day that my father and I have been praying for, individually and together, for fifty years."

It seemed an ideal time to liberate that big Baptist X-ray machine and to take it to his Chinese brothers.

He started north for Sian accompanied by two travelling companions. One was Peter Tennant who wanted to inspect some flood relief work that F.A.U. members were doing in Shensi. The other was a Mr. Heath, a British embassy official who wanted to make a first hand reconnaissance of the famine that was reported to be raging in Honan. (He was *really*, as it turned out, an ex-Shanghai policeman, now a British commando, engaged on an intelligence mission.) Heath was a pleasant chap and McClure had no objection to the idea of company to the vicinity of Chengchow.

They went via Chengtu which was still managing to avoid the ravages, if not the overflow, of war. The F.A.U. was now well entrenched on the campus and was getting full co-operation from the University in space for godowns and a hostel. Some of the members were getting more co-operation from the female students than was perhaps good for their powers of concentration, but such were the hazards of civilization. There was also an R.A.F. squadron billeted on campus and, taken all in all, McClure thought the place showed some signs of joining the real world.

Bob had had word that his sister, Janet, was seriously ill. He was pleased to find her much recovered, able to sit up for lengthy periods and to walk a few steps. It was their first opportunity for a visit since Bob had been in the Red Cross trucking business.

He also had his first visit with Bruce and Marnie since their return to China in 1940. They had two children now—John, about five and a half years old, and Peggy, four. They were not living on the campus but were off in the city. Bruce was not working with the mission but directly with the Chinese church. As usual, it was a delight to see the Coplands. Marnie was always such a good hostess, always so full of information on local customs and manners, so full of anecdotes about *people*, that she could help one keep the war in perspective as being a temporary political aberration. On the other hand Bruce, with an almost encyclopedic memory and a scholar's concern for accurate detail, never failed to amaze Bob with his grasp of issues. A visit with the Coplands was always a feast for both heart and mind, but it said much for the breadth of both men that two such different personalities, the activist surgeon and the intellectual clergyman, should have developed such a firm friendship.

Marnie was again pregnant and, as Bob reported to Amy, "taking on the contours of a barrage balloon". As Bob took his leave there was some joking about the Hsiu-wu miscarriage episode. He warned them that since they had a medical college and hospital almost on their doorstep they could not expect the same instant night time service-by-bicycle that they had received in Honan.

Tennant, Heath, and McClure hitch-hiked from Chengtu to Sian.

At Sian, Loa Tai-fu began to meet old friends from Honan. It was almost like a home-coming, or like Hwaiking on a Christmas morning. He met former amahs, cooks, gardeners, and their children, many of them now grown up. He wrote to Amy, fairly bubbling with the pleasure of having seen old Chinese friends, and listed their names as though hoping that Amy, too, could share the pleasures of reunion. He heard news of others. Chou Teh-kwei was surviving and still running a clinic in the Wen-hsien area, so the Hwaiking Rural Medical System still had one practitioner left.

These people were in Sian as double refugees. Not only were they fleeing the Japanese but they were also fleeing from famine in Honan. The Yellow River had flooded near Tung-kwan inundating hundreds of square miles of agricultural plain. Farther east there had been no rain and the drought only compounded the problems of man-made devastation. Several years earlier, the Yellow River dikes below Chengchow had been blown by the Chinese in a move that had all but wiped out an entire Japanese division, and had plunged its eminent commander into career oblivion. Now the price of that military victory was famine. It was heaviest in Japanese territory, so militarily the gain was still positive, but the human costs were enormous. "All along the road," Bob told Amy, "one can see the people with their little bundles, all from Honan. They are from places like Wenhsien, Menghsien, Hwaiking, Sihswei, and Chengchow. One somehow feels some sense of personal responsibility for these people. When you meet them on the road you cannot just pass them by. Somehow or other they seem to be our folk."

He was depressed because his own mission seemed to have no rallying point for these people. It was a problem he and Bruce had already been discussing back in Chengtu. Now that he was seeing it first hand he urged Amy to conduct some more gentle lobbying in Toronto suggesting the church establish a rallying point up in the Sian or Loyang area rather than far away at Chengtu. "After all," he pointed out, "we know that the war is going to end sometime and when it does we shall have to start (again). These people and the children of theirs who have come through our mission schools are, after all, the harvest that we have to show for years of work in Honan and we should do a lot more to hang onto them and to really act as pastors. I do hope . . . that some salvage work of this type is undertaken before it is too late . . . It could be done in the form of a co-operative establishment in which the people could work, their children could go to the local schools, a church could be operated and the group could be held together . . . When one sees this gang from the old field one realizes that it is in these people . . . that rests the germ of what The United Church of Canada has done in 50 years. They may be weak in many ways but they have tremendous amount of guts to them, and they have on them that Christian mark. That Christian mark makes them different from others whether in war or famine. We taught them to play the game of life by the new rules, and it is up to us to stick by them now . . . at times when rules are hard to stick to, and are hard on those who stick to them."

Bob felt that in Sian the English Baptists were doing an impressive job of sticking by their people and he was more than impressed by their hospital. He sat up late one night writing to Amy at length about the English Baptists and their accomplishments in Sian: "Handley Stockley* in particular and his mission generally are doing a magnificent bit of work under very great difficulty. The way one has to scrounge to buy drugs on the street from thieves and smugglers is terrible. Yet Handley is doing it and is running at a very high standard the largest civilian hospital in North West China. They still do a tremendous amount of charity work at great cost . . . He has a fine anti-syphilitic clinic run on the 'Hwaiking plan' and has run it longer that we did in Hwaiking. It really does work and he is getting a fine reputation for that work. He is still doing more kala-azar work than any other mission hospital in China . . .

*Dr. Handley Stockley, the Baptist, who married Jean Menzies of Hwaiking.

He certainly is one of the medical heroes of this war in the way he has stuck with the game . . . Stockley is absolutely tops with everyone in the district. It is seeing him that one is again confirmed in the idea that the doctor who wants to work in China *after* the war has a priceless opportunity to work his way into the minds of the people *during* the war."

This was becoming a recurring theme for McClure. All around him the Chinese were changing, becoming more self-confident, less willing to be subservient to Westerners, more responsive to being treated as colleagues. McClure was desperately concerned that the missionaries who did not adapt to these changes, or who were not working in China now to witness the changes occurring, would never be able to function constructively in China after the war. Right now, however, it was good to be back near his own part of the country where he was recognized by old patients and old friends and where he felt at home with the flat plains and the dust and the North China food. He pushed on eastward, toward 'home', travelling by rail.

Peter Tennant's destination was the flood area where the F.A.U. were working on relief. He dropped off, and McClure and Heath continued. Soon they were at Tungkwan, where Bob had met Bethune at what now seemed some remote far away time. At Tungkwan the train was shelled by Japanese gun emplacements on the high bluffs of the north shore of the Yellow River. From there on, travel conditions deteriorated. McClure and Heath found themselves for the next twenty-four hours travelling on top of a load of broken stone in an open freight car in the clear cold air of March. The end of the rail run was at Loyang. From there to Chengchow the tracks had been destroyed. It would be a three day walk to the final destination and the giant X-ray. In the meantime they went to earth at the Catholic mission station with Msgr. Megan, once of Hwaiking, now the Bishop of Loyang. The Bishop and one Chinese padre were hanging on, forming the rallying point that Bob felt his own mission so sadly lacked. (Within six months time the United Church would remedy that lack, by posting a missionary to Loyang.)

As usual, the Catholic hospitality was warm and open. The Bishop provided more than hospitality. He provided bicycles. McClure and Heath pedalled on toward Chengchow.

The roads were crowded with refugees, walking, riding bicycles, or pulling carts and rickshaws loaded with personal belongings. There were corpses by the roadsides, and broken carts, and abandoned belongings. Several times, while pushing through groups, Bob heard his name called and invariably met acquaintances from Hwaiking. He heard stories that would bring tears to a strong man's eyes. There was a mother with a six year old child and one four years old, and carrying a nursing infant. Like others, she was trying to get to a land of food before her children died of starvation. She could carry the infant, the six year old was walking well, but the four year old could not keep up. The mother was afraid they would all perish. She tied the four year old to a tree so he could not follow, and struggled on westward. Fortunately the child was rescued, and fortunately there were happier scenes as well. Bob witnessed a roadside reunion between a rickshaw puller and his sister. She had been sold by their parents into prostitution at the age of twelve and the older brother had not seen her, or known of her whereabouts, for five years. That he recognized her now was a miracle. He made room for her on his freight rickshaw and jogged off down the road looking stolidly happy, with his sister in tears. It was the kind of scene that Bob was sure would be disbelieved as "another McClure story". He made a note that he had witnesses.

From what he could learn, Bob decided the famine in Honan was at least 50 percent man-made, thanks to incredibly corrupt and inefficient Chinese government. The harvests had failed but there were 1,200,000 Nationalists troops in the province doing very little except eating. Altogether Honan was in a mess.

Chengchow was a ghost city. The Japanese had overrun the city first away back in 1938. It was about 95 percent destroyed; 85 percent evacuated. The homes of departed refugees were sitting roofless, their rafters gone into the winter fires of those who stayed behind. Since then the amorphous 'lines' of the Sino-Japanese War had fluctuated over and around Chengchow. Even as Bob arrived now, toward the end of March, 1943, the guns could be heard firing just a few miles to the east.

It was a miracle that the big X-ray was still in the hospital. Six hours before the Japanese had first arrived the Chinese had blown up the hospital power plant, including Dr. Ayers big cantankerous Diesel that Bob had laboured over during his days as a Red Cross man. The hospital was deserted now except for a wraithlike caretaker staff. No building could survive totally abandoned—it would be dismantled for firewood. Bob walked the fracture ward where Donald Hankey had soothed his traction patients through a bombing. Nothing was left but memories. He found a trunk with some clothes in it and, pleasure of pleasures, they were his own! He was led to a spot in the yard and, upon digging, found the laboratory microscope. It was in good condition after a five year interment. He decided to take it to Loyang and help the Catholics and Lutherans establish a little co-operative laboratory around it. But the real prize, the big X-ray, the object of his quest, was a puzzler. Without power he could not test it. Without testing it he had no way of knowing if it still functioned. He decided he had to take it, as one took many things these days, on faith. He dismantled it.

The X-ray was a large, expensive machine of German make. It weighed about three thousand pounds. McClure had to break it down so that it became portable. He took it apart into literally hundreds of pieces, much the way he and Yang Yung-lo had attacked the ambulance after its immersion in sand. He was finally left with one big piece weighing four hundred pounds, the transformer. He then went out and hired a fleet of nine freight rickshaws.

A freight rickshaw, although large, was pulled by one man. The transformer was a maximum load for one rickshaw. Other parts were distributed evenly. The screen for the X-ray was a delicate commodity. McClure hired a refugee to carry it by hand. The tube, too, was fragile. To begin with it was packed, well padded and cushioned, in a rickshaw. The caravan's departure was delayed two days by heavy rain, a not unwelcome occurrence in a time of drought and famine. The delay gave Bob a little more time to inspect Chengchow.

There were still missionaries in the city, a corporal's guard representing five missions, and Bob had great admiration for their courage and stamina. Their average age, however, was sixty years and he felt their approach to famine and flood relief was pre-1900. He chafed with frustration at the fact that his own mission had none of its young bloods in here to spark some action.

The city was mired in inflation. The rule of thumb, at the moment, for calculating prices was to take the pre-war cost as of 1937 and multiply it by 100. The rule of thumb applied to food (when available), to bicycles, to drugs, to almost anything. A little simple talcum powder that used to be 4¢ per lb. (U.S.) now retailed at $4.00 per lb. But of course Chengchow had no monopoly on inflation.

There was much disorder in the city, as was to be expected with refugees, food riots, and war. Every second morning there were public executions, but Bob was relieved to find they were seldom for the theft of food. The firing squad was reserved mainly for crimes of violence. The one exception while he was there had to do with cannibalism. There was a meat jelly being sold that was made of mule, donkey and horse meat. Bob ate it quite regularly and found it tasty until another customer found a child's finger in it, complete with fingernail. There was a round-up of people engaged in the meat jelly trade and the firing squad put five of them out of business. McClure lost his liking for meat jelly.

By the time McClure and his rickshaws were ready to leave Chengchow the Southern Baptists had rounded up more precious cargo for him. It consisted of medical drugs that had been cached away awaiting 'liberating' into hands that knew how to use them. The only stipulation on the drugs was that he must not give them to the Catholics at Loyang. It was a request that depressed McClure but did not surprise him. The extreme denominationalism among the Chengchow Christians had always depressed him. He swore faithfully to take the drugs safely beyond Loyang to Sian where, he promised, he would enter them into the International Red Cross storeroom. What he did not say was that the Loyang Catholics, namely friendly Bishop Megan and his Chinese padre, could then requisition those same drugs back down the line again.

By Saturday night Bob had cycled as far as the river crossing of quicksand memories. The rickshaws, delayed by mud, had fallen half a day behind. He watched the sun set over distant Hwaiking City and then bedded down in a barren room attached to the chapel of a fundamentalist mission. The next morning, the rickshaws still not having caught up, he attended the church service, which he enjoyed, and communion, which he was not permitted to enjoy. It never failed to amaze him that any group of Christians could exclude other Christians from joining them in communion.

The rickshaw caravan finally arrived at Loyang with everything apparently still intact. From here there was rail transportation. The rail cost would normally have been prohibitive but McClure found that the railway officials, with so many refugees on the move, were terrified of their line becoming a carrier of epidemic diseases. By the time McClure had broken his trip long enough to give them extensive instruction on the establishment of delousing and inoculation stations they were willing to ship the X-ray free. Back-scratching was an old Chinese art and McClure was one of its most adept practitioners.

Bob felt it was unwise to leave the X-ray tube to the tender care of the railway employees. After all, he himself had apprenticed in 'baggage-smashing' in Toronto Union Station. He left Loyang carrying the precious X-ray tube in his arms. It was about the size of an eight year old child. The rest of the freight was to follow on a later train. Near Tungkwan, at nightfall, the journey was interrupted. Japanese artillery had destroyed a section of the railway. There was now a 15 mile gap that had to be traversed on foot. Bob hired a man to carry his personal baggage, while he himself continued to cling to the X-ray tube. The next few hours were spent in crossing a mountainous ridge of hills by a path that climbed some 1,500 feet above the railway elevation. He finished the night sleeping on a station platform so crowded with refugees that people were sleeping everywhere except between the rails. He still had the X-ray tube cradled in his arms. There were rats, dogs, people and bugs, and all were friendly.

McClure's destination lay well beyond Sian at a place called Paochi. There the ton and a half of X-ray equipment overtook him a few days after he arrived. By that time he had established liaison with a hospital belonging to the Chinese Industrial Co-operatives, had repaired their sterilizer, and had located a site for the X-ray in a cave. It was a beautiful cave, about a hundred feet deep, twenty feet wide, fifteen feet high, with a brick floor. It had already had electricity installed, and at the deep end there flowed a spring of clear water, ideal for the developing of X-ray film. What was more, it was bomb proof. Japanese bombs had hit it three times without disturbing so much as a brick.

Bob painstakingly assembled the hundreds of pieces of the X-ray and wired in the big transformer. The second night after it all arrived he turned on the power. It was not until that moment that he knew whether he had been carrying an incredibly useful machine or high priced junk. It was not junk. Everything worked!

McClure headed south, warm in the knowledge that the Chinese co-operatives and his Chinese brothers had access to the largest X-ray machine in Free China. It was one of the most satisfying things he had done for a long time.

Bob was still in high spirits as he arrived at Chengtu, but he was far from happy after he had seen Bruce and Marnie. Marnie was no longer trying to imitate a barrage balloon because the baby had come. She wrote about it years later in an autobiography as delicately flowered as a Chinese painting:

"That night I felt bare and empty and cold as death. Dr. Gladys* brought my son to me in the morning. He was so little. I touched his brown hair, his eyelids that had never lifted, his nose that was so like father's, and the gentle curve of his fingers. He was perfect. Except he wasn't alive."

Marnie did not cry but for days her eyes were full of tears. "It is *my* sorrow," she wrote, echoing Jeremiah, "therefore there *is* no sorrow like it." She knew, of course, that there was much sorrow like it. The mothers of China had been weeping for their children, born and unborn, throughout all these weary years of the twentieth century. Now, with a global war raging, Rachel's tears were universal. What was not universal was the love that surrounded Marnie, flowing to her from her friends and her children and her husband. She wrote of that, too: "Peggy said, 'I'm very sad of the baby.' Their affection and their matter of fact acceptance, and Bruce's strength and steadfastness restored me. 'Underneath are the everlasting arms.' I can't explain it. The arms were there, and I was upheld."**

*Dr. Gladys Cunningham, West China Mission, The United Church of Canada.

**ature *Moon cakes and Maple sugar*, an autobiography by Marnie Copland, (unpublished).

Bob could explain it and did, to Amy, in the direct but somewhat awkward style that characterized his letters. With Marnie and Bruce in mind, he wrote: "It shows up so much out here that there are certain people who can take anything that comes . . . while others try to blame someone for everything that happens and feel that their luck is particularly bad. It is great in times like these to see those people who have a philosophy and a religion that can let them take it on the chin and not be worse for it but be better because of it."

He met Bill Mitchell's wife, Dr. Helen, up in Chengtu on a visit, and was pleased to learn that finally the Mitchells were on the point of departure for furlough. He remembered how he himself had been borne down by the weight of the I.R.C. transport job, and he had not had family worries on top of it. He wrote of the Mitchells with the same warm generosity that characterized so much of his assessment of others: "She and Bill have carried a tremendous amount of weight in China in the war. They have both paid for it in their health, but it is a job well done under difficult conditions and few can have more justifiable satisfaction."

McClure's own big satisfaction, at the moment, was still the warm glow from having liberated the giant X-ray from Chengchow. The people at Loyang, and Sian, and Paochi, and at Chengtu all proclaimed it as a most triumphant feat. He arrived back at F.A.U. headquarters in Kutsing to find that some of the members of the China Convoy were not as impressed. They were, in fact, ready for the semi-annual staff meeting, and were after McClure's head.

The F.A.U. issues, gripes, grievances, and problems were, as usual, complicated. But many of the members were chafing over the fact that their Chairman, the Commandant, always seemed to be absent. If he was not off with one of the surgical units, or drifting into Himalayan valleys on a parachute, he was off to places they had hardly ever heard of rescuing things like X-rays. The Chengchow venture had been the last straw. He had been away from his desk at H.Q. since mid-February and here it was now almost the end of May. The China Convoy debating society corralled the Commandant and talked its way to a consensus.

Following a system that was incomprehensible to the military people, with whom they were in constant liaison, they held an election (without actually casting votes) and demoted their own Commandant. Major McClure was now responsible for purely medical matters; Major Tennant was in charge of transport; over all was a Chairman, Mr. Leonard Tomkinson. The new chairman was described, in retrospect, by one of the China Convoy pioneers as "a staid and conventional Quaker Missionary who performed the useful, but unromantic, function of limiting our ambitions to the carrying out of the programme which Bob had initiated".

Everyone seemed pleased with the new arrangement, and the most pleased of the lot was McClure. The incredible Quakers had made the switch without suppressing the whirlwind. Bob reported frankly to Amy that he "did not have their confidence except in medical things". That was something of an overstatement. He went on to say: "I do feel that now with my attention to medical work only I can go ahead with an assurance that I've never felt before. I really think I know something about this wartime medical work in China." The thought of McClure not having assurance would have astounded all but his wife and his intimate friends. The idea that he knew something about wartime medical work would have met with universal agreement.

Just at the time the China Convoy demoted him, Bob was accredited to the British Red Cross with some sort of rank, he did not know what. It did not matter anyway because he had no uniform on which to wear anybody's rank, honorary or otherwise. His windbreaker was in tatters. He had one good tweed jacket, which he loaned to one of the fellows who was worse off than he was. Then Dr. Bill Service, a young Canadian surgeon (born and raised in Chengtu) who was working in Chungking, came in from India bringing a windbreaker that Amy had sent out for Bob. It was warm and beautiful. Then the tweed jacket was stolen and Bob, remembering the Biblical exhortations in such matters, loaned the new windbreaker to replace the jacket.

Everything was back to normal.

There was just one problem. Some of Bob's China Convoy doctors were beginning to come unstuck.

32

General Ming-yuan McCurdle

The China Convoy medical situation around the end of May, 1943, was indeed desperate. Dr. Hank Louderbough had gone home, soured on China. It seemed to him, as it had so often appeared to others, that with all the best intentions in the world a miniscule group like the F.A.U. could accomplish nothing worthwhile amidst millions of people who seemed dedicated to crime and corruption. It was an extreme view. McClure could understand it while not agreeing with it. From the mellow plateau where he now stood he looked back upon his own audacious assault upon China twenty years earlier. "I can only imagine how green I must have been when I was out here first," he wrote to Amy, ". . . on the other hand one realizes more and more (the wisdom of) the method of approach that was given us at Language School in Peking and it is just in such things that missions avoided much of the trouble with personnel 'bedding in' that we have struck in the F.A.U. This the-Chinese-are-a-bunch-of-crooks idea that some of the men get who come out here in wartime is a big handicap . . . They get it of course from seeing the type of merchant they do, in these big profiteering cities like Chengtu, Chungking and Kunming, and also by meeting a bunch of grafting drivers on the motor road. Then, too, I think most of our chaps had the entire China picture painted in rosier colours before they came. The disillusionment is, therefore, all the worse for them when they get to it. Nearly all of our men take well over a year to get a happy balance and some of them . . . have not yet got it."

Some of them never got that "happy balance", and went

home. Dr. Louderbough was only one of them. Dr. Handley Laycock (F.R.C.S.), he of the immortal truck journey to Imphal, departed, too, but in the opposite direction. Laycock converted from pacifism and joined the British Army. Nor in this was Laycock alone. Some of the non-medical volunteers took the same non-pacifist path. Dr. Terry Darling, the youthful lanky Irishman, was not weakening in dedication but was sick with pleurisy and what Bob suspected was probably early tuberculosis. Dr. Quentin Boyd was suffering from mental depression and was generally feeling rotten. At the moment there were only two young American doctors, both relatively inexperienced but keen. They were Dr. Ernie Evans* and Dr. Arthur Barr. And there was McClure.

More doctors, however, were about to come out and some were already en route. One of them was Donald Hankey. The news that Hankey was coming was like a shot of adrenalin to Bob. True, Hankey was returning under the British Red Cross, but their China Director, Dr. Flowers, had picked him from a stack of applicants because he recognized the name from McClure's Reader's Digest "Unforgettable Character" article. Flowers was soon having his arm twisted by McClure to second Hankey to the F.A.U. There was little doubt that Donald Hankey would soon be with one of the China Convoy surgical teams.

McClure threw himself into a flurry of re-organization and re-grouping of medical personnel. By now the China Convoy was very strong in medical support people. Some of the young men had become impressively experienced as jacks-of-all-trades, being able to function as steam fitters, X-ray technicians, orderlies, and even anaesthetists. There were a number of qualified female nurses with the Convoy. The senior O.R. nurse was Sheila Yiu, a twenty year old girl from a wealthy Chinese family. She had trained in Hong Kong's famous Queen Mary's Hospital. For all her youth, Sheila supervised O.R. in a way that reminded Bob of his intern's terrors at Toronto Western.

From the information McClure could glean around Chungking it appeared as though a push would soon be launched against the Japanese 'somewhere' in the south-west

---

*Not to be confused with the Evans brothers from Wales.

along the borders of Burma and Indo-China. New doctors began to arrive and it looked as though he would have his surgical teams re-organized and ready to go when the time came.

McClure and Dr. Art Barr took a team off to Hsiakwan, on the Burma Road. It was only about 100 miles east of Paoshan. Even though the H.Q. of the Chinese Sixth Army was in the Hsiakwan area, the military hospital there was in terrible shape. McClure estimated there were about 12,000 men under that H.Q. command. The Hsiakwan hospital had beds for about 500 patients, but was only using 180. And no wonder. There was not a single graduate doctor in the entire Sixth Army. Once again the F.A.U. had to start in helping to organize and to upgrade the system. As was so often the case they had to begin with teaching basics—basics as simple as the fact that boiled water and well cooked food helped prevent dysentery.

The hospital was typical in that it was pretending to be a village and was complete with animals. (McClure was beginning to find that any farming instincts he had ever had were disappearing.) There was a laboratory with a microscope that had no fine adjustment, and there was an operating room that had never been used. These were defects that the army confidently expected the F.A.U. would remedy, and the army was not disappointed.

McClure found himself giving lectures every morning, doing most of the lab work himself, and supervising the training of medical assistants. They had to be trained in making distilled water and in the preparation of intravenous saline and glucose solutions. To them the art of creating an aseptic operating room was a mystical cult. It was shades of the Hwaiking training system all over again. Among the students in a lecture class was an army 'surgeon'. She was a girl, about twenty years old and seven months pregnant. Bob assumed she was the wife of one of the officers, but asked no questions about the presence of a semi-qualified, pregnant army surgeon. She was keen, full of spirit, and highly intelligent, and that was good enough for him.

As was customary, wherever the F.A.U. functioned, they reached beyond the military precincts and drew in civilians. Around Hsiakwan they launched public health work and conducted an X-ray survey for TB. One day McClure found himself being asked to X-ray the knee of a fourteen year old high school student. The lad had been suffering from numbness down the front of his thigh and over his knee, but what had really sent him to the Big Nose doctor was a series of festering burns on the affected areas. McClure soon diagnosed that Chinese 'doctors' had been burning incense on the boy's leg to drive out evil spirits. He then submitted the boy to a few Gu-shue-Taylor tests and diagnosed nerve leprosy. Both diagnoses would have baffled many a high powered Western doctor.

As soon as the Hsiakwan team was functioning properly McClure was off again, this time to lead a nine member team down into the hills and jungles near the Indo-China border. Their destination, highly classified at the time, was the Chinese town of Yenshan, headquarters for the Chinese Ninth Army Corps.

Their route took them about 150 miles south on the Indo-China railway. Then they travelled on foot, with a mule train, another hundred miles to the east of the railway. With two tons of medical supplies, six men, and three women, the China Convoy group with its mule drivers made a picturesque cara-van. The men were outfitted in khaki coloured tropical work uniforms, the three nurses were in dark blue overalls. They were beginning to look like a drill team. For McClure, wearing the semblance of a uniform was a strange sensation but they had been warned that the C.O. of the Ninth Army was a bit of a stickler for appearance.

It was quite a team. The senior nurse was young Sheila Yiu. Bob gave Amy a thumbnail sketch of his whole team, be-ginning with Sheila: "She is like all Cantonese, quite temper-mental, but is very energetic and is fine when she is up to her gills in work and gets good and tired. The other two (nurses) are just graduated and came with us the day they finished . . . One is a Canadian-born Chinese, Rosina Luey.* She has fluent English but strange to say can barely get along with Mandarin at all. The other is Joyce Li who has fluent Cantonese, moder-ate Mandarin and no English at all. Here we are in a territory where all the influential people speak in French. What a mix-up this language can be at times! The rest of our team is Ernie Evans the doctor from an old Quaker family in Philadelphia.

*From Calgary, Alberta.

He has been out some 10 months and did a turn on the Kwang-
tung front before coming here. Then there are three English
boys. Sidney Walker is head of the team. We do not make the
doctor head of the team any more. Sid was in Paoshan for
nearly a year and knows a lot about military medical work as a
result. He is good stuff in the operating room too. Jack Skeel
was with the Cambridge Physics labs working in television before the war and is an ideal naturally born lab man. He does lab
and X-ray, both of which he knows fine but claims that he
knows nothing at all. He is more typically English than the rest,
does so much each day, won't do bit more than he can do well,
and then he grouses all the time when he is happy. Systematic
as all get out, and beautiful and accurate notes on everything
that he has done or heard about. His note book is better than
any textbook. Then there is Robin Eden who is a relative of
Anthony's in the foreign office. Robin was an artist before the
war and has tried to fit in to each part of the Unit in China but
has been chucked out as being too artistic. He is now on his last
trial in medical work. He has had a course in anesthetics and he
ought to be good at judging the patient's colour. The other
member is Bill Rahill, one of the latest of the Americans to come
out. Bill is a big husky chap who is rather over his depth in
medical work, for he has only seen a bit in New York. He is
coming along as a whirlwind in Chinese. He is a husky sort of a
basket baller and he ought to do well. We have a good gang but
they are certainly going to a hard job."

The team arrived in Yenshan just three weeks after the
army's Third Field Hospital had moved in. The F.A.U. quarters
were stark, bare, and totally unfurnished but the same applied
even to the Officers' Mess, so they had no complaints. As before they were to integrate with the military hospital, but the
F.A.U. immediately began to set up a civilian out-patient department on its own, something the military could not do.
They found it almost pathetic the way the townsmen gathered
around to know when that O.P.D. would be ready. Until then
the only way the townsfolk could get medical assistance was to
take a three day pony ride to the nearest Provincial Health Station.

The army field hospital was equipped and staffed about on
a par with the one at Hsiakwan. It had an O.R. and very little
staff trained to use it. What staff there was seemed cool and re-

served, but thawed enough to throw a welcoming party in the
spartan Officer's Mess. The party started very formally and
each of the China Convoy men had to make a brief speech.
Then the food was brought in and along with it came the wine,
a potent brew made from corn and sorghum. Bob tried it and
the first swallow made the room rotate. It reminded him of
fusel oil, the poisonous by-product left over from the distilling
of whisky. It also reminded him of his 'tsai-li' vow. The host
hospital staff seemed to be under no such self-imposed restrictions. Their coolness thawed with remarkable speed. Bob noticed that the F.A.U. crew seemed to be building up some sort
of immunity, and that buxom Sheila Yiu was apparently inde-
structible. He wondered if her imperviousness had to do with
her drinking technique. "The stuff just never touches the sides
of her oesophagus," he told Amy, "but you can hear a faint
splash at the bottom of the trip." Apparently the only thing
that prevented the hosts from ending up under the tables was
the lack of tables. After the jollifications were over, all the participants either slumbered on where they were or, like the
China Convoy men and women, rose with studied dignity and
withdrew to the equally hard floors of their own quarters.

The F.A.U. team had not been asleep more than an hour
before their first emergency arrived.

The emergency came in the form of a soldier suffering
from numerous cuts, one of which had mangled the artery in
the palm of his hand. He had been rushed in from a village several miles out and his friends carried him straight into the
F.A.U. 'bedrooms', spattering blood as they went. McClure,
Sheila Yiu, and two of the men hurried him to the hospital
O.R. At the hospital they found that the few orderlies who had
made it back on duty were present in body only. The F.A.U.
quartet had to take over. The only lights were bean oil lamps,
each one somewhat weaker than a candle. The man was cut so
badly that McClure felt it best to use a general anaesthetic, not
knowing that a general was almost unknown in that field hospital. They managed to tie off both ends of the arterial arch,
and all went well. The next day they found the personnel of the
Third Field Hospital were warm and friendly, and apparently
more than willing to co-operate with their new associates.

That opening party, McClure discovered, was not the correct basis on which to judge the Yenshan field hospital. It had,

he discovered, the best disciplined patients, orderlies, and male nurses that it had been his good fortune to see in any military hospital in China. It did not have much medical know-how, but it had pep and it had zing. Bob discovered why when he and Bill Rahill managed to struggle out of bed at 5:15 a.m. for a flag raising ceremony. Amy, too, was permitted to participate in that ceremony: "The super gave the men the talk. I thought it was the talk for the week, but found out since that he gives them hell every morning. This was the first time that he had had them all together since they moved back 40 kms from their former place where they had been for two years. It was a big job to move and has taken over 3 weeks. During the process there was discovered that two men had deserted and got away with several days start before their absence was detected. Boy! Did he light into them! He said he had been a superintendent for umpteen years and had never had it happen before—of course he had. He said now they were a front line unit getting ready for big things ahead, and in the future there would be, if any were caught, a very brief trial at which he would be the judge. He said following that there would be an execution before the firing squad, and he went over in front of the flag and drew a circle on the ground and said that was where the victim would be standing when they shot him. It was a bit gruesome but it seems to work."

The hospital party had been on a Thursday. The following Saturday, General Chou, Commander of the Ninth Army, turned up after a survey to the front and he, too, gave a party to welcome the newcomers. This time the F.A.U. went at the fusel oil with even more care, and the three F.A.U. nurses, all of whom were of Cantonese origin, made the happy discovery that the General, too, was Cantonese. After the ice was broken they chatted away happily to him most of the evening. The idea of female nurses at the front was a new one to the general. He took to it most happily. By the end of the evening he seemed willing to grant the F.A.U. anything they requested, and had committed himself to approving their out-patient department and allowing some use of the hospital O.R. for civilian work.

General Chou had no flair for formal speeches but liked to drink toasts. The gathering drank the more obvious toasts—to Chiang Kai-shek, to Roosevelt, to Churchill—and then moved on to the less obvious ones. It was the only time Bob had ever heard a toast proposed to Franklin Roosevelt's mother-in-law, and he wondered for weeks afterwards who she was. The general was not a man to be defeated by running out of personalities. He decided he would like to hear everybody's national anthem, beginning with his own. By this time the windows of the hall were lined with faces pressed to the panes—the General had an appreciative audience. He called the Third Field Hospital to attention and announced to all who cared to hear that the Third Field Hospital was about to sing the Chinese national anthem. The hospital sang, and drank another toast to Chiang Kai-shek. The General then announced the national anthem of the great British Empire. The English members of the F.A.U. led the way through "God Save the King", after which everybody ignored the King and drank another toast to Churchill. The General then fixed his eyes on McClure and announced the national anthem of the great democracy of Canada. The only other Canadian in sight was Rosina Luey. Neither she nor McClure were quite sure whether there really *was* an official Canadian national anthem, and anyway the Brits had just rendered "God Save the King". Nor could Bob and Rosina decide how many times one had to "stand on guard" in "O Canada". They settled for a verse of "The Maple Leaf Forever". It should have been followed by a toast to Mackenzie King, but Bob still choked a little on the name (and did not want to take the time to explain that W.L.McK. was a kind of permanent Prime Minister) so he proposed a toast to "King of Canada" instead, and left everyone nicely confused. The General then moved on to Dr. Ernie Evans and ordered up the national anthem of the great Republic of the United States of America. Evans held a little conference with his compatriot, Bill Rahill. The two of them decided that, although lubricated with fusel oil, the high notes of "The Star Spangled Banner" were too much to inflict even upon a Chinese army. They wondered about "God Bless America" but did not want to turn the party into a prayer meeting. By this time, while Evans and Rahill were conferring, the party was in a fair way of dying and General Chou was beginning to look annoyed. Inspired by desperation, Dr. Evans turned to his Canadian and British allies and said, "Come on, fellows, let's sing 'I've Been Working on the Railroad'."

The China Convoy team came to attention and gave a rousing rendition of the old folk classic.

"Now *that*," said the General, "is a great national anthem!

Dr. Loa, be so generous as to translate for this unworthy person the meaning of the words of this most honourable anthem."

McClure decided he had better avoid a translation and give a precis, "Well, sir, it's uh—it's all about railroads. Railroads, as one of such brilliance as yourself well knows, contributed very much to the building of the most illustrious United States."

"How practical," said the General. "Just like the Americans. We shall all sing that honourable song again so that I and my unworthy men may learn it."

They all sang their way through the new American National Anthem, right through to Dinah in her kitchen. The General was very pleased, while Evans and Rahill were very nervous. They wondered if they had just sown the dark seeds of some future international incident. Their worries were not unfounded, because in the weeks and months ahead the Commanding General of the Chinese Ninth Army never held a party without ordering up the American National Anthem as a kind of dessert.

McClure remained with his F.A.U. team at Yenshan on the original trip for some three weeks. By the final week they were fully functional with their forty F.A.U. beds set aside for post-operative patients, the O.R. itself in reasonable shape (although still without electric lights) and the out-patient department in full swing. To begin with the principal military work lay in cleaning up a backlog of old cases—wounds that had never been attended to by a surgeon but had simply been treated medically and had moist bandages applied every day, serious eye cases that should have been operated on long ago but were now simply lying in a thousand bed hospital and receiving one eye washout a day and slowly going blind. McClure had no eye instruments with him and had to do the best he could with regular surgical equipment. There was no one else in the entire area who had done any eye work, including his own men. Once again he found himself operating and instructing at the same time. On later trips he would bring better eye equipment with him, and would have two tables going so he could turn from one patient to the next with no loss of time.

The team took cholera vaccine to the school and vaccinated

350 children and a class of adults. Word spread, and on market day they vaccinated another 350 civilians. The out-patient department began sending patients to the O.R. Soon, the log book almost balanced between civilian and military surgery. General Chou was appalled. He had agreed to an O.P.D. because he did not think it would be used, the people were so backward. One of the nurses baked him a chocolate cake and calmed his worries.

At the end of the O.P.D.'s first week they received a patient whom McClure had heard about, but had hoped would not come in until such time as they had better surgical tools. It was the six year old son of a local head man and the boy's fate could make or break the future of the out-patient department. The boy arrived after a four day trip on horseback. After examining him McClure decided there was no way he could, or should, postpone surgery. The boy had had a bladder stone growing for more than two years and was now suffering terribly. He could only ride or walk a few paces without having to squat down and dribble. They scheduled him into O.R. for a general anaesthetic. The day got off to a bad start because Robin Eden, their anaesthetist, was in an artistic mood that day and showed up late. He received a bawling out from McClure that he undoubtedly remembered. (It was well known in the China Convoy that the best way to enrage McClure was to mess around with the O.R. One of the wags had once said that the sight of McClure in an O.R. rage was enough to make the blood mc'curdle. They called him "Old McCurdle" in their genial, insubordinate way.) Anyway, after McCurdle had curdled Robin they set to on the boy with the bladder stone and did, what McClure considered to be, "a dandy job". Unfortunately, the delay in starting meant that they finished O.R. that day doing another extremely delicate operation by the light of the bean oil lamps, which did little to soothe Old McCurdle.

It was difficult to remain angry with Robin Eden. In the months ahead he was always good for morale. When the going got tough, and he felt the team needed a party, he would decide it was Anthony Eden's birthday, or that of some aunt not even Mr. Eden had heard of, and they would all have a little celebration. And he was quite talented as an artist. He was fascinated by the tribal people he had met in the course of his various postings, and lugged portraits with him in his personal

pack. He was entranced by the scenery of China, and particularly so down here near Indo-China. This southern scenery had
even fascinated McClure when he first saw it. It was not mountainous country but was hilly. They were not ordinary hills.
They were the little sugar-loaf variety that Bob had seen in
Chinese paintings and had always thought were figments of
the artists' imaginations. There was ample opportunity to
enjoy the scenery because the officers' latrine was on a hillside,
with a view, and they all suffered, frequently, from dysentery.

General Chou liked Robin's paintings, too, and one day
demonstrated his knowledge by identifying various tribal portraits, and even the scenery. "Ah," he said, "that man is of the
Lisu tribe—ah yes, that is an unwed girl. She belongs to the
Flowery Miao tribe, see that skirt she is wearing?—Let me see,
don't tell me, ah yes that scene is near Precious Mountain, and
the one next to it is near Eternal Peace air base." General Chou
was very, very good, and his knowledge of his country and his
people was quite impressive, but there was one painting that
baffled him. He identified it as being in the Yenshan area but
he could not pin point its location. "And yet," he said, "it is
one of the most familiar of all scenes. It is as though it were part
of me and yet I cannot place it!" He finally gave up and asked
to be enlightened. They told him it was called "View From the
Latrine". That day the nurses gave him kaopectate instead of
chocolate cake.

Robin Eden did some artwork for McClure. Bob had been
enjoying his new 'uniform'. It was cool and comfortable, having a kind of cellular shirt, and a bush jacket and shorts that actually matched. He asked Robin if he would label each item of
kit for him with indelible ink. Whether it was to fend off thieves
or borrowers Bob did not know, but thought it would be nice
for once to have his personal gear identified. The bush jacket
came back with the name in large letters across the back—
"General McCurdle". Each item of kit bore the same identity.

Old McCurdle had been marked, but he had also left his
mark. During the last evening of his first visit to Yenshan he
was sitting tapping out a letter to Amy on his little Hermes
typewriter, when there was a sound of shouting and general
turmoil from the sentries at the gate of what the F.A.U. were
pleased to call their 'fort'. After dark was not a healthy time to

tamper with Chinese sentries. The team hurried to see what devastation was underway, but by the time they got there the gates to the courtyard had been thrown open to the invaders. An hour or so later Bob resumed his letter to Amy: "We saw coming in a long line of people with little bean oil lanterns and carrying things on poles. Of course in our bloodthirsty way we hoped it was a multiple stabbing or something for us to do. However we were all very surprised to find it was a deputation of six of the local gentry. They knew of our school health work and all, and had found out a few hours before that I was off tomorrow, so they rustled around and got 5 chickens, 50 eggs, 100 chin* of potatoes and huge baskets of fruit. It looked like the Sunday School pictures of spies returning from the promised land . . . It was a fine gesture. We are using all of this as an opening for our special diet work for soldiers. Eggs, chicken and potatoes will give a marvelous kick off to the old show. These things go a long way to make one feel that our work is welcome and that we are really getting some place."

McClure returned to Yenshan several times that year and for stays of varying lengths.

A new doctor joined the Yenshan team. He was Dr. John Thompson of the British Red Cross. He was a tall man, standing six feet four inches, with a head bald as a boiled egg, and an enormous fund of stories adaptable for all occasions. He was not only a good doctor but an accomplished magician. He gave the team an aura of wizardry that enhanced their image in the eyes of the local populace.

They built up an enormous out-patient department. As far as McClure could tell, from any figures he had ever seen, they were handling twice as many patients as any other Red Cross team in China. Patients were coming in on journeys that took almost a week on horseback. Some of their ailments were awesome. One woman came in after a five day ride and McClure diagnosed her problem as an ovarian cyst. She was in a terrible way and there was no alternative but to operate. He removed a cyst that weighed forty pounds. (She died twelve hours later for lack of blood transfusions.)

A group of army recruits arrived. The sight of young recruits could be heart-rending at most times. They would plod

*About 133 lbs.

along in their hundreds, often roped together to prevent desertions. This batch had been on the march for fifty days without receiving immunization shots. Two hundred of them were seriously ill and seventy-six stretcher cases were taken immediately to hospital where there were not sufficient beds. They were laid on the dirt floor. They were dying of relapsing fever and typhus while admission papers were being made out, and McClure was distraught at the bureaucratic ruthlessness of it all. Those who died were put in a tower at the corner of the 'fort' from where they were buried when a wind change made it necessary. The F.A.U. team heard noises late at night and found one youth in the tower who had not died. They took him into the F.A.U. ward and tried to get some nourishment into him. It was all ghastly, and reminded McClure that there were indeed cultural differences in the way his two homelands looked at human life.

Most of the work, fortunately, was less frustrating. A transport 'plane crashed nearby and they went off on an aluminum salvaging trip, something none of them had done for some time. The hospital sterilizer was about to give up, but the results of that trip put it back into full operation. "You can't make plowshares," said General McCurdle, "without a goodly number of swords."

General McCurdle also went off with Robin Eden on a ten day trek along the front where they virtually immunized an entire army with a new tetanus and typhoid vaccine, "T & T", that had been perfected after experience in Africa. As yet no other Red Cross team in China had taken it seriously. McClure had a row with his own doctors who claimed there was no need for it. The argument ended abruptly when a wounded cavalryman was deposited in their midst suffering from advanced tetanus.

The immunization field trip was in October, and just as he completed it Bob realized his seventeenth wedding anniversary had rolled around. Instead of waiting a day for army transport he hurriedly walked twenty-seven miles back to base, in order to have access to his writing materials, so he could at least write to Amy on their anniversary day. It was a little thing but somehow important that that letter be written on the exact date. Amy received the letter nine weeks later and forgave him for writing so triumphantly on the 6th when their wedding had actually been on the 5th. It was a letter that did not talk of medical or military matters but of love, marriage, forced separation, and duty: "I'm thinking about our married life a great deal at this time. There are a lot of people around us who seem to be able to carry on their married life in a much more normal and routine manner—as such I envy them. However, there are also many of the army people around us now, too, and I'm sorry to say that while they all seem to love their wives, write to them often, and talk about them a lot, yet there are also a good many times when they forget about them in their behaviour . . . I can say that since I came out this last time there has scarcely been a time when any queer thoughts have even crossed my mind. The answer of some to that would be that perhaps I did not meet much temptation and while that may be partly correct I think there has been a bit of the old serpent with the apple come my way too.

"Two things I do regret about our 17 years are that we have not been together as much as we should have been. I may be changing my ideas about that, too, a bit now . . . When one thinks of the sacrifices in flesh and blood that this war makes on others then for us to make that of separation does not seem much or too much by comparison. The other day I saw five corpses beside a burned out transport plane, and since then when people talk of sacrifice I feel that none of us really know much about what it is. Our discomfort is spread out over years; theirs was but for a few minutes . . . The other feature that I cannot feel clear about is that I am not taking my share in raising the kids. I really do feel it and feel it much more now than I have ever done before."

He reminisced about their courtship days, about their wedding in Tientsin, their honeymoon, nights in Taiwan, and reunions in Canada.

"It may be a sign of age but I go over these things rather often in my mind in these past months. What makes me feel secure is the fact that these are the memories that now crowd out others in my mind. Others used to thrill me but they no longer do so. Only those of you. These as I say may be a sign of age but they at least are signs that our love is ripening with that age and so long as it is the case then I don't care."

Bob McClure may have missed his wedding anniversary by one day, but there was a much more public event around that same time that General McCurdle did not miss. The story that came out of Yenshan was a little confused, but it had to do with railroad birds coming home to roost.

American army machinery had finally punched a usable road into the Yenshan area and General Chou announced, with a great deal of pleasure, that an American unit was coming in to help train his men in the use of American weapons. Everybody seemed to think it was good news—except Dr. Ernie Evans and Bill Rahill. They had a hasty conference and approached Old McCurdle. "Look," said Ernie, "we've taught a whole Chinese army that the American National Anthem is 'I've Been Working On the Railroad'."

"Yes," said McCurdle, "I believe we have."

"But," said Ernie, "don't you realize what this means? Bill and I are Americans. We've disgraced our country."

"Oh, that," said McCurdle. "We can talk our way out of that."

"Well, if anybody can," said Ernie grudgingly, "perhaps you can."

The day the Americans were expected McClure borrowed enough uniform to make himself look quite military, feeling that his General McCurdle outfit lacked something in impressiveness. He then walked several miles out the new motor road and positioned himself where he could be the first to accost the new arrivals. He was not disappointed. The American convoy arrived—motor cycles, staff cars, half-tracks, armoured cars, anti-aircraft guns—the works. Everything was so new even their uniforms smelled of fresh paint. McClure spotted the C.O. in the second jeep and stepped forward smartly, waved the jeep to a halt, and saluted. The C.O. had never heard of McClure, McCurdle, or the Friends Ambulance Unit, but he listened patiently while McClure briefed him on the fact that his odd assortment of Yanks, Brits, Canucks and Chinese had run into a problem that had to do with the high notes in "The Star Spangled Banner". McClure pointed out how inconvenient it was that a Chinese general and his entire army were under the impression that the American National Anthen had to do with railroads, and that it would be terribly bad in the face department if the general were disillusioned.

The C.O. made a few choking noises about having no authorization to change the American National Anthem and forced McCurdle to become political. "Look," Bob said, "I don't want to blackmail you but there is no use contradicting me. Your interpreter here, I see, is Cantonese Chinese from San Francisco. Well he's going to have an awful time with the local language. General Chou will take my word. I'll just have to explain when you trot out another anthem that you were a rebel in the civil war and *you* lost, and that *our* anthem is authentic." McCurdle paused for a moment, and then added, darkly, "—or that you belong to the wrong political party and that our anthem is Roosevelt's anthem. Roosevelt is very big around here."

The C.O. eyed the strange roadside apparition for a few moments, no doubt wondering whether what he had just heard was some bizarre Canadian re-write of American history. But the C.O. was a civilized man with a university background and believed in adaptability. "You know, McClure," he said, "I've heard my men sing 'The Star Spangled Banner' and it's not a pleasant experience. I think they'll do much better with Dinah."

The next morning at 5:30 there were 20,000 Chinese soldiers lined up in the Yenshan parade square and faced by the spotless American unit. To one side stood the Chinese men of the Third Field Hospital and with them the men and women of the China Convoy surgical team. General Chou strode out and, to the accompaniment of the Chinese National Anthem, the Chinese flag was hoisted proudly to the top of its pole. Then, while the whole world seemed to stand to attention, Old Glory was unfurled to the winds of China while a Chinese military band played "I've Been Working On the Railroad".

General McCurdle and his boys and girls all stood to attention and saluted with the best of them.

That was the story that came out of Yenshan. There has been no indication that it was documented in any military log, which is not surprising. There are those who have implied that the scene by the roadside and the flag raising ceremony were the figments of a mc-curdled imagination while others maintain that even Bob McClure and his gang would not have fabricated a story that had a potential twenty-thousand witnesses.

33

The Return of Hankey

In the summer of 1943 while McClure was on one of his forays out to headquarters, or between forays into Yenshan (it was sometimes difficult to know in which direction a McClure foray was headed), he met Donald Hankey. It was a reunion to which McClure had been looking forward for years, but when it came it was too emotional to rate more than one short paragraph in a letter home: "It is the first time we have been face to face since 1938. It was good to see him! All kidding aside, the eyes of both of us were just a bit weepy for awhile. It is so funny to have tried to think just what he would be like, or what he was like before. Well he is just as I wrote about him and just as he used to be. There is not a spot of change in him at all."

McClure and his British Red Cross counterpart, Dr. Flowers, lost no time in sending Hankey into action with a combined B.R.C.S. and F.A.U. team on the Salween front. Seldom was any team doctor anywhere held in such high esteem by his Chief Surgeon as was Dr. Hankey.

McClure had hardly turned around from that reunion than he enjoyed another one, this time with his sister Janet. Dr. Janet, complete with children and husband, was headed for the 'outside'. McClure was in transit through Kunming by land when he was told that the Kilborns were about to land at the airport in transit by air. He rushed to the airport to meet them. Their landing was delayed by an air raid warning, and Bob had a half hour of mixed emotions. On the one hand he worried about the safety of the airborne travellers. On the other, he took immense enjoyment from the spectacle of the American

P38s and P40s hurtling down the field in formation and hurling themselves into the air. It was a spectacle that never failed to exhilarate the flyer in him. It was enough to make him join up, had it not been, as he once said, that he "would have to put Christianity into storage".

The passenger 'plane carrying the Kilborns was the first to land after the raid. There was a brief family reunion while Liberators and Fortresses revved their huge engines outside on the tarmac and the returning fighters swooped in as though to raise the tiles off the control tower roof. The children were wildly excited. It was a confused, noisy visit. Bob felt very homesick as he saw the Kilborns leave with Canada as their final destination. He had a feeling that Janet would never return, and he was right. Bob McClure was now the last of William and "Maggie" McClure's family still to have his feet on the soil of China.

What a strange China it was, and what a strange war! Now, entering the last half of 1943, there were few real pushes on anywhere in China. Everybody was talking about a big drive in the south-west, but as yet it had not materialized. The Nationalist forces were still following their policy of trying simply to hold what they had without worrying about regaining territory. Ever since the Communists' Fourth Route Army had tried to infiltrate heavily into the south-east and had been stopped by Nationalists the same Nationalists had been blockading the major Communist units to keep them in the north and to keep supplies, even Red Cross shipments, away from them. An American estimate said that almost half a million of the Generalissimo's best troops were engaged in this blockade instead of fighting the Japanese. By September Chiang's American second in command, General "Vinegar" Joe Stilwell, was demanding that the Generalissimo lift the blockade, get together with the Communists, and proceed with the war.

The Generalissimo was still shackled by the dilemma that the Communists' style of warfare called for the organizing of guerrilla bands inside enemy territory. That meant training and arming the peasantry. Chiang knew that in the long run an armed peasantry could destroy the Second Revolution. The fact that the peasantry would want to destroy the Second Revolution, because it had obviously stopped far short of any real revolutionary objective, was apparently not given great weight. President Roosevelt was an admirer and supporter of the Generalissimo. He, like many Americans, after feeling the weight of the Japanese steamroller themselves, had gained retroactive respect for the valiant Chinese struggle of the opening years of the Sino-Japanese war. And there was that whole image so beloved by the Western press of the Generalissimo and Madame as being such a civilized, well educated, Christian pair. And Madame spoke English so beautifully. Roosevelt was siding with Chiang rather than with Stilwell and was making moves to have China recognized as one of the Big Four. The British were cool to this idea because it conjured up the spectre (or spectacle), vividly described by Foreign Minister Anthony Eden, of China "running up and down the Pacific". The Russians, presumably, did not mind the thought of China scurrying around the Pacific but had no intention of giving her any say in Europe. On the other hand, the Generalissimo was distrustful of Moscow because Moscow was supposedly friendly with the Chinese Communists, although the Russians were on record as saying that Mao and his people were "radishes", being red on the outside and white within. At any rate, by November 1st, 1943, the Four Powers managed to agree in the Moscow Declaration that they would all fight unceasingly toward final victory and would sign no separate peace treaties.

The unceasing waging of the war down in McClure's area seemed, at the time, to be a matter of a military stalemate. The biggest inroads were being made by typhus, dysentery, malaria, relapsing fever, inflation, corruption, lice, malnutrition and all the other woes attendant upon a wartime population where even the government was a refugee. What it all meant was that no matter how much the political powers might stall and temporize, McClure's war continued to be an exceedingly hot one.

As chief of the China Convoy's medical services he continued to visit the surgical teams—to inspect, to consult and, always, to assist at the operating table. More and more, Michael Harris was serving as McClure's liaison man, often going on administrative assignments in one direction while his chief went on surgical tours in the other.

McClure returned to Hsiakwan. There he caught typhus,

and went to bed with a raging fever. Four members of the China Convoy had already died of typhus fever. The mortality rate from typhus among the general populace was alarmingly high, with as many as three dying out of every four infected. The team at Hsiakwan rallied around to make certain Old McCurdle did not become one of the statistics. It was a hard struggle but McClure came through it only slightly weakened and showing very little lessening of general vitality. He climbed out of bed and went back on the road again.

Whether as a hold-over from the predestinarianism of his Presbyterian youth, or as a matter of simple Oriental fatalism, McClure was paying less attention than ever to personal dangers. When two trucks immediately preceding him and one following him on the Burma Road were all waylaid by bandits (one truck was sent over a precipice and the occupants killed) he simply wrote: "God keeps us as long as he wants to use us and when our time's up it doesn't make much difference where we are, in how safe a spot, we're due to be taken."

By the fall of '43, things were looking very good. McClure felt the team leaders were turning out to be more "high-powered" than he had dared hope. More doctors were arriving and others were on the way. It appeared that he would soon have difficulty finding enough support personnel to accompany the doctors, which was a total reverse of the situation that prevailed as recently as the previous May. It was good timing because in October an offensive started on the Burma front, although not quite as planned. This was a Japanese offensive.

McClure headed down to the Salween area to lend a hand to the combined B.R.C.S. and F.A.U. surgical team under Donald Hankey and a China-born British doctor, "Billy" Toop.

Just one month earlier Hankey's Mobile Team No. 5 had travelled in to the Salween on foot, with their medical and surgical supplies being carried by coolies and pack mules. It had been a grim trip, along narrow mountain paths bordering the precipices of the Salween gorge, and had been accomplished for the most part in pouring rain. They had lost one driver and a mule in a dizzying 300 foot fall. Now, when McClure went in, the same paths had been 'improved' by the army and were supposed to be roads. They were improved to the point that

Bob was able to ride horseback instead of walking. He thought that if those were improved trails he would have hated to have travelled them before.

Bob found his men at work in the most vigorously active combat zone any F.A.U. team had been in since the escape from Burma. He also found morale very high, not only among his own men but among the Chinese troops. He thought the Chinese soldiers were better equipped and looking more fit than he had ever seen them at any previous time.

It was real jungle country and a very bad malaria region, but now every man had his own mosquito net. The incidence of malaria was down to about one tenth of what it had been a year before when McClure and Louderbough had made a Salween survey. So important was the mosquito net that the scene every morning at every sentry post, bivouac, and camp, as the men rose and folded their nets with reverential care, reminded Bob of some vast mystical religious rite.

Hankey's team had commandeered three Chinese temples as a hospital. Two temples were wards. The third was the operating theatre and 'administrative' centre. These were not abandoned temples. One could still burn incense at the altars, cast fortune sticks, and pray to the gods. The gods were still present, inhabiting ferocious looking statues. Some of these gilded deities looked so fearsome they had to be discreetly draped to prevent the more seriously wounded men from having waking nightmares.

Here, working under the eyes of the supernatural supervisors, with drugs in short supply and no X-ray with which to inspect fractures or trace shrapnel, Dr. Hankey, the imperturbable Englishman, was in his element. He and his men had Japanese gunfire for breakfast every morning, but they also had a foreign breakfast of porridge, with bean milk, followed by local eggs and ham, and topped off with toast. The U.S. Army sent some coffee in with McClure. The team used that as a change from Hankey's chrysanthemum tea. Hankey shaved every morning before breakfast and spent at least ten minutes every day polishing his shoes. He insisted that the men take a short break for tea in the afternoon. He taught the cook to make an English supper. (It reminded McClure of a shilling meal in a pub—nourishing, but as tasteless as only an Englishman could make it.) Hankey created a civilized veneer that sustained the team of two doctors and three support personnel in the midst of interminable hours of heavy surgery.

McClure arrived just as casualties were pouring in from a raid, and once again he found himself in the operating room with his friend. It seemed like years since he had decided away back in Chengchow that Hankey had the makings of a good surgeon. He found now that he had been right.

McClure came out from the Salween and headed back along the Burma Road. He had urgent things to attend to, not the least of which was the rounding up of a portable X-ray from somewhere, anywhere, and getting it in to Hankey and Mobile Team No. 5. He was hitch-hiking, as usual, by truck. He began to get hot flashes, followed by dizzy spells. The dizziness increased to the point where he was having difficulty maintaining consciousness. He asked to be deposited at a small way station. There he struggled to organize his thoughts and just managed to send a telegram to the nearest F.A.U. post asking his boys to come and get him. It was the first time anyone had ever received an out and out call for help from Bob McClure. After he had sent the message he collapsed, and lost consciousness. That was the last he remembered for several days.

Bob came to in a little hospital at an American Air Force base. He had relapsing fever. He came out of that session with a weight loss of thirty pounds. The China Convoy debaters deliberated and speedily reached a consensus. McClure was to be flown home for a brief rehabilitation period. McClure agreed, on condition he could find free transportation. The Chairman put in a request to the American Air Force for a travel priority.

Between Christmas and New Year's, 1943, McClure decided he would not wait for travel clearance. He contacted some of the American pilots with whom he had worked in establishing the Air Rescue scheme. Almost instantly, he found himself at a little fighter base about 20 miles from Chabwa, in India, with a New Year's Eve party just getting underway. He recruited a young lieutenant as a driver and conned the base commander into providing a jeep to get him to the main air base at Chabwa. Since the lieutenant wanted to spend New Year's Eve with his girl in Chabwa it was a cheerfully satisfactory arrangement. When they reached the Chabwa base they realized neither of them knew the password. McClure lurked in the shadows until he heard the word "snowball", which could only be a password in that climate, and he and his driver entered. An air force B24, converted for mail and V.I.P. use, was scheduled to leave Chabwa for Miami in a few hours. The brass were all off celebrating but McClure found a sympathetic sergeant who put his name on the manifest list. The 'plane flew to Karachi and there everybody's papers were rigidly inspected. McClure had no papers, no pass, no travel priority. He came up against another sergeant, but this one wanted to get a belated Christmas gift to his girl in Detroit. McClure verified that the gift was not drugs and accepted the errand. He arrived in Toronto, via Miami, during the first week of January, 1944. The whole trip had been an oriental back-scratching tour de force. The precious gift that had secured his passage from Karachi to Miami was a made-in-the-U.S.A. alarm clock from the American military PX.

Back in China, the Convoy lads and lasses were singing a ditty* to the tune of "The Mountains of Mourne":

> You've heard of McCurdle, alias McClure,
> Our medical chief who is always on tour.
> He's never stayed more than two weeks in one place
> And with all the Chinese he's got plenty of face.
> Just now he is flying to visit his wife
> But's he's sure to come back for the rest of his life.

Bob arrived in Canada to find his countrymen's eyes all riveted, as usual, on Europe. The previous July, Canada had been electrified by the news that the First Canadian Division and a Tank Brigade had landed with the British and Americans on the island of Sicily. Since then the whole country had followed the exploits of their boys in the capture of Sicily and the push up the 'boot' of Italy. Their thoughts had been with the regiments with the strange colloquial names—the Princess Pats, the Hasty P's, the Carelton and Yorks, the R.C.R.s, the Edmontons, the West Novas, the Ontarios, the Van Doos, the Three Rivers, the Seaforths, the 48ths—names their grandchildren might never hear but which now carried the hopes and prayers of a nation. As Bob was reunited with his family in Toronto (Norah, the eldest, was now sixteen) the country was

*By Brandon Cadbury.

heaving a sigh of relief that the Canadians had just successfully completed the fierce battle of Ortona and were moving into winter lines.

For 'Rest, Recreation and Rehabilitation', McClure went on the campaign trail to remind his countrymen that China, too, was still part of the real world.

At that same time, in January, 1944, Dr. Donald Hankey left his temple O.R. and went on a field trip into the jungle to vaccinate front line troops. It was not an idle trip. A typhus epidemic was creating more slaughter than were the Japanese. Hankey and an assistant, working at an exhausting pace, saw to the vaccination of some ten thousand men. In his haste, Hankey did not take the time to vaccinate himself. He caught typhus. He died in the arms of his China Convoy companion. Dr. Donald Hankey, known as "Noble Soul" to the Chinese, was buried by a lonely lake in that almost forgotten corner of the world where he had gone because it was "the right thing to do".

34

The City of Jade and $(a=r+p)$

McClure was in Canada for little more than four months. His Rest, Recreation, and Rehabilitation leave did not take the form of quiet days puttering around the house, of early evenings spent helping the kids with their homework, and of late evenings sitting ensconced in an easy chair in the dimly lit living room with a fire in the fireplace and Amy cuddled on his lap in something diaphanous. The longing for such a delectable ending to a day had been expressed by him in more than one letter written from lonely wayside inns and beside Himalayan campfires. But there never had been any way Bob McClure could spend three months at either Rest or Recreation and, as his friends all knew, he was hopelessly beyond any chance of Rehabilitation. With the war still underway, and with the men and women of the China Convoy teams preparing for 'the big push' it was inevitable that Amy would have to share her husband with Canadian audiences. Bob threw himself into what amounted to deputation work for the F.A.U.

The message McClure brought was a new one to many Canadian conscientious objectors. Their options had been severely limited. They could either go to work camps or be conscripted into the army for home service. It was a time when doctors were in short supply, both overseas and at home. Medical students were on accelerated crash courses, driving through to completion without benefit of long Christmas breaks or summer holidays. And yet a medical student who refused to enroll in the Officers Training Corps at university could find himself twiddling his thumbs behind barbed wire, and a number did. Then along came McClure telling of a unit that offered opportunity for adventure, danger, *and* service that was all in line with the most demanding conscience. Before Bob headed back to China, applications to join the China Convoy were already beginning to roll in from young Canadians. McClure was elated, not knowing that various bureaucracies would see to it that it would be almost a year before any of those volunteers could arrive in China.

McClure had also been fund raising. He had been given a particularly earnest hearing by the Canadian Red Cross. When he headed back for China in mid-May, 1944, he was the bearer of stupendous news for the F.A.U. The Canadian Red Cross was giving half a million dollars in Canadian funds to the work of the China Convoy. It was a transfusion that was destined to give the Convoy new impetus just as it was about to begin a new phase of its work. It also reassured Bob that the tree which bore the maple leaves was still healthy. The response from volunteers, the donation from the Red Cross, combined with the fact that the United Church, the Bloor Street congregation, and numerous schools, service clubs, and individual donors had never failed to back him, all served to reassure Bob on a point he had long suspected—in the long run one could count on Canadians, just don't count on their governments.

McClure arrived back in Asia in June just as the Allied armies arrived on the beaches of Normandy. There had been no other military news since the Battle of Marathon to equal the tidings of the D-Day invasion of Europe. Once again the Western world was paying scant heed to events in China. But in that country the Japanese had already launched an attack on what was called the Changsha front, driving south and west from the Hankow area. They were said to be using twenty-seven Manchurian Divisions. And while the Allied soldiers were still pouring from landing craft onto the beaches of Normandy, the Japanese began another major drive north and west from Canton. If the Changsha drive and the Canton drive should meet it would mean the final isolation of the entire eastern areas of China. It would leave pockets of guerrillas totally cut off from outside aid. It would leave millions of civilians cut off from relief supplies. It would leave missionaries trapped behind enemy lines. It would leave F.A.U. transport personnel, who had been hauling medical supplies to eastern epidemic areas, also trapped behind Japanese lines.

On the other side of the ledger the Chinese were finally launching the long expected push along the Burma and Indo-China front. Two of the China Convoy surgical teams were moving with the army westward along the Burma Road. A third team was back-packing its O.R. gear ever deeper into the jungles of the south-west. Another Convoy team had finally taken over the hospital in Kutsing and were doing more and more civilian work. Yet another team was doing strictly civilian work as a result of the civilian needs uncovered by the Yenshan unit. McClure felt the whole medical thrust was encouragingly diversified, but he received his biggest boost from observing a change in attitudes among Chinese *and* Westerners. *Some* Western doctors were beginning to treat their Chinese hospital staff like colleagues rather than employees! Even the Canadian Embassy in Chungking was adapting to new attitudes and new conditions. It had just made a name for itself as being the first embassy in China to abolish alcohol and to forego the dubious pleasure of throwing cocktail parties. This was, perhaps, not the most warlike of contributions, but it was original.

In some ways the Chinese were changing faster than the Westerners. Bob reported to Amy, with considerable enthusiasm, that the Chinese military medical facilities were vastly improved, the morale higher, and that senior medical officers were actually moving their offices to within "only a few tens of miles" of the fighting.

"There are some other changes in Chinese attitudes," he wrote. "These are (a) desire for large scale training of 'quack' doctors. Surprisingly enough the Rockefeller man on medical education in China is keen on it . . . What a chance to say 'I told you so'. (b) Whereas before they were sticky about nursing schools, now they want every hospital with a couple of doctors and a couple of trained nurses to become a nurses' training school, and they will even give an elaborate government subsidy to keep it going. This is part of China's post-war program that is to begin at once. The prospects then for mission hospitals are very bright indeed."

What was becoming almost an obsession with him, however, was the fear that the old crop of missionaries would not adapt to new attitudes and that a new crop, who had not participated in the war experience, would be unacceptable to the Chinese. He was beginning to picture the F.A.U. as having a vital role to play in the transition to peace time. He hoped that some of the F.A.U. people would move on into mission work when their term of service expired.

He had several talks with the United Nations Rural Rehabilitation Association people in Chungking and found that they were also eyeing the China Convoy as a prospective talent pool. And it began to look as though U.N.R.R.A. might be willing to follow up on projects that the F.A.U. could begin. Postwar planning was beginning to make progress, leaving only one small problem—that of everyone, including China herself, surviving until the end of the war.

The B.R.C.S. had had to evacuate Changsha in the face of the Japanese advance. McClure borrowed some British nurses from them to reinforce his own teams, and headed for the Burma front. He found that the Precious Mountain team had been running two operating tables in its one small O.R. and had been working all out for seven days a week for several months. He arrived in time to run into disaster. Dr. Quentin Boyd was in the midst of a nervous breakdown. He had begun to suffer from 'depression' a year before, but depression seemed to overtake everyone at some time, even McClure. Now, however, it was more than depression. Dr. Boyd was uncontrollably violent. McClure rushed him to the nearest American airbase. Space was made available on a transport headed for India. McClure wanted to get his patient to a hospital, in Assam, which was under Dr. Isidor Rabin of the University of Pennsylvania. It was the nearest point where good psychiatric treatment was available.

It was necessary to confine Boyd in a straight jacket. The jacket did not restrict the patient's legs. En route over the Hump he became so violent he managed to crack two of McClure's ribs while the latter was trying to inject a sedative. In desperation, in order to quieten his patient, the doctor had to withold oxygen as the 'plane climbed to 15,000 feet, and beyond.

They reached the hospital in Assam. It was a 350 bed hospital that had had 5,000 wounded pass through it in the last two months, but they accepted a mental patient as calmly as they would a fractured femur. McClure was surprised at the speed of their diagnosis. The patient had developed a very noticeable yellow hue and almost the first question asked was, "Has he been taking atabrin?"

He had indeed. Atabrin was the current anti-malaria wonder pill. If one took it regularly it gave an immunity to the disease. In the American Army in China it was not by a Health Order that atabrin was issued but by a Command Order, which meant that in theory it was a commander's responsibility to see to it that each man actually took his daily pill. McClure himself took atabrin whenever he felt a malaria attack coming on. Acting purely on instinct, he had never taken it on a regular basis. Many others had done the same. Dr. Boyd, however, had been meticulous in his use of the drug. He had been taking it steadily now for almost two years.

The doctors told McClure that there was no doubt Boyd was a victim of atabrin poisoning. They could quote chapter and verse on other case histories to prove it. They also told him it was classified information and that he was not to say anything about it. The British and American military authorities knew all about atabrin's dangers but they also knew it was saving immeasurably more men than it was killing.

A few days later Dr. Quentin Boyd was dead.

McClure flew rather pensively back to China pondering the unpleasant decisions that wartime leaders had to make in the name of the 'greater good'. He was jarred out of his pensiveness when the 'plane's brakes failed on landing. The machine ended up off the end of the runway, standing on its nose in a mudhole, with its props bent.

By the end of the summer of 1944 Bob was peering into the future and beginning to panic. Many of the China Convoy members were due for repatriation after three years of work. By November, McClure was to lose thirteen of his fifty-four medicals and his twenty Canadians had not yet arrived. He had hoped they would be arriving hard on his own heels so he would have had time to train them before November. As it was now he could see the work having to be cut by as much as 40 percent and then being laboriously rebuilt. What made it even more galling was the fact that now, at last, there was no shortage of supplies. But the problem was not all in Canada. Part of it lay with the various liaison committees in Chungking who had a habit of countermanding each other's orders and of changing priorities. The F.A.U. pulled McClure back to the capital to join in the bureaucratic 'battle of Chungking'. They managed to keep him in the area for almost a month.

Mid-September found McClure hurrying back along the Burma Road to rejoin his teams. He found that Paoshan had been saving surgery for him. It ranged from genitourinary wounds to chest, eye, and brain. One of the brain cases came to the hospital with maggots in the wound which, although visually unpleasant, was probably fortunate for the patient. It never ceased to be amazing the way maggots could clean up a wound. Bob seemed to be doing more and more brain surgery. He had had to do two brain operations at mission hospitals along the way. He gave thanks that he had had the presence of mind to see Dr. Wilder Penfield again in Montreal during the last visit home. Among other advice, Dr. Penfield had counselled that brain wounds be closed very quickly. It was advice that ran contrary to current practice in China but it was advice that McClure followed. He reported excellent results.

It seemed the year had hardly begun before it was October and Bob was writing another anniversary letter to Amy.

Bob nearly always incorporated at least one sentimental paragraph in his letters to Amy and was meticulous in ensuring that that section was always written by hand even though the letter was partially typed. Away back in the early days of their separation, in '37 and '38, the sentiment never seemed to come easily. The phrases were awkward, often almost gauche, not as though he did not mean what he was saying but as though he were extremely uncomfortable trying to verbalize personal feelings. It was seldom in the early days that he could even manage to write the straight-forward, 'I love you' of a marital sign-off, although he would occasionally make allusions to their nights together that must have given the censors insomnia. It was inhibiting, of course, to know that ones' letters would be read by a censor in the F.A.U. office and probably by a Chinese censor in Chungking and by a British censor in India. He had confessed to the fact that it was the F.A.U. censor that was most inhibiting. Now, however, in 1944, the awkward self-consciousness was gone: "I believe that even in our loneliness we've been drawn closer together. I admire you now more than ever and I love you with a love that is all the deeper because of our forced separation. My love is like a hunger almost—not just sexual hunger but that deep hunger of one partner for the other. As hunger drives you to walk faster to the next stop so this love drives me to work harder for the time when the job will be done and we shall be together again."

McClure then joined his Salween team which was with the Chinese army that was laying siege to the City of Jade.

Since time immemorial the Chinese had held jade, that hard, beautiful mineral, varying in colour all the way from off-white to dark green, in high esteem. To them jade represented the essence of hill and water solidified into precious translucent stone. Jade quarries had been developed in nearby Burma and one of the cities that had been given over almost wholly to the manufacture and sale of jade ornaments was the Chinese city of Tengchung. Tengchung was located in a Himalayan valley about fifty miles north-west of the Burma Road and west, too, of the Salween River. It was within about thirty miles of the Burma border. It seemed a strange place to find a sophisticated trading city, until one realized that although Tengchung had been missed by the Burma Road it had been on the old silk trail that led from Peking to Mandalay. Tengchung had been the outpost city, a gateway of trade, and its people for centuries had been familiar with the outer world. Even so, the British Consulate that had been located in Tengchung, until the Japanese overran the place, had had the unenviable reputation of being the loneliest consulate of the British Empire. But now, in the late fall of 1944, there was nothing remote, or weirdly beautiful, or romantic, or even lonely about Tengchung. There was a Japanese garrison entrenched behind the ancient walls. There was a Chinese army on the outside blasting its way in by means of mountain artillery and trench mortars.

The China Convoy surgical team had been here for some weeks with its O.R. established up in the hills overlooking the City of Jade. Here, at last, the surgeons' macabre prayers were being answered—they were getting to treat wounds early. The action was all around them and wounded were going onto the tables only minutes after being hit.

The Japanese garrison, short of both food and water, made a break for freedom. It was a futile effort. The tribesmen followed them through the hills and the valleys in a savage manhunt. There were virtually no Japanese survivors. Now, as the

Chinese were re-occupying the City of Jade, McClure and the Convoy surgical team entered with them.

As the F.A.U. entered Tengchung, the work changed. From here on the China Convoy emphasis would be on Rehabilitation.

The team set out to establish a hospital where none existed. Almost nothing existed. They had intended to commandeer a building, but Tengchung was in ruins. It rained, and there was no shelter larger than an umbrella. Corpses of people and horses lay everywhere. The air was foul, and vultures sat bloated on the ruins of the temple walls. Just outside the battered city gate was a small schoolhouse that was, incredibly, almost intact. The Convoy team moved into the school and began, methodically, to create a modern hospital from the seeds of a front line surgery. Since every modern hospital was based on three prime requisites—trained personnel, electricity, and the facility to boil water in quantity—the F.A.U. personnel now set out to salvage anything and everything that could be of use. As usual, generators, wiring, and aluminum from crashed airplanes proved to be invaluable.

It was an interesting team. The doctor was John Perry, son of the Episcopal Bishop of Boston. There were two English nurses, Rita Dangerfield and Margaret Briggs. Margaret Briggs, a rather large, good-natured woman, was the senior nurse and quite old by F.A.U. standards, being in her thirties. The X-ray technician, anaesthetist and general mechanic was a Scotsman, Doug Crawford. He had spent seven years in a bank in some previous life and was a dour, dependable type. There was a Chinese lad, Henry Yu, from North China. He talked good English but found the language so absurd that he took pleasure in deliberately tying it in knots. There were two Chinese married women from Tengchung who were working as volunteers and there were two teenage Burmese sisters, who were poor as mice, worked like Trojans, were light of heart, immaculately clean, and wore colourful sarongs that made everyone else look drab and bulgy. The presence of the Burmese girls and of the two Chinese women made it obvious that one of the early services offered by the emerging hospital should be that of a nurses' training school.

What Dr. Perry, Nurse Briggs, and Bob McClure had in mind was somewhat audacious. McClure spelled it out in a letter in October, just after the city fell: "Here we are going to set up what we think is an U.N.R.R.A. hospital but as yet U.N.R.R.A. isn't functioning . . . The work gets going first and finally the parent organization that should do it extends its big-hearted recognition."

McClure intended to use some of the Canadian Red Cross money to equip the hospital. He felt that the organization should be congratulated for its far-sightedness. "This really is an original job they are going to be doing. No other organization in China has tried to do this type of work." The Canadian Red Cross, like U.N.R.R.A., was still blissfully unaware that it had gone pioneering with McClure.

Bob went off to Chungking and contacted what he called "The Tengchung Old Boys' Association", a group of wealthy merchants all of whom claimed to have their business and family roots in Tengchung. He found them to be amazingly generous. They donated money for the hospital with no strings attached, other than that they wanted its services to be free. (One merchant called his donation a "loan" but was so surprised when McClure turned up several months later to pay it back that he promptly re-donated it as a gift.)

The building of the Tengchung hospital was a milepost for McClure. He was finally feeling the exhilaration of dreams come true. The Westerners were finally not only working *for* the Chinese but *with* the Chinese.

The team had hoped to have the hospital functioning properly by January but were well ahead of schedule by December. U.N.R.R.A. had still not caught up. "As I told you before," Bob wrote to Amy, "this is our idea of what an U.N.R.R.A. hospital should be, and the fact that it is not yet adopted or recognized by its rightful parent does not bother us in the least. Up in Chungking they are all talking about an U.N.R.R.A. program for China which will begin early in 1946 and here we are with one going in 1944."

In the process of this Tengchung experience he miscalculated Amy's birthday, this time being off the mark by precisely one month. She forgave him this, too, when it became apparent that another endeavour at Tengchung had been forcing him to concentrate his mind even more than usual. It was an experiment in what McClure catalogued as 'preventive medicine' and what others would call 'bomb disposal'.

The problem had been brought forcefully to their attention. Even while they were founding a hospital they were running an emergency surgery and many of the emergency patients were children who had lost at least one hand. For a period of almost six weeks the O.R. had been treating an average of one such victim a day. Then it escalated to two a day, then four, then five. It was obvious that the children were collecting un-detonated primers, hand grenades, shells, and other assorted explosives. As the pathetic parade continued, the doctors were becoming desperate.

A team of American engineers turned up. They were just passing through on a road construction project, but they were explosives experts. McClure took three days off from the O.R. while the engineers taught him the demolition trade.

There were times when McClure could become so caught up in a project that he would become insensitive to the feelings of others. This was one of those times. The enthusiasm with which he reported this new venture to Amy demonstrated total insensitivity to the fact that his news might cause nervous prostration among his loved ones: "It is very exciting and has everything that flying has. To step up on a ladder and pick an unexploded but activated '75' shell out of a mud wall knowing that the old thing may go off any time and then walk carefully down the ladder and take the thing along 200 yards to a pit and lay it down carefully is quite a thrill . . . We got an American '75' sticking in the city wall with its nose in the wall and its rear sticking out 10 feet above the ground . . . I went up on the wall and dropped bricks on its rear and knocked it loose but it did not go off . . . We got two Japanese unexploded '75's too and a couple of unexploded bazooka rockets which are very hot stuff. We picked up three hand grenades to add to the pile. Then we put in three packages of TNT of 1/2 lb. each, like cakes of butter only hard, and packed the lot in together . . . Was it ever an explosion . . . It makes 4th of July seem tame indeed to see a mushroom of black smoke go up 300 feet and then taste the bitter taste in your mouth as it drifts down on you."

Amy almost wept as she read that letter. Her madman of a husband had found a new way to apply his own formula for adventure—a formula that could be expressed quite simply: $a = r + p$, "*a*dventure equals *r*isk with a *p*urpose". And there was no doubt as to what he was up to. He spelled it out: "I still have about 12 packages of TNT and some fuses and stuff and when in Tengchung I shall make it a practice to carry that stuff with me and do some useful work . . . It is all a matter of knowing how, and doing enough of it, that one does not get excited at all."

There were many people who were sure that McClure's self-confidence would be the death of him, and he seemed in a fair way to proving them right. He was in and out of Jade City frequently over the next six months and all that was required to send him off on a new surge of demolition work was the sudden appearance in O.R. of several children with their hands blown off or their eyes out. He substituted electrically detonated sticks of dynamite for the cakes of TNT and decided it was now safer but still exciting work. It was more than exciting. McClure went after unexploded shells and booby traps as though conducting a personal vendetta against death. In spite of his efforts there were 150 deaths and 300 wounded in that one small city. Most of the wounds were amputations. Most of both wounds and deaths were among children.

McClure uttered a plea that relief doctors should all be taught bomb disposal if they were to function properly in the reclamation of China's cities. He also tried to talk his peers in the F.A.U. into establishing a trained demolition squad, but that suggestion was side-tracked by other priorities.

By the end of March, 1945, U.N.R.R.A. caught up to the Tengchung hospital and adopted it. It was to be used as a demonstration hospital where U.N.R.R.A. teams could gain field experience before going out to found other hospitals. Bob could not help crowing, slightly—at least to Amy: "Again we have been right, if a little ahead of others, in planning for this work." The hospital already had thirty-seven beds functioning out of a planned sixty-five. It had two foreign doctors (not counting McClure) and seven foreign nurses on staff. A nurses' training scheme was underway. The O.R. work was still mostly on those chronic explosion cases, but two thirds of the hospital's work was medical, with the old familiar enemies predominating—malaria, dysentery, typhus. When Yang Yung-lo came in to be the hospital mechanic, McClure was sure that God was still in Heaven.

About this time both the British Red Cross and

U.N.R.R.A. were beginning to make quietly seductive noises designed to lure McClure away from the F.A.U., but he was not to be easily lured.

On the Burma front the Japanese appeared to be on the run. They were *not* on the run back in Central China. There they had closed the pincers on the Changsha front and had penetrated to within a few miles of Kweiyang, the city which had been McClure's headquarters back in his Red Cross trucking days. In that area the Japanese presence had been causing consternation and turmoil, with the usual increase in refugee traffic to the west.

Out in the Pacific, the Americans had been on the move in the Philippines for quite some time.

In Europe, the whole show was just about wrapped up. By May 8th, 1945, it *was* wrapped up.

The announcement of Victory in Europe came while Bob was in Tengchung. It seemed almost as remote as the declaration of war had seemed five years earlier. "There is such a long way to go yet," he wrote to Amy. "Here we are in a city that has been completely knocked out in order to get victory. People know that there has to be a lot more like this. The hillside is covered with graves of those who helped to retake the city. Somehow it seems difficult to celebrate victory of this kind in the ordinary way. On the other hand everyone is delighted that in one sphere the mess is over."

He was quite right. In China, "the mess" was far from over. There was indeed a long way yet to go.

For McClure himself, there was no respite. While his friends in Canada were still celebrating VE Day, he went off to fight a plague.

35

Plague Valley

While the F.A.U. surgical team had been awaiting the fall of Tengchung, and after that while they had been establishing the Tengchung hospital, they had been acutely aware of the fact that plague was stalking the tribesmen of a large jungle valley. It was the bubonic plague, the Black Death of mediaeval Europe.

McClure went out on several expeditions to inoculate the people against the dread disease. His first foray coincided with the Japanese flight from Tengchung. Both the doctor and the plague were hunting tribesmen while the tribesmen were hunting the Japanese. It made for some rather tense moments on the trail.

Inoculation was a defence, but not a perfect one. Even with inoculations the bubonic plague could achieve a 50 percent mortality rate. Without inoculations it often managed 100 percent. Bob always carried a New Testament in his pack, but there was something about the plague that made him reach into his memory for solace from the Old Testament. He found it among the Psalms: "A thousand shall fall at thy side, and ten thousand at thy right hand; but it shall not come nigh thee." Plague made a man thoughtful. It did not stimulate the adrenalin the way bomb disposal did.

In his reports to Amy, however, Bob was matter of fact, almost jocular: "Many have had inoculations before. They take to it like ducks to water. I had . . . only one needle for 1,200 people. It was a sort of horse needle though, and in the evening and at noon I sharpened it on my razor hone, but it was a tough job putting that needle into so many people—tough job for the people perhaps, too."

The plague refused to be stamped out. After the Tengchung hospital had been established, after VE Day had come and gone, the Black Death was still there in the jungle-lined valleys between Tengchung and the Burma border.

McClure went back to headquarters for more supplies, determined to make another assault upon the disease. While in the Kutsing area he received a ride from a Free French army officer who drove a jeep like a madman. The officer swerved to miss a pothole, an almost useless manoeuvre on China's roads, and the little machine rolled into the ditch. Both men were badly shaken up. McClure dislocated his left shoulder. That shoulder continued to bother him for some time, but did not prevent him returning to Plague Valley.

This time he came well armed. He had a supply of the new drugs, sulpha-thiazol and sulpha-diazene. These had been hailed as 'miracle drugs', and indeed they were. If one could get a high concentration of sulpha into a victim's bloodstream, and hold it there for just a few hours, bubonic plague could be conquered.

Bob knew there was a small Catholic mission out in the plague area. He sent a runner with a supply of the sulpha tablets to give to the priests so they, too, could begin treating victims. He himself set off with two Chinese assistants, inoculating and treating as he went. They walked for eight days on a trek that took them across the Burma border.

It was the rainy season and Bob found himself being soaked one minute and roasted the next. His clothes never dried out. Mould grew on the back of his shirt. Giant leeches clung to the tall wet grasses and transferred to passing legs, penetrating clothing. One of Bob's companions pulled one off, and the spot bled for eight hours. McClure was more scientific. He removed the leeches with a touch of a glowing cigar, and the spots only bled for five hours. Tigers coughed within twenty-five yards of the campfires. One night a leopard took a chicken from the very hut in which the three men were sleeping. Ming-yuan longed for the dry, open, wind-swept plains of North Honan.

They could tell when they reached the Burma border because there had been a rudimentary Burmese road here, years

before, that ran to the border and stopped. When the Japanese
had captured Bhamo, motorists had fled, following the little
road to its very end, and even beyond. The two vehicles that
had gone the farthest had been a Baby Austin and a Jeep. Both
were still there in the jungle. The Austin had beaten the Jeep by
some twenty-five yards.

From the border the medical team doubled back, still inoculating the well and treating the victims as they went. As
they came into the area served by the Catholic mission Bob sent
a runner ahead to arrange a rendezvous with one of the
priests.

To understand McClure's first impression of the man he
was about to meet it is necessary to understand one simple fact
about the bubonic plague. It was carried by fleas. The *best* protection was to wear clothing that prevented flea bites. Since a
flea could only jump about thirteen inches the leather high cuts
that McClure favoured were good protection.

McClure and the priest met in a tiny village of thatched
huts in the heart of the plague area where the rats were beginning to die. (Dying rats were always a sign of approaching
plague. First the rats died and then the children. It hit the children more swiftly than adults because up to the age of twelve
the children slept on the floor with the fleas.)

Bob was ushered into the presence of a tall, thin, French
priest of the Order of St. Bernard. His name was Pierre Lacoste. He was wearing a long black mandarin robe and baggy
Chinese trousers with wide leg openings. He wore no socks
and on his feet were thin Chinese slippers. When McClure first
saw him, Pierre Lacoste was squatting on the ground brewing
coffee over a small fire. He was a prime candidate for flea bites,
and yet McClure knew that the man had survived in this area
for years. It seemed obvious that the Good Lord was protecting
Pierre Lacoste.

It was a protection that had not been afforded to all the
members of his mission. Two of his associates had recently
been captured by the Japanese. When last seen they were being
dragged across the hills by the retreating soldiers. The priests
were tied together by wires threaded under their collar bones.
Their eyes had been put out. The only other survivor was, like
Father Lacoste, out in the villages trying to stem the plague.
The tribesmen had not betrayed the priests for the sake of a

Japanese reward, and the priests had no intention of deserting the tribesmen.

Lacoste had run out of sulpha tablets and he and McClure spent several days together treating people in the area that Lacoste had just traversed.

Finally, on the outskirts of one village, Lacoste hesitated. It was a village that was neatly divided in half by the main trail down the valley. The priest seemed reluctant to enter it. After some hesitation, he explained why.

"When I arrived here I was running out of sulpha tablets. I went through the village first, looking in each house. On that side of the street," he waved his hand to indicate one collection of mud huts, "I found twenty-two children with the plague. On the other side, almost as many. I had only eighty-eight tablets left." He paused, as though thinking back to that very day.

McClure needed no further explanation of Lacoste's predicament. It required four tablets to cure a child. Lacoste's eighty-eight tablets had been just enough for half the victims.

"What did you do?"

"I gave the sulpha tablets to the twenty-two children on that side of the street." He waved his hand again, but vaguely, as though afraid to be so specific. "To all the others I gave aspirin."

Bob could feel his heart hesitate and his chest muscles tighten. Suddenly, out here in the jungle near the Burma border, he and Father Lacoste were about to walk into a living laboratory. On the one side of the street were those who had been given the new drug. On the other side was the traditional 'control group'—those who had been given aspirins for placebos. But here the guinea pigs were children and the unwilling scientist was a priest. It was all far too real.

They entered the village together, doctor and priest. On the sulpha side of the street there had not been a single death. On the other side of the street there had not been a single survivor.

36

General McCurdle and the Relief of Honan

By the spring of 1945 the war in China had finally begun to turn around. The Chinese had begun recapturing cities in the interior. Out in the Pacific the Americans had captured Iwo Jima and then Okinawa. Just after VE Day they launched an enormous air offensive against the Japanese navy and Japan herself. It all climaxed in August, as the Americans dropped the first atomic bomb on Hiroshima, and followed with the second on Nagasaki.

When VJ Day arrived, McClure was on a heavy stint in an O.R. and did not celebrate. Besides, there had already been several premature celebrations, which he had observed with a clinical eye, and he had come to the conclusion that too many victories were hard on the liver. After VJ Day, with the world supposedly at peace, he went off to the south-east toward Canton to help put together the people of the city of Liuchow. It was a city that had been almost totally destroyed by liberating American bombers and McClure could not help a feeling of special responsibility toward people who had been hammered by their own side. They were truly victims of victory.

The trucks of the China Convoy were now hauling approximately 95 percent of the medical supplies being distributed to civilian hospitals in Free China, and the Convoy was committed to rehabilitation work. This work expanded into other cities which, like Tengchung and Liuchow, had been demolished in the process of liberation. The plight of the people in recently destroyed cities was obvious. It was an area of work where agencies of the Nationalist Government and of U.N.R.R.A.

were willing to follow once the F.A.U., British Red Cross, and others had shown the way. But McClure knew of an entire area of the country that was being overlooked. It had not been devastated by 'liberation' and so far had only been liberated on paper, since the Japanese were still in control. It was the 'forgotten' Province of Honan.

McClure threw himself so whole-heartedly into turning the China Convoy's thoughts toward Honan that he caused Doug Crawford, the dour Scots hospital mechanic of Teng-chung, to write poetry. The writing of poetry (using the term very loosely) had become a Convoy habit. It was an outlet that protected those who were still rational against both creeping insanity and Bob McClure. Crawford summed up McClure's new plans in a few succinct verses:

Old McCurdle has a plan,
Based upon Chengchow,
To save the people of Honan,
Starting with Chengchow.
With the Unit here and the Unit there,
    (which of us knows where we are?)
We save the people of Honan,
Starting with Chengchow.

Old McCurdle will expect
When he's in Chengchow
Hospitals to resurrect
All around Chengchow.
With a medmech* here and a medmech there
Here a med, there a mech, everywhere a medmech,
Hospitals we resurrect
All around Chengchow.

Old McCurdle has a scheme,
Centred in Chengchow,
Surgical technique to redeem
All around Chengchow.
With a little op here and a big op there,
Here an op, there an op, every blooming where an op,

---

*A medical mechanic, or technician.

Surgical technique we redeem
All around Chengchow.

Crawford was absolutely right. McClure did want to help
Honan and his plan did call for the work to begin in Chengchow, using the big Baptist hospital as a base. Before Crawford
penned his way to some final verses old McCurdle's plan had
been endorsed by the F.A.U., and Bob was en route to Honan.
The word went out to numerous China Convoy members scattered throughout south-west China that they were to rendezvous at Chengchow. How they got there was up to them. As it
turned out, within six months time the whole China Convoy
headquarters would follow.

If Old McCurdle seemed to be in haste, he was. For a brief
few weeks after victory in Asia there had been a somewhat
euphoric feeling that China was on the upswing. Inflation,
which had soared well beyond the bounds of reason, began an
almost immediate nose dive. The Nationalist Government and
U.N.R.R.A. and everybody else were talking great plans for rehabilitation. But the euphoric feeling soon evaporated as inflation began to soar even higher than before, and as the struggles
began among Kuomintang officials to enrich themselves personally from the vast amount of American supplies that were
now up for grabs. Chiang Kai-shek's armies began to disinte-
grate, and to slip away from the Generalissimo's control. Some
of the Kuomintang generals began to show alarming tendencies to resume the old role of warlord. The Americans were en-
dorsing the Chiang Kai-shek regime as the government of all
China, and were beginning to airlift Nationalist troops into
cities that had been under Communist domination. The Communists were not amused. A whole garden of dragon teeth was
just beginning to sprout as McClure headed for Honan.

His intentions were not complicated. He wanted the
F.A.U. to be on the spot so it could move in and reclaim mission hospitals as the Japanese moved out, and *before* the Chinese military had a chance to move in and use them as barracks. McClure had had occasion to notice that the Japanese
often left a hospital stripped but in reasonably good shape
(being themselves hygienic to the point of obsession), whereas
Chinese soldiery too often treated their barracks like stables,
chopping furniture up to burn in campfires on the floors. If the

Honan mission hospitals were not saved so they could be handed over to their parent churches and quickly put back into operation, McClure foresaw a long continuing period of misery and suffering for the general populace.

On VJ Day the Japanese had been in control of Chengchow and, as far as anyone knew, were in fact using the Baptist hospital as a headquarters. Under the rules of war a defeated army was responsible for maintaining both law and order *and* the status quo in the area it occupied, until it could be relieved by the victors. This meant that the men and women of the F.A.U. were hoping to relieve a Japanese general of his Chengchow headquarters before the Generalissimo's men got there.

There was some doubt whether the Japanese in Honan would be willing to recognize the fact that they had been defeated. If they should opt for independent action in order to save face, while the Communists and Nationalists went for each other's throats across the Yellow River, there could still be very interesting times in Honan.

McClure travelled by way of Paochi and collected the big X-ray machine to return it to its original home base. This time he broke it into seventy-five pieces of baggage, all of which he sent by train. He took faith, and consigned the X-ray tube to the hands of the baggage smashers.

At Sian he made connections with other United Church of Canada people who were also headed into Honan to consolidate liaison between their own mission, the Chinese Church, and the F.A.U.

As the group left Sian the Generalissimo's troops were building pillboxes in the streets in preparation for a civil war.

From Loyang to Chengchow the railroad was under the control of polite and efficient Japanese who were running a strange locomotive with retractable rubber tired wheels and powered by the engine from a tank. What was more important, and a considerable relief, was the fact that the Japanese commanders in Honan were obviously accepting defeat.

Once again Bob passed almost within sight of Hwaiking without being able to approach it. There was absolutely no communication with the north side of the Yellow River. Tension between the Communists and Nationalists had Hwaiking as isolated as it had been at any time during the war.

In Chengchow the F.A.U. vanguard found the Baptist hospital occupied by the Japanese Group Commander for the area, a man of Field Marshall rank. There were no Chinese officials who were willing to ask him to move out. McClure could tread softly when he had to. He did so now. After some delicate negotiations the Japanese withdrew from the Baptist compound and the F.A.U. moved in. The Japanese general kept one small cottage for himself. He had had it fixed up and rather liked it. He was in no hurry to return home to Japan because his wife and five children had been killed in the bombing of Tokyo.

McClure was favourably impressed by the efficiency, punctuality, and honesty of the Japanese commander and his men. He was disgusted by the high ranking Chinese officers who were arriving in Honan to take over from the Japanese. He described them to Amy: "Verily it is as the people say that there are four kinds of disasters that come to Honan. Droughts, floods, locusts and soldiers and this is the latter that is with them now. For those of us who have worked with the re-vamped Chinese armies in south-western and south-eastern China it is hard to realize that this is the type of soldier that those re-vamped armies started with. Here it is the old warlord type. The generals and all their staff and many of the junior officers move with their families . . . They commandeer trains and upset all transportation just as they did in the warlord days. They have never built so much as a field latrine, but move into other people's places and just live off the people. Chiang Kai-shek has said that he hoped the generals would avoid as far as possible taking any taxes from the people this year, to allow the people to recover a bit. Instead of that, while they told us about hearing the broadcast, the general told us that because of the 'special circumstances' in Honan they were taking the usual taxes, all of them plus 35 percent because Honan seemed to have a decent harvest this year! Really one feels when one sees these conditions that if we were them (the people) we should probably be interested in some new political experiments too."

Bob re-assembled the big X-ray where it had stood in Dr. Ayers' days. When he opened the case that contained the precious X-ray tube he found that the tube was rubble. Other equipment, and even clothing, was slow arriving. Most of it he had ordered months ago, anticipating its need here in Honan. But the Unit had used its grant money for the year and supplies were being withheld until the calendar showed it was again time to proceed. Bob was furious with what he saw as a chain of bureaucratic incompetency which stretched all the way across the Pacific, even to the offices of the Canadian Red Cross. The hospital had no power plant, no sewing machine, no blankets. Bob and his men had no winter clothing. He sounded off to Amy: "Even our winter battle dress for the boys that we ordered has only been shipped to Shanghai in October, if they were sent then. Here we are with cold weather upon us and we still have to go around in shorts with one woollen battle dress tunic per three men. We take turns wearing the top, and whoever has to call on the Japanese general wears the battle dress top to make it look official. The Japanese have their winter uniforms, but the people of the nations that won the war run around in shorts. Well such is life when people do not trust us enough to fill the orders that we send in to them."

Two weeks later, still without the necessary supplies, he had decided to go back into the producer gas business and to improvise. He was plagued with boils behind his right knee, was cold, and was prophesying that it was "going to be one hell of a winter". His hair was beginning to turn grey and was thinning out on top.

By December, more of the F.A.U. team were arriving. There was by now quite a leavening of new blood in the China Convoy and most of it was Canadian. Twenty Canadians had finally arrived in China back in the spring and had been scattered around to receive their training in the field. McClure had been more than pleased to see them. "The Canadian boys are the finest lot of new recruits that the F.A.U. has ever received," Bob told Amy, succumbing for once to the unpardonable sin of nationalistic pride. He added, hastily, "It is the comment one hears on every side." He mentioned that one of the new men had grown a "crazy beard" and then added, innocently, "Hope he will get over it for I don't like the F.A.U. to be known as a bunch of eccentrics."

Eccentrics or not, the F.A.U. China Convoy was converging on Honan. Among those who arrived in December was an English doctor, John Wilkes, and a Chinese nurse, Doris Wu. McClure had the highest respect for both of them. He began to relax a little.

Two days before Christmas, 1945, the Chengchow O.R.

had its first big emergency operation. It was on a man who had
been terribly crushed in an accident. They still had no electric
lights and no electric heating but they operated by the light of
Coleman lanterns and in the warmth of a wood stove. It was an
explosive environment in which to use ether anaesthetic, but
they worked in the midst of sandbags and all went well. Things
were still primitive but Chengchow Baptist hospital was open
for business. Before long McClure was modestly claiming that
it was probably the best rehabilitated hospital in China.

In the meantime he made several trips down to Hankow.
A passenger train was running in the daytime. It consisted of a
couple of coaches hauled by one of the Japanese automotive
contraptions, and was usually overloaded to the point that the
passengers felt as though they had been packed in with a hammer. Trips were restricted to daytime on most of the railroads
in the north. The guerrillas had become used to blowing up
tracks at night, and were still at it.

In Hankow, McClure acted as consultant with U.N.R.R.A.
and the co-operating missions that were busily rehabilitating
the Hankow Union Hospital. He was soon doing surgery in
their refurbished O.R. In Hankow even the Nationalist army
was co-operating to the full and on his first visit McClure was
able to lay the ground work for setting up a lab course. It was
the rebirth of the work of the Institute of Hospital Technology.
"Hankow," Bob reported, "was like a wild dream and everything one did came true."

As the early months of 1946 rolled by, McClure went on
forays out of Chengchow with Convoy units that were working
on rural rehabilitation projects up and down the south shore of
the Yellow River. One project that fascinated him was a peanut
co-operative. It centred on a crushing mill that was built by
F.A.U. mechanics from the hydraulic landing system of a Lib-
erator that had crashed in the backyard of the Chengchow hospital. The giant press was set up in a village temple. McClure
was present on opening day.

It was a gala event. Not only had the Convoy men salvaged the hydraulics, they had also salvaged the pilot seat and
controls. There were four hundred villagers crowded into the
temple to watch the mayor, suitably clad in ceremonial robes,
climb up onto the pilot seat. He looked like an Oriental wizard

out of Buck Rogers. It was a high point in his official career as he moved the lever that had once lowered a heavy bomber's great wheels. There was a sigh of admiration from the audience as the hydraulic arms stretched downward with deliberate but unrelenting force. Those arms crushed the peanuts all right, but since they were braced against the roof beam they also began just as unrelentingly to lift the roof. There was a moment of consternation as timbers began to creak and as roof tiles began to shift. One of the mechanics leaped unceremoniously into the mayor's lap and de-activated the monster machine. In one fleeting moment Bob had realized what it must have been like in the temple when Samson had seized the pillars.

The mechanics re-thought their design. A few weeks later the peanut co-operative got off to a less spectacular start.

McClure travelled by bicycle along the dike to the place where an American U.N.R.R.A. engineer, Oliver Todd, was masterminding the closing of the great gap in the Yellow River dikes. Todd's second in command was Don Faris, the United Church missionary who had bicycled down across Japanese lines with Bruce Copland away back in January of '38. Other United Church people were returning to North China. Bruce Copland turned up, and Bill Mitchell. Both were looking well and going strong. By this time McClure considered Bill Mitchell to be the most knowledgeable relief expert in China.

As soon as travel conditions permitted, Bob went north to Hsin-hsiang, where his blood brother, George Wang, had been walking a political tightrope all through the war.

In the early days of the war the Chinese puppet government had pressured George to take on county administrative duties. George had developed a convenient case of diabetes and had sent himself off to recuperate, leaving his hospital in the care of Bishop Megan. After Pearl Harbour the Bishop was no longer a neutral and had to take to the hills (en route to Loyang) so George returned and took over his hospital again. He used the hospital profits to help support the Catholic fugitives. He kept quietly crossing the lines to tell the Nationalist Government and the Nationalist troops what he was doing. It got even stickier when a Japanese H.Q. moved into his premises. But George never 'took his shoes off to the Japanese', and he came through with his hospital and his honour intact. Ming-yuan was pleased to see that his brother had completely recovered from diabetes. That, too, was an achievement.

The local presbytery of the Chinese church was accustomed to holding its meetings in George Wang's house. Bishop Megan had returned and was opening a little Catholic hospital. George loaned his lab man to the Bishop and was acting as consultant. McClure moved a kala-azar team into the area and George built team housing for them in his hospital compound. Before long the F.A.U. was launching the biggest kala-azar drive ever organized. George and Bob agreed that the housing for the team was suitable repayment for the personal loan Ming-yuan had extended years ago for the founding of Dr. Wang's hospital.

McClure organized a refurbished mobile surgical team. The doctor was Dr. Philip Hsiung, a Chinese member of the F.A.U., and the O.R. nurse was Margaret Briggs, recently of Tengchung. McClure worked with them. One of their first cases turned out to be a 45 lb. fibroid uterus. It was a messy, depressing case where the surgeons had no alternative but to press on. The patient was a widow, with a young daughter, and when she died McClure felt terribly depressed. And then the relatives sent in a message: "We wish the honourable surgeon to know," so ran the gist of it, "that our sister has suffered greatly for six years and she herself did not expect to live. We hope her lamented dying will not prevent the honourable surgeon from having good heart for the very much work that is to be done."

McClure was no longer doing wartime surgery where the surgeon first scrubbed up and *then* saw what case was on the table. Now he could consult with the patient, and both patient and surgeon could plan ahead. Bob was particularly impressed by one of Bishop Megan's parishioners: "The prize piece was a mixed parotid tumour on the right side of the face of a young married farm girl . . . It was pretty tight and went up to above the back of the ear, behind to the mid line and down to the shoulder muscles and angle of the jaw. It was at least a 50 percent risk operation and I told her and Megan . . . She went back home, fixed up things, had her religious blessing, then came down as cool and settled a patient as I've ever had. We had to ligate first common carotid and internal jugular vein and the deep section of the tumor was attached to the cervical vertebrae. We got it all away and she recovered fine . . . and of all things she has not even got a facial nerve gone. She had a mass before her rectal ether began and on 2nd day they had a thanksgiving mass at her bedside. Not for years have I seen one whose religion helped both patient and doctor as much as did hers. She's just a peasant woman but she sure has something."

McClure was intrigued by young Dr. Hsiung whom he found to be "bloodthirsty" but bright. He commented about Hsiung in a letter to Amy that took them both back seventeen years in memory: "History seems to repeat itself for he is now in about the same position in his work that I was in Formosa, and if I do say it myself I think my surgery is about as good as G.G.T.'s* ever was." That one comment was almost the only time McClure had ever written such a precise evaluation of his own surgical skills.

He could still be incredibly generous in his evaluation of other people. Owen Evans turned up. He was the quiet Welshman who had been captured in Hong Kong while on F.A.U. business and had refused every opportunity to escape because he felt he could be of service to his fellow prisoners. Evans was a graduate of Cambridge University, with a B.Sc. in engineering, and a law degree. Now that he was again a free man he had travelled all the way to Honan to confer with McClure because Owen had decided to spend the rest of his life working with the Chinese. McClure could hardly find terms adequate to describe Owen Evans: "A man with loads of courage, never gets down, never gives up, and never any recriminations . . . one of the most humorous and humble men I've ever met . . . He makes a trail of friends wherever he goes. Few people whom I know have given up as much to do as great a service to their fellow men as has Owen Evans. He has no grudge against the Japanese and pities them . . . Yet he was eyewitness to the crucifixion of a U.S. Army aviator and saw a negro member of an air-crew tied hand and foot and dragged through the streets of Hong Kong behind a horse-cart until he was literally peeled like a potato and died . . . He is one of the finest chaps I know and one of those who really makes you feel proud to say 'Owen Evans is a friend of mine'."

*Dr. G. Gushue-Taylor.

McClure was overwhelmed that Evans had travelled to Honan in February just to see him, travelling in boxcars and without an overcoat. He promptly gave Owen his own great-coat, which he had just acquired. "Possessions," wrote McClure, "make one comfortable but the comfort one gets from sharing them is so much greater. Before another winter comes around I shall have another coat and it need not be brown col-ored." Unwittingly, McClure, while trying to describe some-one else, had put his own philosophy into a footnote.

"Owen Evans," said McClure, "is one of the most Christ-like men I know."

McClure had also been buoyed up by the way things had survived and were progressing at Chengchow, Hankow, and Hsin-hsiang. But he was plunged into deep gloom by the situa-tion in his boyhood compound of Weihwei.

The Weihwei hospital, that pioneer of 'modern' hospitals in Central China that had been built by his father's successors, Drs. Struthers and Auld, had been left in the hands of the Chinese church after Pearl Harbour. But there had been an error in communications. It was thought that the compound it-self was the responsibility of the church, but that the hospital was the responsibility of its Chief, Dr. Tuan. Dr. Tuan had has-tened to make his staff sing the Japanese National Anthem and had quickly denounced any who objected. He had also sold drugs and instruments and had used hospital income to buy copious quantities of land in his own name. It was now a sticky and delicate problem in diplomacy that the United Church mis-sionaries had walked into. They were trying to get the Weihwei hospital back under the full control of the Chinese presbytery, but Dr. Tuan did not wish to let go. He was demanding pay-ment for having saved the buildings and, in McClure's estima-tion, had gone quite money-mad.

Since Tuan had been a collaborator, he was afraid to move far from the compound for fear that either Nationalists or Com-munists would have at him. As a result he was claiming to be more devoted to the 'service' of the church than ever before. It all enraged McClure and he resigned from the Church Synod medical committee: "All their problems for the next few years are going to be problems of diplomacy and politics, and no doc-tors have time nor qualifications for that line. There is plenty of other work that takes medical skill for me to do and it is work that leaves a decent taste in one's mouth too." He went on reporting to Amy in terms that even McClure would not have used in a formal report. "If there is one form of diplomacy that is low it is church diplomacy. I leave it entirely to others. In every other line that I am following, and there are several of them, I seem to get marvelous results and win all the breaks except in this church politics stuff. I will say this, though, that with all its difficulties our Honan church is better off than any other church of its kind I have seen in China. It is certainly much better than anything down . . . south of the river. It is at least now possessed of a great spirit of independence and the leaders feel that it is up to them to work through their problems. Of course the Chinese way of working through a problem is radically different from ours. They slide round problems rather than smash into them but they skid on the corners often, according to my lights."

Before long he was reporting that the only hope for Weihwei would be to clear out all the staff who had remained throughout the war, since there was no spirit of service left. He regretted that the hospital had not been destroyed. The staff had saved the bricks but lost the essence.

The situation up in The United Church of Canada's northern station of Changte was quite different. Here the compound and the hospital had been very roughly used. An F.A.U. team settled in to rehabilitate the Changte hospital, with a missionary lady acting as their mother hen.

Changte was in a strange situation. It was a little island of Nationalist control in a sea of Communism. To get there from the south one had to travel through Communist territory. One could only go a few miles from Changte in any direction without running into Communist sentries. In the villages these sentries were often old women and they had the habit of stripping wayfarers of everything except their basic clothing. McClure had to negotiate with the Communists before his kala-azar team could work in the countryside. Before long there was fighting between the Communists and Nationalists right at Changte airport but, in spite of it all, McClure's Convoy team pushed forward with hospital rehabilitation.

The whole political scene in North China was very confused and getting more so. Ming-yuan was beginning to think that he had merely dreamt that the war in China was over.

Fortunately for all of them life was not all church politics, heavy surgery, civil war and relief. For the first time in years Bob began to relax on Sunday afternoons. Sometimes he read and sometimes he went duck hunting. One memorable afternoon he turned up in the Chengchow compound astride a Mongolian camel. And romance was blossoming within the Unit. Dr. John Wilkes was showing signs of falling for nurse Doris Wu, and in May, nurse Briggs married Al Matheson, the head of the China Convoy garages. By this time McClure considered Margaret Briggs to be the finest O.R. nurse he had ever worked with, and he had developed great affection for her. He tried to describe his feelings to Amy: "As you know people cannot work together as we do in medical work . . . without coming into a pretty close fellowship. It is never an affection such as one has for one's 'girl'. Neither is it just a platonic friendship, but it is something that I think we only get in medicine and nursing and it certainly is fine."

The Briggs-Matheson wedding was a happy occasion. As, the couple emerged from the chapel, an F.A.U. honour guard formed a triumphal bridal arch by crossing the weapons with which the China Convoy had waged the war—bedpans and monkey wrenches.

The only sad thing about the Briggs-Matheson wedding was that although McClure had been asked to give away the bride, he was not able to be present. He had finally headed for Hwaiking.

37

Requiem for Hwaiking

McClure had heard various accounts of conditions around Hwaiking. Some of them were first hand and some of them came via the grapevine. None of them was cheerful. Subconsciously he had been postponing a visit to Hwaiking, even though he knew in his heart that such a visit was inevitable. His term with the F.A.U. was to expire in June, and it was now May. The rapid approach of his departure date, combined with the desire of the F.A.U. to extend medical assistance into Communist territory, finally gave him a positive reason to go on what he was afraid could be a rather sombre trip.

To reach Hwaiking he would have to cross from Nationalist into Communist territory and consequently he had to negotiate with both sides for passes and safe conducts. Both sides seemed willing to have him travel, and both promised that their outposts would be notified of his arrival. Even so, it took him several days to acquire clearance papers and when he arrived at the Nationalist lines there was a great deal of telephoning in many directions to verify instructions that had never been received. He almost wished he had not helped to pioneer the 'phone system in the North Honan triangle and decided, in some despair, that there was no hope of the Chinese ever doing anything with any semblance of efficiency or precision.

The spurline railway had been thoroughly torn up by the Communists, so McClure made the trip by truck. Between the military lines he drove across a no-man's land of waving wheat fields. The wheat was ripe for harvest but here those usually teeming plains were barren of human life. Behind the military lines, in both directions, peasants were close to starvation, and yet any peasant who dared walk out to harvest these particular fields was shot. McClure found himself thinking cynical thoughts about the warring factions, both of whom loudly protested their deep concern for the peasant farmers, while their outposts gunned them down.

He reached Communist territory. The outposts here, too, had received no word of his coming, although he had been assured that all were prepared. Inefficiency, he decided, was not a monopoly of either the Right or the Left. His clearance eventually came through and he continued, accompanied by a "guide".

He travelled through the bamboo area near Chinghua, where he had once gone journeying to search for Moslem bandits. This time the Moslems came searching for him. He was intercepted by a messenger who invited him to elude surveillance and come to a meeting. McClure did so. In a quiet meeting in the shelter of a bamboo grove Moslem elders, some of whom he had saved as children from kala-azar, asked him if the Christian church was going to found an underground for the people who still worshipped God. They wanted the Christians to know that Moslems would be part of any such underground. McClure did not know what the Christian church was intending to do. All he knew was that times had changed and it was no longer up to the missionaries; the initiative was no longer in their hands.

He went on toward the city of Hwaiking. The road was bumpy and he drove slowly. Workers by the roadside recognized him and raised their hands in greeting. Peasants in oxcarts looked up and smiled in sudden recognition. It was a good feeling, but it was short-lived.

The old city wall that had sheltered Hwaiking city was gone. There was nothing now but a swelling mound, like an old dike. The ancient city looked somehow naked and exposed. Beyond the outskirts of the city, across the open fields, Bob could see the Hwaiking mission. It stood even more naked than the city. The compound walls were mere jagged remnants. Even from a distance he could see daylight through the walls of the big square mission homes built by Dr. Menzies. As he came closer he could see that there were really no houses at all, merely fragments. There were no sheltering roofs, no chimneys, no people, no children. There was no bell tower, and no bell tower gate through which a cavalcade could march on its way to tent meetings as they had done twenty years ago. The house where he had brought his bride was rubble. The power plant where he had worked with Chou Teh-kwei before turning him into a medical practitioner was gone. The school where he and Yang Yung-lo had dissected the ambulance was in ruins. The section of wall he had scaled with Sun during the pre-revolutionary siege was a pile of dust. The O.R. where Loving Lotus had learned to be a scrub nurse was an empty shell, and so was the ward where she had lectured bandits on the evils of theft. The Japanese had stripped everything out of the mission—the Chinese Communists had destroyed it.

He suddenly felt very tired, and made his way into the city to the Catholic mission. At least it had survived, thanks to being occupied first by the Japanese and then by the Hwaiking Chamber of Commerce.

That evening, many quiet figures moved in and out of the Catholic mission. They began to come at dusk and were still coming and going long after it was dark and far into the night. They had heard that Loa Tai-fu had returned. They were former patients, old friends, associates. Dr. Loa heard many stories and was told many tales. The Japanese and Communists, so he was told, had warred over Hwaiking all through the war years. After VJ Day, Nationalist troops had occupied the city and the Communist troops had immediately laid siege to it. It was during this period of a three month siege that the Hwaiking mission had finally been destroyed. In the later stages of their attacks upon the city the Communist troops had driven masses of peasants before them to absorb the defenders' fire. Some said that 10,000 peasants had been killed while being used as human sandbags. So went the stories. He was told that Christians were being liquidated. He was told they were being permitted to worship openly. Dr. Loa did not know the truth of any of it. Instead of listening too closely to the words, he remembered the little tribesman on the Burma Road and watched the speakers' sad eyes. What he saw there confirmed a feeling that had been growing upon him all that long day. He was still heavy in his heart when he finally reported to Amy: "As people now say, the communists in their territory have been able to do what the Japanese could not do in seven years of war—make the Chinese quit smiling. There is no smiling inside this huge prison of the Hwaiking area which includes one and a quarter million people."

That was not quite true. There was one cheerful moment in the course of that evening. Elderly Mr. Li Hung-ch'ang, one time principal of the mission boarding school in Hwaiking city, came in quietly for a chat. He still wore a flowing mandarin gown and still observed the Confucian courtesies.

"This most unworthy person is honoured to be in the presence of Loa Tai-fu."

"My miserable self is enlarged by the very presence of Principal Li."

The two of them talked of days past, the old Christian scholar in his hand-tailored Chinese robe and the forty-five year old Christian doctor in his Canadian battle dress with F.A.U. insignia. They talked of the Warlord of Hwaiking, and of the honorific plaque—of how Loa Tai-fu and Principal Li had connived with the Master Woodcarver of Hwaiking to save the Menzies Memorial Hospital from bankruptcy. They laughed as they talked, and Loa Ming-yuan felt much better for having been in the presence of Li Hung-ch'ang. The serene Mr. Li was the only visitor during that long remarkable night who did not ask Dr. Loa for help in leaving the area.

Loa Tai-fu had one other encounter in Hwaiking territory. It came as he was walking down a city street. It was crowded, as usual, like any city street in China. But past the people and across the street he saw a familiar face. He struck across the cobbled road, dodging mules, rickshaws, trucks and bicycles as he went, until he came to the far side. The man was almost up to him and there was no doubt of his identity. It was Chou Teh-kwei. Loa Ming-yuan stepped toward him, smiling, his hand outstretched. Chou Teh-kwei looked through him and beyond, and passed on by, his face like wood.

McClure returned to Chengchow with much to think about. It had been a strange trip indeed, that return to Hwaiking. It had depressed him mightily until he began to put it into perspective. The Boxer Rebellion that had put his parents to flight had not been a happy period either. Nor had the time of the First Revolution when he and his father had returned to China together. An image of firing squads on station platforms still figured in his memories of boyhood. And the warlords' rape of China had not been pleasant for the peasants, although it had contributed greatly to the surgical education of a young doctor. The summer riots and the strikes and the Second Revolution had been desperate times for everybody, and yet his sympathies had certainly been with the Chinese Nationalists who had finally had enough of foreign domination. He still admired the achievements and the courage of the Generalissimo and his brilliant lady. If only they had continued the revolution instead of pausing to slaughter communists. And how one's sympathies had gone with Mao Tse-tung and his comrades on that Long March into the hills of Shensi, and what desperate months for the peasant marchers! And through all the indignities suffered at the hands of the Japanese, from the time of the Manchurian 'incident' on through the endless years of the Sino-Japanese war, the peasants of China had been under the lash of it all. And now less than a year after the world had finished with the second war to end all wars the Chinese peasants were being caught up in the first swells of what appeared to be an all-out civil war. How on earth could one criticize the Communists of Hwaiking if they had not instantly created a heaven on earth in this special hell that was China? How could he even criticize Chou Teh-kwei for choosing to ignore him? All the other old friends had weighed the odds and had come quietly at night. But Bob, a Westerner from across Nationalist lines, had suddenly accosted Chou in public! In retrospect, he had to admire the man's self control, while his heart wept for a world in which such control was necessary.

Loa Ming-yuan returned to Chengchow with no criticism in his heart but only a prayer for his people. He, like the folk he had met in Hwaiking, had had enough of the politics of both Right and Left. He had had enough of Imperialism, enough of Nationalism, of Communism, and all the rest of it. Shakespeare had the words for it, a plague on all their houses! Bob expressed his political views on China to Amy in one sentence: "99 percent of the people do not care two hoots who wins but only hope for a reasonably decent government under any system that will give them some peace."

The wartime F.A.U. became the peacetime Friends Service Unit and the work of the China Convoy continued until 1950. Its kala-azar teams drove deep into the hill country of the north-west and a mobile medical team went to Communist headquarters in Yenan, where it served with distinction. But McClure's time with the Friends Unit had come to an end.

At the end of June, 1946, Ming-yuan sailed for Canada.

Although McClure's F.A.U. term had expired, he had an open-ended term with The United Church of Canada. Under its auspices he would return to his beloved China one more time.

38

The Last China Year
of Bob McClure

Even as Bob McClure left China in that summer of 1946 an American general was trying to talk the Communists and Nationalists into forming a coalition government, and thus ending the civil war. The general's name was George Marshall. He was noted for his un-warlike qualities of compassion and diplomacy. His name would be associated with the successful rehabilitation of many a war-torn country, but not with that of China. Neither Mao Tse-tung of the Communists nor Chiang Kai-shek of the Kuomintang was interested in a coalition which, by its very nature, would give tacit recognition to the other party as a legitimate power. Neither party was democratic. Neither leader had been voted into office. Both ruled by virtue of the authority vested in them by armed might.

Prior to VJ Day the Russians had moved quickly to take over Manchuria. They were now in a position to hand over most of the province to the Communists. Instead, they stripped Manchuria of its industrial machinery and pulled out, magnanimously leaving the province up for grabs. The Nationalists grabbed for the major cities and the Communists grabbed for lesser cities and the rural areas. It was a pattern that was being repeated throughout much of China. Mao Tse-tung and his people were consolidating their hold on rural China while the Generalissimo and his people were attempting to control China by holding its cities.

While these campaigns were underway McClure was off on a strange campaign organized by The United Church of Canada. It was called "Cavalcade". Its battle plan called for an all-out onslaught from the autumn of '46 until the late spring of '47. The terrain for this campaign was the whole broad expanse of Canada.

The front-line troops of "Cavalcade" were veteran missionaries of the United Church who were home on furlough, or who had been recalled for temporary home duty. Their assignment was to take part in a highly organized, sophisticated, educational blitzkrieg aimed at stimulating Canadians with the challenge of mission. It was, in a way, a kind of nine-month-long, high-powered, mobile tent meeting without the tent.

For McClure, that long winter of "Cavalcade" turned into an endless blur of towns, church basements, pulpits, platforms, and faces. Most of the events were relegated to an area of limbo in his memory from where they refused to move. All except a meeting in Rosetown, Saskatchewan.

By the time he *arrived* at Rosetown, McClure already knew where he was going after furlough. He was going back to China under the auspices of the United Church, and he was going to accept an invitation to work at the Union Hospital in Hankow. Before he *left* Rosetown, he knew that an important part of his work in Hankow would be on cancer, because a well-to-do widow lady, challenged by McClure's platform presentation, had volunteered to purchase radium for him.

Just as he had pioneered the use of radium in China in 1931 so did McClure again pioneer its use in post-war China. He returned to Hankow in November of 1947 armed with 55 mg of radium (a very respectable amount) with which he proceeded to establish a cancer detection and treatment centre at the Hankow Union Hospital.

McClure lured a young Canadian doctor and his wife out to Hankow, Douglas and Frances Dalziel. Dr. Dalziel had just graduated in surgery, would later specialize in gynaecology, and was destined to become superintendent of Toronto's Grace Hospital. He, too, came out under the auspices of the United Church.

McClure and Dalziel devoted themselves to the three phases of cancer work; detection, treatment, surgery. Their cancer clinic was the only one in the whole of Central China and served an area with a population of some 200 million people. The widow in Rosetown had had no idea what she was setting in motion by the simple act of opening first her heart and then her cheque book.

For almost the first time since he had interned McClure was spending all his working time within the walls of one institution. It was just as well. Outside was chaos.

Inflation was not soaring, it was rocketing. When people went food shopping they quite literally carried suitcases full of millions of Nationalist paper dollars. Business men hoarded U.S. dollars, gold bars, Chinese silver coins, and rice. Leading Kuomintang families became enormously rich. University professors and students feared for their very lives as the Kuomintang secret police terrorized intellectuals and succeeded in driving undecided scholars into the Communist camp. The age-old recipe for a successful Chinese revolution had not changed. It still called for support from both the peasants and the scholars. The Kuomintang policy of repression provided the Communists with the scholarly ingredient that might otherwise have been missing.

In the autumn of 1948 the Communists launched a major offensive. They already controlled the province of Shantung and all of rural Honan. Now they captured Tsinan and swept into the Yangtze Valley. Up in Manchuria they completely defeated the cream of the Kuomintang troops. The Generalissimo fled from Peking in October, never to return to the ancient capital. In December, 1948, the Nationalist defenders of Peking retreated behind the fourteen mile barricade of the old city's sixty-foot high walls. The attacking Communist general was so confident of winkling them out that he consulted with architects and archeologists to make certain that in the process he caused no unnecessary damage to China's cultural heritage.

All during that same Fall of 1948 the work of the Union Hospital in Hankow had been proceeding much as usual. The new class of nurses-in-training had had one somewhat unmanageable student—a peasant girl about twenty-one years old who did not take easily to authority, was often absent without permission, and often checked into residence after lights-out. She had a habit of prowling through the hospital and of snooping in areas and departments that should have been none of her concern. McClure had advocated her expulsion and, when she did not make her grades, that was done, but he had thought no more about it.

By mid-December, about the time the siege of Peking was taking place, it was obvious to all that it was a mere matter of a few weeks before the Communists would take over Hankow. A meeting was held of the Union Hospital staff. McClure gave them all a pep-talk.

"I don't know exactly what the Communists are like," he said. "It's going to be tough. Anytime there is a military take-over it's tough. There's no reason this time should be any different. But I do know that the Communists will need medical services, and so will the people of Central China. No take-over can change that need. When the Communists see that we are dedicated to giving medical service to the people, I am sure they will be decent to us. We certainly mustn't be like a bunch of rats. We can't leave a sinking ship."

As usual, McClure's enthusiasm, confidence, and general optimism created an upswing in morale among both the foreigners and the Chinese.

And then, just a few days before Christmas, Bob received a cable from Amy. There had been telegrams from other people in earlier days telling him he should go home for one reason or another. Throughout the years there had been the occasional letter from Amy suggesting that it was time he thought about coming home. This cable, however, was not making a suggestion. It contained an order. Twenty-year old Norah was seriously ill and in hospital. Bob was required at home, "immediately".

Bob had been conscience-haunted for the last ten years by the fact that Amy had had to raise the children almost single-handedly. He could cite chapter and verse to himself about his medical-missionary "duty" and about the demands of "service", but at the same time he would tell himself that he was "a rat", "a stinker", and "a piker". There had been no evidence that Amy thought him any of those things, and much evidence to support the idea that she believed in the value of his work even more strongly than he did himself. But it had been there just the same, that nagging conscience.

When Amy's peremptory cable arrived Bob packed a few of his clothes, but left most of his belongings lying wherever they happened to be. He caught a 'plane at Shanghai.

As McClure left China the Revolution was moving into its final stages. Within two weeks Hankow was taken over.* The

*Early in 1949 Chiang Kai-shek and the Kuomintang withdrew to Taiwan where they continued to claim to be the legitimate government of China. On October 1st, 1949, the Communists established the People's Republic of China on the mainland.

young nurse-in-training, who had been ejected from the hospital, turned up and laid a gun on the superintendent's desk. She introduced herself as the new hospital administrator. It was a good thing that McClure was not there.

It was just as well for other reasons. Reliable sources informed Bob, during the next few months, that he was on a Communist list of wanted (or unwanted) persons. Apparently he had been in too close contact with the Kuomintang, the Generalissimo, and Madame, and with 'imperialist agencies' like the International Red Cross, the Royal Air Force, the American Army, and the Christian church. Loa Ming-yuan had been contaminated by association and was proscribed.

That his name could be on such a list was a possibility that Loa Ming-yuan could well believe, and could even understand. He bore no rancour.

As forty-eight year old Bob McClure left China on that December day in 1948 he was typical of hundreds of other missionaries from many countries who were leaving behind their life's work. There would be many who would say that that life's work had come to nothing; that the fifth wave of Christian endeavour in China had been broken, absorbed, and was now evaporating like all the others. In twenty years' time it would be accepted by many informed people that the Christian church in China had ceased to exist. Other informed people would continue to debate it, because it all depended very much upon semantics and the precise meaning one gave the word 'church'.

It was just possible that McClure and his associates and their predecessors had left a legacy to China so big that few of them then, or later, could see it. Bruce Copland* put it in writing not long after:

"The influence of the church, especially the Protestant church, in bringing about this revolution, has been very great, though probably not always recognized by the communists . . . Let it not be forgotten that most social progress in China, now often credited to Communism—witness popular education, rural reform, medical services, participation of women in public life—began quietly many years ago in the Christian church."

*Marnie and the children flew home in December, 1948. Bruce spent the next 2-1/2 years in Hong Kong.

To McClure it was inconceivable that his life's work could be in ruins. In his philosophy such an eventuality was not possible. He had already explained why in a letter to Amy almost six years earlier:

"When it is all added up the only thing a doctor leaves behind him in this country is not grateful patients, as so many people think, but it is a trail of men who have worked with him, who have got something that took time to give them. These are what one leaves behind."

What a trail he had laid. He had criss-crossed China from Peking in the north-east to Tenchung on the Burma border; from Paochi in the north-west to Yenshan in the south and on to Taiwan; Chengchow, Hankow, Chungking, Kweiyang—all were in McClure territory. With X-ray, radium, bicycle spokes, the 'loop', scalpel, and wrench he had pioneered, adapted, improvised, taught, and practised.

There was no doubt in Bob's mind that he was now heading for a major crossroad. It was just possible he might have to pause at this one; perhaps even glance sideways. But he certainly was not going to look backwards.

McCLURE-CHINA CHRONOLOGICAL TABLE

1888   Dr. William McClure goes to China as one of four pioneer missionaries appointed by the Presbyterian Church in Canada.

1900   The Boxer Rebellion. Missionaries flee from the interior of China. Robert McClure is born while his mother is en route home to the U.S.A.

1901   The McClure family returns to China.

1910   The McClures leave China and live in Ohio during the period of the doctor's study furlough.

1911   The First Chinese Revolution. The fall of the Manchu Dynasty. China becomes a republic, first under Sun Yat-sen and then under Yuan Shih-k'ai.

1912   Bob McClure and his father return to China.

1914   World War I begins in Europe.

1915   Bob and his father go to Canada. Japan issues "Twenty One Demands" on China and the Chinese generals revolt.

1916   President Yuan Shih-k'ai dies of "chagrin and rage". The Age of the Warlords is beginning.

1920   Dr. James Menzies is murdered by bandits at Hwaiking.

1922   Bob McClure graduates in medicine from the University of Toronto.

1923   Bob interns in surgery in Toronto. He leaves for China to take the place of Dr. Menzies at Hwaiking.

1926   The Second Revolution is underway, with Nationalists and Communists in alliance. Amy Hislop goes to China and she and Bob McClure are married.

1927   General Chiang Kai-shek breaks with the Communists. Missionaries again flee from the interior. Bob and Amy McClure go to Taiwan, where their first two children are born.

1928   Chiang Kai-shek is made President of the new Republic.

1931   Bob gets his F.R.C.S. at Edinburgh. He and his family return to China. Japan occupies Manchuria.

1931- Bob McClure is Chief of Surgery at the Menzies Memorial
1937   Hospital, Hwaiking. Two more McClure children are born.

1934- The *Long March* of Communists from Kiangsi Province to
1935   Yenan, in Shensi Province.

1936   Chiang Kai-shek is kidnapped by his own troops. He is forced into an uneasy alliance with the Communists to oppose Japanese encroachments.

1937   Outbreak of the Sino-Japanese War. Bob and Amy are separated by the war zone. Bob becomes Field Director for the International Red Cross in Central and North China.

1938   The Japanese control most of North China. Chiang Kai-shek and the Nationalist government withdraw to the west, to Chungking. Bob is sent to England, Europe and Canada by the Red Cross. Amy and the children return to Canada, along with Dr. Wm. McClure.

1939   Bob returns to China to take charge of transportation for the International Red Cross in West and South-West China and along the Burma Road. He is seriously injured in December. In Europe, World War II has begun.

1940   Bob is invalided home. France falls. Bob takes flying lessons. He meets Prime Minister Mackenzie King.

1941   Bob McClure returns to China as Commandant of the Friends Ambulance Unit's *China Convoy*. Their territory is the Burma Road and all of Free China. Japan attacks Pearl Harbour, Singapore and Hong Kong.

1942   Burma falls to the Japanese. The Burma Road is closed. Supplies are flown in from India via the Himalayan "Hump". McClure becomes involved in air-to-ground rescue work.

1943   No longer Commandant of the F.A.U. Bob is free to concentrate on the medical and surgical services of the China Convoy. Chinese Nationalist troops are blockading Chinese Communists.

1944   Bob is in Canada briefly to recuperate from relapsing fever. He recruits personnel and raises funds for the F.A.U. and returns to China in June. D-Day in Europe.

1945   Victory in Europe and Victory in Asia. The Americans recognize the Nationalists as the government of China and Chiang Kai-shek moves to consolidate his hold on all major cities. McClure and the F.A.U. move into rehabilitation work.

1946   McClure and the F.A.U. concentrate upon the rehabilitation of North Honan. China moves into a state of open civil war between Communists and Nationalists. McClure completes his term with the F.A.U. and returns to Canada.

1947   Bob returns to China, to Hankow.

1948   Communists are consolidating their hold on North and Central China. McClure returns to Canada in December for family reasons.

1949   Chiang Kai-shek and the Nationalist government flee to Taiwan. On October 1st, the government of The People's Republic of China is established in Peking.